Experiencing Empire

Early American Histories

Douglas Bradburn, John C. Coombs, and S. Max Edelson, Editors

Experiencing Empire

Power, People, and Revolution
in Early America

Edited by PATRICK GRIFFIN

University of Virginia Press
Charlottesville and London

University of Virginia Press
© 2017 by the Rector and Visitors of the University of Virginia
All rights reserved
Printed in the United States of America on acid-free paper

First published 2017

ISBN 978-0-8139-3988-9 (cloth)
ISBN 978-0-8139-3989-6 (ebook)

9 8 7 6 5 4 3 2 1

Library of Congress Cataloging-in-Publication Data is available
from the Library of Congress.

Cover art: Detail of *A New Generall Chart for the West Indies of
E. Wright's Projection vut. Mercator's Chart, Sold by W. and I. Mount
and T. Page on Tower Hill, London.* (Courtesy of the Osher Map Library,
University of Southern Maine)

Contents

Acknowledgments

The essays in this collection have their origins in a conference held at Northwestern University in June 2013 in honor of T. H. Breen. The conference would have never come off without the work of Elizabeth Lewis Pardoe. A first-rate historian and an able administrator (a *rara avis,* in other words), Beth helped shape the intellectual content of the conference and saw to the logistical details. No Beth, no volume. I also owe a great debt to Sam Fisher, who helped me with a great many details. Lisa Gallagher similarly did yeoman's work on formatting the essays.

The contributors deserve a special word of thanks. They were delightful, and they met deadlines! I doubt I will ever utter that phrase again. Dick Holway was his usual enthusiastic, visionary self. This does not surprise me, as I have known Dick for so long. He is a pro's pro and knows a good collection when he sees it. He, too, is a delight to work with. The external reviewers gave me some sage advice. I was impressed with how closely they read the essays and the introduction. I found their insights invaluable, and I think the collection is much stronger for their efforts.

I learned after the fact that the late Drew Cayton was an earlier reader. His reading had a great effect on how I framed the introduction. Such was always the case whenever I gave Drew anything to read. There was no scholar more selfless than Drew Cayton. He is terribly missed, but I would like to think in some way his thoughts live on in this volume.

Finally, I would like to thank Tim Breen. I first got to know Tim as a mentor. Now I regard him as a dear friend. There is really little I could do to thank him for all he has done for me over the course of my career. This volume is but a small token.

Experiencing Empire

Introduction

Imagining an American Imperial-Revolutionary History

Some questions never change. For the period of the American Revolution, they remain fixed and can be summed up in the invocation of key years. How do we get from 1763 to 1776? And from 1776 to 1787? These simple questions, the sort that are standard issue for any American history survey course, preoccupy historians. They do so for a good reason. We tend to use dates as shorthand for fundamental dynamics that have characterized how we view the American Revolution. They tie together pre- and postrevolutionary events and processes in manageable, memorable, and symbolic ways and give us a consensual method of bookending a defining period of time.

The hinge date speaks for itself. The year 1776, of course, refers not only to the Declaration of Independence but also to the end of British America and the beginning of an American national story. It represents a death and birth, and as such all fix their eyes on it. It is what we could usefully call the "vanishing point" of American history, the date to which all things in the distant past point toward and from which all events in the more recent past emerge.[1]

The other dates require little more explanation. Let's start with 1787. This date, of course, refers to the Constitution. By convention, the document—and more critically the act of drafting it—marks the end of the American Revolution. For better or worse, and gallons of ink have been spilled on this either/ or formulation, a period of hope, fear, and uncertainty came to a conclusion, and from this point we could measure how what was imagined in 1776 was or was not realized. It represents the proverbial measuring stick moment.

As any early Americanist knows, 1763 might be the most critical, but underappreciated, of the three. It stands for the signing of the Treaty of Paris, the formal end to the Seven Years' War. It was the time, as we have begun to appreciate only recently, that Americans considered themselves to be the most British. Hence the conundrum of getting from this date to the national vanishing point. We now know that throughout the eighteenth century, the descendants of English colonists became British provincials. They consciously thought of themselves as members of a larger imagined community, one that stretched across an ocean that by this point, as one scholar argues, functioned more like a highway than a saltwater curtain.[2]

The dates also suggest a strange disjunction. In fact, they point to a set of questions that do not fit together comfortably. Put simply, understanding the dates, as well as why we deploy them, does not help us solve the riddle of how we get from one defining moment to the next. Historians have characterized the earlier period, the time before 1763, as one of processes leading to self-definition. Through work on Atlantic history, we have reconstructed an eighteenth-century provincial world defined by the movement of people, goods, and ideas. A generation ago, we referred to this as "Anglicization." Now we reckon it as part of the process of America "becoming British."[3] What had been English colonists were now becoming Britons, with all the cultural baggage such a potentially loaded term conveyed. In other words, we have a keen sense of how British Americans conceived of themselves by 1763 and how they formed an integral part of a broader Atlantic system that was being consolidated throughout the eighteenth century.[4] The question, then, that we address here, perhaps now the most significant in American history, is how the most British people in the world threw off their older allegiances to become American. The issue of identity defines the thirteen years between 1763 and 1776.

The period from 1776 to 1787 has always focused on a completely different set of concerns. Scholars have been enthralled with power within the newly independent states: how it was used, who had it, the principles that underscored it, and its implications. Through the work of neo-Whigs and neo-progressives, we are still fighting battles to explain who won and lost the Revolution and whether it constituted a success, albeit measured, or a failure. On the one hand, as Gary Nash contends, we have to appreciate how the "sparks from the altar of 1776" did or did not set off a conflagration of liberty that empowered all.[5] On the other, as Gordon Wood argues, the Revolution may, in fact, have succeeded. It accomplished its radical intent. Wood, however, defines "radicalism" less as liberation and more as a change in defining ideology. Liberty for some would come in the wake of revolution; liberty for the rest would only come later.[6] The two positions ask the basic question we have been posing for some time: "Whose American Revolution?" The imaginative space between 1776 and 1787, therefore, suggests a referendum on revolution and new power relations, far different than the questions focused on process and identity that define the period just before.

The cost is clear. We have an American Revolution that represents a threshold not only historically but also interpretively. On one side of that liminal space, early American historians look backward and out to Britain and its historians for inspiration; at the other end, historians of the early republic peer inward and ahead to the Civil War. One school studies origins and ideas; the other focuses on interests and outcomes. The period between 1763 and 1787 not only delineates two distinctive fields of study; it also presupposes two distinctive understandings of what happened in the middle. In between lies a Revolution, which looks—moving toward it—like a bid for independence within what could be construed as a British civil war, but as we head out seems like an American revolutionary moment, achieved or aborted. We, therefore, have two 1776s: one focused on independence, the other used as a revolutionary litmus test.

For some time, though, a few voices have been calling out of the wilderness to make straight a path between 1763 and 1787, offering as they do so a third way of thinking about revolution in America. Though stars in the field, they have been outliers, scholars who have eschewed the conventional narratives of idealist origins and interest-laden outcomes. They focus on the meanings of the critical dates but in a different way and with a different set of interpretations. It has, therefore, proven difficult to figure how they fit into the debates over the Revolution. Though working on different topics and with distinct sets of interests, the outliers, unbeknownst to each other, have been doing something quite similar and quite fashionable. For some time, three scholars have been urging us to consider empire as the answer.[7]

T. H. Breen would be one. In the late 1990s, Breen published an essay entitled "Ideology and Nationalism on the Eve of the American Revolution: Revisions *Once More* in Need of Revising."[8] In it he updated an older piece by his mentor Edmund Morgan, one that had then tried to figure how Americanists could incorporate what at the time was some of the latest scholarship of English political culture.[9] Morgan saw how Sir Lewis Namier's work could shake up the field of revolutionary America in fundamental ways. He proposed a new imperial approach to the Revolution. Breen did much the same, but he did so in the wake of the rise of the "new" British history and "new" imperial history in Britain. He asked us "once more" to bring empire and sovereignty back into the study of the American provincial culture and revolutionary origins and to mesh it with all the emerging work by Atlantic historians.

Breen answered his own plea in *Marketplace of Revolution*.[10] In it he looks at the Atlantic processes that made America British before the Seven Years' War and how they became the very stuff of politicization by 1763. Empire allowed him to make such a leap between process and identity, on the one hand, and power, on the other. As successive British ministries tried to map power onto the Atlantic system by regulating trade, asserting Parliament's supremacy over the colonies, and constructing a new ideology of how empire had to function, they began to transform what had been a cultural and economic arrangement of interests into a political union, but one in which the colonies would serve subordinate roles. From the center, such a program made a great deal of sense. In a world of heightened competition, because of the integration of the Atlantic, imperial states could only manage an anarchic world. State capacity, amplified through global war making, had grown to allow statesmen to imagine empire in these new ways. As Breen argues, power and process became entangled after 1763 through the imposition of empire. Whereas 1776 stems from this dynamic, empire created the problem.

Others have followed suit. And we are beginning to recognize for the period before revolution that what Parliament did and how English society was enmeshed in American culture mattered for the colonies. We are not, however, returning to such understandings through a narrow Namierite framework. The latest scholarship on political culture, such as that of Eliga Gould or Brendan McConville, brings together all of the fine work done on Atlantic processes—the movement of people, goods, and ideas—with the new political history we see blossoming in English, Scottish, and Irish eighteenth-century history.[11] Fred Anderson does much the same for war making, tying it into an imperial story that Breen and others have been laying out.[12]

A similar though disconnected phenomenon has occurred for the period after revolution. Led by Peter Onuf, a new generation of scholars is beginning to look beyond the winners-and-losers model that has defined the field and instead explores how empire mapped onto power relations after the war.[13] Cognizant of how framers had to wrestle with so many unmanageable dynamics after the 1770s, Onuf argues that state power was the answer to many problems. Ensuring the West lay open as a safety valve to demographic growth, developing a vision of political economy that could knit the new nation together, keeping slave economies intact, recognizing the democratic ethos of the postrevolutionary society, and maintaining independence in an anarchic and competitive international order needed a state that functioned almost like Breen's British empire. And as Onuf has shown, thinkers such as Thomas Jefferson functioned as imperial architects. They devised blueprints of empire to bring revolution to a close, to codify older arrangements, and to rationalize new realities.

Onuf has been followed by other thoughtful scholars, such as Max Edling and Frank Cogliano, both of whom consider America an imperial state after the Revolution.[14] Far from weak, the new federated leviathan proved able and adaptable. It could bring focused power to bear in protecting its borders and in policing its citizens. The term "empire of liberty," these scholars propose, was neither an empty rhetorical flourish nor simply an oxymoron. It speaks to how Americans had to reorder society in the wake of war. We now know that the new United States were not exceptional in the world of geopolitics. They too comprised an empire. This for these scholars working on what we could call the "new history of the state," one clearly imperial in scope and ambition, stands as the story after the War of Independence, and charting who won and who lost stems from these critical questions.

A final voice has also been working as a prophet of sorts. Jack Greene could hardly be considered marginalized in the profession, and he could hardly be considered cutting-edge. Yet he has proven difficult to pigeonhole, mainly because he has consistently worked on something that has not captured the attention of the reigning interpreters. Throughout his career he has stood at the intersection of early American history and British imperial history, looking at Britain from the periphery and peering at America from the center. Unsurprisingly, imperial sovereignty has long transfixed Greene: how it was articulated, how it varied from place to place, and how it was exercised. Greene's Revolution, pure and simple, revolved around the concept and how it could and could not rationalize the whole.[15] And others follow him as well, in this case scholars like Peter Miller, John Philip Reid, and Steve Pincus.[16] Though as prolific as any scholar of the past half-century, Greene has proven an iconoclast because of his emphasis on empire, but with Breen and Onuf, he finds himself in good company.

Apart, these perspectives help explain what our dates mean. If Breen explains 1763 and Onuf 1787, Greene sets his sights on 1776. Yet their imperial perspectives do much more. They bind the dates together in a continual arc. Wedding them together promises to create a more integrated narrative moving from 1763 and 1787. It also reorients our understanding of what happened in the middle. For Breen, Onuf, and Greene, the Revolution represented more than a war of independence and more than a referendum on the spirit of 1776. If we move forward from Breen, what we find is that a newly politicized people became insurgents within an embattled empire. They lived during a period of promise and of great fear. They struggled, in short, during a revolutionary moment, one that saw a contest over the meaning of sovereignty, as Greene argues. If we move back from the "empire of liberty," we see a period that appears remarkably similar. It is, as Onuf has argued, a moment that teetered between anarchy and sovereignty, with common people existing on the horns of this dilemma.[17] Between the British empire and the American empire, Americans descended into the anarchic abyss. The death of one empire and birth of the other empire would prove daunting.

What we could refer to as the "imperial-revolutionary" approach of Breen, Greene, and Onuf, however it diverges from the conventional narratives, is not altogether new. In fact, it resurrects the broad super-structure created by an earlier group of scholars, the so-called old imperial school. Though not portrayed as an inspiration for Atlantic history, its adherents had simple but profound things to say about transatlantic connections. The institutions of empire, and the ideas of sovereignty that sustained them, bound America to Britain before the Revolution, lay at the heart of American resistance to Britain, and would leave a lasting legacy for the new nation. Breen, Greene, and Onuf do work remarkably similar to that of Charles McLean Andrews, Lawrence Henry Gipson, and Charles McIlwaine.[18] By going back to the future, the modern troika comprises the core of a movement for which empire is striking back.

This volume is animated by this seamless imperial-revolutionary sense of the period, and in it we start to see how such an approach is beginning to characterize how we conceive of revolution in America. If these essays are any indication, this sensibility informs the ways we think about the eighteenth century, the Revolution, the period after 1787, and the relationship between them. The contributors are driven by some traditional understandings of how empire worked and what it meant in much the same way Greene's work is. Empire conventionally understood broadly serves as the backdrop to each of the essays. But they are in keeping with the newer ways we consider a very old topic, which would put them in line with Breen and Onuf. What we see in the essays is how empire has once more become a hot topic, and the new approaches to it animate the ways the contributors consider power and its implications.

The contributors find themselves in what seems a burgeoning (or reburgeoning) field of study. Since Breen published his plea for a new early American imperial history, British historians have continued to rediscover empire and have argued that the domestic cannot be divorced from imperial ambitions. One merged into the other. They have also started to craft a seamless narrative of their own for a revolutionary age. Following on the heels of Linda Colley, David Armitage and especially Eliga Gould and Richard Bourke have set out an ambitious agenda to rediscover the ideas and sensibilities behind a "Greater Britain."[19] This emphasis has led to a rather traditionally defined project: the "Oxford History of the British Empire" series.[20] Nonetheless, the editor for the eighteenth-century volume has moved from it to penetrating studies of British imperial ideology and ambitions. The work of P. J. Marshall, tying the first to the second British empire, serves as a perfect example of how exciting the field has become.[21] He has pushed well beyond Colley and pointed us toward a heightened awareness of how the first British Empire and the so-called second were not as distinctive as we had thought. Moreover, he has demonstrated how even in the Atlantic the echoes of empire remained after the revolutionary crisis. Indeed, he sees British empire as the story of continuity between early modern and modern eras.

All of these scholars use the idea of "empire" in a number of complementary ways. It can be an intellectual concept and a justification or rationalization for the expansion of power. It can be employed to suggest an aspiration for greatness and expansion, proclaiming, for instance, the birth of an empire that does not yet exist. "Empire" can mean a cultural sense of superiority, the notion that an imperialist is bringing "order" to the benighted peoples of the globe. Or, most conventionally, the term connotes a fiscal/military structure that projects the power of the core to distant places. That structure can take on many guises. It can take the shape of a collection of holdings with different institutional ties to the center bound together by a commercial ideology and a common identity. It can be a political unit across vast space that is bound by centralized authority and by a clear expression of sovereignty.[22]

The concept of empire is now employed in even more fascinating fashion. Indeed, Native American historians have made "empire" downright fashionable. About a decade ago Gregory Dowd argued that, akin to Armitage, Native American cultural change, such as seen at the time of Pontiac's War, made no sense without reference to empire.[23] More provocatively, Pekka Hämäläinen has applied a concept of empire any nineteenth-century Europeanist would be comfortable using to characterize a people normally construed as the victims of empire. His "Comanche Empire" controlled space, law, and allegiance. It had boundaries and ambassadors. It was, in a word, sovereign and unambiguously so.[24] However controversial his interpretation, what he has done is make scholars appreciate empire anew. State and sovereignty matter, even for those normally deemed on the margins.

The renewed fascination points to the innovative ways scholars from around the world are exploring this most traditional of concepts, which is beginning to shape how Americanists understand their own field. Historians working on any number of places and topics now emphasize empire as lived experience, and they attend to the cultural consequences of power. They do not do so to restate the obvious: that empire often exploited and oppressed "subaltern" peoples. Power in the hands of the "new-new" imperial historians works in a much more subtle fashion. Indeed, no field is more fertile than imperial history today. Those studying Spanish and Portuguese empire, for instance, have recovered how the Bourbon reforms of the 1760s, focused on the person of the king, buttressed rule for some time but ultimately attenuated imperial bonds. Work on Spain, particularly by Gabe Paquette and Jeremy Adelman, has broken new ground on this theme.[25] Portugal, far from an inexplicable exception to a larger imperial rule, now seemed to try to weather the crises of the late eighteenth and early nineteenth century by combining state and empire into a complex and efficacious whole.[26] And this dynamic stemmed from a distinctive imperial culture that had dramatic implications for the period after the age of revolution. Sir John Elliott has done more than any other scholar of tying the history of the Iberian "exception" into the mainstream. Spain's experiences seem typical—but not identical—once we consider them from an imperial perspective used to understand Britain. Elliott's Atlantic empires appear as variations on a common theme.[27]

Even those nations whose imperial ambitions shrank before Spain and Britain's have their "new" imperial history.[28] In their work we find, perhaps, some of the most intriguing examples of the reconsideration of empire. Take the French case as an example. Though the French created a more centralized empire than Spain and Britain—in terms of how it was to be managed and how it had to be justified—power on the peripheries remained weak. Pretensions gave way to sordid realities. Yet, as scholars have recently shown, the French proved adept at sustaining an empire in the New World that relied on native ways, on accommodation, on limited but focused coercion, and most vitally on information networks. French empire worked. Though they lost empire in 1763, or at least the mass of their territory, the French demonstrated themselves to be able imperialists, using power in supple ways. Like the Spaniards, they too initiated drastic reforms for how empire would function after 1763, leading to the preconditions that would spark revolution in Saint-Domingue by dividing groups in new ways and leading to ill-fated alliances of power.[29] Scholars, then, have recovered the varied means through which power was employed and its kaleidoscopic implications. They have looked at master-slave relations through the prism of empire, sexual relations, and intercultural conflict. To appreciate empire is to gauge how common people understood it.[30]

British scholars have followed suit, considering the projection of power and sovereignty over space in innovative ways that build on, say, the Oxford History but that also move well beyond it. Cultural patterns from the high style to the vernacular, we now know, were suffused with empire. To cite just a few examples, David Shields has examined the ways Scottish enlightenment sensibilities, particularly the ideal of sociability, penetrated popular culture. Tavern gossip, popular ballads, and *belles lettres* constituted the venues and modes to debate empire and province.[31] Scholars have of late explored imperial ideology and employed Atlantic perspectives to uncover the cultural costs of empire within the provinces. The creation of identity involved those excluded from the traditional story of the provincial dilemma. As Susan Scott Parish argues, British American understandings of their status in the empire depended upon the labor of slaves, as well as the exclusion of women from the body politic.[32] Recent studies also suggest that the only way to understand provincial cultures is to widen the lens to incorporate the whole empire. Maya Jasanoff reminds us that empire encompassed the exotic East. Collecting the curiosities from places such as India, just as an empire was collected, shaped British conceptions of the self. The English, the Scots, and even some Irish developed their understandings of their status within the state and the empire as they thought of the East.[33]

Empire has opened a new world of possibilities beyond the strictly political and the simply subaltern for appreciating the British center and the peripheries. As Kathleen Wilson finds, Britons of all stripes performed empire through ritual and theater. Exploring rites of celebration and commemoration, as seen in the materials produced for everyday consumption, offers as reliable a measure of what it meant to be English or Scottish in the eighteenth century as high-flying intellectual life.[34] And Colin Calloway has argued that the ways Highlanders did and did not fit into empire paralleled the ways that Indians participated.[35] Tom Bartlett has done the same for the Irish, explaining that the critical difference for them stemmed from how both Indians and Highlanders were fetishized in the military, while the Irish soldier was not.[36] These scholars point to a new way of thinking about empire, one with a focus on common people but one that up to this point has not animated an empire-less America.

The essays of this collection embrace older and newer understandings of empire, while paying deference to the questions raised by Breen, Greene, and Onuf. They still work with an understanding of empire as the term is traditionally and still usefully used, that is, by placing states with expansive overseas agendas and with subjects far away from the metropole in geopolitical competition. Empire does not only concern "powers" but "power" as well, how it is justified and applied by metropolitan authorities intent on control over spaces and peoples removed from the center. This observation is especially true in prerevolutionary and postrevolutionary contexts. Both were imperial ages, punctuated by an age of revolution. In the former, Britain was engaged in a process of heightened imperial rivalry occasioned by the consolidation of the Atlantic that led officials in the metropole, forced them really, to try to reform empire. In essence, they made the arrangements that had bound the colonies to Britain more systematized to create an Atlantic empire that could withstand the challenges of the time. A similar dynamic held after the Revolution, when a new American state, focused on the West for its imperial ambitions, now stood among the nations of the earth.[37] Though republican, this empire proved more durable than the last. It was propelled, not stymied, by popular sovereignty. And ingenious federal arrangements, which allowed new republics to replicate and multiply, allowed it to grow across the Continent. The so-called empire of liberty was an empire in every sense of the word, improving on the older British model by unleashing settlers' and speculators' energies, displacing indigenous peoples, and expanding the domain of slave labor.

The essays, though, view empire as a protean concept. It took on a wide variety of improvised forms. It was imagined on the margins as much as it was at any center. It incorporated all sorts of people in its web. It had as much to do with attitudes of subordination, something we could call "imperialism," as it did with the formal structures and centers of power. It could include those who were technically stateless, who sought to dominate neighbors without the presumption to rule, as well as those who were the agents of European imperial agendas, those intent on making dominance over space and peoples permanent and politically unambiguous.

Moreover, at key moments, the formal and the protean collided, forcing all to articulate what power meant, how it would be channeled, who could wield it and who could not. Questions of sovereignty could not be avoided when geopolitical realities dictated otherwise. Often, in the meantime, power had become diffused through all sorts of informal arrangements and local institutional life. Once debates about formal sovereignty began, the informal had to be rationalized anew, erased, fought for, and fought against. And we could peg such moments to our dates.

In other words, the authors acknowledge traditional markers of sovereignty but they refuse to be held captive by them. The varied places they study and the topics that capture their attention as they explore sovereign power in its many dimensions speak to how the "imperial-revolutionary" way is beginning to shape the field. The essays range from the late seventeenth to the early nineteenth century. They move from the American northern frontier and St. Louis to the streets of Edinburgh and Paris—and all points in between. They cover Indians, American colonists, slaves, Britons, Frenchmen and women, Spanish colonists, speculators, loyalists, insurgent patriots, traders and merchants, theorists, lawyers, officials, commanders, wealthy women, poor women, Huguenots, construction crews, antiquarians, and diplomats. But they demonstrate how the field of early America, the American Revolution, and the early Republic is changing. I say "field" in the singular because the essays illustrate a converging sensibility about contexts and power. All deal with empire or state power, the veritable old questions. All contend with these sorts of questions in light of the work done by social and then cultural historians.

Together they suggest an old sensibility in a new form, as well as a new narrative that captures the meanings of 1776 and helps us move from 1763 and before to 1787 and beyond. What we see in these essays is people reckoning with the meanings of British empire before revolution and American empire after. In between, they managed the abyss. Invoking "people" may sound trite, but it most assuredly is not. As most of the recent work on empire testifies, it is men and women, particularly the common sort, who create, sustain, or contest empire. In these contexts, people are ever negotiating. The term has been overused and abused, a cheap way to gesture toward something happening on a human level. Here it suggests something else. In the essays, men and women find themselves in constrained circumstances, sometimes of their own making, and have to act. The times, especially in and around imperial-revolutionary moments, call for decisions and conscious actions. The relationship between sovereignty—the stuff of empire—and how people manage it, even if they have to choose between competing programs, is the dynamic each of these scholars find meaningful. Like the latest work on Native American empires and their European counterparts, they point to more nuanced ways of thinking about negotiations. Far from invisible, once we look for it, imperial power had many manifestations and varied implications.

In America, common men and women created, resisted, and struggled with empire before 1763, between 1776 and 1787, and after 1787. Indeed, the revolutionary period was, in many ways, a moment when Americans accommodated themselves to successive empires and their demands in quick succession. The study of America after the imperial turn usefully blurs the distinction between the prerevolutionary eighteenth century and the crisis that brought revolution. The debate over power and empire began in the 1760s, escalated in the 1770s, and led to profound changes in the 1780s. But how did the preceding experience with empire shape these pivotal decades? How did men and women then see postrevolutionary processes? How would they remember these? This issue of memory proves critical for exploring the topic of empire in America in large part because, as Americans were constructing their own empire in the early nineteenth century, they had to forget their own imperial past in the eighteenth century.

The first set of essays, in a section entitled "Empire and Provincials," explores the intersection of British empire and American provincial culture. Each asks how eighteenth-century immersion in a British Atlantic world and initial British attempts to integrate the colonies politically and economically challenged Americans to consider who they were. Imperial power is understood to work in complex ways. Each of the scholars in this section looks at what we would consider a traditional concern of Atlantic historians, especially the movement of commodities, to demonstrate how the process of Atlantic consolidation had political implications that cannot be disentangled from imperial concerns. In this way, the Atlantic, usually understood geographically, was becoming politicized in the eighteenth century well before the crisis of sovereignty.

Timothy Shannon explores the question of British perceptions of North America during the late eighteenth century by looking at the career of a Scottish collector. This essay opens the collection for one reason: it considers power in its many manifestations at a time before formal projections of power enveloped the colonies in prerevolutionary crisis. Shannon offers a working-man's guide to the colonies, a way of gauging how far or how close Americans were to Britain and Britons to America on the eve of Revolution. Britons were discerning shoppers of all things American. They knew America and could discriminate. Intellectual ferment of Enlightenment, Shannon tells us, flowed both ways across an ocean, but it also flowed through or around the center, and sustained and reflected power relations. Empire, before the crisis of the 1770s took hold, was something built in the provinces and at the center. It was the work of officials, of course, but also involved ordinary people. And Britishness was sustained by the production and consumption of the idea of a British empire on the part of common men and women. Construction of empire, and of the ideas that rationalized it, Shannon suggests, was no simple, straightforward matter.

Owen Stanwood trods similar ground. For him, goods could unite as much as they could complicate. They could help unify an empire and heal the political rift that was developing in the 1770s. He turns what would appear a dead-end—Americans making wine—into a fascinating foray of political possibilities and imperial visions. Notions of political economy were not set; rather, as Stanwood suggests, the period of the eighteenth century led to deliberations over how the imperial economy should be organized in light of the integration of the Atlantic during the period. From this essay we are left with perplexing questions about identity (who were Americans?) and about the hows and whys of the imperial crisis that would start in the 1760s. The contradictions of being provincials in a dynamic empire still searching for a theory of political economy that worked (a postmercantilist, pre–Adam Smith world) and the political paradoxes engendered by the tug between center and periphery were evident by the time Americans experienced a renewed mania for winemaking. The efforts at winemaking, he concludes, failed because Atlantic tensions proved too great.

Patricia Cleary takes us right to the heart of the struggles that define the period with a study of sex. Sex, she tells us, is about power. It goes to the tension between personal autonomy and the prerogatives of state power. European women, as she argues, embodied—quite literally—the tensions between empire and provincialism because their "ability to have fully European offspring positioned them differently in the social and biological calculus of empire building." Instead of abstractions about political economy, Cleary examines "officials" looking to police. These officials were also involved in a process of negotiation. Eager to control, they often tolerated. And what we find in this essay is a creative dance between state power and individual autonomy, a dance happening during a period of profound flux. Imperial power, she reminds us, does not work in a straightforward fashion. It mapped onto the processes that consolidated the Atlantic but did so in surprising ways.

Cleary introduces us to the theme of imperial surprises and how once we stand at the intersection between power and process, the unexpected often results. Ian Saxine's essay takes us to Maine where contestation between various subjects in a context of imperial imperatives was a way of life. As he argues, the struggle between speculator, colonist, and Indian defined the eighteenth century and represented the very stuff of colonies becoming provinces of empire, but in anything but straightforward ways. In fact, the process of Atlantic consolidation that led to some sort of stability in many places led to tension here; at the same time, the process created strange convergences in the process of empire building. Earlier on, landowners tried to assert a vision of an orderly society on a motley assortment of men and women, who themselves were in conflict with one another. This accounted for the kaleidoscopic nature of imperial state formation in Maine, a place where no one had the upper hand but where many had pretensions to having an upper hand. The disjunction between expectations and experience made for a place defined by the sort of flux that only a war could ease. Frontiers, Saxine reminds us, are different sorts of places, where we see some of the fundamental issues gripping all regions but in greater relief. In Maine, as he shows, the violence and disorder that defined the eighteenth-century frontier would "blend into" the violence and disorder of the Seven Years' War and, of course, that of the imperial crisis that would lead to revolution. Warfare would, however, lay siege to the strange sort of cooperation that saw officials in Massachusetts siding with Indians to curtail imperial expansion.

Reimmersion in a broader British Atlantic, then, also entailed new systems of power and had unexpected results. And America's imperial moment took place well before 1763, requiring even those on the metaphorical and physical margins of society to reconsider who they were. Empire was not, after all, merely an abstraction or a cultural ideal. It confronted all with dilemmas, challenges, and possibilities. These essays pick up on the dynamics Breen explores. Indeed, it's fair to say his general approach, as well as that of others such as McConville, serves as an inspiration, though here complexity defines all. With people, goods, and ideas came notions of power relations that would, of course, be fully realized in the 1760s and 1770s with the crisis that led to revolution. To cite the simplest example, the Seven Years' War confronted Americans with the bluntest of all power, and Americans had to make peace with it.

The next set of essays, in a section called "War, Revolution, and Empires," moves to the unsettling transition from one empire to the next. Like Greene, the authors work with the concept of sovereignty. Indeed, it forms the basic idea that they see animating the struggle that was the Revolution. Yet they move far beyond the legal ideas that Greene and Reid focus on by looking at their implications on the proverbial ground. Against the backdrop of the contest for sovereignty, they explore the difficult choices people made in constrained circumstances when dealing with elemental state power or its absence. These essays confront power in a straightforward way, understandably so as the Revolution revolved around power relations. We see here a revolution that was first and foremost a process that began once imperial power collapsed. It hinged on sovereignty—who controlled it and how it was rationalized—and how this abstract concept was embodied. People in difficult straits, concerned with peace and security, struggled to create the institutions that could tame the process of revolution. Revolution did not only center on aspirations. It also represented a period veering wildly between the extremes of fear and hope. We have long appreciated the French Revolution in this regard.[38] But the American? Hardly. These essays, which bring process and power together and try to judge how people made sense of it all, point toward a new way of thinking of this seminal moment.

James Coltrain's essay explores the formal projection of power and how it manifested itself in an American context. As he argues in this essay, the British were able to harness the forces of the Atlantic and use them to build forts on even the furthest reaches of the frontier. More to the point, Coltrain brings us back once more to that time in place when the Atlantic became enmeshed with empire. At Fort Stanwix, process met power. Because the British demonstrated flexibility in navigating a world commercial, maritime, and free, they could construct the sinews of power on the frontier. In so doing, he suggests, they were able to map the apparatuses of sovereignty onto a system. The French, presumably because of hyper-centralization, had put the cart before the horse. Power preceded process, and because of this, they failed. Coltrain reminds us that for whatever reason it is the period around the time of the Seven Years' War that brought the two dynamics together, as now that space became as never before a locus for the contest over sovereignty. In combining the two, the British enjoyed unparalleled success, the sort of success that, as Coltrain suggests, would cost them dearly.

As Chris Hodson reminds us, what happened to the mainland North American colonies during the eighteenth century represented a British variation on a common Atlantic theme and was more complicated than we had believed. His essay offers the French example (or counterexample) as a means to see the British American dynamic of coming to terms with power in stark relief. Hodson's exploration of the French experience of empire forces us to not only consider the whole—the whole Atlantic that would be rocked by struggles over power, commerce, slavery, and revolutionary ferment—but also the American provincial chapter of the story. As he explains, the French story moves us beyond simple tales of imperial success and failure to bring us to fundamental questions of process and power. Hodson brings the looming question of the state back into a field where it has been constructively missed. What does power mean in the wake of the new social history, the shift to ethnography, and the linguistic turn? Hodson's essay quite consciously brings the reader to traditional questions of power in a field of study transformed by all sorts of new approaches. And, as he shows, our understandings of power are more nuanced because the worlds we encounter today as historians working on Atlantic subjects are, as he suggests, extraordinarily complex. Hodson's essay serves as a vivid reminder that imperial power—formal, informal, negotiated, unmediated, implemented, failed—created problems and opportunities for all men and women at both the center and the margins.

The complexity only increases as we ask what made people revolutionaries. We could, of course, explore ideas. We could also examine material interests. Michael Guenther is interested less in the substance of revolutionary sensibilities than the question of "how" they came to be. But in so doing, he reminds us what happens to societies when empire is reeling. The collapse of imperial sovereignty presented people on both sides of the ocean with new challenges and new possibilities, especially as transatlantic debates on what constituted empire began to fixate all in the late 1760s and early 1770s. Guenther reconstructs the world of one London printer, John Almon, to demonstrate what happens during such moments. Well situated in an "imperial" network, Almon was able to make opposition more a practice than a prescription, an idea avidly adopted by Americans as they struggled with the sharp end of empire. Although in Britain, such networks would sustain reform movements, in America revolution was the answer to the question of an imperial dilemma. By creating an ecosystem of relationships like Almon's in the colonies, Americans were unwittingly not only crafting the bases of revolution, they were also developing the quasi-institutions that would allow them to wield power as imperial power fell to pieces. Together with Hodson's piece, Guenther reminds how imperial dynamics function outside of formal institutionalized lines of authority. They work through networks, circulation, and intelligence.

Power functioned most vividly when empire was absent, especially during the war. And here we get to yet another theme covered in this section. A number of the essays try to help us understand what revolutionary tumult entailed or how power or the lack thereof confronted ordinary people with difficult choices. Here we witness a contradiction about the power that a number of the essays explore. Sometimes power was to be resisted; at other times it was desired. Such moments, in the time between sovereignties, remind us that reckoning with power is not straightforward and that simplistic answers cannot do justice to social realities during periods of profound flux.

Donald Johnson's essay is a case in point. It serves as a transition piece in the collection, dwelling on the war but moving us toward its tangled but forgotten legacy. It is the fitting start to the last section of the collection. In fact, his essay explores how revolution became the American Revolution. Contemporary historians, looking at the tumult they and their neighbors had survived, sanitized what had happened, turning a time of uncertainty and vacillation into a narrative of certainty and well-defined allegiances. They also absolved many of the taint of loyalism, allowing such men and women to wish away collaboration with the British imperial state. Johnson, then, introduces us to how revolution came to an end. It did so as long as Americans forgot their recent past and recast the crisis that had led to an imperial impasse. The act of forgetting, as he argues, would have dramatic implications for how Americans would craft their own empire, for American empire would be constructed on the pedestal of a narrative of uncomplicated virtue.

The remaining essays ask us to consider the implications that Johnson encourages us to wrestle with. As power reemerged after a period of flux in new guises, how did Americans grapple with what might have been? How were they haunted by the ghosts of old empires and older provincial identities in a world characterized by a new empire? Power, this section entitled "The Ghosts of Empire" reminds us, is a complicated thing. Americans needed to forget an older empire as they created a new one to contain the tensions that had not been rectified by revolution. Like Dickens's Scrooge, they would be haunted by ghosts of past, present, and future.

David Gellman argues that a more conventional notion of ambivalence—which by its nature leaves questions unanswered—defined the period and explains a great deal of what we would regard as contradictory behavior. To our eyes owning slaves and posing as an abolitionist smacks of perversity. Alas, in the period near the end of revolution, it was not so surprising. Though confronting power and the contradictions of freedom and unfreedom through their revolution, Americans did not so much do away with tensions as they reordered them. Creating a new empire placed them in a bind similar to the one the British had to contend with. Having to attend to the process of constructing their own state, they found themselves in the position of signing onto a new devil's bargain to ensure the survival of a republic, to hold the whole together, and to maintain stability. Gellman's essay illustrates how such choices were becoming defining features of a postcolonial, postrevolutionary world, in which white elites now had to reckon with the fallout of a process of Atlantic consolidation that was sustained through the institution of slavery. The revolution did not undo such perversities. In fact, Gellman suggests, it may have sustained them as imperial people learned to live with ambivalence.

For Seth Cotlar, a sense of American haunting had as much to do with what had occurred in America during revolution—especially perceived discontinuities of time that he calls "ruptures"—as it had to do with the pace of change in the then-present. On the face of it, his essay explores nostalgia. It is easy to regard nostalgia as a retreat from history, a safe space once the past no longer matters urgently for sense of self. Cotlar suggests the opposite is the case. The nostalgia of the frenetic period of the early republic stands as a vital counterpoint to the celebratory narratives of the then-present—creating relics of a world contemporaries felt they were losing—not to go back to that past, but to address the uncertainty and paradoxes of the present. Nostalgia, it seems, was not nostalgic, but it did stem from feeling and perception. It also bespoke ambivalence. Cotlar here gives us a needed antidote to more celebratory takes on the period after revolution. But that's what the Revolution, one presumably that was meant to destroy power but rationalized it in new ways, wrought. Nostalgia, like memory, fit itself around this paradox of American empire. In this regard Cotlar's essay does something quite interesting with the familiar trope of ambivalence. It ties it into time when it is usually employed to consider condition, the disjunction between what it hoped for and what is achieved. His is one of how the past is reimagined in light of the present.

In a world still politicized, Americans understood processes, such as westward movement, the acceleration of the slave trade, the whipsawing effect of economic stagnation and opportunity, with the discourses of power: who ruled and who did not; what sovereignty entailed and how it would be justified. The essays also suggest that leaving one empire behind, with much of its injustice still animating the newly independent states, and bringing into being a new one that enshrined some of the same injustices required men and women, the sort we have been looking at throughout this long period, to remember and to forget. What we see in this section is common people creating and struggling to understand the empire Onuf writes about. As much as Jefferson and Hamilton, they too tussled with the period's ambiguities and came up with ideas of their own to deal with them. Whether they wanted to or not, they had to wrestle with ghosts and demons. Such is the lot of any imperial people.

T. H. Breen concludes the volume by reflecting on the essays of the collection. He does so by examining the ways the authors are pursuing themes— and a timeline—that continue to transfix American and British historians. In it, he suggests that once we slip out of the prevailing narrative and break it into discrete segments, different stories emerge that challenge that very framework. The origin myth of the Revolution begins to appear less compelling when we frame the 1760s as part of a broader imperial story. The years of revolution become more revolutionary. And the 1780s appear less troubling than we could have believed, revealing a seamlessness to the period impossible to see with the older undeconstructed narrative structure. He does this in light of the essays in the collections and reaffirms the utility of the imperial-revolutionary arc to reknit the deconstructed segments.

Ultimately, Breen reminds us that the dates we choose determine what we see, and that when it comes to America's Revolution, the dates we use have an extraordinarily powerful pull, that unless carefully dealt with will lead to celebratory narratives and lend an air of inevitability. Once we disentangle these dates from American exceptional myths and tie them to imperial moments or windows of time, however, they resonate in new and enlightening ways. The American origin story seems less exceptional, as Britain's imperial crisis paralleled the struggles of other powers. The revolutionary years appear more tumultuous and less predetermined, less tied to the patriot narrative. And the end came only when ordinary men and women reckoned with the realities of and need for power in a postrevolutionary society. The narrative Breen describes is still pinned broadly to the three moments the other authors hold to; however, he demonstrates that they have relevance far beyond the confines of the conventional story of the Revolution.

Because in many ways the approach that these essays embrace was shaped by the work of T. H. Breen, we have asked a prominent scholar to write an "afterword" on how his work grew over a career to find its fullest and clearest expression on power, process, and people through empire. One of Breen's most renowned students, Joyce Chaplin, explores how his work, as well as his assumptions about the past, has been animated by this focus on power and ordinary people. She argues that Breen has consistently been transfixed by discovering how people found meaning in shifting contexts. In exploring Breen's career, Chaplin hopes to understand how people in the past learned to live with or contested authority. How did men and women—of all races—navigate systems of oppression? How do we explain the sometimes rather unexpected ways they worked within the constraints imposed by predominant power relations? How did distance from the metropole complicate relations of power? How did common people participate in and create empire? And how do we make sense of power during periods of profound instability, be that instability material or ideological? These questions, she contends, fascinate Breen.

Together the essays point to a compelling way of thinking about the period of the American Revolution. For a start, call the time instead the "imperial-revolutionary" moment. The fundamental signposts of the period remain. The date 1763 still represents the apogee of British sovereign control of its New World holdings, 1776 stands for the moment British sovereign contentions were shaken as a new notion of sovereignty was poised to replace it, whereas 1787 marks the rise of an expansive American state. These dates speak to moments of geopolitical reckoning when formal imperial power had to be realized, when it was rejected, or when it had to be resurrected in new form. But the years 1763, 1776, and 1787, and more critically the relationship between them, take on new, subtler meaning in these essays. At their most basic, the contributors point to a more seamless period of time bookended by two dynamically changing empires. Ironically, in increasingly competitive worlds on either side of revolution, elites structured power in similar ways to address broad processes, both their constraints and their possibilities. Common people participated and shaped these processes in both contexts, but they reacted differently in each. Empire on one end created for many insuperable problems; on the other, it presented the only viable alternative to the world's troubling dynamics. On the one side of the revolutionary divide, the concept of empire could not provide interpretive order, much less sovereign order, to the changes gripping the Atlantic system in 1763; on the other side, it could.

The period in between proves just as critical to our understanding of the beginning and the end and helps explain the fall of one empire and the rise of another. The Revolution changed basic categories of political belonging but not the need for order and control. If power, as the essays suggest, mattered before in deep but subtle ways, after the Revolution it did so transparently and overtly. This reality, as much as any other, demonstrates the difference between an empire of subjects that could not stand and one of citizens that did. This is the essence of the "imperial-revolutionary" approach.

At each of the critical junctures of this moment in time, officials and ordinary men and women struggled over how power would be actualized, or how the protean ways power operated in colonial settings could and could not jibe with formal imperial sovereignty. In 1763, those negotiations centered on how an Atlantic empire could rule places far removed as well as subjects of all sorts, the most powerful of whom had created autonomous settler societies through exploitation and through commerce. In 1776, after the failure of the British state to create empire, those same settlers elected to enter a state of nature and construct a state that could ensure their happiness and allow for government with minimal power. In 1787, after more than a decade in a near-anarchic state, they opted to compromise and to construct a new empire that could deliver them from disordering effects of ungoverned power and promise happiness for many at the expense of marginalized groups.

What we have, then, is a world before the Revolution that looks like a "colonial" society of imperial subjects and a postrevolutionary world that functions as a "postcolonial" world of imperial citizens. Americans usually invoke one term in nostalgic ways—think here of tricorn hats and muskets—and the other never at all. When empire meaningfully enters the equation, the terms have new purchase. The colonial condition of provincial America was shaped by empire. But most did not experience empire as a subject people. Power empowered them to subject others, especially Indians and Africans. And so most common settlers found themselves in a colonial world as a privileged people, that is, until the years just after 1763. And we see in these years not so much the clear-cut stories of "colonial" oppression but a narrative of ambiguity, explaining of course why such a term does not quite seem to fit. The postcolonial world for Americans proved just as ambivalent but in a different way. Heirs to the ambiguities of the colonial past, they had not vanquished these ghosts in the crucible of revolution. Instead, they created institutions and new sets of rules, especially the one of 1787, which canonized the ghosts and which would haunt the new empire. Of course, America was and was not an "empire of liberty." The ambivalence of the postcolonial had less to do with the Revolution than with the colonial holdovers that defined postcolonial empire.

The notion that a revolution brought one empire to an end and another into being suggests continuities over the *longue durée.* Or does it? The American republican empire, like its British precursor or the Comanche empire for that matter, controlled space, subjected peoples, demanded allegiance, and used power to protect its interests and expand its ambit. Yet the culture had experienced a sea change. Empire had to be legitimated in new ways to reflect its republican bases as well as the fact that people had been politicized by war and the overturning of an old order. Popular sovereignty was no abstraction but animating fact. A politicized people rationalized power in new ways, requiring different cultural responses to broad processes, such as demographic shifts. One could not impose, say, a Proclamation Line in place to keep subject peoples apart. One had to work through new institutions and appeal to new ideas to restrain or, more likely, channel expansion. The American state had to be an "empire of liberty" to reflect broad changes and maintain order. As opposed to the British Empire, which situated sovereignty in Parliament in a centralized state system, the American empire, federal and democratic, was a many-headed hydra.

Empire allows us to understand stability and instability, power and impotence, and limits and possibilities in a tumultuous age. Because the United States became the first empire to emerge out of an age of imperial intrigue, crisis, and revolution, and because Americans had fastened on a way to manage power effectively, they were able to forestall the most destabilizing excesses of the age. They avoided the furies that pulled down the Spanish and Portuguese empires, that decimated France and created Haiti in a baptism of bloodshed, that imperiled Britain and leveled Ireland. Therefore, the transition from a British empire to an American empire proved less violent and more seamless than in any of these places. The new national, democratic empire was far more adept at managing space and handling internal challenges, such as frontier intrigue or slave resistance, than any monarchical empire ever could. At least until the Civil War.

Through the "imperial-revolutionary" lens, therefore, we have a 1763 that looks far different than the one we have grown accustomed to, one that illustrates how power functioned in many guises and which would have profound implications for formal debates about sovereignty. At the time, through their participation, common people sustained imperial power. Soon they would contest it because of the disjunction between how power had operated in the provinces and the ways it was imagined in the metropole. Here 1776 appears less about a document than the manifestation of the tangled ways empire could not work. It represents a moment when imperial sovereignty fractured, leaving a vacuum in its wake and plunging America into a sovereign abyss of competing programs to reconstitute it. And 1787 marks not an end to this process but a window of time when Americans had to construct and then make peace with the simple fact that for revolution to end, a government needed power and had to expand. All would be haunted because of it. For these essays, the questions do not change, but because of the focus on the relationship between people and empire, the answers do.

Notes

1. On this, see Patrick Griffin, *America's Revolution* (Oxford, 2012). The idea of a vanishing point in history is developed by H.W. Smith, *The Continuities of German History: Nation, Religion, and Race across the Long Nineteenth Century* (Cambridge, 2008), 13–38.

2. Frank Thistlethwaite, "Migration from Europe Overseas in the Nineteenth and Twentieth Centuries," in Comite International des Sciences Historiques, Xie Congres International des Sciences Historiques, *Rapports: V: Histoire Contemporaine* (Stockholm, 1960), 32–60.

3. The concept of Anglicization is John Murrin's and forms a keystone of his work. For a series of recent reassessments—and the thoughts of Murrin himself—see Ignacio Gallup-Diaz, Andrew Shankman, and David J. Silverman, eds., *Anglicizing America: Empire, Revolution, Republic* (Philadelphia: University of Pennsylvania Press, 2015). The term "making British" is Nicholas Canny's—see his *Making Ireland British 1580–1650* (Oxford, 2001)—but I have adapted it to America in *America's Revolution*.

4. Joyce Chaplin, "The British Atlantic," in Nicholas Canny and Philip Morgan, eds., *The Oxford Handbook of the Atlantic World, 1450–1850* (New York, 2011). On the broader Atlantic dynamics, of which the British theme forms one variation, see Jack Greene and Philip Morgan, "Introduction: The Present State of Atlantic History" and Trevor Burnard, "The British Atlantic" in *Atlantic History: A Critical Appraisal* (New York, 2009), 18–20, 118–19.

5. Gary Nash, "Philadelphia's Radical Caucus That Propelled Pennsylvania to Inde-

pendence and Democracy," in Nash, Alfred Young, and Ray Raphael, eds., *Revolutionary Founders: Rebels, Radicals, and Reformers in the Making of the Nation* (New York, 2011).

6. Gordon Wood, *The Idea of America: Reflections on the Birth of the United States* (New York, 2011). On these debates, see Al Young and Gregory Nobles, eds., *Whose American Revolution: Historians Interpret the Founding* (New York, 2011).

7. In a thoughtful essay advocating this sort of approach, Edward Larkin argues, "It would seem logical therefore that we ought to be able to construct a longer term narrative that flows smoothly from the Anglicization thesis's account of the colonies' relationship to the British Empire in the eighteenth century to the postnationalist American studies' vision of the US as an incipient imperial power in the nineteenth century." He also sees the work of T. H. Breen and Jack Greene as helping to do so. See "Nation and Empire in the Early US," *American Literary History* 22, no. 3 (2010): 501.

8. T. H. Breen, "Ideology and Nationalism on the Eve of the American Revolution: Revisions Once More in Need of Revising," *Journal of American History* 84, no. 1 (June 1997): 13–39.

9. Edmund S. Morgan, "The American Revolution: Revisions in Need of Revising," *William & Mary Quarterly*, 3rd ser., 14 (January 1957): 3–15.

10. Breen, *Marketplace of Revolution: How Consumer Politics Shaped American Independence* (New York, 2004).

11. Eliga Gould, *The Persistence of Empire: British Political Culture in the Age of the American Revolution* (Chapel Hill, NC, 2000); Brendan McConville, *The King's Three Faces: The Rise and Fall of Royal America, 1688–1776* (Chapel Hill, NC, 2006).

12. Fred Anderson, *The Crucible of War: The Seven Years' War and the Fate of Empire in British North America, 1754–1766* (New York, 2000).

13. Peter Onuf, *Jefferson's Empire: The Language of American Nationhood* (Charlottesville, VA, 2000).

14. Francis D. Cogliano, *Emperor of Liberty: Thomas Jefferson's Foreign Policy* (New Haven, CT, 2014); Max Edling, *A Revolution in Favor of Government: Origins of the US Constitution and the Making of the American State* (New York, 2003); and *A Hercules in the Cradle: War, Money, and the American State, 1783–1867* (Chicago, 2014).

15. See, for example, his *The Constitutional Origins of the American Revolution* (Cambridge, 2011) and the collected essays in *Creating the British Atlantic: Essays on Transplantation, Adaptation, and Continuity* (Charlottesville, VA, 2013).

16. Peter Miller, *Defining The Common Good: Empire, Religion, and Philosophy in Eighteenth-century Britain* (New York, 2004); John Phillip Reid, *The Ancient Constitution and the Origins of Anglo-American Liberty* (DeKalb, IL, 2005); Steve Pincus, *The Heart of the Declaration: The Founders' Case for an Activist Government* (New Haven, CT, 2016).

17. See his "Afterword" in Griffin et al., eds., *Between Sovereignty and Anarchy: The Politics of Violence in the American Revolutionary Era* (Charlottesville, 2015).

18. Bernard Bailyn has claimed that the Atlantic approach owes little to these scholars in *Atlantic History: Concept and Contours* (Cambridge, MA, 2005).

19. Colley, *Britons: Forging the Nation 1707–1837*, 3rd ed. (New Haven, CT, 2009); David Armitage, *The Ideological Origins of the British Empire* (Cambridge, 2000); Gould, *Persistence of Empire*; Bourke, *Empire and Revolution: The Political Life of Edmund Burke* (Princeton, 2015).

20. Greene covered America for the eighteenth-century volume. See P. J. Marshall, ed., *The Oxford History of the British Empire: Volume II: The Eighteenth Century* (New York, 2011).

21. P. J. Marshall, *The Making and Unmaking of Empires Britain, India, and America, c. 1750–1783* (Oxford, 2007); see also *Remaking the British Atlantic: The United States and the British Empire after Independence* (New York, 2012).

22. See, for instance, Lauren Benton, *A Search for Sovereignty: Law and Geography in European Empires, 1400–1900* (New York, 2009).

23. Gregory Dowd, *War under Heaven: Pontiac, the Indian Nations, and the British Empire* (Baltimore, 2002).

24. Pekka Hämäläinen, *The Comanche Empire* (New Haven, CT, 2008).

25. Gabe Paquette, *Enlightenment, Governance, and Reform in Spain and Its Empire, 1759–1808* (New York, 2008); Jeremy Adelman, *Sovereignty and Revolution in the Iberian Atlantic* (Princeton, 2006).

26. Paquette, *Imperial Portugal in the Age of Atlantic Revolutions: The Luso-Brazilian World, c. 1770–1850* (Cambridge, 2013).

27. John Elliott, *Empires of the Atlantic World: Britain and Spain in America, 1492–1830* (New Haven, CT, 2006).

28. Dutch scholars, for instance, who study the question, tell us empire matters but not, alas, for the Dutch. See Pieter C. Emmer and Wim Klooster, "The Dutch Atlantic, 1600–1800: Expansion without Empire" in *Itinerario* 23, no. 2 (July 1999): 48–69.

29. Michael Kwass, *Privilege and the Politics of Taxation in Eighteenth-Century France: Liberté, Egalité, Fiscalité* (Cambridge, 2000); Laurent Dubois, *A Colony of Citizens: Revolution and Slave Emancipation in the French Caribbean, 1787–1804* (Chapel Hill, NC, 2004).

30. And this is exactly where Chris Hodson and Brett Rushforth are taking it with their new volume on the French Atlantic empire; for a preview see their essay "Absolutely Atlantic: Colonialism and the Early Modern French State in Recent Historiography," in *History Compass* 8, no. 1 (2010): 101–17.

31. Shields, *Civil Tongues and Polite Letters in British America* (Chapel Hill, NC, 1997). On these themes, see also my essay "The Birth, Death, and Resurrection of the Provincial Dilemma" in *History Compass* 9, no. 2 (2011): 134–46.

32. Parrish, *American Curiosity: Cultures of Natural History in the Colonial British Atlantic World* (Chapel Hill, NC, 2006).

33. Jasanoff, *Edge of Empire: Lives, Culture, and Conquest in the East, 1750–1850* (New York, 2005).

34. Wilson, *The Sense of the People: Culture and Imperialism in England, 1715–1785* (London, 1995); *The Island Race: Englishness and Gender in the Eighteenth Century* (New York, 2003).

35. Colin Calloway, *White People, Indians, and Highlanders: Tribal Peoples and Colonial Encounters in Scotland and America* (New York, 2008).

36. Tom Bartlett, "Ireland in the Era of Total War," forthcoming in the *Cambridge History of Ireland.*

37. On this, see Eliga Gould, *Among the Powers of the Earth: The American Revolution and the Making of a New World Empire* (Cambridge, 2012).

38. See Timothy Tackett's recent book, *The Coming of the Terror in the French Revolution* (Cambridge, 2015).

Part I

Empire and Provincials

The Baubles of America

Object Lessons from the Eclectic Empire of Peter Williamson

Timothy J. Shannon

In October 1776 a curious advertisement appeared in the *Scots Spy*, a magazine published by Edinburgh publican and printer Peter Williamson: "To be Sold by way of Lottery; a pair of American gray Squirrels, about eighteen Months old, are very tame and tractable, and need no confinement in cages, as they are used to run about the house: Those animals generally live long, and are two years old before they begin to breed." Williamson informed his readers that the squirrels could be seen at his "Penny-post-office" inside Edinburgh's Royal Exchange building, where the curious could also purchase tickets for the drawing.[1]

Williamson did not advertise the squirrel lottery again, and his magazine ceased publication not long afterward. So we do not know how the squirrels came into Williamson's possession or where they ended up. It is tempting to think that this lottery was ground zero in an invasion that plagues Britain to this day. Since the nineteenth century, the American gray squirrel has been pushing the British red squirrel out of its native terrain. The American squirrels are larger and more ravenous than their British cousins. They are also transmitters of a disease known as squirrel pox to which they are immune but red squirrels are not. Although the two species are incapable of mating, the male American squirrels can exhibit behavior that intimidates their British counterparts and prevents them from reproducing with the females of their own species. British wildlife experts have decided that the problem with gray squirrels is similar to that of American GIs stationed in Britain during World War II: they are overfed, oversexed, and over here. Concerned citizens have organized a campaign known as "Save Our Squirrels" (SOS) to protect red squirrels from impending doom. Bringing us full circle from Williamson's gray squirrel lottery in 1776, the British National Lottery appropriated over £600,000 in 2006 to fund sixteen red squirrel wildlife reserves in northern England.[2]

Some historians might interpret this tale as a reminder of the continuing consequences of the Columbian Exchange; for others, it might serve as a metaphor for British national identity under siege in a post-imperial, globalized world. In this essay, however, I would like to use it to frame a less obvious topic, that of British perceptions of North America during the late eighteenth century. Historians of material culture have already explored how consumer goods that American colonists imported from Britain helped shape their political ideology and experiences in the years preceding the American Revolution. In particular, the consumption of these "baubles of Britain"—clothing, ceramics, tea, and other items—gave colonists from widely divergent religious, ethnic, and economic backgrounds the common frame of reference necessary for them to express and unite around their shared grievances with British rule.[3]

But what of the baubles of America? Did colonial goods imported to Britain have a similar impact there, shaping how Britons interpreted their relationship with America? After all, the American colonies had been founded to export products to Britain, which was engaged in its own consumer revolution during the eighteenth century. A number of consumer goods associated with overseas trade became attached to British national identity during this era, including sugar from the West Indies, tea and ceramics from China, and coffee from Turkey. With the exception of Virginia tobacco, however, the products of the North American colonies did not seem to have the same imaginative impact.[4] Fish and furs were staples of the American colonial trade, but they did not inspire new consumer habits or social customs among everyday Britons. Likewise, North American wheat, rice, and pork were profitable commodities in Atlantic markets but appear to have had negligible impact on British identity, perhaps because so much of that trade went to parts of the empire other than the mother country.

The baubles of North America were of a different kind. They were exotic, and in some cases they were animate. From the very beginning of American colonization, European explorers brought back examples of the strange and new plant and animal species they found there. They also brought back Indians, some willingly and some not, for public exhibition. By the time of Williamson's squirrel auction in Edinburgh, the first wave of British fascination with America had long since passed, but Williamson himself was a product of a second wave that crested during the Seven Years' War, when the British struggle against France in North America generated renewed demand among British consumers for information about the colonies.[5] Williamson had arrived in Edinburgh in 1759 as a bit of human flotsam from that conflict. He was a disbanded soldier, a survivor of the French siege of Oswego on Lake Ontario in 1756 who had been sent home as a repatriated prisoner of war on a French cartel ship.[6] In a narrative he published in York in 1757, he also claimed to be the victim of a childhood kidnapping from Aberdeen in 1743; the survivor of a shipwreck off Cape May, New Jersey; a former indentured servant in Pennsylvania; and a captive who had lived among Delaware Indians. During the 1760s and 1770s, he operated two Edinburgh coffeehouses, in which he performed live exhibitions of his story, displayed objects purported to be of Native American origin, and sold subsequent editions of his narrative and other books.[7]

The gray squirrels Williamson tried to sell by lottery in 1776 were just one example of the way in which he marketed objects from America, including himself. These baubles of America were not the ubiquitous goods of Anglo-American consumer life. For the most part, they were the opposite: one-of-a-kind (or in the case of the squirrels, two of a kind) items that Williamson advertised and displayed as curiosities. Individually they appeared to be novelties of dubious provenance, but collectively they provide a valuable plebian perspective on the British Empire in North America, a sort of workingman's guide to the colonies based on lived experience that combined autobiography, ethnography, and natural history. Williamson's American adventures may have been singular, and in some cases even fabricated, but the objects he used to convey them to his audiences were real enough, and they tell their own story about how everyday Britons imagined America during the tumultuous years between the Seven Years' War and the American Revolution.

"The Royal Family of the Mohawk Indians"

The earliest reports of Williamson's activities in Edinburgh date to 1758, when he began hawking his narrative and engaging in his coffeehouse performances there. Advertisements in Edinburgh's newspapers described him as an "unhappy sufferer" of Indian captivity who was now telling his story in print and in person to raise "a little money to carry him back to America." The advertisements emphasized Williamson's familiarity with the Indians' methods of warfare: he would demonstrate the "manner of their scalping . . . the Nature of their painting . . . the Form of all their War-Dances," and their "several Cries, as the War-hoop, the Death-hollow, &c."[8]

In other words, the first and most important bauble of America that Williamson presented to his British audiences was himself as a self-proclaimed expert on American Indians. In his narrative and performances, he described the colonies as the strange and often murderous place where he had been buffeted about by what the title of his narrative called the "vicissitudes of fortune."[9] It is noteworthy that from the very start, Williamson chose to make his fabricated Indian captivity the defining feature of his performance, rather than his experiences as a kidnap victim, servant, or soldier, all of which were more firmly grounded in reality. The details of his fabricated Indian captivity and the novelty of his Indian costume usually took top billing in the advertisements. The *Newcastle Courant* introduced him as "Peter Williamson, who wears the surprizing Indian dress," and the *Caledonian Mercury* described him as "Peter Williamson, [who] by residing so long among the Indians, has acquired a particular knowledge of their Customs, Manners, and Dress."[10] An image of him that first appeared in a London magazine in 1759 and that served as the frontispiece for subsequent editions of his narrative depicted him in Indian dress and war paint, clutching an unsheathed "Scalping knife" in one hand and smoking from a pipe tomahawk held in the other, while in background scenes, Indians paddled a canoe, danced around a captive tied to a tree, and skulked single file through the woods (fig. 1).

As these advertisements indicate, Williamson crafted his performances to take advantage of a fascination with Native Americans that the Seven Years' War ignited among the British public. Newspapers and periodicals significantly expanded their content on North America after Anglo-French hostilities broke out there in 1754, and within that coverage, the presentation of Native Americans changed as well. The generic Indian of an earlier age, depicted in feathered skirts and headdresses and often conflated with Africans, Turks, and other exotic foreigners, was replaced by Indians who were now identified by their nations, allegiances, and geographic locations. During the 1750s British readers gained access to information about Native Americans that was richer and more ethnographically detailed than what had been previously available.[11] Williamson's exhibitions offered them another means of consuming that information in a manner that moved off the printed page to incorporate more visual, tactile, and auditory input, such as the chance to run a finger along the sharp edge of a tomahawk or to hear the piercing cry of a war whoop. A savvy marketer, Williamson exploited the British public's curiosity about all things Native American by focusing his story heavily on the intercultural violence Britons associated with warfare in North America. Although he was never an Indian captive, he was a veteran soldier who had likely witnessed the work of enemy Indian warriors at the siege of Oswego, and he had no doubt heard tales and rumors about Indian warfare and captivity from his comrades in arms. He also read the same press coverage of

the war in North America as his British contemporaries, as evidenced by his plagiarism of at least two London magazines in his narrative.[12] Although he played fast and loose with the facts of his own life, Williamson did not invent what he knew about Native Americans so much as he repackaged input he received from other sources, whether American or British in origin, for the pleasure of his audiences.

That process was illustrated by his incorporation of alleged Indian artifacts into his performances. In December 1759 an advertisement in Edinburgh's *Caledonian Mercury* announced a new addition to Williamson's exhibitions. Under the headline *"Just arrived from North America,"* the advertisement described a "noble and curious set of figures" of Native Americans. These included a life-sized statue of King Hendrick, the British-allied Mohawk chief who had been killed at the Battle of Lake George in 1755. The other figures were miniature models of an "Indian Queen" with her child, sitting in a "true Indian canoe" being paddled by two other Indian figures. Williamson described the figures collectively as "the royal family of the Mohawk Indians, in all their proper uniforms and dresses, adorned with their instruments of war. . . . The like not to be equalled in Europe." The advertisement urged the curious public to view the figures at the same venue where Williamson was exhibiting himself in Indian dress and selling the most recent edition of his narrative.[13]

How had such an exotic collection of Indian artifacts come into Williamson's possession? As a former prisoner of war, he presumably returned to Britain with only the clothes on his back. In the same advertisement, Williamson explained that the "group of figures" had originally been erected by the Mohawks themselves in honor of their deceased king. The figures had been acquired by Miss Long, an Indian captive from Boston who had been rescued by Williamson and other British soldiers in 1755 (the advertisement provided page references for readers interested in the account of this episode given in Williamson's narrative). The appreciative Miss Long sent the figures to Williamson as a present and to "gratify the curiosity of the publick in Europe." These very same figures had already been viewed by the Prince of Wales and "a great number of the principal nobility and gentry at the court of Britain." They could now be viewed in Edinburgh for a mere six pence admission charge.[14]

As discerning readers of this advertisement may have suspected, Williamson's explanation of the provenance of these figures was dubious at best. First, there was no Miss Long. Of all the questionable passages in Williamson's narrative, his account of her captivity and rescue is the most easily debunked.[15]

Second, no similar reports of these figures appeared in other British newspapers indicating that they had been exhibited in London or before audiences of the royal family or other nobility. Nevertheless, these objects had to come from somewhere, and their likely origins shed light on the consumer market in Britain for Native American artifacts.

Williamson's inspiration for these figures likely came from London, where the exhibition of objects, figures, and people associated with Native Americans experienced a revival during the Seven Years' War. When Parliament established the British Museum in 1753 by acquiring the collection of Sir Hans Sloane, it set a precedent for turning privately owned "cabinets of curiosities" into publicly accessible collections of ethnography and natural history. On a smaller and more down-market scale, this trend also occurred in coffee-houses, taverns, and fairs, where proprietors displayed for paying customers artifacts commonly associated with Native Americans, such as tomahawks, wampum beads, calumets, snowshoes, and drums. Model canoes, such as the one referenced in Williamson's advertisement, were circulating in Britain during this period. Made by Native American and French women in Quebec and Montreal and sold to European collectors as American curiosities, these model canoes sometimes included doll-sized figures of Indians and such accoutrements as miniature paddles and cradleboards, making them in essence portable dioramas of Indian domestic relations and material culture (fig. 2).[16] Williamson's "Indian Queen" and "true Indian canoe" were undoubtedly a version of these popular souvenirs brought back to Britain by veteran officers returning from the war in America. Life-sized figures of Indians could also be found in eighteenth-century Britain. In 1762 Mrs. Salmon's Waxworks in Fleet Street, a popular London attraction, featured wax models of three Cherokee chiefs who visited the city in that year.[17] Williamson's figure of King Hendrick was most likely an adaptation of the generic wooden Indian figures used by tobacconists to advertise their shops. Thomas Constable, an Edinburgh publisher who came of age during the 1790s, remembered seeing Williamson's Indian statue after it had been retired to a garden in the city's Canonmills neighborhood; he described it as "a wooden figure with all his dress and paraphernalia, which I have been told, used to stand at the sign-post of his [Williamson's] exhibition."[18]

Williamson's identification of these generic Indian figures as "the royal family of the Mohawk Indians" is another indication of his savvy as a commercial promoter. Hendrick was the most famous Indian known to Britons at the time. His death at the Battle of Lake George had been reported widely in the British press, and he had been memorialized in multiple posthumous

FIG. 2.   Miniature canoe with Native American figures. (Canadian Museum of History, CMC III-M-10 a-n, IMG2009-0063-0017-Dm)

images published in magazines and prints.[19] Taking advantage of Hendrick's fame, Williamson turned the miniature Indians attached to the model canoe into Hendrick's wife, child, and attendants, in the same manner that the proprietors of waxworks attracted customers by exhibiting figures in the likeness of British and foreign royalty. Williamson also exploited British fascination with Native American celebrity when he exhibited in his Edinburgh coffeehouse the "night-cap" of Captain Jacobs, a Delaware chief whose death at the hands of Pennsylvania militiamen in 1756 had been reported in the British press. Although Williamson never elaborated on what the "night-cap" looked like, it was in all likelihood a genuine or imitation human scalp, another war souvenir brought back from America that Williamson had managed to acquire, although with a provenance as suspect as that of his statue of King Hendrick.[20]

Williamson's marketing of himself involved multiple and overlapping representations of Native Americans. The artifacts he displayed, including himself, gave physical form to the savagery Britons associated with Indian warfare, and his personal story illustrated Britain's star-crossed fortunes at the outset of the war. His sufferings in America were those of the empire writ small. But by donning Indian dress and war paint, he also transformed the captive into the captor and turned his tale of woe into one of patriotic conquest and triumph. Nor was it all blood and guts. His performances also promised customers ethnographic information about the Indians' history, families, and such nonmartial elements of their material culture as wampum beads, pipes, and canoes.

Williamson's New Machine for Reaping of Corns

During the early 1760s Williamson's entrepreneurial energies found new outlets. In June 1760 he advertised in the *Caledonian Mercury* that he had opened his own "American coffeehouse" in Paterson's Court in the Lawn Market section of Edinburgh, where he continued to display his "Groupe of Statues" representing King Hendrick and the Mohawks.[21] In July 1762 he advertised the fifth edition of his narrative, this one featuring "a new and correct whole sheet map of North America." The book could be purchased at his coffeehouse in Paterson's Court or at his new shop in Parliament House, the Scottish Court of Session building in the heart of Old Town Edinburgh.[22] City tax records indicate that Williamson was one of several merchants who kept small shops within the Parliament House, catering to the judges, attorneys, clients, spectators, and other hangers-on who conducted business there. Most of these merchants were listed as booksellers; Williamson was the only one identified as "bookseller & Coffeeroom," giving him, in effect, the Starbucks concession in one of Edinburgh's busiest public buildings.[23] James Boswell noted drinking a dram at "P. Williamson's Coffee-house" while engaging in court business in December 1774.[24]

As Williamson settled into his coffeehouse business, he took up another venture that attempted to capitalize on his American experiences. News items that appeared in Edinburgh periodicals in summer 1762 announced "Williamson's New Machine for Reaping of Corns" (fig. 3). The reaping machine was a scythe featuring several long "fingers" that ran parallel to the blade, designed to catch and deposit grain in neat rows as it was cut. Williamson described the scythe as his own invention, one that would help farmers who faced a "scarcity of hands, on account of the present war" at harvest time. He claimed that one field hand working with his reaping machine could do the work of six men, and he offered to give an "ocular demonstration" to that effect for any interested parties. A testimonial included in the news story confirmed that "in the presence of many gentlemen of character," Williamson had cut down in an hour and twenty minutes "a full quarter of an acre of barley measured out for that purpose, which he laid in the most regular order." Williamson hoped to receive a "suitable encouragement" for his invention from gentlemen

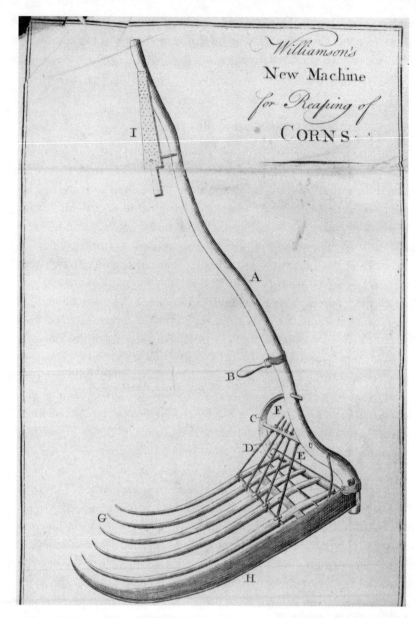

FIG. 3. *Williamson's New Machine for Reaping of Corns,* from Peter Williamson, *The Travels of Peter Williamson* (Edinburgh, 1768). This image first appeared in *Scots Magazine* (Edinburgh) 24 (August 1762). (Library of Congress, Washington, D.C.)

patrons interested in "the encouragement of arts and sciences," and he offered "for a moderate premium" to teach any "overseer, or principal servant on a farm, how to handle the machine."[25]

At first glance the provenance of Williamson's reaping machine seems as specious as that of his Mohawk figures or Captain Jacobs's "night-cap." After all, Williamson was an urban tradesman who mostly peddled coffee and tall tales for a living. Up to this point, he had exhibited no talent or interest in farming or the mechanical arts. Edinburgh was, however, the seat of the Scottish Enlightenment, and in 1762 Scottish farming was on the verge of its great transformation, as the principles, methods, and technologies of England's agricultural revolution were adopted by "improving" landlords in the north. Between 1760 and 1825, many Scottish landowners and farmers abandoned the traditional system of open-field farming in favor of consolidation and enclosure. They required tenants to adopt new methods and improvements, such as crop rotation, drainage, and hedge-planting, and these changes pushed cottars and other rural poor out of the countryside and into cities or onto ships filled with overseas migrants.[26] The most famous improver of this era was Sir Archibald Grant of Monymusk, an Aberdeenshire laird with whom Williamson had a brief encounter after his return from America, but Williamson had left Aberdeen at a young age and returned there only briefly as an adult. In either instance, it is unlikely that he spent enough time in the company of Grant or his tenants to absorb much expertise or enthusiasm regarding their innovative practices.[27]

Furthermore, the reaping machine had no antecedents in Scotland. Williamson's invention was modeled after a scythe, whereas the reaping tool of choice for Scottish field workers in the eighteenth century was a handheld sickle or reaping hook. When operated by an adult male, the scythe did cut fields more quickly, but if not wielded properly, it shook the grain out of the stalk prematurely. Sickles were more easily handled by women, who made up the majority of reapers at harvest time, and they were more portable than the scythe, a significant consideration for the seasonal Highland laborers who carried their own tools with them when they came into the Lowlands to work the harvest. Lastly, sickles worked better for grain planted in Scotland's traditional runrig style, which produced a corrugated pattern of ridges and furrows, while scythes worked most effectively with grain sown on level ground.[28]

So where then did Williamson's idea for the reaping machine come from? The answer rests in his American sojourn as an indentured servant. In his narrative Williamson claimed that he had been sold as a servant in Philadelphia in 1743 to a Scotsman named Hugh Wilson, who had also come to

America as the victim of a childhood kidnapping.[29] Williamson offered little other detail about Wilson or where he lived, but through tax lists and genealogical sources, it is possible to locate him in Chester County. Wilson owned seventy-five acres in Radnor Township, about fourteen miles west of Philadelphia. Court records indicate that Wilson had indeed arrived in Pennsylvania as a twelve-year-old servant in 1697.[30]

Williamson spent six years in Wilson's household. Judging from the estate described in Wilson's will, the young servant would have been put to work on the family farm, tending crops and livestock. Southeastern Pennsylvania had a prosperous and diversified economy. When Swedish naturalist Peter Kalm passed through Chester County in 1748, he noted that practically every farm had an orchard, "sinking under the weight of innumerable apples." Wheat was "sown everywhere," and swine "went about in great herds in the oak woods," feeding on acorns.[31] In this world, far removed from Scotland's runrig fields of barley and oats, it is possible that Williamson encountered a tool known as the basket cradle or cradle scythe (fig. 4). In design and purpose, it is the obvious inspiration for his reaping machine. Eighteenth-century German migrants brought it to North America, and it was likely being used in southeastern Pennsylvania during Williamson's servitude there. It remained a common agricultural implement in the region until the advent of mechanized reaping machines in the mid-nineteenth century.[32] It is impossible to know if Hugh Wilson owned one (his will refers only to "implements of Husbandry"), but Chester County in the 1740s was home to a diverse population of Welsh, English, Scots Irish, and German farmers. Radnor Township stood alongside the Great Wagon Road, the east-to-west route that carried immigrants from Philadelphia to the Susquehanna Valley and points beyond. Even if Williamson rarely got off Wilson's farm, he was still likely to have engaged in the diffusion of material culture made possible by this promiscuous mixing of immigrant groups in southeastern Pennsylvania.

Alas, Williamson did not strike it rich marketing his reaping machine in Edinburgh. In subsequent advertisements, he offered it for sale in his coffeehouse, but his promotion of it ceased during the 1770s.[33] Despite the progress of the agricultural revolution in Scotland during Williamson's lifetime, the sickle remained the tool of choice for harvesting grain, and the scythe was confined mostly to mowing grass and hay.[34] As a bauble of America, Williamson's reaping machine failed to find a market among British consumers, but it is a reminder that the intellectual ferment associated with the Enlightenment flowed both ways across the Atlantic. Williamson may have lacked the formal education, academic affiliations, and elite status of his more famous contem-

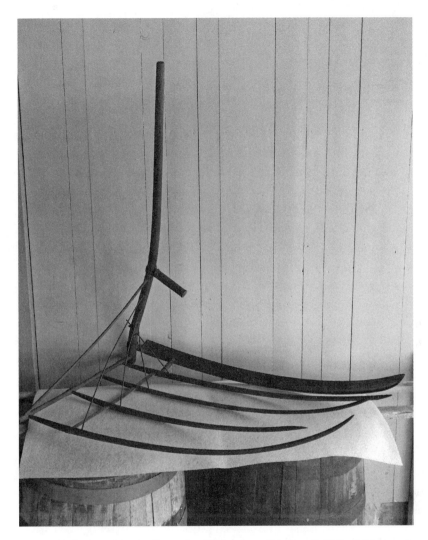

FIG. 4.   Early American cradle scythe. (Collection of the Landis Valley Village and Farm Museum, Pennsylvania Historical and Museum Commission, photograph by Bruce Bomberger)

poraries in eighteenth-century Edinburgh, but his business there put him at the center of the city's economic and political life, where he imbibed the improving spirit of the age. His promotion of the reaping machine calls to mind the workingman's Enlightenment lived by his American contemporary Benjamin Franklin, who used a similar language of private enterprise and civicmindedness to promote his own inventions and projects.[35] Like Franklin's lightning rod (a much more successful bauble from America), Williamson's reaping machine embodied the Enlightenment marriage of the mechanical arts with the public good.

Peter Williamson, Printer and Publisher

The comparison to Franklin is worth expanding upon, because like that famous colonial American, Williamson seemed intent on harnessing his social and economic advancement to his city's burgeoning print culture. Franklin's fortunes in Philadelphia had risen on the back of his success as the printer of the *Pennsylvania Gazette* and *Poor Richard's Almanac*. In a similar manner, Williamson set himself up as a printer and publisher in 1768. His ride in Edinburgh's marketplace for the printed word was bumpier than Franklin's, and ultimately his success there came to rest on concerns more local than imperial. Yet one work that he produced in this period offered an omnibus of American curiosities that bridged his American and British worlds.

Williamson's entry into the publishing business was spurred by his acquisition of several portable printing presses from London, one of which he taught himself to use and the others which he offered for sale. In one of the first items to come off his press, a satirical poem by William Meston titled *Mob contra Mob*, Williamson included his own mocking dedication to the printers of Edinburgh, whom he chastised for refusing to admit him into their guild. During the 1760s Edinburgh's printing industry was dominated by a few leading figures who cooperated in limiting the access that potential competitors had to readers and advertisers. As a result, the city sustained only two profitable newspapers and magazines, despite its large and literate population.[36] Projecting a do-it-yourself ethic that challenged the monopoly of his competitors, Williamson noted that his new portable printing press was so easy to use that "gentlemen, nay ladies, may perform with it in their closets."[37]

Williamson displayed admirable gumption in starting his printing business, but his output never seriously challenged Edinburgh's reigning publishers. Between 1768 and 1779, he published a small range of titles, including plays by Shakespeare and Voltaire, pamphlets concerning Scottish religious controversies, a history of Scotland, and psalm books. Not much of this output has survived, indicating a small circulation.[38] Despite the currency of colonial affairs in British news at this time, Williamson showed no particular inclination to publish on topics related to the American crisis. In 1776 he launched his own weekly magazine, the *Scots Spy*. Consisting of prose and poetry written in a colloquial style, the magazine avoided politics and religion in favor of essays on moral instruction, satirical verse, and bawdy humor. Occasionally content appeared that hinted at Williamson's experiences in America, such as the advertisement for his gray squirrels lottery and the fictionalized memoir of a Mohawk Indian visitor to Britain, but for the most part, Williamson did not promote or fill his magazine with references to his adventures abroad.[39] He was pursuing a local readership, and judging from his constant pleas for subscriptions and the magazine's lack of advertising, he had difficulty finding it. The magazine ceased publication within the year. Williamson revived it as the *New Scots Spy* in 1777, but that version also folded after a few months.[40]

The one work that Williamson published during this period that might rightly be called a bauble of America was *The Travels of Peter Williamson, Among the different Nations and Tribes of Savage Indians in America,* which appeared in 1768. The most recent edition of his captivity narrative had appeared two years earlier in Dublin, and his touring days as an Indian impersonator were over. His coffeehouses in Edinburgh were well established, and his printing business was getting under way. With this new book, Williamson's perspective on North America changed from a place of plebian tribulation to a continent-sized cabinet of curiosities.

The Travels of Peter Williamson was not a rehash of Williamson's narrative. Although it referenced his Indian captivity in its preface, this book devoted most of its pages to descriptions of Native Americans and exotic American fauna. It was, unsurprisingly, an exercise in wholesale plagiarism, which borrowed most heavily from several travelogues and histories of North America that had been published in London during the Seven Years' War. For material on the Mohawks, Williamson plundered stories that had appeared in the *Gentleman's Magazine* in 1755 concerning Hendrick's death at the Battle of Lake George. He copied his descriptions of the Iroquois confederacy from William Smith's *History of the Province of New-York,* which had been published in London in 1757. Williamson also devoted considerable space to the Cherokees, a group with which he had no direct experience during his American servitude and military service, but which loomed large in British popular imagination after Cherokee embassies to London in 1762 and 1765. For this material, Williamson borrowed without attribution from the posthumous memoirs of Henry Timberlake, the Virginia militia officer who had led the Cherokee delegations. Williamson also incorporated into this book material on Algonquian Indians of the Great Lakes, who had allied with the French during the war but were now familiar to Britons from news coverage of Pontiac's War. This material he took directly from French traveler Pierre Charlevoix's *A Voyage to North-America* (1744), which had been published in English translation in London in 1761.[41]

Williamson devoted considerable space in his *Travels* to the natural curiosities of North America. His account of Niagara Falls, which he claimed was "according to my own observations," he copied verbatim from Swedish botanist Peter Kalm.[42] For descriptions of the opossum and buffalo, he borrowed again from Timberlake's memoirs of his time among the Cherokees. His catalogue of American snakes took up almost a quarter of the book's text to describe twenty-two species. This material included an account of the rattlesnake's ability to hypnotize its prey that was based on a similar report published in the *Gentleman's Magazine* a few years earlier.[43] Williamson also described two mythical serpents that he claimed were indigenous to America: the horn snake, which could kill with strikes from its venomous tail, and the cockatrice, which had a cock's head and snake's body and moved about "half upright" rather than by creeping on the ground (fig. 5).[44]

Williamson's *Travels* did not have a wide circulation. Unlike his narrative, it was not published in other editions in other cities, and it was not advertised in newspapers beyond Edinburgh.[45] By notice on the book's title page, Williamson offered to distribute it on commission to booksellers in Britain and Ireland, but he found no takers. *The Travels of Peter Williamson* ended up being a curiosity in its own right, a stitched together act of multiple plagiarisms that sealed Williamson's subsequent literary reputation as a travel liar.[46] Within this one volume, an interested reader could find the speeches of King Hendrick, read a translation of a Cherokee war song, marvel at the spectacle of Niagara Falls, and discover such wonderful and strange creatures as rattlesnakes, alligators, and opossums. Williamson may have lacked the status and wealth of other British travel writers of his era, but he knew their books and shared their penchant for conflating natural histories of North America with ethnographies of Native Americans.[47] With his *Travels*, he offered readers a plebian appropriation of this work, one that presented the spectacle of America without the pretense of understanding it.

Enlightenment and Empire

During the 1770s, Williamson's career shifted away from its American origins. Although his coffeehouses and public persona remained linked to his alleged Indian captivity, he earned his living less sensationally as a civic-minded entrepreneur. He finally found success by publishing the city's first directory. *Williamson's Directory, for the City of Edinburgh, Canongate, Leith, and Suburbs* appeared in fifteen editions between 1773 and 1793, providing residents of the rapidly growing and famously overcrowded city with an essential

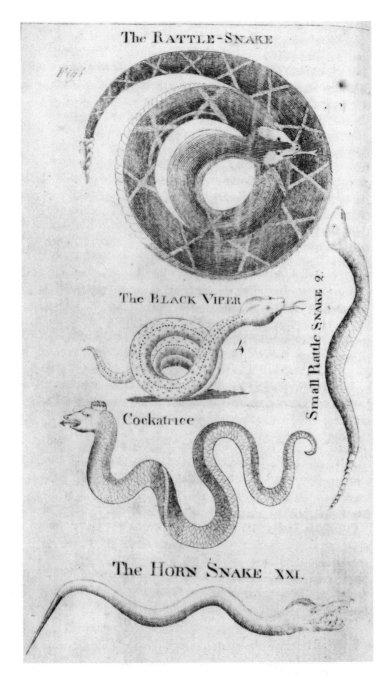

FIG. 5.   *The Rattle-Snake, The Black Viper, Cockatrice, The Horn Snake, Small Rattle Snake,* from Peter Williamson, *The Travels of Peter Williamson* (Edinburgh, 1768). (Library of Congress, Washington, D.C.)

guide to its streets and residences.[48] The directory worked hand-in-hand with another business Williamson launched during the 1770s, a penny post that used runners to deliver mail throughout the city and its suburbs on a daily schedule. In addition to providing Williamson with material security in his later years, the directory and penny post gave him a hard-earned respectability. When the royal postal system took over Williamson's penny post in 1793, Parliament granted him an annual pension of £25 in recognition of his public service.[49] Six years later, Williamson's obituary—initially published in Edinburgh and reprinted in London newspapers and periodicals—noted his "various adventures" in North America, but also commended him for the penny post and directory, public works "so essentially useful in a large city."[50]

What then should we make of Williamson's baubles of America? He certainly never made a fortune selling gray squirrels, reaping machines, or his books, but he did succeed in marketing himself as an American curiosity, and he eventually parlayed that notoriety into a quieter and more sustainable career as an Edinburgh tradesman and citizen. That he did this in the city that was home to Scotland's great age of intellectual ferment should remind us that the Enlightenment came in more varieties than one. North America played an important role in the Scottish Enlightenment. When luminaries such as Adam Smith, William Robertson, John Millar, and Adam Ferguson contemplated human society's development from savagery to civility, they looked across the Atlantic and described American Indians as peoples still in the starting blocks of this progression, the living examples that allowed European observers to study the origins of society and the stages of human improvement. But none of these thinkers had been to North America, and they gleaned their knowledge of Native Americans from the works of such second-rank Enlightenment writers as Charlevoix and Cadwallader Colden.[51] They may have read Williamson or even witnessed one of his coffeehouse exhibitions, but they did not cite him or consider him a part of their scholarly conversations. The North America they presented to their readers was as much a philosopher's conjecture as it was a home to flesh-and-blood human beings.

The North America Williamson presented to his audiences was different. It was a product of his lived experience, and it took tangible form in the objects he displayed in his coffeehouse. As a publican and printer, he inspired conversations about America, Indians, and empire that transpired not in university lecture halls or learned texts but over punch bowls and coffee pots, knit into the fabric of life and business in a busy, vibrant city. People curious about America and its indigenous inhabitants had their questions answered by attending Williamson's performances or reading his books. While those answers may have been more sensational than accurate, they reflected an emerging British identity rooted in encounters with strange lands and peoples that attached cultural and racial inferiority to the inhabitants of those distant places regardless of their point of origin.[52] The American Revolution may have been sparked by the colonists' insistence that they were the constitutional equals of their fellow subjects in Britain, but from the perspective of Williamson's Edinburgh, America was still a place filled with exotic fauna and forest-dwelling savages. Even after American independence, a British consumer market for American exotica remained, and entrepreneurs claiming firsthand expertise with Native Americans continued to exploit that curiosity by publishing autobiographical narratives and engaging in public exhibitions.[53] As Britain's imperial interests moved eastward, the same process occurred as adventurers, captives, and other travelers returned to Britain from the South Pacific, India, and Egypt with their own tales to tell.[54] The political and military fortunes of empire ebbed and flowed, but the impulse to collect, display, and consume the objects of empire steadily expanded during the nineteenth century, and it was not confined to elites.

We usually think of empire as something imposed upon the working peoples of the British Isles. They were the ones who endured the risks of transatlantic migration, who labored as servants in colonial fields and workshops, who served as the rank and file in military and naval expeditions, and who suffered and died by the thousands for the sake of extending British profits and power in distant lands. Williamson reminds us, however, that common folks shaped that empire in countless smaller transactions as consumers and as entrepreneurs, as conduits for the passage of information and objects from the colonies back to Britain, and as interpreters of the world abroad for audiences back home. Williamson's baubles of America—gray squirrels, Mohawk statues, reaping machines, and his own well-embellished travels—were idiosyncratic, but collectively they told the story of an empire that was packaged, communicated, and consumed in myriad everyday acts shared by everyday people.

Notes

1. *Scots Spy* 2 (18 October 1776): back cover advertisement, Edinburgh Room, Edinburgh City Library.

2. See Peter Coates, "Over Here: American Animals in Britain," in *Invasive and Introduced Plants and Animals: Human Perceptions, Attitudes, and Approaches to Management,* ed. Ian D. Rotherham and Robert A. Lambert (London, 2011), 39–54, and D. T. Max, "The Squirrel Wars," New York Times, 7 October 2007.

3. T. H. Breen, "'The Baubles of Britain': The American and Consumer Revolutions of

the Eighteenth Century," *Past and Present*, no. 119 (May 1988): 73–104, and T. H. Breen, *The Marketplace of Revolution: How Consumer Politics Shaped American Independence* (New York, 2004). See also Richard L. Bushman, *The Refinement of America: Persons, Houses, Cities* (New York, 1993).

4. See, for example, Sidney W. Mintz, *Sweetness and Power: The Place of Sugar in Modern History* (New York, 1985); Brian Cowan, *The Social Life of Coffee: The Emergence of the British Coffeehouse* (New Haven, CT, 2005); and Troy Bickham, "Eating the Empire: Intersections of Food, Cookery, and Imperialism in Eighteenth-Century Britain," *Past and Present*, no. 198 (February 2008): 71–109.

5. On Indian visitors to Britain during the colonial era and the British fascination with North America sparked by the Seven Years' War, see Alden T. Vaughan, *Transatlantic Encounters: American Indians in Britain, 1500–1776* (Cambridge, 2006), and Troy Bickham, *Savages within the Empire: Representations of American Indians in Eighteenth-Century Britain* (Oxford, 2005).

6. Timothy J. Shannon, "French and Indian Cruelty? The Fate of the Oswego Prisoners of War, 1756–1758," *New York History* 95 (Summer 2014): 381–407.

7. For an overview of Williamson's life and a debunking of his Indian captivity, see Timothy J. Shannon, "King of the Indians: The Hard Fate and Curious Career of Peter Williamson," *William and Mary Quarterly*, 3rd ser., 66 (January 2009): 3–44.

8. *Edinburgh Evening Courant*, 7 October 1758, and *Caledonian Mercury*, 16 November 1758.

9. Peter Williamson, *French and Indian Cruelty; exemplified in the life and various Vicissitudes of Fortune, of Peter Williamson, a Disbanded Soldier* (New York, 1757).

10. *Newcastle Courant*, 27 May 1758, and Caledonian Mercury, 16 November 1758. I would like to thank Peter Rushton for sharing the advertisement from the *Newcastle Courant* with me.

11. See Bickham, *Savages within the Empire*, 21–109; Kathleen Wilson, *The Sense of the People: Politics, Culture, and Imperialism in England, 1715–1785* (Cambridge, 1995), 29–54, 178–205; and Laura M. Stevens, *The Poor Indians: British Missionaries, Native Americans, and Colonial Sensibility* (Philadelphia, 2004), 84–110.

12. In his narrative Williamson lifted his description of the siege of Oswego from the *Gentleman's Magazine* 27 (February 1757): 73–78. He also plagiarized descriptions of Indian warfare on the Pennsylvania frontier from the *Magazine of Magazines* 11 (February 1756): 161–63.

13. *Caledonian Mercury*, 3 December 1759.

14. Ibid.

15. See Shannon, "King of the Indians," 15–16.

16. See Ruth B. Phillips and Dale Idiens, "'A Casket of Savage Curiosities': Eighteenth-Century Objects from North-eastern North America in the Farquharson Collection," *Journal of the History of Collections* 6 (1994): 21–22, and Ruth B. Phillips, *Trading Identities: The Souvenir in Native North American Art from the Northeast, 1700–1900* (Seattle and Montreal, 1998), 81–86.

17. On the display of artifacts associated with Native Americans, see Troy Bickham, "'A Conviction of the Reality of Things': Material Culture, North American Indians, and Empire in Eighteenth-Century Britain," *Eighteenth-Century Studies* 39 (2005): 29–47. On

the role of ethnographic collecting in shaping British perceptions of empire, see Maya Jasanoff, "Collectors of Empire: Objects, Conquests, and Imperial Self-Fashioning," *Past and Present*, no. 184 (August 2004): 109–35.

18. Thomas Constable, *Archibald Constable and His Literary Correspondents*, 3 vols. (Edinburgh, 1873), 1:538–39.

19. On posthumous news coverage and the image of Hendrick in Britain, see Eric Hinderaker, *The Two Hendricks: Unraveling a Mohawk Mystery* (Cambridge, MA, 2010), 267–73.

20. Williamson claimed to possess Captain Jacobs's scalp in his *Brief Account of the War in N. America* (Edinburgh: printed for the author, [1760]). Williamson said he had received it as a gift from Benjamin Franklin, while both were serving in Pennsylvania's volunteer forces during the winter of 1755–56, but there is no corroborating evidence that the two ever met, and Captain Jacobs was not killed until the raid on Kittanning in September 1756, at which time Williamson was confined in Quebec as a prisoner of war.

21. *Caledonian Mercury*, 11 June 1760.

22. *Edinburgh Evening Courant*, 3 July 1762.

23. See Extent Rolls, SL35/2/3 (1769–1770) in Edinburgh City Archives.

24. Hugh M. Milne, ed., *Boswell's Edinburgh Journals, 1767–1786*, rev. ed. (2001; Edinburgh, 2003), 180.

25. "An account of a Reaping-Machine, invented by Mr Peter Williamson," *Scots Magazine* 24 (August 1762): 404–5. A similar report on the reaping machine appeared in the July 1762 edition of the *Edinburgh Magazine*. The article from the *Scots Magazine* was reprinted in North America in the *Boston News-Letter* on 23 December 1762, the only mention of Williamson that occurred in an American newspaper during his lifetime.

26. For the agricultural revolution in Scotland, see T. M. Devine, *The Transformation of Rural Scotland: Social Change and the Agrarian Economy, 1660–1815* (Edinburgh, 1994), and T. C. Smout and Alexander Fenton, "Scottish Agriculture before the Improvers—an Exploration," *Agricultural History Review* 13 (1965): 73–93.

27. Williamson was born in Aboyne, a village in Aberdeenshire, and his father was a tenant farmer there, but at a young age he was sent to live with an aunt in Aberdeen, so it is unlikely that he encountered anything like the basket scythe before his passage to America. When he became embroiled in legal troubles after his return to Aberdeen in 1757, he sought and received from Sir Archibald Grant, who was then a justice of the peace, a certificate testifying to the truth of his birth in Aberdeenshire, but there is no evidence that his contact with Grant went beyond this brief meeting. See *Edinburgh Evening Courant*, 7 October 1758.

28. For Scottish reaping tools and practices before the age of mechanization, see James E. Handley, *The Agricultural Revolution in Scotland* (Glasgow, 1963), 256–58.

29. Williamson, *French and Indian Cruelty*, 5–7.

30. In my search of Chester County's tax lists, I consulted the microfilm copies available at the Pennsylvania State Archives in Harrisburg. See roll #6437, Chester County Archives, County Taxes, 1718–53. Hugh Wilson (sometimes spelled "Willson") appears on every extant tax list (fifteen in all) for Radnor Township between 1720 and 1747. The tax lists are also available in a searchable database from the Chester County Archives and can be found online at www.chesco.org/archives. For Wilson's landownership in Radnor, see Katharine

Hewitt Cummin, *A Rare and Pleasing Thing: Radnor Demography (1798) and Development* (Philadelphia, 1977), 280, 294. For Wilson's will, see "Last Will and Testament of Hugh Willson . . . of Radnor in the County of Chester" in the Register of Wills Office in Philadelphia's City Hall, room 185, in Will Book G (1743–1748/49), 325. An abstract of the will may be found in *Abstracts of Philadelphia County, Pennsylvania Wills, 1726–1747* (Westminster, MD, 1995), 171. For evidence of Wilson's arrival as a child servant in Pennsylvania in 1697, see David Dobson, *The Original Scots Colonists of Early America, Supplement: 1607–1707* (Baltimore, 1998), 181.

31. See Peter Kalm, *Travels into North America: The English Version of 1770*, ed. Adolph B. Benson (1937; New York, 1987), 86–87.

32. On the basket scythe and eighteenth-century Pennsylvanian agricultural implements, see Graeme R. Quick and Wesley Fisher Buchele, *The Grain Harvesters* (St. Joseph, MI, 1978), 8–10; Beauveau Borie IV, *Farming and Folk Society: Threshing among the Pennsylvania Germans* (Ann Arbor, 1986), 37–45; Eric Sloane, *A Museum of Early American Tools* (New York, 1964), 102–3; and Stevenson Whitcomb Fletcher, *Pennsylvania Agriculture and Country Life, 1640–1840*, 2 vols. (Harrisburg, PA, 1950–55), 1:98–99.

33. *Caledonian Mercury*, 29 June 1771.

34. For a discussion of the merits and uses of the sickle and scythe in Scottish agriculture, see Alexander Fenton, *Scottish Country Life* (Edinburgh, 1976): 52–64, and Quick and Buchele, *The Grain Harvesters*, 10.

35. On Franklin's self-promotion through civic-mindedness, see Gordon S. Wood, *The Americanization of Benjamin Franklin* (New York, 2004), 41–54.

36. On Edinburgh's printing industry and Williamson's competitors during this era, see Stephen Brown, "Indians, Politicians, and Profit: The Printing Career of Peter Williamson," in *Book Trade Connections from the Seventeenth to the Twentieth Centuries*, ed. John Hinks and Catherine Armstrong (New Castle, DE, 2005): 115–34.

37. [William Meston], *Mob contra Mob; or, The Rabblers Rabbled, Wrote by a Buchan Poet, in the Style of Hudibras, in Six Cantos* (Parliament-House: Printed by Peter Williamson, in one of his New Portable Printing-Presses, 1769), i. Williamson advertised his portable presses as for sale during the 1770s and 1780s. See, for example, advertisements in *Caledonian Mercury*, 29 June 1771 and 29 June 1782.

38. The National Library of Scotland and Edinburgh City Library have copies of most, but not all, of the extant works published by Williamson. Most of what he produced appeared in inexpensive duodecimo editions; an exception to this trend was his miniature book of Psalms: *The Psalms of David, Fitted to the Tunes Used in Churches* (Edinburgh, 1779).

39. See "Observations of SAG A YERN QUA RASH TOW, one of the Indian kings, on the Manners and Customs of GREAT BRITAIN," *Scots Spy* 1 (29 March 1776): 45–48, Edinburgh Room, Edinburgh City Library. This story, which continued over several editions of the magazine, was clearly modeled after the visit of the four Indian kings to London in 1710, and it was likely written by Williamson himself.

40. On the *Scots Spy* and *New Scots Spy*, see Brown, "Indians, Politicians, and Profit," 126–32, and W. J. Couper, *The Edinburgh Periodical Press: Being a Bibliographical Account of the Newspapers, Journals, and Magazines Issued in Edinburgh from the Earliest Times to 1800*, 2 vols. (Stirling, 1908), 2:138–40.

41. Peter Williamson, *The Travels of Peter Williamson, Among the Different Nations and*

Tribes of Savages in America (Edinburgh, 1768). For the sources Williamson plagiarized, see *Gentleman's Magazine, and Historical Chronicle* 25 (June 1755): 252–56 and (November 1755): 519; William Smith, *History of the Province of New-York* (London, 1757); Henry Timberlake, *The Memoirs of Lieut. Henry Timberlake* (London, 1765); and Pierre de Charlevoix, *Journal of a Voyage to North America* (London, 1761).

42. For Peter Kalm's description of Niagara Falls, see [John Bartram], *Observations on the Inhabitants, Climate, Soil, Rivers, Productions, Animals, and other Matters Worthy of Notice, made by Mr. John Bartram, in his Travels from Pensilvania to Onondago, Owego and the Lake Ontario, in Canada, to which is annex'd, a curious account of the cataracts at Niagara by Mr. Peter Kalm* (London, 1751).

43. J. B. [John Bartram], "Remarkable and Authentic Instances of the Fascinating Power of the Rattle-Snake over Men and Other Animals," *Gentleman's Magazine* 35 (1765): 511–14.

44. His source on the horn snake was Mark Catesby, *The Natural History of Carolina, Florida, and the Bahama Islands*, 2 vols. (London, 1754), 2:43, and for the cockatrice, Charles Owen, *An Essay towards the Natural History of Serpents* (London, 1742), 78–80.

45. Williamson advertised the publication of *Travels* in the *Caledonian Mercury* on 16 November and 12 December 1767, but it otherwise does not appear to have received notice in British newspapers or periodicals.

46. See Percy G. Adams, *Travelers and Travel Liars, 1660–1800* (1962; New York, 1980).

47. See Susan Scott Parrish, *American Curiosity: Cultures of Natural History in the Colonial British Atlantic World* (Chapel Hill, NC, 2006), 215–58.

48. The most complete collection of Williamson's directories can be found in the Edinburgh Room of the Edinburgh City Library.

49. For Williamson's penny post, see F. T. Green, "The Penny Post and Postmarks of Peter Williamson," *Philately in Scotland* 1 (1933): 8–9. For his pension, see *The Parliamentary Register, or History of the Proceedings and Debates of the House of Commons*, 12 vols. (London: 1797–1802), 5:106.

50. For Williamson's obituary, see the *Edinburgh Evening Courant*, 21 January 1799. It was reprinted in several other newspapers and periodicals, including the February 1799 edition of the *Gentleman's Magazine*.

51. See Joseph S. Lucas, "The Course of Empire and the Long Road to Civilization: North American Indians and Scottish Enlightenment Historians," *Explorations in Early American Culture* 4 (2004): 166–90, and Roger L. Emerson, "American Indians, Frenchmen, and Scots Philosophers," *Studies in Eighteenth-Century Culture* 9 (1979): 210–36.

52. See Linda Colley, *Britons: Forging the Nation, 1707–1837* (New Haven, CT, 1992), 101–45, and Kathleen Wilson, *The Island Race: Englishness, Empire, and Gender in the Eighteenth Century* (New York, 2003), 1–28.

53. See, for example, J. Leitch Wright Jr., *William Augustus Bowles: Director General of the Creek Nation* (Athens, GA, 1967), and Benita Eisler, *The Red Man's Bones: George Catlin, Artist and Showman* (New York, 2013).

54. See Wilson, *The Island Race*, 54–91; Linda Colley, *Captives: Britain, Empire, and the World, 1600–1850* (New York, 2003), 239–346; and Maya Jasanoff, *Edge of Empire: Lives, Culture, and Conquest in the East, 1750–1850* (New York, 2005), 241–74.

Imperial Vineyards

Wine and Politics in the Early American South

OWEN STANWOOD

Louis de Mesnil de Saint-Pierre had a simple vision: to turn the American South into a vast vineyard. In 1770 the French gentleman and Protestant refugee traveled from his adopted home of New Bordeaux, South Carolina, to sell his dream to possible English benefactors. One of the leaders of a settlement of Huguenots and Germans on the Savannah River, Saint-Pierre believed that planting vineyards would solve virtually all of the empire's looming problems. "The Vine is a native of America," wrote the Frenchman. "And this divine plant may be found throughout that vast continent, from the mouth of the Mississippi to that of the St. Lawrence, where it is as common as now, and much more so than formerly in France and Italy." With the help of foreign experts, Americans of all classes could turn their energies to the cultivation of this valuable commodity that would provide the entire empire with lucrative products and give employment to thousands—and put a stop to the political divisions that threatened to tear the empire apart. "Perhaps Government may find out, *when too late,*" Saint-Pierre scolded, "that the number of *emigrants* daily resorting to *America,* as well as the *natives* of our colonies there, would have been much more usefully employed for the *benefit* of the *mother* country, by the cultivation of the lands, in producing *Silk,* and raising *Vines,* &c. than in the *rivaling* of the *mother* country in *arts* and *manufactures.*"[1]

This was not the first time that an ambitious European proposed making wine in North America. In fact, such designs had appeared since the sixteenth century, when European explorers noticed the vast amounts of wild grapes that grew across the continent. From John Smith to William Penn, dozens of projectors experimented with wine making, some using native vines, others acquiring cuttings from Europe. Hundreds of migrants, mostly French Protestants and Germans, devoted themselves to the schemes. As more than one visitor noted, however, the results of these experiments were not the best. Despite being on the same latitude as the Mediterranean, the southern colonies stubbornly failed to produce drinkable wine. American varieties of grapes proved too sweet, and the soil and high humidity made the southern colonies less than ideal wine country. And yet the dream never died. When Thomas Jefferson planted his vines at Monticello, there was nothing revolutionary about it. He was heir to a long tradition of agricultural experimentation in the American South.[2]

The early American obsession with vineyards appears at first glance to be just another dead end in colonial agricultural history—a false start on the way to finding successful staple crops. But the persistence of these schemes suggests that vineyards were more than historical footnotes. The long-term obsession with grapes and wine presents a vision of colonial America not as it was but as imperial planners wished it would be. The real story of American agriculture was the rise of a "plantation complex" centered on staple crops like tobacco, rice, and in the linked Caribbean island colonies, sugar. These commodities made planters and merchants very rich and also brought about a massive revolution in labor practices, as Europeans turned from indentured servitude to more profitable enslaved African labor.[3] As central as this system became, it was not without its detractors, and the persistence of wine schemes provides one look at a persistent vision of a different America. The champions of wine advocated an American agriculture more attuned to England's political economic needs. They also envisioned a more diverse workforce that included European expert laborers and hoped that the economic center of gravity could move away from swampy lowlands toward the milder upcountry. All of this would lead to a better, more virtuous empire: one in which laborers of all nations worked in tandem to improve the mother country's place in the world order.[4]

In the end, climate and geography made such visions impossible, but their failure should not blind us to the imperial visions that they represented. In the eyes of Louis de Saint-Pierre, only the lack of the right vine cuttings and the right (French) laborers prevented America from becoming a new Mediterranean, a new France under the protection of a benevolent English monarch.

There was hardly a European in North America who did not notice the grapes. Exploring what would later become South Carolina, for instance, the Frenchman René Goulaine de Laudonnière noted that "the trees were all entwined with cords of vines, bearing grapes in such quantities that their number would be sufficient to render the place habitable."[5] Several decades later and a few hundred miles to the north, John Smith marveled at vines that "climbe the toppes of the highest trees in some places."[6] Indeed, Virginia's first historian noted, in a refrain that could be found in almost any description of the region, that the region possessed "Grapes in such abundance, as was never known in the World."[7]

Europeans interpreted the grapes in a variety of ways. For French visitors like Laudonnière, they signified habitability. It was the Huguenot settlers in La Caroline in the 1560s, supposedly, who produced the first North American wine, and they appeared to do so for their own sustenance. How, after all, could French people live without wine? Others could view vineyards as signifying the Edenic plenty of the new world, a sign that life would be easy for those who settled there. For many English, who imported wine anyway, grapes appeared almost as alluring as the tantalizing glimpses of silver and gold they sometimes saw in American landscapes. As Thomas Harriott reported from the soon-to-be Lost Colony at Roanoke, "When [the grapes] are planted and husbanded as they ought, a principall commoditie of wines by them may be raised."[8] The grapes could make money, and from the 1610s onward English projectors sought to find ways to turn the natural resources of these new places into a financial windfall. Doing so, however, proved far more difficult than they imagined.

From the first decade of settlement, Virginia Company officials tried to turn the wild grapes into commodities. In one of their many missives to their Company overlords insisting on the colony's promise of profitability, the Council noted that "in every boske and common hedge, and not far from our pallisado gates, we have thousands of goodly vines running along and leaning to every tree, which yeald a plentifull grape in their kind." All that they needed were "skillfull vinearoons" to make a "fruitfull vintage."[9] Around the same time, a worried Spanish official passed on a report that the Virginians had already produced wine and that it "resembles much the wine of Alicante."[10]

In fact, the Spanish reporter was probably exaggerating the success of these early efforts. Virginia's first leaders did all they could to encourage the industry, even passing laws encouraging all householders to make at least a small quantity of wine.[11] Some colonists evidently answered the call. John Smith reported that Virginians made 20 gallons of wine from "hedge grapes" that was "neare as good as your French Brittish wine," that is, wine from Brittany, but would prove better if it were "well manured."[12] In mentioning husbandry, however, Smith gestured toward the problem with Virginian viticulture, which was readily identified by the councilors when they reported back to the Company. Virginia had nature's bounty but not the human ingenuity to make it profitable. English people simply could not master the complicated process by which grapes became wine. As a later commentator noted, "we of the Northern Climate are neither Artists, nor curious, in propagating that pleasant and profitable Vegetable."[13] The answer, of course, was to import laborers who did know this ancient art, and from the 1610s onward Virginians began a long search to find the "vinearoons" that could jump-start the industry.

There was an obvious problem that complicated the search for expert laborers. Most Europeans skilled in wine making lived in Catholic countries. Not only were they unlikely to make the trek to English America; many of the English colonists had no desire for them to do so. Virginia's ministers thundered against the evils of Catholicism, identifying the pope as Antichrist and Spain as "the sword of Antichrist," the earthly enforcers of evil.[14] In fact, one reason to produce wine in the colonies was to compete with Catholics and take a portion of their profits. But there were other possibilities. Further east, Greek vintners lived under the oppression of Ottoman Turks—and as Orthodox Christians, they appeared more desirable than Catholics. Increasingly, however, champions of colonial wine looked to the French, and specifically to France's Protestant minority, the Huguenots.

The Huguenots were in many ways the most logical people to grow wine in Virginia. Protestants dominated French merchant communities in Normandy and La Rochelle and had played a disproportionate role in early French colonization and overseas trade, including early colonial experiments in Florida and Canada. The Edict of Nantes of 1598 guaranteed limited toleration of Protestantism in France and made some Huguenots secure, but the Thirty Years' War and policies of Cardinal Richelieu inspired others to take their talents elsewhere—just in time to help English colonizers in their efforts to produce Mediterranean commodities in America.[15]

The first French colonists arrived in Virginia sometime in the 1620s, and while few records document their activities, they definitely came to make wine, but with little success. In 1621 the French were already there—Company officials instructed Governor Francis Wyatt to "take care of the vignerons"—but by 1628 the General Assembly asserted that the French "either did not understand the business, or concealed their skill; for they spent their time to little purpose." In 1632 the House of Burgesses passed an act prohibiting the French from planting tobacco, claiming that they "not only neglected to plant anay vynes themselves, but have also spoyled and ruinated that vyniard, which was, with great cost, planted by the charge of the late company and theire officers here."[16] During the same era, another Huguenot, the Baron de Sancé, petitioned the secretary of state for aid for a new French colony in Virginia, one that would "settle French Protestants in Virginia in order to plant vines and olives there and make silk." All he asked for in return was denization for himself and his family, but this plan, like others, did not come to pass.[17]

Despite all encouragement from authorities, tobacco, not wine, eventually found its place as Virginia's cash crop. It was well after the turn to tobacco, however, in 1650, that the most coherent statement of the colony's wine ambitions appeared in the London press. In his book *Virginia, Especially the south part thereof, richly and truely valued,* the planter Edward Williams made a case for Virginia wine that predicted many of the political economic screeds of the next century and a half. His argument began with latitude; Williams claimed that "whatever *China, Persia, Japan, Cyprus, Candy, Sicily, Greece,* the South of *Italy, Spaine,* and the opposite parts of *Africa,* to all which she is parallel, may boast of, will be produced in this happy Country."[18] Williams identified a number of crops that would make Virginia the most productive corner of the empire, including silk and olives, but wine was perhaps his chief obsession.

If climate provided the means to make wine in Virginia, political economy provided a reason. In a classic, early expression of mercantilistic theory, Williams alleged that when filled with people, Virginia would project English power around the world and, perhaps more important, fill the national coffers with customs duties. This could only be done, however, if Virginians produced things that could actually make money, and wine was one of those things. Williams suggested that Virginia would soon produce "the Noblest Wine in the World," which would corner the northern European market and make Virginia "the envy of France and Spain." In his most unorthodox suggestion, Williams even suggested that Virginians could market their wine to the Chinese, "the richest and mightiest Empire in the world." In brief, Virginian wine revenues would turn England into "the happiest Nation in Europe."[19]

For whatever reason, Williams's suggestions went largely unheeded. A few Virginians experimented with silk production in the 1650s, but that commodity proved even more difficult than wine, and the fever for tobacco infected the minds of Virginians and transformed the colonial landscape. In a response to queries from the Lords of Trade and Plantations in 1671, Governor William Berkeley blamed the Navigation Acts for the failure of the colony's wine, silk, and other experiments, since the restriction of commerce to English ships prevented colonists from acquiring materials necessary to further the industries, such as the vine cuttings that Williams believed would bring Virginia wine to perfection. Berkeley himself believed in economic diversification and attempted to raise grapes on his own plantation. The wine was as good "as ever came out of Italy," but transporting the wine across the ocean proved difficult, and few of his neighbors wanted to imitate him.[20] Restricted in their activities, English Virginians became slaves to tobacco and the cultural transformation that the crop required.

Only a few years after Berkeley wrote, the English philosopher and polymath John Locke traveled around France. Among other tasks, Locke collected the wisdom of *vignerons* across the kingdom. In his manuscript notes on his journey, Locke described how vineyards grew in different provinces of France, the proper time of year to plant, the effective use of fertilizer, and how to turn the grapes into proper wines. He presented his observations to his employer, Anthony Ashley Cooper, the Earl of Shaftesbury, one of the proprietors of the new colony of Carolina and a leading colonial theorist, noting that "I should scarce have ventured to trouble your Lordship with these French trifles, had not your Lordship yourself encouraged me to believe, that it would not be unacceptable to you." Evidently, Shaftesbury encouraged Locke to uncover secrets of the trade that could be applied in Carolina. The earl hoped, like the Virginia Company before him, that his new colony would soon rival France in the production of wine.[21]

Locke's treatise provides a window into a period that might be considered the golden age of wine experiments in the southern colonies. The founding of Carolina in the 1660s expanded the geographic bounds of English settlement in the region and brought about another period of agricultural speculation as planters searched for a profitable staple. At the same time, the expansion of Virginia into the Piedmont—lands less suited for tobacco—renewed hopes for wine there. Beyond the colonies, meanwhile, imperial and global events spurred on these hopes. Political economic writers became increasingly breathless about the dangers of a negative balance of trade, and many of them began to theorize that colonial products could help to close that gap. Finally, the changing political situation in France provided a new population of possible laborers for these colonies, as tens of thousands of refugees fled that kingdom and scattered around Europe and the world.[22]

The renewed push for colonial wine responded to common concerns among late seventeenth-century political economists. The great ambition of states, according to theorists, was to maintain a positive balance of trade. As Carew Reynall put it, "Where a Nation Imports by its voluptuousness more than it Exports, it must needs come to ruine." Sadly, England was becoming the most voluptuous nation of all, awash with wine, silk, and other "*French Toyes*" that "fetch away our Money and solid wealth."[23] Reynall's answer was more domestic manufacturing and eschewing foreign luxuries like wine, but others took a different tack. According to the East India Company president

Josiah Child, for instance, maintaining foreign plantations that shipped raw materials home could build the national economy, especially since colonists would consume English manufactures and provide employment for thousands in shipping.[24] In addition, as Charles Davenant later added, "our Tobacco, Cotton, Ginger, Sugars, Indico, with other Commodities, if we take Care to secure our Plantations, will create us Business in all the Ports of *Europe.*"[25]

At the same time that economists obsessed about balance of trade and colonial commodities, they also fixated on population and the movement of peoples. Common wisdom stated that a nation's strength lay in its people and that any drain on population—whether to rival nations or colonies— weakened the realm. Some political economists, most notably Josiah Child, disputed this notion, but they also proposed another way around the problem. Seventeenth-century Europe abounded with religious dissenters: persecuted people who desired opportunities to practice their faiths freely and would offer their labor and talent to any nation that offered them freedom of worship. Child and others strongly advocated for naturalization of "strangers" with particular talents—not just Protestants but Greeks and Jews as well.[26]

This combination of political economic theorizing and politico-religious drama led to a proliferation of wine schemes in the late 1600s. The key players, once again, were the Huguenots, nearly 200,000 of whom fled France during the 1680s as Louis XIV revoked the Edict of Nantes and banned the practice of Protestantism. At least initially, the key theater for this speculation was Carolina, a new proprietary colony directed, at least in its early years, by Locke's employer, the Earl of Shaftesbury. Carolina's proprietors intended their colony to combine the two dreams of the political economists: it would provide a refuge for religious dissenters while bringing new, valuable commodities into the empire. The many Carolina promotional tracts of the 1680s reflected these concerns. Most of them mentioned wine among possible staple crops in the new colony, and the proprietors specifically courted religious dissenters, especially Huguenots, to create the vineyards.[27]

Like the early travel accounts, Carolina promotional tracts stressed the proliferation of wild vines. As one propagandist asserted, the possibility of a colony based on wine, silk, and olive oil attracted a "great Concourse" of people to the colony. These migrants had already experimented in harvesting both the wild grapes and cuttings from Europe, with promising results. Indeed, the first wine sent back to England "was well approved of," and without doubt more industry would make Carolina "a *Magazine and Staple for Wines* to the whole *West* Indies." Of course, Carolina could not realize its promise without skillful vignerons, and so the author noted that the proprietors had already offered free passage to a number of Huguenots to relocate to Carolina, "they being most of them well experienced in the Nature of the *Vine*, from whose Directions doubtless the *English* have received and made considerable Advantages in their Improvements."[28]

French-language tracts repeated the common encomiums to American grapes and encouraged French migrants to devote themselves to wine making. As the Huguenot minister Charles de Rochefort declared in an emigration guide to the colonies, vines "grow naturally there without any human labor," while another author described wild vines as thick as a man's arm.[29] A detailed tract instructing Huguenot gentlemen in forming their "establishments" in Carolina suggested finding laborers in Europe who had particular expertise in the culture of the vine and listed the French provinces that would be most likely to produce such laborers. "If one can achieve a wine harvest and it is abundant," the tract concluded, "there is no doubt that it will provide a very good living."[30]

As the latter tract uncomfortably revealed, not all French migrants had the requisite knowledge to create a productive vineyard. Many of the kingdom's Protestants worked in commerce or manufacturing rather than agriculture, and a substantial number came from regions, Normandy in particular, where wine making was a marginal pursuit. Nonetheless, many leaders in the Huguenot community were all too willing to play into the English belief that all French people instinctively understood viticulture. The first Huguenot appeal to the proprietors for land in Carolina stressed that the migrants were natives of a similar climate and therefore "accustomed to the culture of vines."[31] Indeed, Huguenots stressed their agricultural skills as much or more than their status as persecuted Protestants in their many petitions for land and good treatment.

While most of the wine schemes of the late 1600s centered on Carolina, the fever spread to other colonies as well. Even in Pennsylvania, William Penn experimented with vines and publicized his experiments in a tract targeted specifically to Huguenot migrants.[32] The most ambitious plans, however, occurred in Virginia, encouraged in particular by the travels of a Huguenot gentleman known to posterity as Durand of Dauphiné. A refugee from southern France, Durand originally intended to move to South Carolina and set himself up in the silk industry, but when his ship blew off course, he found himself converted to wine and Virginia. Traveling through the Piedmont with his Virginian hosts, Durand noticed the proliferation of grapes. While staying on Ralph Wormeley's plantation on the Rappahannock River, he went so far as to pick some of the fruit and ferment it outside his room, pronouncing the result "very good." He speculated, "Good wine could certainly be obtained if on arriving the branches were pruned & cultivated; at least there would be enough for one's own use, & yet low grape-vines could be planted, the wine would be better, & it would bring a very good income."[33]

Durand's hosts, either inspired by his enthusiasm or of their own volition, chose to encourage the Frenchman's efforts to jump-start Virginia's wine industry. Traveling on the upper reaches of the Rappahannock, Durand "was extolling upon the beauty of the place we had just seen, the same lovely hills whence flow fountains & brooks, & broad meadows below, always covered with wild grapevines; I was saying that fine vines could grow upon these slopes & that doubtless the wine would be excellent." Wormeley "replied that if I could find some means to bring Frenchmen there, he would sell the whole of those ten thousand acres of ground he owned on both sides of the river for one écu an acre," including the houses.[34]

Durand returned to England convinced that Virginia was the most salubrious climate for Huguenot refugees. They would not have to face the relentless rain of London, the cold winters of New England and New York, or the deadly heat of South Carolina. Moreover, the climate was perfect not just for French people but for their grapes, and the vineyards would make Virginia both habitable and profitable for its new French colonists. Contrasting Virginia to New York, for instance, Durand noted that "wine can be made in Virginia in large quantities, & very good, while [in the north] the climate is colder than in England, & grapes will not ripen easily."[35]

Durand's interest in vines may have primarily served to convince French people that they could survive in Virginia. But his patrons clearly saw visions of great wealth in these plans to offer their excess lands to tenants who could develop a new cash crop. William Fitzhugh of Stafford County was one of these projectors. One of the county's leading landowners, Fitzhugh lobbied Durand to bring his countrymen to the Potomac River valley, and he confided to his English partner that the land was "more proper for French men, because more naturally inclined to Vines than yours or any about our Neighbourhood."[36] There were many issues at play. English officials needed settlers for frontier regions, away from the lucrative tobacco fields of the Tidewater, but the obsession with that single crop tended to keep the English migrants clustered in the Tidewater scrambling for their share of the tobacco profits. By encouraging French emigration and the wine industry, the colony's leaders aimed to bring about a more diverse and secure Virginia.

Whether in Carolina, Virginia, or Pennsylvania, most of these wine schemes remained just that: dreams with little hope of success. Pennsylvania never attracted many Huguenots at all, and only a few answered Durand and Fitzhugh's calls to settle in Virginia—at least during the 1680s. Nonetheless, Huguenots did migrate, and the few surviving letters provide evidence that a few of them did experiment with vineyards. The most enthusiastic evidence came from Louis Thibou, a Parisian wine merchant who worked assiduously to make wine on his Carolina plantation. "I have tried growing vines which do wonderfully well," Thibou wrote back to contacts in Europe, noting that he used cuttings of European grapes to produce his wine. "They produce excellent grapes which are sweet, wine flavored (*vineux*), and full of juice," he continued. "There can never be a lack of them since they are nourished by warmth and soft rain; that is why I am sure of producing here better wine than could be produced in Europe." As with so many similar missives, Thibou lamented that only the proper cuttings prohibited him from realizing the soil's true potential, and if he had "good vine-stock from Champagne, Suresne and Argenteuil I would very quickly do well in this country for wine is very dear and sells at 20 sous a bottle."[37]

Other letters made clear that such experimentation was widespread among French residents of South Carolina during the 1690s. A Swiss settler, Jean-François Gignilliat, tried growing several types of grapes and found that those from Bordeaux worked best, but he hoped for even better results once he obtained cuttings from Spain, Portugal, or Madeira, after which "we will infallibly make very good wine."[38] The following decade the Charleston minister Paul Lescot reflected on these various experiments, noting that vignerons had made "a small quantity" of wine but continued to experiment with different varieties of grapes, first with grapes "from our continent," which did not succeed, but finally with native grapes, "which have found success here." Lescot's conclusions seemed to contradict those of Thibou and others and probably reflected the significant confusions and difficulties that French vignerons went through in their attempts to make wine in a humid subtropical climate that, whatever protests to the contrary, was nothing like Languedoc.[39]

As South Carolina planters, Huguenots included, turned to rice in the early eighteenth century, wine speculation returned once again to the Chesapeake. In 1700 and 1701, a large retinue of Huguenot refugees arrived in the colony after a global drama that included the failure of similar refugee schemes in Ireland and on the Gulf of Mexico.[40] The French settled on the upper reaches of the James River in Manakin Town, and while wine did not feature in planning for the colony, the refugees quickly began some of the same kinds of experiments that proliferated in Carolina. A Swiss traveler noted in the early eighteenth century that "the most awful wild grapevines" surrounded Manakin Town, but that the refugees had already made "fairly good wine" and had started grafting European grapes to the wild ones that grew around them.[41] The planter and historian Robert Beverley raved more enthusiastically about Huguenot wine efforts. "The *French* Refugees at the *Monacan* Town have lately made a sort of Clarret," Beverley wrote, referring to the variety of red Bordeaux wine favored by the English. Though the grapes came from "the wild Vines in the woods," Beverley "was told by a very good Judge, who tasted it, that it was a pleasant strong, and full body'd Wine. From which we may conclude, that if the Wine was but tolerably good, when made of the wild Grape, which is shaded by the Woods, from the Sun, it would be much better, if produc'd of the same Grape cultivated in a regular Vineyard."[42]

Beverley went far beyond the usual optimistic predictions to discover why previous hopes had failed and how future attempts could succeed. He noted that many people had tried to make wine in both Carolina and the Virginia Tidewater, but that these essays had failed due to local environmental conditions. Vineyards thrived best "on the Sides of Hills, Gravelly Ground, and in the Neighbourhood of fresh Streams," Beverley asserted, but most of the American vignerons had planted their vines in the only cleared lands available, which were usually in the lowlands "near the salt Rivers, in Piney Ground."[43] Beverley was stumbling toward a very astute environmental observation: wine grapes needed particular conditions of soil, sun, and lower relative humidity to succeed. At the same time, it was a self-serving observation, as Beverley himself owned land in Virginia's hilly Piedmont, and like Wormeley and Durand several decades earlier, he hoped to use wine to move Virginia's economic center of gravity away from the Tidewater.

Beverley also experimented with making wine on his own plantation. According to the Anglican minister Hugh Jones, Beverley began by studying vintages, but then attempted to plant a small vineyard to test his theories. "He bragged much of it in publick," Jones continued, and apparently received many skeptical responses. Being a typical Virginia gentleman, Beverley encouraged his challengers to offer a wager: "he proposed to give each of them a guinea down, if they would give him ten, if he made a certain number of gallons of pure wine that vintage," Jones reported. "They accepted the proposals, and he distributed . . . one hundred guineas, made the wine and won his wager." He then invested his winnings back into his vineyard, finally making enough wine to supply his own household—even the slaves—as well as many neighbors.[44] Another traveler, the Irish Huguenot John Fontaine, observed Beverley's vineyard in person in 1715—a three-acre plot situated, of course, "upon the side of a hill." From Fontaine's reports, Beverley had invested much into wine efforts: he had transplanted French cuttings and even built a cave and wine press. In the end, however, Fontaine remained unimpressed. His vineyard was "not rightly managed," and when Fontaine tasted the wine he pronounced it "good," but "I found by the taste that he did not understand how for to make it."[45]

Beverley was not the only English gentleman in Virginia or South Carolina to invest significant resources in wine making during the first decades of the 1700s. They did so, to be sure, to make money, but their wine experiments also reflected a larger political economic vision, one that imagined a new place for the colonies as producers of new commodities, beyond tobacco and rice, that contributed to the national interest. Thus imperial officials like Virginia governor Alexander Spotswood signed on enthusiastically to Beverley's plans. Spotswood sponsored a settlement of Germans in the Piedmont called Germanna, and "These are encouraged to make wines," according to Hugh Jones.[46] William Byrd II presented a similar plan in a promotional pamphlet intended for Swiss migrants, noting that "nothing is lacking but good grape people, who could plant and make it correctly." With the right laborers, "one would then doubtless get good wine."[47]

For officials around the South, wine schemes represented dreams of diversification. On one hand, diversity meant an economy not so dependent on the fluctuations of one staple crop. But it also meant bringing in new people and developing different types of landscapes further in the continent's interior. In short, Spotswood and Beverley wanted to create a new South, but as long as connoisseurs like Fontaine remained skeptical, there was no way that Virginia or Carolina wine could survive in a European market—or even a colonial one. With French claret and Madeira flooding colonial markets, Beverley and other colonial vintners had few prospective customers.[48]

In 1768 the "Honourable Society for the Encouragement of Arts, Manufactures, and Commerce" (later known as the Royal Society of Arts) published a lengthy summary of the various attempts to make wine in America. Founded about a decade earlier, the Society represented a push from the imperial center to encourage new projects in agriculture and manufacturing. The purpose of these efforts, as they put it, was "to encourage the growth of those Commodities in our Plantations which we take from Foreigners," which would undoubtedly lead to "the encrease of our manufactures at home, and consequently our Navigation and Commerce by supplying the Colonies with our own Commodities in exchange for this New Produce of theirs."[49] Among many other things, the Society resolved in 1758 to encourage the projects that Beverley and others had pioneered, "deeming it not impracticable" to encourage the growth of "the Vines of the Eastern continent into our American Colonies." The Society offered premiums for nearly a decade, and unlike its essays in silk and olive oil manufacturing, it dubbed the wine bounties successful, as "the introduction of vines into America is known, by the Society, to have taken place." In 1763, for instance, Charles Carter made a "spirited attempt" to produce wine on his Virginia plantation and took a gold medal for his troubles. Four years later, a Connecticut farmer took a medal as well. The Society admitted that the American wine industry experienced "frequent miscarriages" but insisted that colonial wine could be a great commodity.[50]

The Society's efforts served as a backdrop for the last, and in some ways most ambitious, period of wine speculation in the southern colonies. With new encouragement from London, and a large influx of new migrants from wine regions like the Rhine River valley, dozens if not hundreds of projectors tried their luck at planting vineyards. These efforts never entirely stopped at any point in the 1700s. During the 1730s, for instance, an eccentric Swiss wine merchant named Jean Pierre Purry had received a substantial grant in South Carolina for promising to bring "Foreign Protestants" who were "well Skill'd in the Production of Silk & Wine."[51] The founders of Georgia had a similar vision of creating a southern colony that eschewed the slave-based monoculture of the South Carolina low country. As a Boston newspaper reported, "There will be Attempts made for raising Raw Silk, Vines, Olives, and other things which succeed very well there, and do not grow well in England; and the People will be encouraged in bringing Raw Silk, Wine, and Oil to Perfection, and be prohibited from making any manufactures that may interfere with Great Britain."[52] But while some did cultivate vines in Georgia, most of the trustees' energy went toward silk; indeed, the colony's seal even featured a silkworm.

Finally, some Virginia planters continued with Beverley's efforts to make wine in the Virginia Piedmont. Philip Ludwell attempted, with the Society's aid, to acquire vine cuttings from Greece that he believed would perfectly suit Virginia's climate.[53] A member of one of the colony's leading families, Charles Carter, dedicated himself to diversifying Virginia's economy, fearing that "if the common Consumers were sensible of the great proportion of poysonous Quality" of tobacco, "they wou'd be induced to lay it aside, to preserve their Healths & save their Money." He worked on a number of projects intended to "add greatly to the Strength and Riches of our Mother Country, by bringing the Ballance of Trade now carried on with Foreigners in Favour of Britain." Carter acquired all of the vine cuttings he could and experimented with a variety of techniques on his plantation, preferring French, Spanish, and Portuguese vines to Ludwell's Greek ones. He hoped that the many Chesapeake merchants in France could bring back cuttings. He also mentioned wild grapes, noting that "many People have accidentally without makeing any Observations made delicious Wine from them," but adding that the cuttings rarely took root and the quality was uneven. In the end, the Society awarded Carter one of their gold medals for his "noble speculations," hoping that Virginia wine could resemble the "Rhenish sort," as "German Wines are in much Vogue amongst us at this time."[54]

While Virginia's planters continued their quest for diversity, new wine efforts began in South Carolina during the 1760s. As in Virginia, these attempts took place in a political context, especially the design by successive governors to encourage settlement in the colony's upcountry, a region of great strategic importance but without the economic rewards of the low country. In addition to the Scots-Irish settlers who flowed down the Great Wagon Road from Pennsylvania, South Carolina officials encouraged German and French Protestants to make their way to the colony, offering them land and assistance in the Bounty Act of 1761. Thousands of Germans and a smaller number of Huguenots answered the call and headed for the Carolina Piedmont.[55]

One of these newcomers, a German named Christopher Sherb, attracted the attention of South Carolina governor William Bull. A resident of Berkeley County some miles upriver from Charleston, Sherb began producing wine on his farm in the 1760s. In 1768 Sherb made twenty-five gallons of wine, but increased the yield to eighty gallons the following year. Bull tasted Sherb's vintage and admitted that the wine was "not yet very good," but instead of blaming the climate, he pointed the finger at "the young people in the Neighbourhood" who stole grapes and thus necessitated Sherb to pick them before they were ready. The governor recommended Sherb for the Royal Society of Arts's bounty.[56] In 1770 Bull personally visited "the poor German at Broad River" and "saw 1600 Vines neatly planted, cleared from weeds and well inclosed." From five cuttings, Bull reported, Sherb had produced 500 vines, and also distributed cuttings to his neighbors. This all served to demonstrate, Bull asserted, "what industry and perseverance can perform when assisted by a fertile soil, and a benign climate."[57]

The German never lived to see his efforts lift him out of poverty, as he died in the early 1770s, but Bull's interest in South Carolina wine lived on. He soon moved his efforts several hundred miles west to New Bordeaux, a settlement of Huguenots and Germans founded in 1763 by a French minister who arrived with part of his congregation and received land along the upper reaches of the Savannah River. Bull convinced the General Assembly to pay to send a number of different vine cuttings there, including some from France.[58] By 1773, Bull reported, one of the town's leading lights, Louis de Mesnil de Saint-Pierre, had become "very sanguine in pursuing the object." Saint-Pierre had already planted four acres of vines, and "the success of a few," Bull predicted, "will soon invite many to follow the example."[59]

With Bull's encouragement, Saint-Pierre embarked on the last and most ambitious attempt to gain support for wine culture in colonial America. There is no evidence that Saint-Pierre had any particular expertise in wine making. He came from the Norman port town of Honfleur, a place with long-standing connections to Atlantic trade but no traditions of viticulture. According to a French report, most of Saint-Pierre's fellow colonists were "workers of various trades" from the Norman seaside region of Coutances, not farmers from wine country.[60] Nonetheless, Saint-Pierre, perhaps inspired by Bull, dedicated himself to turning a profit from New Bordeaux's vineyards. Apparently not finding enough financial help from the Assembly, Saint-Pierre returned to London with Bull's blessing, hoping to procure funding from investors there. He presented a petition to the king complaining that he had not been able to find a suitable tract of land to bring his project to fruition. He claimed he needed five thousand acres but had only been able to find a few noncontiguous plots. Since the governor only had the power to grant Saint-Pierre one plot, the Frenchman asked the king to directly grant him more. He had already invested much of his own money in obtaining the proper vine cuttings, and it would be a shame to let them go to waste.[61]

Apparently this petition went nowhere, as Saint-Pierre soon moved to a new tactic, putting his case in print in a search for sponsors. In two separate publications, Saint-Pierre repeated many of the commonplace assumptions about the benefits of an American wine industry. He began with the usual platitudes about balance of trade. Anyone "really concerned for the *true* interest of this country," Saint-Pierre asserted, "grieves to see it pay such enormous sums to the *Italians, Spaniards, Frenchmen,* and ungrateful *Portuguese,* when it is so apparent in our power to be supplied, in the course of a very few years, with the greater part of our wines from our own *American* Colonies." Saint-Pierre understood that many had tried and failed to make domestic wine before, but his plan would succeed, he claimed, due to the superior skills of his countrymen. "The present Settlers at *New Bourdeaux* were all bred up in *Vineyards,*" he claimed rather incredibly, "and understand the culture of *Vines* as well as any of their countrymen."[62]

If Saint-Pierre's arguments were commonplace, even boilerplate, he adapted them to the peculiar circumstances of his time. The empire was in crisis, he pointed out, and Saint-Pierre identified the troubles as economic and demographic in nature. An "infinite multitude" of new migrants settled in the colonies, and the old plantation economy could simply not provide work for all of them. In such circumstances the people would naturally tend to "set up manufactures"—thus competing with the mother country and negating the very purpose of the colonies.[63] If these multitudes could be put to work in vineyards—directed in their labors by French and German experts—then they would fulfill their proper role as producers of raw materials and consumers of English goods. After all, as Saint-Pierre wrote, "the number of people necessarily employed in the cultivation of the Vine supposes a vast consumption of European manufactures."[64]

Saint-Pierre envisioned a harmonious, integrated empire—one in which metropolitans and colonials understood their proper roles in the imperial system. And it would all be made possible by vineyards. Indeed, the wholesome grape would literally guarantee the health of the body politic. Like many Huguenots, Saint-Pierre held up the example of France as both a model and a warning. The kingdom's large population, which allowed it to build a powerful army, came about because "the wholesomeness of this divine liquor" provided both employment and health to the population. The British Empire stood in a position to inherit this wealth, because France's foolish persecutory policies pushed its people away, while Britain's guarantees of freedom of religion brought people in. People were the "only true riches of a nation," Saint-Pierre concluded, and by providing jobs and freedom, the British Empire stood poised to bring many of the world's peoples into its benevolent union.[65]

By 1774, however, the empire that Louis de Saint-Pierre hoped to save with wine no longer had much of a future. Probably weary of colonial projects, investors stayed away from the Frenchman's scheme, and he returned home to New Bordeaux by 1775 at the latest. By this time the Continental Congress was on the verge of declaring independence, and like most of his French and German neighbors, Saint-Pierre chose the patriot side. He died in 1776 fighting the British-allied Cherokees on the upper reaches of the Savannah River.[66] Meanwhile, further to the north officials in Virginia turned the last page on the imperial wine experiment. In October 1776 the now independent House of Burgesses voted to sell land and slaves in York County that the House had established as a vineyard in 1769, in one of the last organized attempts to turn Virginia into wine country. The land, the act declared, "is unfit for that purpose," and the slaves "are become useless, and of no advantage to the publick."[67] Vines would grow in Virginia, but the imperial dreams of southern vineyards, which persisted in the face of dozens of false starts, did not survive the turmoil of revolution.[68]

Notes

1. Louis de Saint-Pierre, *The Art of Planting and Cultivating the Vine; as also, of Making, Fining, and Preserving Wines &c. According to the Most Approved Methods in the Most Celebrated Wine-Countries in France* (London, 1772), xx–xxi; [Saint-Pierre], *The great Utility of establishing the Culture of Vines, Silk, Indigo, and Fruit Trees, in such parts of North America, where the Climate is particularly favourable to those Productions* ([London], 1772), 3.

2. There has been very little work on early American wine making, but for a brief overview, see Thomas Pinney, *A History of Wine in America: From the Beginnings to Prohibition* (Berkeley, CA, 1989). On British and American wine consumption, see David Hancock, *Oceans of Wine: Madeira and the Origins of American Trade and Taste* (New Haven, CT, 2009); and Charles Ludington, *The Politics of Wine in Britain: A New Cultural History* (Basingstoke, 2013). On Jefferson, see John Hailman, *Thomas Jefferson on Wine* (Oxford, MS, 2009). The story of early American wine is closely tied to the better documented history of silk experimentation. See Ben Marsh, "Silk Hopes in Colonial South Carolina," *Journal of Southern History* 78 (2012): 807–54.

3. The term comes from Philip Curtin, *The Rise and Fall of the Plantation Complex: Essays in Atlantic History* (New York, 1990). For various perspectives on plantation agriculture, see Richard S. Dunn, *Sugar and Slaves: The Rise of the Planter Class in the English West Indies, 1624–1705* (Chapel Hill, NC, 1972); Alan Kulikoff, *Tobacco and Slaves: The Development of Southern Cultures in the Chesapeake, 1680–1800* (Chapel Hill, NC, 1986); S. Max Edelson, *Plantation Enterprise in Colonial South Carolina* (Cambridge, 2006); and on slavery, see Peter Wood, *Black Majority: Negroes in Colonial South Carolina from 1670 through the Stono Rebellion* (New York, 1974); Philip D. Morgan, *Slave Counterpoint: Black Culture in the Eighteenth-Century Chesapeake and Lowcountry* (Chapel Hill, NC, 1998); and Lorena S. Walsh, *Motives of Honor, Pleasure, and Profit: Plantation Management in the Colonial Chesapeake, 1607–1763* (Chapel Hill, NC, 2010).

4. In this emphasis on the "culture of agriculture" I draw especially from T. H. Breen, *Tobacco Culture: The Mentality of the Great Tidewater Planters on the Eve of Revolution* (Princeton, 1985).

5. Rene de Laudonnière, *Three Voyages*, ed. Charles Bennett and Jerald T. Melanich (Tuscaloosa, AL, 2001), 65.

6. Karen Ordahl Kupperman, ed., *Captain John Smith: A Select Edition of His Writings* (Chapel Hill, NC, 1988), 214.

7. Robert Beverley, *The History and Present State of Virginia*, ed. Louis B. Wright (Chapel Hill, NC, 1947), 16.

8. Thomas Harriott, *A Brief and True Report of the New Found Land of Virginia* (1588; New York, 1871), 9. (Electronic edition at http://docsouth.unc.edu/nc/hariot/hariot.html.)

9. Council in Virginia to the Virginia Company, 7 July 1610, in Alexander Brown, ed., *The Genesis of the United States* (New York, 1890), 409–10.

10. Report of Francis Maguel, 20/30 September 1610, in Brown, ed., *Genesis of the United States*, 395.

11. Pinney, *History of Wine in America*, 16.

12. Kupperman, *Captain John Smith*, 215.

13. John Lawson, *A New Voyage to Carolina*, ed. Hugh Talmage Lefler (Chapel Hill, NC, 1967), 57.

14. On the religious context of early Virginia, see Douglas Bradburn, "The Eschatological Origins of the English Empire," in Bradburn and John C. Coombs, eds., *Early Modern Virginia: New Essays on the Old Dominion* (Charlottesville, VA, 2011).

15. On the larger context, see Janine Garrisson, *L'Édit de Nantes et sa révocation* (Paris, 1985).

16. William Waller Hening, ed., *The Statutes at Large, Being a Collection of all the Laws of Virginia, from the First Legislature in the Year 1619* (Richmond, VA, 1809–23), 1:115, 136, 161. For other glimpses of these vignerons, see Susan Myra Kingsbury, ed., *The Records of the Virginia Company of London* (Washington, 1936), 3:240.

17. Antoine de Ridouet, Baron de Sancé to [Sec. Dorchester], June 1629, CO 1/5, no. 14, National Archives, Kew; Paul E. Kopperman, "Profile of Failure: The Carolana Project, 1629–1640," *North Carolina Historical Review* 59 (1982): 1–23.

18. [Edward Williams], *Virginia. Especially the South part thereof, Richly and truly Valued* (London, 1650), 11. On the origins of Virginia's tobacco regime, see especially Edmund S. Morgan, *American Slavery, American Freedom: The Ordeal of Colonial Virginia* (New York, 1972).

19. [Williams], *Virginia*, 16. There has been a robust debate on "mercantilism" as an analytical category; compare Steve Pincus, "Rethinking Mercantilism: Political Economy, the British Empire, and the Atlantic World in the Seventeenth and Eighteenth Centuries," *William and Mary Quarterly*, 3d ser., 69 (2012): 3–34, with Philip J. Stern and Carl Wennerlind, eds., *Mercantilism Reimagined: Political Economy in Early Modern Britain and Its Empire* (New York, 2013).

20. Enquiries to the Governor of Virginia, 1671, in Hening, *Statutes*, 2:515–16; Berkeley to the Earl of Clarendon, 18 April 1663, in Warren M. Billings, ed., *The Papers of Sir William Berkeley, 1605–1677* (Richmond, VA, 2007), 193.

21. Locke's manuscript was published the next century as *Observations upon the Growth and Culture of Vines and Olives: The Production of Silk: The Preservation of Fruits* (London, 1766). See pp. 1–24; quotation on xiii. On the context of the tract, see David Armitage, "John Locke, Carolina, and the Two Treatises of Government," *Political Theory* 32 (2004): 611–12.

22. On the larger economic context, see Andrea Finkelstein, *Harmony and the Balance: An Intellectual History of Seventeenth-Century English Economic Thought* (Ann Arbor, MI, 2000); Carl Wennerlind, *Casualties of Credit: The English Financial Revolution, 1620–1720* (Cambridge, MA, 2011). On how the Huguenots fit, see Owen Stanwood, "Between Eden and Empire: Huguenot Refugees and the Promise of New Worlds," *American Historical Review* 118 (2011): 1319–44.

23. Carew Reynall, *The True English Interest* (London, 1674), 10, 12.

24. Josiah Child, *A New Discourse of Trade* (London, 1693), 164–91.

25. [Charles Davenant], *Discourses on the Publick Revenues, and on the Trade of England* (London, 1698), 2:120.

26. [Child], *A New Discourse of Trade*, 187. On the politics of population in England, see Daniel Statt, *Foreigners and Englishmen: The Controversy over Immigration and Population, 1660–1760* (Newark, DE, 1995); Mildred Campbell, "'Of People Either Too Few or Too Many': The Conflict of Opinion on Population and Its Relation to Emigration," in William A. Aiken and Basil D. Henning, eds., *Conflict in Stuart England: Essays in Honour of Wallace Notestein* (London, 1960), 171–201.

27. Much of this history is ably covered in Bertrand Van Ruymbeke, *From New Babylon to Eden: The Huguenots and Their Migration to Colonial South Carolina* (Columbia, SC, 2006), esp. 40–49. On the founding of Carolina more generally, see L. H. Roper, *Conceiving Carolina: Proprietors, Planters, and Plots, 1662–1729* (Basingstoke, 2004), and M. Eugene Sirmans, *Colonial South Carolina: A Political History, 1663–1763* (Chapel Hill, NC, 1966).

28. *Carolina; or a Description of the Present State of that Country, and The Natural Excellencies thereto* (London, 1682), i, 9–10; *Description du Pays nommé Caroline* (London, 1679), 2.

29. Charles de Rochefort, *Histoire naturelle et morale des îles Antilles de l'Amérique*, ed. Bernard Grunberg, Benoît Roux, and Josiane Grunberg (Paris, 2012), 2:257; Extrait d'une lettre de Mr. Lescot ministre de l'Eglise françoise de Charlestown en Caroline du Sud, du 6 d'Avril 1701, Archives Tronchin, vol. 81, f. 194, Bibliothèque de Genève.

30. *Plan pour former un Establissement en Caroline* (The Hague, 1686), 7, 9.

31. Humble Proposition faite au Roy et à Son Parlement pour donner retraite aux Etrangers protestans et au proselites dans ses Colonies de L'amerique et sur tout en la Carolina, March 1679, in A. S. Salley, ed., *Records in the British Public Record Office Relating to South Carolina, 1663–1684* (Columbia, SC, 1928), 63.

32. *Recüeil de Diverses Pieces, Concernant la Pensylvanie* (The Hague, 1684), 58–60.

33. Durand of Dauphiné, *A Huguenot Exile in Virginia; or, Voyages of a Frenchman exiled for his Religion with a description of Virginia and Maryland*, ed. Gilbert Chinard (New York, 1934), 126–27.

34. Ibid., 154.

35. Ibid., 172.

36. Fitzhugh to Hayward, 20 May 1686, in Richard Beale Davis, ed., *William Fitzhugh and His Chesapeake World, 1676–1701: The Fitzhugh Letters and Other Documents* (Chapel Hill, NC, 1963), 189.

37. Lettre de Louis Thibou, 20 September 1683, South Caroliniana Library, Columbia. Many thanks to Bertrand Van Ruymbeke for sharing the original and his translation of the letter.

38. Robert Cohen and Myriam Yardeni, eds., "Un Suisse en Caroline du Sud à la fin du XVII siècle," *Bulletin de la Société de l'Histoire du Protestantisme Français* 134 (1988): 68.

39. Extrait d'une lettre de Mr. Lescot ministre de l'Eglise françoise de Charlestown en Caroline du Sud, du 6 d'Avril 1701, Archives Tronchin, vol. 81, f. 194, Bibliothèque de Genève.

40. On these migrants, see David E. Lambert, *The Protestant International and the Huguenot Migration to Virginia* (New York, 2010); James L. Bugg Jr., "The French Huguenot Frontier Settlement of Manakin Town," *Virginia Magazine of History and Biography* 61 (1953): 359–94.

41. "Report of the Journey of Francis Louis Michel from Berne, Switzerland, to Virginia,

October 2, 1701–December 1, 1702," ed. and trans. William J. Hinke, *Virginia Magazine of History and Biography* 24 (1916): 123.

42. Beverley, *History and Present State of Virginia*, 134.

43. Ibid., 134–35.

44. Hugh Jones, *The Present State of Virginia, From Whence Is Inferred a Short View of Maryland and North Carolina*, ed. Richard L. Morton (Chapel Hill, NC, 1956), 140.

45. Edward Porter Alexander, ed., *The Journal of John Fontaine: An Irish Huguenot Son in Spain and Virginia, 1710–1719* (Charlottesville, VA, 1972), 85–86.

46. Jones, *Present State of Virginia*, 91.

47. Richmond Croom Beatty and William J. Mulloy, eds., *William Byrd's Natural History of Virginia, or the Newly Discovered Eden* (Richmond, VA, 1940), 32–33.

48. On colonial wine consumption, see Hancock, *Oceans of Wine*, esp. 275–392.

49. John Ellis to the Society, 2 November 1758, Royal Society of Arts Archives, London. On the background of these efforts, see Joyce E. Chaplin, *An Anxious Pursuit: Agricultural Innovation and Modernity in the Lower South, 1730–1815* (Chapel Hill, NC, 1996).

50. Robert Dossie, *Memoirs of Agriculture, and Other Oeconomical Arts* (London, 1768), 1:242–43.

51. Report to ye Lds of the Committee of Councl on ye Peticon of Colo Purry to His Maty relating to ye Settlemt of Some Foreign Protestants att ye New Town called Purrysburgh, 5 September 1734, CO 5/401, f. 106, TNA. For background on Purry and his settlement, see Arlin C. Migliazzo, *To Make This Land Our Own: Community, Identity, and Cultural Adaptation in Purrysburg Township, South Carolina, 1732–1865* (Columbia, SC, 2007).

52. *Weekly Rehearsal*, no. 51, 11 September 1732, 2.

53. Francis Fauquier to Peter Wyche, 22 April 1760 (extract), RSA Archives.

54. Carter to Peter Wyche, recd. 6 May 1761, RSA Archives; Peter Wyche to Carter, ibid.

55. On this migration in general, see Janie Revill, ed., *A Compilation of the Original Lists of Protestant Immigrants to South Carolina, 1763–1773* (Columbia, SC, 1939; repr., 1968). On the development of the Carolina backcountry during this period, see Peter N. Moore, *World of Toil and Strife: Community Transformation in Backcountry South Carolina, 1750–1805* (Columbia, SC, 2007), and Robert L. Meriwether, *The Expansion of South Carolina, 1729–1765* (Kingsport, TN, 1940).

56. Bull to Hillsborough, 6 December 1769, CO 5/393, f. 9, TNA.

57. Bull to Hillsborough, 6 June 1770, CO 5/393, f. 130–131, TNA.

58. Bull to Hillsborough, 6 March 1770, CO 5/393, f. 45, TNA. New Bordeaux has attracted little scholarship, but see Arthur H. Hirsch, *The Huguenots of Colonial South Carolina* (1928; repr., Columbia, SC, 1999), 34–46; Owen Stanwood, "From the Desert to the Refuge: The Saga of New Bordeaux," *French Historical Studies* 40 (2017): 1-28.

59. Bull to Hillsborough, 15 May 1773, CO 5/395, f. 74, TNA.

60. Dumesnil Saint-Pierre, Gentilhomme en environs d'Honfleur refugié en Angleterre, où il intrigue contre la colonisation francaise, 1772, E 154 (Personnel colonial ancien), Archives Nationales d'Outre-Mer, Aix-en-Provence, France.

61. Petition of Lewis de Mesnil de Saint-Pierre to the king, 28 February 1772, CO 5/396, f. 17–18, TNA.

62. [Saint-Pierre], *The great Utility of establishing the Culture of Vines*, 1–2.

63. Saint-Pierre, *The Art of Planting and Cultivating the Vine*, xii.

64. Ibid., xvi. Saint-Pierre's statements fit well with the argument in T. H. Breen, *The Marketplace of Revolution: How Consumer Politics Shaped American Independence* (New York, 2004).

65. Saint-Pierre, *The Art of Planting and Cultivating the Vine*, xvi–xviii.

66. On Saint-Pierre's death, see Nora Marshall Davis, "The French Settlement at New Bordeaux," *Transactions of the Huguenot Society of South Carolina* (1951): 51.

67. Hening, *Statutes*, 9:239. The vineyard in question was the subject of a great debate between André Estave, a French emigrant vintner, and the planter Robert Bolling. See Bolling, "Essay on the Utility of Vine Planting in Virginia," *Virginia Gazette*, 25 February 1773, and Estave's response, *Virginia Gazette*, 18 March 1773.

68. On nineteenth-century wine efforts, see Erica Hannickel, *Empire of Vines: Wine Culture in America* (Philadelphia, 2013). In recent years Virginia vineyards have experienced a resurgence, including one in Fauquier County that "follows in the footsteps of the Carter family and their dream for wine making in Virginia." See www.pcwinery.com.

Sex and Empire in Eighteenth-Century St. Louis

Patricia Cleary

Sex matters. Sexual conduct, misconduct, and reputation; sex inside and outside of marriage; the legal, religious, and demographic repercussions of sexual activities: all of these preoccupied European authorities. With European migration bringing more men than women to colonial outposts in North America, particularly French and Spanish ones, European men sought sexual partners from among the indigenous populations they encountered, as well as from among the peoples—indigenous, African, and mixed race—whom they held in bondage. Given the skewed sex ratio, such interracial and intercultural liaisons come as no surprise, and scholars have interrogated them in depth in recent years, grappling with the evolution of racial identities and attitudes in colonial contexts and exploring issues related to desire and the formation of gender.[1] Sometimes less examined in such contexts is the sexual misconduct of European women outside of the Anglo-American sphere, women whose ability to have fully European offspring positioned them differently in the social and biological calculus of empire building.

A useful site for exploring such issues is colonial St. Louis, a place where the political affiliations and cultural identities of its inhabitants in the age of Atlantic empires points to what was shared and what differed, according to which European power claimed control, and how much distance from the center of empire mattered. With differing understandings of what empire entailed and whose needs should prevail, colonists and officials attempted to put their competing visions into practice, with those on the ground ultimately triumphing. Neither fully French nor Spanish in its imperial character, St. Louis occupied a peculiar position. The capital of Upper Louisiana was overwhelmingly Francophone, yet administered loosely, first by a French officer of the Illinois Country, Louis St. Ange de Bellerive,[2] and eventually by Spanish authorities, when they could be bothered to seize the reins of government. There, neither French nor Spanish agents were able to exercise the kind of imperial control the British more energetically, if temporarily, pursued along the eastern seaboard. In surveying historians' recent interpretations of the French Atlantic, Christopher Hodson and Brett Rushforth offer a useful framing of that scholarship which seems apt for thinking about St. Louis as well. They describe "two discrete histories: one of unrealized imperial visions emanating" from the centers of authority, "the other of unregulated interactions among peoples who mostly flouted the crown's plans." Hodson and Rushforth note that a seeming sign of imperial failure— unfulfilled state ambitions in the face of local, individual autonomy—can also be seen as indicative of "challenges inherent to colonialism," with new imperial histories evoking "dynamic tensions that reshaped empires even as they reshaped the worlds they colonized."[3] In St. Louis, a settlement very much on the geographic periphery of France and Spain's Atlantic empires, imperial policies and the tensions that arose from them played out on a scale at once grand and intimate, as officials endeavored to regulate sex for the purposes of state building.

"*Gobernar es poblar*" (to govern is to populate), as political theorist Juan Bautista Alberdi put it in the 1850s.[4] But populating was no straightforward matter, and how European or not the colonial populace was concerned authorities when women and men of different backgrounds had sexual relations, whether willingly or through coercion, and procreated. Clerical authorities joined with civil ones to promote marriage, in part because of the apparent lack of interest of male colonists in the institution of marriage on one hand and their clear enthusiasm for nonmarital sex on the other. Scholars like Guillaume Aubert, Juliana Barr, Anne Hyde, Maria Elena Martinez, Brett Rushforth, and Jennifer Spear have done useful work on the racial politics of empire and interethnic liaisons in French and Spanish contexts, exploring contacts especially between European men and indigenous or African women.[5] If we follow Ann Laura Stoler's suggestion to pursue "a scholarship looking to the tense and tender ties of empire and to sex—who with whom, where, and when" in order to arrive at "more effective histories of empire's racial politics," then white women's sexual misconduct merits a strong spotlight.[6] Turning attention to European women's conduct and official views of it helps to clarify the full spectrum of sexual behavior that took place in the colonial context of the Mississippi River valley, a region of vying empires and economic competition. It also, surprisingly, points to a kind of tolerance toward white women's sexual transgressions in sparsely settled European imperial outposts.

In Spanish and French North America, official policies that aimed to promote and control colonial population growth were centered on miscegenation, in what circumstances it was acceptable, and when it was abhorrent. Government officials faced a recurring dilemma: how to create a growing and culturally European population in distant colonies where European men vastly outnumbered European women. In St. Louis, established in 1764 and a Spanish outpost for most of its four decades as a colonial settlement, such issues were of pressing concern, given the demographic peculiarities of the village population of European, Indian, and African inhabitants.[7] Settled by French merchants, farmers, trappers, traders, and colonists from France, New Orleans, Canada, and Illinois, all of whom hoped to capitalize on the fur trade, St. Louis needed the ongoing presence of Indians willing to exchange domestic pelts for European products. To take advantage of the commerce in furs, some Native Americans built settlements near the village, and others regularly visited for diplomatic and economic purposes. Both French and Native American inhabitants and traders did their best to ignore the tenuous administrative authority of first France and then Spain in governing St. Louis and its environs; collaboration and creativity in social and economic arrangements proved the order of the day.[8]

When Spanish authorities assumed control of St. Louis and Upper Louisiana in 1767, five years after they laid legal claim to the territory, they tried to dictate explicitly how the area would be populated; Louisiana governor Antonio de Ulloa wrote:

> The intention is that, inasmuch as the garrison is Spanish, the settlement shall be so also, and that its government, customs, and manners shall be those of that nation. Therefore, it shall be enjoined that if possible the workmen who are requested (brought) from Havana shall be married, and that they shall be accompanied by their families; and measures shall be taken to see that some of the sailors who go are Spaniards, and that they be married and take their wives.[9]

What is striking is how prominently the institution of marriage figured in these directives about building a garrison. The orders went on to say that if the Spanish men refused to marry within two years, they should be forced to leave and never return, a regulation the governor considered "most important to uproot the vice . . . generally reigning in the colony": concubinage with "negro and mulatto slave women."[10]

Interested in the growth of St. Louis, distant Spanish authorities instructed local officials on how to collect, organize, and report population data on an annual basis, including a sample census that modeled the numbers defining an ideal community in terms of age, gender, and race. Authorities envisioned a white population of sixteen adults (nine men and seven women) and fifteen children (seven boys and eight girls), and one person of each sex over fifty; among the enslaved adults, there would be eight men and four women, along with four boys and two girls. In short, there would be a roughly balanced sex ratio among whites and a population among the enslaved in which men outnumbered women 2:1. But this imperial goal proved far from the reality. The demographic data that government agents gathered in the 1770s seriously challenged authorities' expectations of a rapidly growing and balanced European population matched by increasing numbers of enslaved men. Census reports from 1772 and 1773 show that while the population of St. Louis did indeed have more white females than males under the age of fifteen, the adult sex ratio was far from balanced. Further, the numbers of enslaved men and women were far from the 2:1 ratio envisioned and suggest a sex ratio far more equal than that among white colonists.[11] It seems likely that the comparatively smaller numbers of white women likely contributed to interracial liaisons between European men and African and indigenous women, though scholars have rightfully interrogated the practices that informed such relationships and the participants' sexual and cultural identities, weighing into the balance factors such as preference and coercion.

In early St. Louis, efforts to replicate a recognizably European settlement and populace were hampered not only by a skewed sex ratio among its French and Spanish inhabitants but by what authorities deemed a kind of laxness in behavior on these colonists' part that threatened to undermine the village's nascent community life. Officials described villagers as a hopelessly dissipated people, whose "looseness of conduct, . . . dissoluteness and license" could only be deplored.[12] Among the vices that preoccupied authorities, interracial sex proved an especially disturbing and persistent source of concern. For both the Spanish and the French, onetime policies promoting miscegenation between Europeans and Indians for population-building purposes gave way in the face of hardening European beliefs in racial hierarchies and the failure of cultural conversions. That is, authorities ultimately despaired because French men too often tended to "go native" and experience *ensauvagement* when they married Indian women, rather than bringing Christianized Indian wives into colonial settlements that were predominantly culturally French.[13]

In St. Louis, Lieutenant Governor Francisco Cruzat expressed official concerns in a 1776 prohibition on whites and slaves from gathering together, a practice he believed produced only drunkenness, disorder, and scandal.[14] Several aspects of interracial socializing bothered Cruzat. In a statement replete with expressions of racial prejudice, beliefs in innate hierarchies, and notions of profound differences among peoples, Cruzat noted that "while the sole difference in color should be a sufficient reason to keep all whites from getting involved with their slaves, nonetheless, several, without considering the distance which separates them," managed to gain entrance to their meetings. The interlopers' intentions were immoral and their actions illicit: white men attended such gatherings to introduce alcohol and thereby to commit with greater impunity "disorders and scandals that dishonor, at the same time, their own persons and debase the conditions of their fellow men." Such excesses had "disastrous consequences" and had to be prevented. Any white person, "of whatever quality, condition, sex, and state," who was discovered "at any assembly of slaves, whether at night or in the daytime," would be punished "with eight days in prison, and a fine" to be put toward the needs of the church.[15] While the transgressors whom the lieutenant governor was targeting were undoubtedly men, he included both white men and white women in the prohibition.

Cruzat's restrictions point to settings seldom illuminated in the records: places where Africans came together day and night to interact and socialize. (By definition, this provision against socializing with slaves targeted Africans, as Indian slavery had been outlawed. Some French colonists nonetheless thwarted the law and continued to hold Indians in bondage for years afterward.)[16] Where the enslaved gathered in St. Louis is difficult to determine, whether in slave quarters, the few homes of free blacks, or the houses of whites willing to dispense alcohol to all tipplers.[17] Wherever such meetings happened, according to the official view, they witnessed alcohol consumption and interracial fraternizing, factors that made sexual contact across racial lines—initiated by white men—possible. Perhaps anticipating violations, Cruzat emphasized that the order be "read, published, and posted on the front door on the church." As the physical boundary between sacred and secular spaces—the demarcation line for the spheres of influence under clerical and civil control—the church door occupied an important symbolic function in colonial St. Louis. God's dominion was within, and the state claimed all the space without. Thus when their interests intersected, and magistrate and priest sought the same ends, the church door emphasized their mutually reinforcing authority. What is very clear is that in a community in which enslaved Africans congregated outside of masters' presence on a regular basis and European colonists sought entrée by providing a desirable product—alcohol—interracial socializing was a source of potential disorder that merited intervention.

While the sexual misconduct of European men with African or indigenous women preoccupied officials, the sexual conduct of European women also concerned authorities. How the centrality of European women's role in imperial projects—as wives and especially as mothers—affected their lives and official views of them is difficult to assess, but a case related to the founding of St. Louis is worth exploring along these lines. The story begins in 1763, when Pierre Laclède, an immigrant from France who had lived in New Orleans for several years, received permission to trade with Indians along the vast watershed of the Missouri River, home to unknown numbers of tribes at the time. Traveling upriver with a thirteen-year-old boy, Auguste Chouteau, as his companion, Laclède scouted the western banks of the Mississippi between the Ohio and Missouri Rivers. After exploring the area, Laclède selected a raised spot on the western bank and marked some trees on the site that would become St. Louis, later sending Chouteau to direct a workforce of thirty men to construct the first buildings.[18] On the surface, the founding narrative of St. Louis presents a relatively straightforward tale of an ambitious merchant, the fur trade, and a site unsettled at the time by Native Americans (though it had centuries before been a major settlement of Mississippian Mound Builders).[19]

What Laclède did not know when he selected the site of St. Louis was that the territory west of the Mississippi was no longer French but Spanish, an imperial realignment that stemmed from the vagaries of the French and Indian War. Although Spain had joined the war against England in January 1762, the tide of the war was not altered by its entry. The French, accurately anticipating defeat in this war for North American empire, decided to try to conclude the hostilities on favorable terms. To compensate the Spanish for their losses and to persuade their allies to sign peace treaties quickly, the French ceded Louisiana to Spain under the terms of the Treaty of Fontainebleau of November 1762. News of this treaty and its provisions did not reach the area for two years, until after the founding of St. Louis. In the meantime, settlement had begun in earnest, and by the end of 1764, St. Louis had forty to fifty families in residence, many of them francophone transplants from across the Mississippi River.[20]

And, of course, there is more to this founding story than immediately meets the eye, a hidden element of behind-the-scenes personal intrigue that matched the machinations at the political level. As it happened, young Auguste Chouteau was not just Pierre Laclède's right-hand man: he was the son of Laclède's longtime lover, Madame Marie Thérèse Bourgeois Chouteau, the wife of René Chouteau. The adulterous Laclède-Chouteau liaison had begun years before in New Orleans.[21] In 1748, the teenaged Madame Chouteau, a native of that city, had married Auguste René Chouteau, a twenty-five-year-old French immigrant, and their only child, Auguste, was born the following year. Whatever the cause, the couple separated, and no records show René's presence in Louisiana between 1752 and 1767; he returned to France at some point, deserting his young wife and son. Sometime after Laclède arrived in New Orleans in 1755, he became attached to the young Marie Thérèse, and their first child, Pierre, was born in 1758, with three daughters following in 1760, 1762, and 1764.[22]

The lovers maintained the legal fiction of legitimate paternity, with the younger children surnamed Chouteau and acknowledged in baptismal records as René's legitimate children. Although Laclède's paternity was firmly established by John Francis McDermott in the twentieth century, for many years some descendants of the Chouteau family repeatedly attempted to deny the fact the Marie Thérèse gave birth to their ancestors out of wedlock, one even authoring an outraged tract in 1921 entitled "Madame Chouteau Vindicated," which argued that "ignorant closet" "alleged historians" should do research instead of giving the "world barefaced falsehoods" and besmirching the "character of an honorable, respectable, and unordinarily gifted woman."[23] For that descendant at least, a family history that apparently did not trouble its eighteenth-century protagonists—or their friends and community—was a potential source of unbearable shame. Personal relationships informed by elements of expediency—whether formalized or not—fulfilled a variety of contemporaries' needs, and their communities appeared to have largely accepted them, regardless of official prohibitions or laws.

In August 1764 Madame Chouteau and the four younger children journeyed up the Mississippi to join the rest of the family in St. Louis. There they cohabited, sharing Laclède's large house and store until 1768, when Madame Chouteau moved into a new home Laclède had built a block away.[24] In that year Laclède took the unusual legal step of deeding the new house, several slaves, and some land to all of his lover's children. This act ensured that his offspring, as well as Auguste, would all inherit property, despite the fact he was not married to their mother.[25] In the gift deed Laclède glossed over the state of Madame Chouteau's marriage, referring to Auguste and his own offspring as the children of René Chouteau, "absent from this Post." Such evasions in church and civil records, which allowed an element of ambiguity, suggest some degree of complicity on the part of the clerks and participants.[26]

All might have gone on tranquilly for the Chouteau-Laclède family if not for René Chouteau. Returning to New Orleans after more than a decade's absence, he decided at some point that he wanted his wife back at his side. Under the law, he was legally entitled to her presence and also authorized to sue those who detained her or gave her refuge.[27] Regardless of his earlier desertion, René wanted Marie Thérèse, now in her early forties, back in the Crescent City, and he sought the assistance of civil authorities to achieve that goal. Ultimately, his complaint reached official—if not altogether sympathetic—ears. In October 1774 the Louisiana governor wrote about Chouteau's complaint to his second-in-command, upriver in St. Louis.

In his response from January 1775, Lieutenant Governor Pedro Piernas noted that he had just received the governor's letter advising him to send Madame Chouteau to New Orleans on the first boat possible, so that she might there "enter into the power of her husband." It is noteworthy that Piernas emphasized the power dynamic rather than acknowledge any sort of spousal allegiance; legal concerns rather than emotion had to dictate his actions. Piernas went on to assure the governor that Madame Chouteau would not be on that vessel alone; her children, or at least some of them, presumably the girls, still quite young, would accompany her. By this time, *Veuve* Chouteau or "Widow Chouteau," as she styled herself, had been in St. Louis for over a decade, during which she had acquired property, purchased slaves, run a household, and taken in boarders. Not to be trifled with on her own account as a woman of property and substance, Madame Chouteau had additional status, or perhaps some degree of immunity to official interference in her private life, as Laclède's partner, a point on which Piernas maintained silence. Perhaps stalling for time, Piernas promised the governor that he would see to it that she traveled to New Orleans to be delivered to her husband as soon as she had completed settling her affairs.[28]

Whether Piernas ever broached the subject with Laclède or Madame Chouteau is impossible to determine. What is clear is that the situation remained unchanged nearly a year later, when Piernas's successor as lieutenant governor, Francisco Cruzat, took up the matter. In August 1775 Louisiana's governor wrote again, this time to Cruzat, about the couple. Not responding to that missive until December, Cruzat apprised his superior of his progress, noting that he was giving Madame Chouteau the time she needed to conclude her affairs without damaging her finances. Such flexibility was appropriate given her various enterprises and assets. His predecessor's promise of sending her south on the first boat seemed forgotten.[29]

Despite the prominence and influence of the family, Cruzat, unlike Piernas, did not turn an altogether blind eye toward the couple's relationship. He reported that during the time it took Madame Chouteau to settle her affairs, he was forbidding her to have any contact with Laclède. Keeping the two apart would be rather difficult, Cruzat acknowledged, given that they lived in the same house. After Cruzat ordered the two to separate, they agreed to do so, but there is no evidence that they ever ceased cohabiting. The long arm of empire may have proved a phantom limb. Eventually events in New Orleans altered the situation. René Chouteau died, in his will claiming his wife again, adding that legitimate offspring resulted from their union, and naming his survivors as his heirs.[30] With his death in April 1776, the crisis facing the family abruptly concluded.[31]

News of her husband's death must have been, at least in part, a relief to Marie Thérèse, Pierre, and their family and friends. With René's death, Pierre and Marie Thérèse were finally free to wed after roughly twenty years together. Yet *Veuve* Chouteau, as she now truly was, did not remarry, and Monsieur Laclède remained a bachelor. Although their relationship continued until Laclède's death in May 1778, the two never formalized their ties legally, possibly in part to save her any complications arising from his significant mercantile debts.

What should we make of this illicit liaison, which provoked official scrutiny? How was it perceived by their friends and other villagers? Given that Laclède's mercantile associates were present for the baptisms of his and Marie Thérèse's children in New Orleans, it seems likely that they were at least somewhat supportive, with pragmatic recognition of the pair's partnership outweighing religious or legal scruples about its validity or propriety. In St. Louis, Laclède had been a close friend of former French commander Louis St. Ange de Bellerive, who was also boarding at Madame Chouteau's home at the time of his death in 1774; Laclède had been a staunch supporter of both French and Spanish authorities. Thus the pair's relationship, which might have marginalized Madame Chouteau in a more settled, polite society, did not stop her from—and indeed may have assisted her in—becoming one of the most powerful women in the village. Her experience begs the question of what other extramarital or nonmarital relationships were subject to censure in colonial St. Louis. When did they escape condemnation and commentary? Some, such as liaisons between European men and African women, were routinely criticized. Others, such as European women's sexual transgressions, may have been treated differently.

Whereas in the Chouteau-Laclède matter some might try to argue that Laclède's position protected Madame Chouteau from censure, another case, involving the estranged wife of an influential member of the community, reinforces the sense that white women were treated with some flexibility by authorities. For Elizabeth Coulon de Villiers and her husband, Pierre de Volsey, interracial sex lay at the heart of their failed marriage and the very public scandal that erupted in the 1770s. In legal proceedings, husband and wife accused each other of infidelity, and their complaints reached the ears of the governor in New Orleans. Central to the wife's claim was the charge that her husband had committed adultery with an enslaved black woman, Magdalene.[32] According to Elizabeth's complaint, everyone knew of the liaison, and her husband acknowledged it by trying to make his mulatto daughter heir to property that rightfully belonged to her, his legitimate wife.[33] The charge of adultery was supported in other legal records. After Magdalene's death in 1764, Pierre had purchased her young daughter, Françoise, taken the toddler into his home, and in a 1768 will named her as sole heir of goods acquired during his marriage. In 1772 the couple manumitted the ten-year-old.[34]

Madame de Volsey's petition, it should be noted, was partly in response to one written by her husband, in which he accused her of adultery.[35] In his complaint Monsieur de Volsey charged that his wife had been unfaithful with René Kiersereau, the church chorister. When Pierre returned to St. Louis after a two-year sojourn in France, his wife fled in the singer's company, and Pierre initiated proceedings against her. She retorted that she was fleeing her husband's abuse, not running away with a lover, and the local priest, Father Bernard de Limpach, backed her up. Involving himself in the high-profile marital dispute, the village priest upbraided Monsieur de Volsey about his conduct, using "language ill-suited to [the cleric's] character and injurious to [de Volsey's] honor." Receiving the fighting pair's complaints, the governor took advantage of his distance in New Orleans to declare himself too busy to address the matter, and he bounced it back to the lieutenant governor, Fernando de Leyba, on the scene in St. Louis, to handle.[36] He, in turn, responded by telling Monsieur de Volsey to calm down and then eventually decided the problem was beyond his ability to solve, lacking, he declared, anyone with whom to confer to reach a judgment.[37]

Ignoring or tolerating seemingly incontrovertible evidence of white women's sexual misconduct did not happen only with prominent women. Slander cases involving nonelite women demonstrated a similar pattern: official interest or inquiry, followed by dismissal. In slander cases from the 1770s, accusations about women having children fathered by men other than their husbands—whose involvement in the fur trade meant long absences from the village—proved a recurring theme.[38] In 1778 a history of mutual insults regarding sexual behavior was transferred from the streets into the courts, when Madame Montardy lodged a formal complaint against Madame Denoyer for defaming her character, calling her a lifelong prostitute, a *putine* with a bastard daughter. Rather than deny having made such statements, Denoyer defended herself by claiming that she had felt compelled to retaliate against similar calumny from the plaintiff, "*cette Dame Nocturne.*" What prompted the court action was purportedly Denoyer's most recent slanderous declaration that Montardy, whose fur trader husband was frequently far from home, was the mistress of another man. Fearful that such charges would alienate her spouse's affection, Montardy enlisted the apparatus of government in her behalf. If not forgiven by a husband, adultery was grounds for a wife to lose her property rights. Thus the case combined the key elements required for pursuing justice before the law: damaging someone's honor and injuring a slandered person's ability to make a living were both grounds for action.[39] After several women testified about the veracity of the litigants' accounts, as well as to their respective sexual and marital reputations, the proceedings came to a close. Reviewing all of the testimony, the lieutenant governor dismissed the matter, declaring it little more than the old petty quarrels of women and prohibiting both parties from indulging in improper discourse designed to injure another's reputation. In other words, the resolution was court-mandated silence.[40]

Another case involving charges of a woman bearing a child not fathered by her husband was not so peremptorily dismissed. In December 1778 Thérèse Caron charged Baptiste Ménard with spreading the false and malicious rumor that she had had a child by someone other than her spouse. Madame Caron urged that the gossiping Ménard be required to prove his assertion or be imprisoned until he cleared her name. According to the accused man, the impetus for his slander was not ill will but liquor, under whose effects he had sullied an honest woman's reputation. Spirits and slander, both sources of disorder, went hand in hand, or cup and mouth.[41] As part of the guilty man's sentence, he was required to offer a public apology; his retraction of his slanderous speech soon followed.

What do these slander cases suggest? If the government's response was largely to dismiss such cases rather than punish women suspected of sexual transgressions, insisting at most on either public apologies or court-mandated silence, then perhaps part of the answer may be that although European women's intimate behavior became the subject of public interest and debate at times, policy makers had more pressing matters to address. Class status was perhaps less important as a factor in affecting the outcome of such cases than it was elsewhere.

What comes through clearly is that there was no completely consistent response to sexual misconduct or interracial liaisons. In their approach to such matters, officials at times attempted to control colonists' behavior and at other times seemed to tolerate, if not altogether approve, actions and relationships that fell outside of law and custom. Such transgressions were perhaps perceived as of less pressing importance in the face of myriad other challenges facing those who governed the outpost. If the misbehavior of white women was either considered not to have taken place, as was perhaps the case with some slanderous speech, or viewed as not fundamentally damaging to the growth and development of the community, then perhaps it could be ignored or minimized. It is possible that as they navigated controversies over sexual behavior, St. Louisans ignored established rules and acted according to their own judgment. A recalcitrant populace acted to fulfill its own needs.

One important factor was the comparative weakness of institutions that helped ensure social control elsewhere, in particular the church and court. In early St. Louis, civil and clerical authorities moved with care, faced as they were with repeated challenges to their power. As Stuart Banner has noted, the legal culture of colonial St. Louis allowed for the resolution of disputes, the distribution of property, and the completion of private transactions.[42] But these actions were executed "with little formality, with barely any reference to written law, and with almost no resort to any authority beyond the articulated norms of the community."[43] Few officials had copies of the statues, either French or Spanish, and those who possessed such texts nonetheless seemed to act more in accord with local precedents and temper than with legislation handed down from a distance. As Banner put it, "Cases were decided according to an intuitive sense of justice shared by the community, or at least a large enough fraction of the community to make the decision acceptable."[44]

With authorities constantly facing challenges to economic growth and political stability—in matters of trade, diplomacy, Indian affairs, and imperial competition—their desires to promote the growth of a burgeoning European colonial population had repercussions for women in new settlements like St. Louis. There state power laid siege to the personal autonomy of individuals whose relationships defied culturally ordained norms. Who had the right to determine whether a union was legitimate? To a surprising degree, colonists claimed that prerogative for themselves, in defiance of the state. Given imperial authorities' preoccupation with the cultural and economic dangers of mixed-race unions, perhaps it is not surprising that some white women who strayed *within* their race received a temporary pass for their behavior. An exceptional individual like Madame Chouteau was doubly untouchable:

she was not only the consort of the village's leading citizen but a producer of white children. Likewise, Madame de Volsey could run away with a church worker with seemingly few repercussions because she had done nothing to sully the "purity" of the race. Perhaps some officials saw her husband's transgression as greater in that it resulted in him fathering a mixed-race daughter whom he acknowledged. If the primary concerns of imperial authorities were in promoting population growth and more particularly in promoting that increase among European men and women rather than through mixed-race alliances and liaisons, then they might have turned a blind eye to stable, long-lasting nonmarital unions among European colonists like Chouteau and Laclède or even to the occasional illicit acts suggested by Madame de Volsey's flight—or by cases of slander involving only white participants.

In a small new outpost of empire, the process of forging standards and maintaining stability was a complex and unpredictable one. Unsurprisingly, the contests for control were numerous and varied, as well as profoundly important to both officials and the colonists purportedly under their sway. When it came to populating empire, the state's ability to promote ideal sexual and marital relations and to police problematic ones was undermined by numerous factors, chief among them distance and a recalcitrant populace. Imperial sovereignty was fractured, never as omnipotent as officials envisioned it. With their authority diminished by the noncompliance of an unruly people, officials were forced on occasion to stand by when individuals contravened rules and regulations. Popular will thwarted imperial agendas, as individuals deliberated and acted to promote their own interests. In their apparent disregard for conventional and condoned conduct, colonists formulated social arrangements that suited their needs. In the process, as they navigated controversies over sexual behavior, drinking, religious practice, and numerous other matters, St. Louisans regularly reacted against authorities, ignoring established rules and acting according to their own judgment; in so doing, they may have achieved a kind of openness and innovation in racial, social, and sexual dynamics that was potent, if short-lived.

Notes

The author thanks curators of the University of Missouri for permission to incorporate material originally printed in *The World, the Flesh, and the Devil: The History of Colonial St. Louis* by Patricia Cleary, by permission of the University of Missouri Press. Copyright © 2011 by The Curators of the University of Missouri.

1. Kathleen M. Brown, *Good Wives, Nasty Wenches, and Anxious Patriarchs: Gender, Race, and Power in Colonial Virginia* (Chapel Hill: University of North Carolina Press,

1996); Ann Laura Stoler, *Carnal Knowledge and Imperial Power: Race and the Intimate in Colonial Rule* (Berkeley: University of California Press, 2002).

2. In Carl J. Ekberg and Sharon K. Person's *St. Louis Rising: The French Regime of Louis St. Ange de Bellerive* (Urbana: University of Illinois Press, 2015), St. Louis emerges as a settlement very much within French Illinois Country history, with St. Ange, rather than either Pierre Laclède or Auguste Chouteau, as the key early leader.

3. Christopher Hodson and Brett Rushforth, "Absolutely Atlantic: Colonialism and the Early Modern French State in Recent Historiography," *History Compass* 8, no. 1 (2010): 102.

4. Juan Bautista Alberdi, *Bases y Puntos de Partida para la Organización Política de la República Argentina* (1852; Barcelona: Lingkua Ediciones, 2006), 22.

5. Guillaume Aubert, "'The Blood of France': Race and Purity of Blood in the French Atlantic World," *William and Mary Quarterly*, 3d ser., 61, no. 3 (July 2004): 439–78; María Elena Martínez, "The Black Blood of New Spain: Limpieza de Sangre, Racial Violence, and Gendered Power in Early Colonial Mexico," *William and Mary Quarterly*, 3d ser., 61, no. 3 (July 2004): 479–520; Jennifer M. Spear, *Race, Sex, and Social Order in Early New Orleans* (Baltimore: Johns Hopkins University Press, 2009); Juliana Barr, *Peace Came in the Form of a Woman: Indians and Spaniards in the Texas Borderlands* (Chapel Hill: University of North Carolina Press, 2007); Brett Rushforth, *Bonds of Alliance: Indigenous and Atlantic Slaveries in New France* (Chapel Hill: University of North Carolina Press, 2012); Anne F. Hyde, *Empires, Nations, and Families: A History of the North American West, 1800–1860* (Lincoln: University of Nebraska Press, 2011).

6. Ann Laura Stoler, "Tense and Tender Ties: The Politics of Comparison in North American History and (Post) Colonial Studies," *Journal of American History* 88, no. 3 (December 2001): 865. For "racialised anxiety about sex" and concerns about British identity, see Brooke N. Newman, "Gender, Sexuality, and the Formation of Racial Identities in the Eighteenth-Century Anglo-Caribbean World," *Gender & History* 22 (November 2010): 585–602. See also Anne McClintock, *Imperial Leather: Race, Gender, and Sexuality in the Colonial Contest* (New York: Routledge, 1995), and Ann Twinam, "Racial Passing: Informal and Official 'Whiteness' in Colonial Spanish America," in John Smolenski and Thomas J. Humphrey, eds., *New World Orders: Violence, Sanction, and Authority in the Colonial Americas* (Philadelphia: University of Pennsylvania Press, 2005), 249–72.

7. St. Louis and Upper Louisiana during the colonial era have been the subject of numerous scholarly works, including Carl Ekberg, *Colonial Ste. Genevieve: An Adventure on the Mississippi Frontier* (Gerald, MO: Patrice Press, 1985); Carl Ekberg, *French Roots in the Illinois Country: The Mississippi Frontier in Colonial Times* (Urbana: University of Illinois Press, 1998); William E. Foley and C. David Rice, *The First Chouteaus: River Barons of Early St. Louis* (Urbana: University of Illinois Press, 1983). For the early history of St. Louis and its environs, see John Francis McDermott, ed., *The Early Histories of St. Louis* (St. Louis: St. Louis Historical Documents Foundation, 1952); Andrew Hurley, ed., *Common Fields: An Environmental History of St. Louis* (St. Louis: Missouri Historical Society, 1997), and Patricia Cleary, *The World, the Flesh, and the Devil: A History of Colonial St. Louis* (Columbia: University of Missouri Press, 2011).

8. Scholars of French colonialism in North America have posited a view of complicated, interethnic communities shaped by illicit and creative adaptations as distinctive to the imperial system. See Shannon Lee Dawdy, *Building the Devil's Empire: French Colonial*

New Orleans (Chicago: University of Chicago Press, 2008), and Robert Michael Morrissey, *Empire by Collaboration: Indians, Colonists, and Governments in Colonial Illinois Country* (Philadelphia: University of Pennsylvania Press, 2015). For a recent examination of how individuals performed and interpreted identities, see Sophie White, *Wild Frenchmen and Frenchified Indians: Material Culture and Race in Colonial Louisiana* (Philadelphia: University of Pennsylvania Press, 2014).

9. Antonio de Ulloa, excerpt from "Instructions for the expedition to the district of the Ylinneses [Illinois], which is in charge of Captain Don Francisco Rui," March 14, 1767, Archivo General de Indias–Papeles Procedentes de Cuba (hereafter AGI-PC). Translated and reprinted in Louis Houck, *The Spanish Régime in Missouri* (repr., New York: Arno Press and The New York Times, 1971), 1:8–9.

10. Ulloa, "Instructions for the expedition" in Houck, *SRM*, 1:8–11, 15, 18.

11. St. Louis census, 1772, from Houck, *SRM*, 1:53–54n59; St. Louis census, 1773, Houck, *SRM*, 1:61.

12. Pedro Piernas to Alessandro O'Reilly, October 31, 1769, reprinted in Houck, *SRM*, 1:73.

13. Aubert, "'The Blood of France': Race and Purity of Blood in the French Atlantic World," 439–78.

14. Francisco Cruzat, List of regulations from July 15, 1775–June 8, 1778, dated February 18, 1776, AGI-PC legajo 2358, translation and transcription from the John Francis McDermott Collection (hereafter JFMC), Lovejoy Library, Southern Illinois University–Edwardsville, box 45/3.

15. Cruzat decree, February 18, 1776, AGI-PC 2358, JFMC, Lovejoy Library.

16. Russell M. Magnaghi, "The Role of Indian Slavery in Colonial St. Louis," *Missouri Historical Society Bulletin* 31, no. 4 (July 1975): 264–72. Carl Ekberg found abundant evidence of colonists violating the prohibition on holding and selling Indians as slaves. Ekberg, *Stealing Indian Women: Native Slavery in the Illinois Country* (Chicago: University of Illinois Press, 2007).

17. A court case from the period reveals that enslaved women met during daylight hours when they gathered at Mill Creek to do laundry. Litigation collection, January 23, 1779, MHMA.

18. An authoritative new translation and annotation of the founding narrative, including excellent photographic reproductions of the original document, is *August Chouteau's Journal: Memory, Mythmaking, and History in the Heritage of New France*, ed. Gregory P. Ames (St. Louis: St. Louis Mercantile Library, 2010). The significance typically accorded to Laclède's role in shaping early St. Louis is being challenged by new work by Carl Ekberg and Sharon Person, who explore the important contributions of other, largely forgotten early residents, particularly Jean Baptiste Martigny, Joseph Labuxière, and Louis St. Ange de Bellerive, in *St. Louis Rising*.

19. The massive earthen mounds at Cahokia, across the river in Illinois, and the numerous mounds in St. Louis were reminders of populous settlements abandoned centuries earlier. William R. Iseminger, "Culture and Environment in the American Bottom: The Rise and Fall of Cahokia Mounds," in *Common Fields*, ed. Hurley, 38–57.

20. William E. Foley, *A History of Missouri, Volume 1: 1673–1820* (Columbia: University of Missouri Press, 1971, repr., 1999), 16, 18.

21. The best overview of the family's role in St. Louis history is William E. Foley and C. David Rice, *The First Chouteaus, River Barons of Early St. Louis* (Urbana: University of Illinois Press, 1983). A more popular account, published to coincide with the bicentennial of the Lewis and Clark expedition, is Shelley Christian, *Before Lewis and Clark: The Story of the Chouteaus, the French Dynasty That Ruled America's Frontier* (New York: Farrar, Straus and Giroux, 2004). See also J. Frederick Fausz, *Founding St. Louis: First City of the New West* (Charleston, SC: History Press, 2011), and Jay Gitlin, *The Bourgeois Frontier: French Towns, French Traders, and American Expansion* (New Haven: Yale University Press, 2010).

22. John Francis McDermott pieced together the Chouteau family heritage; his papers are now part of the special collections at Southern Illinois University–Edwardsville (hereafter JFM, SIU-E).

23. Alexander N. DeMenil, St. Louis, October 13, 1921, from the *St. Louis Globe-Democrat*, October 16, 1921, "Dr. A. N. DeMenil Writes on History of Early St. Louisans," pamphlet version: *Madame Chouteau Vindicated* (St. Louis: William Harvey Miner, 1921).

24. Katherine Corbett, "Veuve Chouteau, a 250th Anniversary," *Gateway Heritage* 3 (1983): 45.

25. JFM, SIU-E, 47–36 concludes with the 1768 deed of gift materials, document 768, #9.B (recorded vol. 2, page 14), St. Louis Archives, Missouri History Museum Archives, St. Louis (hereafter MHMA).

26. Donation by Laclède, May 12, 1768, Instrument #9B, St. Louis Archives, MHMA.

27. Vaughn Baker, Amos Simpson, and Mathé Allain, "'*Le Mari est Seigneur*': Marital Laws Governing Women in French Louisiana," in Edward H. Hass, ed., *Louisiana's Legal Heritage* (Pensacola, FL: Published for the Louisiana State Museum by Perdido Bay Press, 1983), 12.

28. Piernas to Unzaga, 26 January 26, 1775, AGI-PC 81, MHMA microfilm. See also 47–36, JFM, SIU-E.

29. Cruzat to Unzaga, December 10, 1775, AGI-PC 81–614, MHMA microfilm.

30. René Chouteau, will, April 10, 1776, Chouteau Papers, copy MHMA.

31. He died and was buried in New Orleans on April 21, 1776; photostat of St. Louis Cathedral (New Orleans) church register, vol. 2, p. 42, in Chouteau Papers, MHMA. Death certificate, April 21, 1776.

32. Billon, *Annals of St. Louis,* 435–36. Madame de Volsey was well connected in St. Louis, daughter of one French commandant at Fort Chartres, Neyon de Villiers, and niece to another, St. Ange. Her husband was prominent as well, having served as captain of the French garrisons in Illinois and St. Louis and acting as St. Ange's successor. Certificate of commission for Pedro Francisco de Volsey, June 1, 1777, AGI-PC 190–42 (Price compilation, MHMA).

33. See petition of Elizabeth de Villiers to de Leyba and response, September 7, 1779, AGI-PC 193b-657, MHMA microfilm.

34. On Françoise's life, see Gilbert, "Esther and Her Sisters," 21. Manumission papers of a girl named Françoise, executed by Pierre François de Volsey and his wife, Elizabeth, June 22, 1772, Slave Papers, MHMA.

35. Pierre François de Volsey, petition, October 11, 1777, Chouteau-Papin Collection, MHMA.

36. De Volsey to governor, February 6, 1779, response from governor, AGI-PC 192-1104, MHMA microfilm.

37. De Volsey to governor, July 12, 1779, AGI-PC 192-1106, MHMA microfilm.

38. Research into slander cases in French Canada suggests the importance of the class status of those involved. In France, jurists assumed that only the higher classes cared about claims of honor and that commoners' disputes were unimportant. One lawyer noted that judges in cases involving the lower orders would be tempted to dismiss them out of hand. In addition, filing a slander suit required certain qualifications; married women and single women under twenty-five could not act on their own. Nonetheless, it appears that individuals of low social rank counted for three-fourths of the plaintiffs, suggesting their relatively better access to courts. Only 10 percent of defendants in New France were women. Peter N. Moogk, "'Thieving Buggers' and 'Stupid Sluts': Insults and Popular Culture in New France," *William and Mary Quarterly*, 3d ser., 36, no. 4 (October 1979): 530.

39. Ibid., 536.

40. Moogk found that most female insults in French Canada involved charges of sexual misconduct. Husbands' responses to rumors of their wives' infidelities included violence. Ibid., 542–43.

41. Slander case before De Leyba, folio 18–19, December 3, 1778, St. Louis History Collection, 1762–1843, MHMA.

42. Stuart Banner, "Written Law and Unwritten Norms in Colonial St. Louis," *Law and History Review* 14, no. 1 (Spring 1996): 46. Marriage contracts bore more reference to French than Spanish customs. One survey suggested that the goal was exclusion of Spanish marriage law rather than adoption of it, with the overwhelming majority of marriage contracts showing evidence of following French codes and legal practices outlined in the *Coutume de Paris*. In the *Supreme Court of Missouri, March Term, 1856, Norman Cutter, Appellee, vs. Wm. Waddingham & Others, Appellants*, 9, 22.

43. Banner, "Written Law and Unwritten Norms in Colonial St. Louis," 38; Stuart Banner, *Legal Systems in Conflict: Property and Sovereignty in Missouri, 1750–1860* (Normal: University of Oklahoma Press, 2000).

44. Banner, *Legal Systems in Conflict*, 52.

On Their Own Ground

Native Power and Colonial Property on the Maine Frontier

IAN SAXINE

Joseph Moody, a resident of the frontier community of York, Maine, began keeping a diary in 1720. The son of York's pastor, Moody had begun the project to chart his spiritual progress. But while he contemplated the power of the Almighty, Moody also provided abundant testimony about the power of the neighboring Wabanaki Indians. As colonists and Wabanakis argued over conflicting interpretations of seventeenth-century land sales, the frontier careened toward war. By 1722 noncombatants like Moody's grandmother had already moved to the safety of blockhouse garrisons, and the twenty-two-year-old Moody took turns keeping watch in one of them.[1] On August 27, 1722, just before he observed town leaders gather to plan a campaign against the Wabanakis, Moody "transcribed a deed from the Indians."[2] Such an activity was not uncommon; Moody's neighbors frequently used Indian deeds to prove title to tracts of land in disputes that took up much of the business of the York County Court of Common Pleas. If Moody ever paused to reflect on the irony that he and most of his neighbors living "Downeast" from Massachusetts in the District of Maine could simultaneously use Indian deeds to prove particular land belonged to them, while also engaging in bloody war against those same Indians over competing land claims, he left no record of his thoughts.

For obvious reasons, Moody paid far more attention to Wabanaki military abilities, but his diary provides eloquent testimony about another important source of Native power on the Maine frontier. By the early eighteenth century, Indian deeds like the document Joseph Moody copied served as crucial evidence in numerous property disputes between competing groups of colonists and absentee land speculators. As colonial numbers grew and Native military strength waned, the Wabanakis leveraged their position as former proprietors of large tracts of Maine real estate to ensure that treaties with Massachusetts (which administered Maine until 1820) conformed to indigenous diplomatic expectations of reciprocity. In doing so, the Wabanakis used the colonists' preoccupation with securing land titles to influence Massachusetts's Indian policy.

Wabanaki success in using their status as former proprietors of Maine lands reveals a more complicated relationship between British colonists' quest for landed property and Native power than we might expect. In Maine the dedication to obtaining and protecting property rights that characterized so much of the British imperial drive could also serve as a brake on its expansion. Explaining the counterintuitive relationship between Native power and colonial property on the Maine frontier requires exploring the themes at the heart of this volume. Living on a contested frontier between French Canada and New England, with weak imperial authority, Wabanakis and ordinary colonists took matters into their own hands to obtain security, which, for all groups involved, required control of land and resources. Distant imperial officials in Whitehall seldom interfered in ongoing disputes over overlapping claims, either by force or by law. Left largely to their own devices, Massachusetts elites attempted to acquire vast land titles to the Maine frontier and direct the colonization of the region in a manner that would benefit investors. When both Indians and resident colonists resisted the speculators' claims, they discovered they needed Wabanaki cooperation to make their titles a reality. Paradoxically, the nature of British imperialism in Maine encouraged colonial elites to use Native land rights to certify their legal ownership of territory. Explaining the multifaceted nature of Wabanaki power on the eighteenth-century Maine frontier thus requires accounting both for the character of empire in the region and how ordinary people exploited, challenged, and influenced its exercise.

Eighteenth-century Massachusetts elites depended on the Wabanakis because they had no choice. Seventeenth-century English colonists arrived in the place the Wabanakis called the Dawnland fully prepared to dismiss Native rights to most of their lands. As restated by a later colonial agent of Massachusetts, the king (through his subjects) could take "possession . . . of a Country inhabited by Salvages, who are without Laws and Government."[3] John Winthrop, the second governor of Massachusetts Bay Colony, advanced several challenges to Native American land claims popular among English colonists and their advocates, including John Locke.[4] "That which is common to all is proper to none," Winthrop insisted.[5] Without grants of individual title or permanent dwellings, fences, and livestock to mark their holdings, the Indians could not lay claim to most of their territory.[6] Unaware of the complex networks of indigenous land use, Winthrop called the rivers and forests (often managed by the Indians to promote certain types of plant and animal resources) "wastelands," fit for occupation by English people, "leaving [the Indians] such places as they have manured for their corn." In any case, Winthrop claimed, "there is more than enough for them and us," and "we shall come in with good leave of the natives."[7] Colonial leaders understood that securing this "good leave" might mean paying Indians for the land, but they did not intend to grant the exchanges the weight of law. In this vein, Sir Ferdinando Gorges, the original royal grantee for much of Maine, directed his agents in America to make sure his prospective tenants would sign "Contracts with you" before they "make purchase of the Pretended Title of any of the Sagamores [chiefs] or Indians . . . but after contract made with you," desired "they give some what to the Adjacent Sagamore or Native, for their Consent."[8]

The gaggle of enterprising fishermen, fur traders, and agents of court favorites acting on royal grants that descended on the coast found the resident Wabanakis amenable to newcomers.[9] The Indians had suffered devastating population losses to epidemics in the 1610s and 1630s that left the survivors eager for allies and trade partners.[10] With dwindling populations and a surfeit of land, the Indians had a clear incentive to invite the strangers into the Dawnland.[11]

The Wabanakis signed numerous deeds with the newcomers, intending them as invitations to participate in a reciprocal relationship, rather than in mere economic exchanges. Like other eastern Algonquian speakers, the Wabanakis often described the land as "Wlôgan," the Common Pot, reflecting their view that land use entailed a set of community privileges and obligations.[12] Their approach to property transfers reflected their practice of combining economic and social transactions. For Wabanakis, an economic exchange formed part of an ongoing reciprocal relationship. They viewed politics in a similar light, with relationships requiring regular renewals.[13]

By allowing the English into the Dawnland, the Wabanakis invited them to partake in the Common Pot. As written in seventeenth-century deeds, Native proprietors granted tracts of land to the English, usually in return for an initial payment, often followed by further annual compensation in the form of various goods.[14]

For their part, Indian land deeds offered English colonists in the Dawnland a level of security and stability that they could seldom obtain from the metropole. Provided a competent interpreter could be secured, Indians gave more accurate grants than vague patents drawn up by Englishmen who had never seen the land in question. Although misunderstandings sometimes led to overlapping claims, Indian deeds caused fewer problems than royal patents. The deeds also better corresponded to the political reality on the ground. Since the Indians held physical possession of the territory many colonists had to pay them for, it made sense to treat these transactions as legal. Colonists also found Native deeds useful for circumventing distant English claims to property and authority. Sir Ferdinando Gorges realized that fact from across the Atlantic when he warned an agent in 1664 that Indian land deeds were "Derogatory to the Grant to me made by his s[ai]d late Majesty."[15]

On a practical level, the reduced Wabanaki population still outnumbered English arrivals, and political instability on both sides of the Atlantic meant colonists could ill afford to alienate their Native neighbors. Indeed, seventeenth-century colonists endured a dizzying succession of political and proprietary overlords, inaugurating a pattern of disputed, overlapping claims to Maine that lasted into the nineteenth century. Descendants of Gorges feuded among themselves and with Massachusetts, which annexed Maine in 1658. Under King Charles II and his successor, James II, Maine gained and lost separate status twice until James revoked the Massachusetts charter and incorporated it—and Maine—into the more centralized Dominion of New England. Bridling at the changes imposed by their new governor, Sir Edmond Andros, colonists overthrew the Dominion government in 1689 and received a new charter in 1691.[16] Each seventeenth-century government of Maine had issued grants to colonists, so that by 1691 Maine contained a crazy quilt of royal, proprietary, provincial, and even town grants alongside claims from Indian sales.

Clashes between Massachusetts colonists and Governor Andros during his short tenure underlined the value of those Indian land deeds for protecting Massachusetts property and independence from outside interference. Alongside other controversial decisions, Andros sparked a firestorm of protest by refusing to recognize any land titles that did not originate from the king's patent.[17] Viewing the hodgepodge of town, colony, and Indian deeds prevalent in the colony, Andros and his supporters insisted these claimants apply to the government for new land titles.

Worried about losing their lands, outraged colonists insisted (disingenuously) that Indian land rights had always formed the foundation of the Bay Colony's property regime. The Reverend John Higginson insisted it was "a standing Principle in Law and Reason" that the Indians had owned the land, and it therefore was never the king's to grant.[18] Other writers echoed Higginson.[19] After ousting Andros and receiving a new charter from King William in 1691, Massachusetts leaders set about ensuring that colonists' land titles could never be questioned by a royal official like Andros again. An important part of that task required resolving the validity of Indian land deeds.

The Massachusetts legislature attempted to enshrine the legality of Indian deeds without explicitly contradicting royal sovereignty, and in the process they perpetuated an atmosphere of uncertainty on the Maine frontier that lasted for several generations. A 1701 act let stand any Indian deeds in Maine made "for further confirmation of other lawful titles and possessions."[20] The act appeared to confirm metropolitan views on Native land rights, only granting Indian land sales the status of "quieting" otherwise illegal occupants. However, the General Court had no choice when crafting the legislation, because the King's Privy Council would repeal any law that contradicted royal sovereignty, as it did in 1692, when the General Court passed "An Act for the Quieting of Possessions and Setling of Titles." The Privy Council then insisted that "a clause may be inserted for saving the rights of the Crown."[21] The act of 1701 banning "Clandestine" purchases from the Indians did not specify which "other lawful titles and possessions" the Indian deeds in Maine had ostensibly confirmed. The act's vague language allowed for a range of interpretations, which proprietors and colonists alike took advantage of in subsequent property disputes over the next century.

Although confusion continued to surround overlapping titles in Maine descended from Gorges and other claimants, by the early eighteenth century, Massachusetts elites agreed on the importance of Indian deeds as a foundation for both landed property and freedom from metropolitan interference. During a second period of uncertainty over the Massachusetts charter between 1715 and 1721, Jeremiah Dummer, the Bay Colony's agent in London, articulated this orthodoxy in his official *Defence of the New England Charters.* Dummer denied earlier English monarchs had the authority to grant North American lands, because the continent "was full of Inhabitants . . . and neither Queen Elizabeth by her Patents, or King James by his afterwards, could give any more than a bare Right of Preemption."[22] In fact, the only right to the land came from "what is derived from the native Lords of the Soil, and that is what the honest New England Planters rely on, having purchas'd it with their Money."[23]

Although they never endorsed this interpretation of Native land purchases, neither did imperial officials in Whitehall wish to become entangled in colonial property disputes. When the activities of an ambitious royal agent to build a new colony east of Maine towns threatened the claims of various Boston-based land speculators, they complained to the Board of Trade, and the agent was soon recalled.[24] The Privy Council also refused to rule on the extent of the disputed Plymouth Patent in 1771, returning the case to Massachusetts for retrial.[25]

In an ironic paradox, relations between Massachusetts and the Wabanakis worsened even as colonial esteem for Indian deeds increased. Massachusetts paranoia about a pan-Indian war at the outset of King Philip's War in southern New England became a self-fulfilling prophecy when the colony's abusive treatment of the Wabanakis drove those people to take up arms in 1675.[26] Following the treaty of 1678, ending hostilities, Thomas Danforth, the newly appointed president of Maine, began issuing land grants around what became the town of North Yarmouth on unceded land. Colonists began to trickle in despite Native protests. Other Wabanakis along the Saco and Androscoggin Rivers complained of English stopping fish from traveling upriver with nets and seins and allowing their livestock to roam free, devouring Native corn.[27] By making land around their towns inhospitable for Wabanaki subsistence practices, the colonists violated, at the very least, the spirit of all the agreements guaranteeing the Wabanakis continued use of the land they sold. Seeking to once again restore the balance in their relationship with the English, Wabanaki warriors began to strike Maine towns in the autumn of 1688, sparking two more wars (1688–99, 1703–13) that reduced the frontier to a charred wasteland. The population of English colonists plummeted from a prewar peak of 6,000 to less than 2,000 by 1713, clustered around the three towns of Wells, York, and Kittery, hugging the border with New Hampshire. At another peace treaty signed at Portsmouth in 1713, the Wabanakis agreed to let the British reoccupy their "Ancient Plantations."[28] Successive Massachusetts governors chose to interpret that statement to mean, as the official provincial publication of a 1717 conference clarified, "all the lands which [the British] have formerly Possessed, and all they have obtained a Right and Title unto"—meaning any vague, misunderstood, or forgotten deed they could locate.[29] So fortified, newly formed land companies like the Pejepscot Proprietors and Muscongus Proprietors shipped hundreds of colonists to new towns in Merrymeeting and Muscongus Bay, venturing farther up the Maine coast than ever before. Massachusetts's refusal to entertain Wabanaki complaints led to a new conflict often called Dummer's War (after the acting Massachusetts governor, William Dummer) in 1722.

Although they would not have admitted it, the speculators who dominated Massachusetts government during the eighteenth century owed their vast Maine land claims to Wabanaki military success in the frontier wars. As the fighting dragged on, these men purchased numerous family claims—often at rock bottom prices—from refugees who had given up on ever returning to

Maine. The speculators also benefited from the act of 1701 banning "Clandestine and Illegal Purchases" from the Indians. By effectively freezing new land sales, Massachusetts leaders prevented ordinary colonists from securing title to Maine lands without going through the large-scale proprietors. No longer could men like John Parker—a fisherman active in the Sagadahoc River region during the mid-seventeenth century—hope to amass private estates by negotiating directly with the Indians.[30] Any new colonists to Maine had to buy land at whatever price the speculators would sell. The legislature also enshrined the legal authority of absentee proprietors to thwart nonproprietors' attempts to play an active role in the distribution of land in their communities, further tightening the speculators' grip on Maine.[31]

The colonists who arrived in Maine after 1713 had their own plans for the frontier, however. A collection of hardscrabble Scotch Irish immigrants, returning farmers from before the wars, and poor New England colonists eager for the chance to own a freehold, frontier residents all hoped to achieve what they called "competency," a level of economic independence and comfort usually attained by owning one's own land.[32] As they struggled to claw a living from a harsh landscape, the colonists clashed with absentee proprietors. Frontier residents wanted to attract more colonists to build stable communities, but the absentee owners claiming most land in their communities hoped to hold onto their investment until it appreciated in value.

Throughout Maine, colonists living in frontier towns moved to assert municipal control over the distribution of land, rejecting the attempts of absentee proprietors to direct events from afar. In an extralegal meeting in 1719, the residents of the unincorporated town of Brunswick voted themselves the power to seize any undeveloped individual lots left vacant for six months after purchase.[33] In Scarborough, returning refugees declared themselves proprietors of the town and began illegally issuing grants on the condition that all new grantees "settle in said Town of Scarborough within three months and abide there in seaven years and bare Town Charges."[34]

Clashes between frontier residents and absentee speculators intensified after Dummer's War ended. Colonists asked why a handful of grandees should hold so much property and power on the frontier. While agreeing in theory with English property law, colonists argued in practice that if a person shared the dangers of living in Maine and "improved" vacant land, de facto possession was as good as law.[35] In 1728 the inhabitants of Falmouth admitted fifty families into town without consulting the proprietors. When challenged, Falmouth's residents justified their actions as "fairly and honestly acted," while admitting the law stood on the side of the proprietors.[36] In addition, the inhabitants argued that "with great danger and Expence [they] maintained themselves in their Settlements during the last Indian War . . . during which time they have received no help from the [absentee proprietors], but their pretences."[37] Similar struggles raged in other Maine communities. After touring Pejepscot Company holdings around Topsham in 1749, Belcher Noyes wrote to his fellow proprietors that he "could not but observe in the People a Disposition to lay hold of every Objection to our Title and improve the same to our Disadvantage."[38] Proprietors worried about rival land companies encroaching on their claims, which could spark costly legal battles with uncertain outcomes.[39]

What one Massachusetts writer called the "great Confusion of Claims" in Maine allowed the Wabanakis to exploit British divisions.[40] The speculators who also served as Massachusetts legislators, judges, and occasionally as governor realized that their contested titles required ongoing Native validation to withstand repeated challenges to their legitimacy from *within* the British imperial system. The chaotic nature of the Massachusetts quest for landed property in Maine thus amplified Wabanaki power beyond their military abilities.

These abilities were formidable enough. Military skill allowed outnumbered Wabanakis to punish British aggression during four frontier wars waged between 1675 and 1726. Time and again, the Wabanakis—sometimes in cooperation with New France—reduced colonial towns to ashes, sending hundreds of refugees flooding southward. Wabanaki achievements were all the more remarkable in light of their small population. Repeated epidemics, along with military losses, had whittled the Wabanaki population down from over 10,000 people in 1600 to around 2,500 in 1725, including 500 warriors.[41] By comparison, Massachusetts contained almost 100,000 inhabitants in 1719.[42] However, few of these people lived in Maine (the colonial population reached a wartime nadir of 2,000 people), and Massachusetts struggled to translate its demographic advantage into military victories.[43] Samuel Penhallow, the treasurer for neighboring New Hampshire (which had been drawn into the fighting), marveled in 1725 "that so small a number of Indians should be able to distress a Country so large and populous, to the degree we have related."[44]

Despite their successes, by 1725 the Wabanakis could not hope to rely on military power alone to defend the Dawnland from Massachusetts encroachment.[45] New France was an unpredictable ally at best. While subjects of King Louis kept a clandestine supply of arms and ammunition available for Wabanaki fighters, they refused to join a war against Britain in defense of Native lands while peace reigned in Europe.[46] Massachusetts forces scored a signal victory in 1724, destroying the major village of Norridgewock and killing many of the inhabitants. Although the Wabanakis retained the ability to inflict damage on colonial towns and troops, they could not hope to repeat their earlier feats of arms.

Even as the prospects of military victory dimmed, Wabanaki unity in the face of colonial factiousness gave them a way to augment their declining military power by exploiting their position as original proprietors of disputed Maine lands. The new Wabanaki strategy involved selective acknowledgment of seventeenth-century land deeds. Henceforth, the Wabanakis recognized most seventeenth-century land cessions while confining their objections to a handful of coerced or willfully misinterpreted transactions. Tribal unity on this point was essential; if even a minority faction acknowledged a deed, speculators stood ready to argue that they represented the "true" owners.

The Wabanaki formulation of this strategy took place during innumerable councils—almost all occurring away from the prying eyes of European recorders. In one rare recorded instance in 1720, a trio of agents for the Muscongus Proprietors traveled to the village of Agemoggon on the Penobscot River in an attempt to obtain "the Deed to all the Land within the Limits of their patent" from the inhabitants.[47] When the agents arrived, the sagamores (chiefs) were in council and made their guests wait a day before presenting their proposal, which they did in a large, specially constructed house. In the Wabanakis' consensus-based society, an important decision like this required broad participation. One of the Muscongus agents counted 100 adult men present, indicating perhaps two-thirds of the Penobscots (the largest of several Wabanaki tribes) were represented that day in Agemoggon, where "every one man took his seat according to his quality."[48] After listening to the proprietors' proposal through an interpreter, the Wabanakis held "a long debate among themselves" and made the visitors wait another day before delivering their answer. Sagamores, shamans, heads of families, and ordinary men (Wabanaki women seldom participated in formal politics) had to debate, seek spiritual guidance, and search for common ground before they agreed upon a course of action.[49] The assembled Indians excluded both the proprietors and their own French missionary from the house while they deliberated. The next day, the Wabanakis informed the proprietors that "their Lands belong to their young men and they c[oul]d not dispose of them from 'Em besides they did not care to have the English settle among 'Em," as they knew what "difficultys and inconveniency" that situation had caused Kennebec River Wabanakis.[50] The conference was part of a longer process of the Penobscot refusal to acknowledge a contested 1694 deed that formed the basis of the

Muscongus Patent. Forged in villages like Agemoggon, this Wabanaki strategy crystallized during a series of negotiations concluding Dummer's War between 1725 and 1727.

The trio of conferences that both sides called Dummer's Treaty marked a diplomatic coup for the Wabanakis, who succeeded in transforming English deeds into totems of a reciprocal Anglo-Wabanaki relationship. While compromising on certain land claims, the Wabanakis attached Native expectations of reciprocity onto most of the old land sales, bridging the divide between these cultures of ownership. As long as they continued to recognize Dummer's Treaty, the Wabanakis would acknowledge the land cessions contained in most seventeenth-century deeds. But the Wabanakis tied recognition of the treaty to Massachusetts's performance of its promises, making the practical validity of certain proprietary titles contingent on the province maintaining amicable diplomatic relations with the Indians. As a result, Dummer's Treaty attached Native expectations of reciprocity to the old written deeds that proprietors wished would serve as little more than proofs of purchase.

The success of Dummer's Treaty differed markedly from preceding agreements, which Massachusetts had violated in short order, either in fact or in spirit. But what had changed? Reflecting on its significance during the 1760s, Lieutenant Governor Thomas Hutchinson argued that success could not "be attributed to any peculiar excellency in this treaty, there being no articles in it of any importance, differing from former treaties. It was owing to the subsequent acts of government in conformity to the treaty."[51] Hutchinson was correct in assessing the importance of Massachusetts fidelity to the agreement, but failed to recognize how the speculators' dependence on Native validation of their titles expanded Dummer's Treaty beyond its written "articles" and encouraged Bay Colony cooperation.

As if to prove Hutchinson's point, the process of negotiating Dummer's Treaty contained the same confusion, misunderstandings, and manipulation that had muddied previous treaties.[52] Massachusetts supplied all the translators, colonists who had spent their childhood as captives in Wabanaki villages and who helped Bay Colony leaders manipulate written treaty articles without Native knowledge. The written articles contained the usual proclamations of (unenforced) royal sovereignty over the Indians and pro forma Wabanaki admissions of war guilt, which Native speakers always disavowed when brought up.[53]

Other evidence complicates this picture of Machiavellian deception, however. Eager to frame their achievements in the best possible light, imperial officials in both New France and New England performed claims of supremacy for the benefit of their superiors in Europe.[54] As Massachusetts leaders postured with an eye to Whitehall, in 1725 the legislature took care to investigate "Claims or Titles . . . to the Lands of the Eastern Parts of the Province" for presentation at the planned 1726 ratification, "and take care as far as possible to make out the same to the Satisfaction of the Indians."[55] After Governor Dummer engaged in preliminary talks with the Indians in 1726, the committee took great pains to show the relevant deeds for the disputed lands to the Indians.[56] To further encourage Wabanaki acceptance, Dummer issued a proclamation echoing the advice he had received (which was entered into the written record of the treaty) promising that "care [would] be taken as far as possible to . . . Ascertain what Lands belong to the English, . . . [for] the Effectual Prevention of any Contention or Misunderstanding on that Head for the future," and promised the Indians that "if the English cannot make out and prove their Titles to the Lands Controverted, they shall disclaim them."[57] At several points during the negotiations, Dummer repeated his pledge that only "Lawful Authority" would decide the justice of future proprietary land claims, until the Wabanakis clarified they understood future land disputes would be settled by "Impartial Judges and disinterested Persons appointed to that purpose, to do equal Justice."[58]

When making his promises to the Indians, William Dummer responded not only to pressures from speculators eager to restore order to the Bay Colony's land claims in Maine but also to savvy Wabanaki diplomacy. Loron, the principal speaker in 1726 and 1727, was insistent "That if a Line should happen to be Run, the English may hereafter be apt to step over it," and he sought promises of an enforcement mechanism.[59] After a legislative committee attempted to secure their approval of twenty-nine individual deeds, Native leaders pushed back, asserting "they had been shewn Deeds and papers enough to last them to the fall of the year, and they did not desire to see any more, and they supposed when they should meet [Dummer] again that matters would be adjusted."[60] Rather than validating each individual deed, Native leaders acknowledged most of them at the close of negotiations. The Penobscots—who took the lead in peacemaking after 1725—objected to a particular deed resulting from a controversial exchange in 1694. That year a Penobscot sagamore named Madockawando unilaterally ceded portions of tribal lands along Muscongus Bay and the St. Georges River to Massachusetts governor William Phips for an unknown price. Neither leader had discussed the plan with his followers; Phips acted not as governor but as a private investor, and Madockawando kept the proceedings a secret from the

Penobscots.[61] News of the cession triggered an uproar among the Penobscots, who immediately disowned it along with its author. Madockawando fell from power, and in retaliation the Penobscots broke a truce they had with Massachusetts. The Penobscots participated in Dummer's War in response to trespassers brandishing the disputed deed, and their diplomats spent much of the 1725–27 negotiations pushing for its revocation. When they signed the treaty, the Penobscots permitted two Massachusetts blockhouses to remain on the land, but never acknowledged the deed. After this compromise, Wenemouett, the leading Penobscot sagamore, and Dummer signed not only the written articles of peace (which were more favorable to Massachusetts) but the entire thirty-five-page record of the conference after the interpreters had read it aloud to the Indians.[62]

If Dummer and other Bay Colony leaders hoped to separate his proclamation promising equal justice and a rigorous review of any British land claims from the treaty articles proper, Wabanaki pressure during the negotiations, combined with intense public interest in frontier land disputes, foiled those plans. Continuing its practice, begun in 1717, of publishing all Indian treaties, the Massachusetts General Assembly included Dummer's promises in its published accounts of the 1726 and 1727 negotiations.[63] Anyone who picked up *Conference with the Eastern Indians, at the Ratification of the Peace, held at Falmouth in Casco-Bay* for 1726 or 1727 could read Dummer's promises that "if the English cannot make out and prove their Titles to the Lands Controverted, they shall disclaim them."[64] Widely available published accounts of Dummer's Treaty meant that the governor's assurances became a matter of written record. The Wabanaki decision to ratify most acceptable deeds by signing the treaty, rather than individually, encouraged the speculators to treat the entire record of negotiations as a gigantic deed.

Eager to shore up their claims, proprietors and their agents collected copies of Dummer's and later Indian treaties as evidence of their titles. Belcher Noyes, clerk of the Pejepscot Proprietors after 1739, acquired a copy of the 1726 treaty.[65] Another Pejepscot Proprietor, Henry Gibbs, owned a copy of the 1727 treaty.[66] Other proprietors collected copies of later treaties.[67] The largest Maine land speculators often invoked Native recognition of their claims in subsequent disputes with the royal agents, frontier colonists, and rival land companies. In a typical deposition for the Pejepscot Proprietors in 1753, John Gyles attested that "altho' (at Several Publick Treaties since that time) the Indians have from time to time disputed the English Claim to some of the Eastern Lands, yet they always Confessed that . . . [the Pejepscot deed] was a good and Lawfull Deed of sale of all the lands therein."[68] The practice, which increased after Dummer's Treaty, continued throughout the eighteenth century. The Draper heirs, who lacked more direct evidence of Native acknowledgment of their title in the Sheepscot River region during a 1795 dispute, secured the testimony of seventy-year-old Mary Varney, who told of witnessing "some Indian men (who I understood to be some of their Great men) who acknowledged [Draper] . . . as the owner of the lands."[69]

For the most successful land company in 1727, Dummer's Treaty assumed an outsized importance in subsequent legal clashes. Belcher Noyes, explaining the basis of the Pejepscot title to another proprietor in 1763, noted the company's 1684 Indian deed had been "produced at all the Treaties with the Indians for above forty years past, more especially . . . at Gov. Dummer's Treaty which is now allowed to be the Basis on which all the Subsequent Treaties are grounded."[70] So long as the treaty remained in force, proprietors like Adam Winthrop could point to it, as he did in a 1741 dispute with the town of North Yarmouth, as evidence that his company "have been from time to time treated with and acknowledged as Owners of sd Lands" by the Indians.[71] The Pejepscot Proprietors, along with other companies like them, had a vested interest in upholding the treaty because Wabanaki repudiation would undermine its usefulness. The Pejepscot Proprietors took a particular interest in the province fulfilling its treaty obligations. Copies of the 1726 and 1727 meetings owned by Noyes and Gibbs contain highlighting and drawn hands pointing to portions of the text mentioning company claims as well as Native land rights.[72]

The speculators' influence proved critical in diffusing the crisis of 1735–36.[73] The Muscongus Proprietors, who had purchased the disputed 1694 Madockawando deed, began shipping Scotch Irish families to Penobscot lands in 1735. Led by a Boston merchant named Samuel Waldo, the proprietors dismissed Native challenges to their title. Fearing their young men would resort to violence, Penobscot leaders made their case to Governor Jonathan Belcher and the General Court in Boston during the summer of 1736, warning that this violation of Dummer's Treaty would bring a renewal of warfare. A committee tasked with evaluating the matter reported that "the Right of the Indian Natives to the Lands in this Country has been acknowledged, and in several late Treaties with them the Government has not only given them Assurances of their Justice with respect to their Lands but promised them to disclaim such Controverted Lands, the Title or Right to which cannot be made out or proved." The committee went further, agreeing the Penobscots had never acknowledged the Madockawando purchase, and even denied that the venerable 1629 grant by the Plymouth Council for New England met the standards of the 1727 treaty, insisting that Native lands be "fairly purchased." They asserted that previous royal guarantees of British subjects' private property in Maine against the Crown were not issued "in opposition to the Indian Right."[74]

Although the committee's report did not say so, its members also knew that a new war would threaten many proprietary titles. The speculators had led Massachusetts to war in the 1720s to secure Wabanaki recognition of their claims. With this recognition now in hand, influential companies like the Pejepscot Proprietors and Clark and Lake Proprietors had a vested interest in preserving the status quo. If the Penobscots became disillusioned and disavowed Dummer's Treaty, their influence among the other Wabanakis would lessen its usefulness for the speculators, who would be more vulnerable to rival claims from neighboring companies and squatters. Only the handful of Muscongus Proprietors stood to benefit from Massachusetts's siding with their company.[75] Over Waldo's repeated objections, Belcher and the General Court sided with the Penobscots. The Indian delegation returned home to lead warriors in a bloodless eviction of trespassing colonists.

The 1736 decision demonstrated how the interests of Massachusetts and Wabanaki leaders had aligned following Dummer's Treaty. By defending Indian land rights, Massachusetts elites protected their own investments. Nor was 1736 an isolated event; additional interventions on behalf of the Indians by Governor Belcher (who supported the speculators) during the 1730s further vindicated the Wabanakis' strategy.[76]

As they faced repeated challenges to their investments, the speculators relied on their Indian deeds to bring the power of the courts to bear on obstreperous colonists. For Massachusetts elites, Native land rights helped protect not only the colony charter but also their own property. In such an environment, breaking Dummer's Treaty and violating Wabanaki land rights made little sense. Pressed by the actions taken by ordinary colonists in meetinghouses and taverns in hamlets across the Maine frontier, Massachusetts leaders instead sought cooperation with their Wabanaki counterparts.

The working relationship that developed depended on self-interest. The Wabanakis managed to use the English system of property to magnify their ability to negotiate from a position of strength, but that ability still depended on the credible threat of force should Massachusetts break its promises. Wabanaki military power waned in relation to Massachusetts during the 1740s and 1750s, and growing numbers of colonists strained the relationship by squatting on Native lands. But the Anglo-Wabanaki relationship finally collapsed under pressure from a powerful new land company holding a claim based on an old royal grant. The wealthy and well-connected Kennebeck Proprietors secured the support of a bellicose Governor William Shirley, who led a military expedition up the Kennebec River in 1754 to build forts in the heart of the Dawnland, goading the Wabanakis to side with France against Britain in the Seven Years' War (1754–63). Britain's eviction of the French from North America destroyed Native military power, and the Wabanakis learned that Massachusetts goodwill alone was insufficient to guarantee their lands. After 1763, thousands of colonists, now free from fear of Native retribution, flooded the frontier in defiance of both indigenous and absentee claims on the land.

Yet this is not merely the story of violence and dispossession. The Maine frontier was also a place where the efforts of ordinary Indians and colonists to achieve security in a turbulent world shaped the trajectory of empire. Although carried out with different goals in mind, the decisions made by colonists and Indians in wigwams, meetinghouses, councils, and taverns across the frontier combined to pressure Massachusetts leaders into cooperating with their Wabanaki counterparts in defense of Native land rights. The uneasy alliance between Wabanakis and land speculators forged in Dummer's Treaty achieved real, if temporary, success. By articulating their own vision of landownership and, through deft negotiations and military prowess, influencing Massachusetts's speculator elites, the Wabanakis showed that the logic of Britain's haphazard imperialism in North America did not irrevocably point to a land without Indians. The perennial Anglo-American quest for landed property could, at times, be harnessed in the service of Native power. Conversely, the degree of Wabanaki success within the eighteenth-century British Empire reveals just how revolutionary events following 1763 were for America's Native people and their colonial neighbors.

Notes

1. Philip McIntire Woodwell, ed. and trans., *Handkerchief Moody: The Diary and the Man* (Portland, ME, 1981), 72 for grandmother, 105–6 for mounting watch.

2. Ibid., 109.

3. Jasper Maudit, agent of Massachusetts in London, in Craig Yirush, *Settlers, Liberty, and Empire: The Roots of Early American Political Theory, 1675–1775* (Cambridge, 2011), 3.

4. See, for example, Barbara Arneil, *John Locke and America: The Defence of English Colonialism* (Oxford, 1996), and Yirush, *Settlers, Liberty, and Empire*, 12.

5. John Winthrop, "General Considerations for the Plantations in New England, with an Answer to Several Objections," *Winthrop Papers* (Boston, 1931), 2:120.

6. William Cronon, *Changes in the Land: Indians, Colonists, and the Ecology of New England* (New York, 1983); Virginia DeJohn Anderson, *Creatures of Empire: How Domestic Animals Transformed Early America* (New York, 2004); Peter A. Thomas, "Contrastive Subsistence Strategies as Factors for Understanding Indian-White Relations in New England," *Ethnohistory* 23, no.1 (Winter 1976): 1–18; Allan Greer, "Commons and Enclosure in the Colonization of North America," *American Historical Review* 117, no. 2 (April 2012): 365–86.

7. John Winthrop, "General Considerations," 2:120.

8. Certified extract of "Sir Ferdinando Gorges Instructions to his Agents Thomas Purchas and others, June 21, 1664," in Pejepscot Proprietors Papers (hereafter PPP), Phillips Library of the Peabody Essex Museum, Salem, MA (hereafter PEM), ser. 1, box 1, folder 1.

9. For reception see, for example, James P. Baxter, ed., *Christopher Levett of York: The Pioneer Colonist in Casco Bay* (Portland, ME, 1893), 104–5, 111–12. For the early colonists, Emerson Baker, "Trouble to the Eastward: The Failure of Anglo-Indian Relations in Early Maine," PhD diss., College of William and Mary, 1986, 72–93.

10. Dean Snow and Kim M. Lanphear, "European Contact and Indian Depopulation in the Northeast: The Timing of the First Epidemics," *Ethnohistory* 35, no. 1 (Winter 1988): 15–33.

11. Emerson Baker, "'A Scratch with a Bear's Paw': Anglo-Indian Land Deeds in Early Maine," *Ethnohistory* 36, no. 3 (Summer 1989): 235–56; Alice N. Nash, "The Abiding Frontier: Family, Gender, and Religion in Wabanaki History, 1600–1763," PhD diss., Columbia University, 1997, 174–99; for a similar dynamic in New Hampshire, see Peter S. Leavenworth, "'The Best Title That Indians Can Claime': Native Agency and Consent in the Transferal of Penacook-Pawtucket Land in the Seventeenth Century," *NEQ* 72, no. 2 (June 1999): 275–300. For the traditional view that English arrivals deceived or coerced the Indians in most early agreements, see Francis Jennings, *The Invasion of America: Indians, Colonialism, and the Cant of Conquest* (Chapel Hill, NC, 1975), chapter 8.

12. Lisa Brooks, *The Common Pot: The Recovery of Native Space in the Northeast* (Minneapolis, 2008), 3.

13. See, for example, Querabannit's concern on this account to Governor Joseph Dudley in 1714 in *Documentary History of the State of Maine*, 24 vols., ed. James Baxter (Portland, ME, 1869–1916) (hereafter *DHSM*), 23:52–53.

14. Baker, "'A Scratch with a Bear's Paw,'" 239–44, and Nash, "Abiding Frontier," 151–53, 174–79, 198–99. For one example, see Nanuddemaure Deed to John Parker, June 14, 1659, copy in proprietors' book, entered by Belcher Noyes, PPP, Maine Historical Society, Portland (hereafter MeHS), vol. 1, box 1, pp. 25–26.

15. Certified extract of "Sir Ferdinando Gorges Instructions to his Agents Thomas Purchas and others 21 June 1664," PPP, PEM, box 1, folder 1.

16. Emerson W. Baker, "Formerly Machegonne, Dartmouth, York, Stogummor, Casco, and Falmouth: Portland as a Contested Frontier in the Seventeenth Century," in Joseph A. Conforti, ed., *Creating Portland: History and Place in Northern New England* (Lebanon, NH, 2005), 5–9; Jenny Hale Pulsipher, *Subjects unto the Same King: Indians, English, and the Contest for Authority in Colonial New England* (Philadelphia: University Pennsylvania Press, 2005), 252–56.

17. Pulsipher, *Subjects unto the Same King*, 250–53; T. H. Breen, *The Character of the*

Good Ruler: A Study of Puritan Political Ideas in New England, 1630–1730 (New Haven, CT, 1970), 153–67.

18. Quoted in Edward Rawson, *The Revolution in New England Justified, and the People there Vindicated from the Aspersions Cast Upon Them by Mr. John Palmer* (Boston, 1691), 14, Evans Collection, ser. 1, no. 575.

19. Rawson also cited John Lynde of Charlestown, *Revolution*, 15–16; see also *An Appeal to the Men of New England, with a short Account of Mr. Randolph's Papers* (Boston, 1689), Evans Collection, ser. 1, no. 455; Yirush, *Settlers, Liberty, and Empire*, chapter 2.

20. An Act to Prevent and Make Void Clandestine and Illegal Purchases of Lands from the Indians, June 26, 1701, *The Acts and Resolves, Public and Private, of the Province of the Massachusetts Bay: To Which are Prefixed the Charters of the Province. With Historical and Explanatory Notes, and an Appendix*, 21 vols. (Boston: 1869–1922) (hereafter *Acts and Resolves*), 1:471.

21. An Act For the Quieting of Possessions and Setling of Titles, October 14, 1692, *Acts and Resolves*, 1:41–42.

22. Jeremiah Dummer, *A Defence of the New England Charters* (Boston, 1721), 9, Evans Collection, ser. 1, no. 2216.

23. Dummer, *Defence of the New England Charters*, 9.

24. For the full debate and hearing, see *DHSM*, 11:97–134.

25. Gordon Kershaw, *"Gentlemen of Large Property and Judicious Men": The Kennebeck Proprietors* (Portland, ME, 1975), 190.

26. Christopher J. Bilodeau, "Creating an Indian Enemy in the Borderlands: King Philip's War in Maine, 1675–1678," *Maine History* 47, no. 1 (January 2013): 11–42; Baker, "Trouble to the Eastward," 202–13; Pulsipher, *Subjects unto the Same King*, chapter 9; Kenneth Morrison, *The Embattled Northeast: The Elusive Ideal of Alliance in Abenaki-Euramerican Relations* (Berkeley, CA, 1984), 108–11.

27. Cotton Mather referenced these complaints in *Decennium Luctuosum: An History of Remarkable Occurrences . . . From the Year 1688. To the Year 1698* (Boston, 1699), 15; for another complaint from Falmouth, see Edward Tyng to Gov. Andros, August 18, 1688, *DHSM*, 6:419.

28. Casco Conference with Wabanaki Sagamores to Ratify Treaty, July 21, 1713, *New England Treaties, North and West*, ed. Daniel Mandell, vol. 20 in *Early American Indian Documents: Treaties and Laws, 1607–1789*, ed. Alden Vaughan (Washington, DC, 2003) (hereafter *NET*), 142.

29. *George Town and Arrowsick Island, Aug. 9th, 1717 . . . A Conference* (Boston, 1717), Evans, ser. 1, no. 1894, 12.

30. See, for example, deeds in *York Deeds*, 2:13, 10:252.

31. See An Act For Regulating of Townships, Choice of Town Officers, and setting Forth Their Power, November 16, 1692; An Act to Enable Towns, Villages, and Proprietors in Common and Undivided Lands, etc. To Sue and Be Sued, October 16, 1694; An Act Directing How Meetings of Proprietors of Lands Lying in Common May Be Called, March 25, 1713, in *Acts and Resolves*, 1:64–68, 182–83, 704.

32. For competency, see Daniel Vickers, "Competency and Competition: Economic Culture in Early America," *William and Mary Quarterly*, 3rd ser., 47, no. 1 (January 1990): 3–4. For colonists, see Rev. Henry O. Thayer, "Transient Town of Cork," in *Collections of the*

Maine Historical Society, 2nd ser., vol. 4 (Portland, ME, 1893), 240–65; Henry W. Wheeler, "Brunswick at the Time of Incorporation," *Collections of the Pejepscot Historical Society*, vol. 1, pt. 1 (Brunswick, ME, 1889), 21–45.

33. May 8, 1719, "Leagual Town Meeting," PPP, MeHS, Pejepscot Proprietors Record Book, box 2, vol. 3, p. 9. Brunswick held its first legal town meeting on March 28, 1739. Brunswick Town Records [microfilm], Maine State Archives, Augusta, 5.

34. September 20, 1721, meeting in Scarborough Proprietors Records, MeHS, p. 18.

35. For examples of this viewpoint, see Belcher Noyes to Enoch Freeman, November 8 and December 26, 1762, in PPP, MeHS, vol. 5, box 3, folder 3, pp. 25, 30; Noyes and William Skinner's account of journey to Brunswick, March 28, 1750, in PPP, vol. 7, box 5, folder 11, pp. 431–34; Agents of Falmouth their Answer to the Petition of Thomas Westbrook & others, 1730, in *DHSM*, 11:54–59.

36. Agents of Falmouth Answer to the Petition of the Ancient Proprietors, September 1730, Massachusetts Archives Collection, in Massachusetts State Archives, Boston (hereafter MAC), 6:497–99, quotation on 498.

37. Ibid., 6:498–99.

38. An Account of the Proceedings of Mssrs Noyes and Skinner in their late Voyage to the Eastward, March 28, 1750, PPP, vol. 7, box 5, folder 11, p. 434.

39. See Alan Taylor, "'A Kind of Warr': The Contest for Land on the Northeastern Frontier, 1750–1820," *William and Mary Quarterly*, 3rd ser., 46, no. 1 (January 1989): 3–26.

40. William Douglass, *A Summary, Historical and Political, of the First Planting, Progressive Improvements, and Present State of British Settlements in America* (Boston, 1749), 1:386.

41. Dean Snow, "The Ethnographic Baseline of the Eastern Abenaki," *Ethnohistory* 23, no. 3 (Summer 1976): 303; Snow and Lanphear, "European Contact and Indian Depopulation," 24; David L. Ghere, "Myths and Methods in Abenaki Demography: Abanaki Population Recovery, 1725–1750," *Ethnohistory* 44, no. 3 (Summer 1997): 527.

42. *Calendar of State Papers Colonial, America and West Indies, 1574–1739*, 45 vols. (London, 1860–1994) (hereafter CSP), vol. 31, doc. 564 i, http://www.british-history.ac.uk /report.aspx?compid=74086.

43. Charles E. Clark, *The Eastern Frontier: The Settlement of Northern New England, 1610–1763* (New York, 1970), 336.

44. Samuel Penhallow, *The History of the Wars of New-England with the Eastern Indians* (1726; Williamstown, MA, 1924; repr., 1973), 127–28.

45. Emerson W. Baker and John G. Reid, "Amerindian Power in the Early Modern Northeast: A Reappraisal," *William and Mary Quarterly*, 3rd ser., 61, no. 1 (January 2004): 104.

46. Messrs. de Vaudreuil and Begon to the Council of Marine, October 17, 1722, in *Documents Relative to the Colonial History of the State of New York; Procured in Holland, England, and France*, 15 vols., ed. E. B. O'Callaghan (Albany, NY, 1856–87) (hereafter *NYCD*), 9:911; Louis XV to Messrs de Vaudreuil and Begon, May 30, 1724, *NYCD*, 9:936; Yves F. Zoltvany, *Philippe de Rigaud de Vaudreuil: Governor of New France, 1703–1725* (Toronto, 1974), 149–50.

47. Thomas Fayerweather Diary, Special Collections, Bangor Public Library, Maine, July 29, 1720.

48. Fayerweather Diary, August 12, 1720. For Penobscot population estimates, see Ghere, "Myths and Methods in Abenaki Demography," 516, 527–28. Begon to Monseigneur, September 25, 1715, Library and Archives of Canada, Ottawa, MG1 C11A F-35, f112; Wenogganet, Querabanawit, Nodagombewit, Owanabbemit, and Pear Exces to Gov. Joseph Dudley, February 12, 1713/14, NET, 157, for a Penobscot self-warrior count of "170 men."

49. The best discussion of the intersection of gender and politics among the Wabanakis is in Nash, "Abiding Frontier," 72–74, 76–78, and 156–57 for etiquette and relationships, 151–99 for distinctions by sex and age and a handful of seventeenth-century female leaders. For leadership in Wabanakia, see Alvin H. Morrison, "Dawnland Decisions: Seventeenth-Century Wabanaki Leaders and Their Responses to the Differential Contact Stimuli in the Overlap Area of New France and New England," PhD diss., SUNY Buffalo, 1974.

50. Fayerweather Diary, August 13, 1720.

51. Thomas Hutchinson, *The History of the Colony and Province of Massachusetts Bay*, 3 vols., ed. Lawrence Shaw Mayo (Cambridge, MA, 1936; New York, 1970), 2:241.

52. Scholars debate the extent and nature of Massachusetts mistranslation of written treaties to the Wabanakis. Further muddying the issue, the Wabanakis relied on their resident French Jesuits to serve as occasional scribes and interpreters, and these men had a motive to engage in their own manipulations in the service of king and church. Robert H. Lord, John E. Sexton, and Edward T. Harrington, *History of the Archdiocese of Boston*, 3 vols. (New York, 1944), 1:137; David L. Ghere, "Mistranslations and Misinformation: Diplomacy on the Maine Frontier, 1725 to 1755," *American Indian Culture and Research Journal* 8, no. 4 (1984): 7; David L. Ghere, "Abenaki Factionalism, Emigration, and Social Continuity: Indian Society in Northern New England, 1725 to 1765," PhD diss., University of Maine, Orono, 1988, 174n20; David L. Ghere and Alvin H. Morrison, "Searching for Justice on the Maine Frontier: Legal Concepts, Treaties, and the 1749 Wiscasset Incident," *American Indian Quarterly* 25, no. 3 (Summer 2001): 381–83; and Christopher Bilodeau, "The Economy of War: Violence, Religion, and the Wabanaki Indians in the Maine Borderlands," PhD diss., Cornell University, 2006, 397–98.

53. *George Town and Arrowsick Island*, 6. See also Loron and Lauverjat to Lt. Gov. Dummer, January 28, 1726 (N.S.), MAC, 29: 250; James Baxter, ed., *Documentary History of the State of Maine*, 24 vols. (Portland: Maine Historical Society, 1869–1916) (hereafter *DHSM*), 23:425–26.

54. See, for example, Traite de Paix entre les Anglois et les Abenakis, 1727, *Collection de manuscrits contenant lettres, memoires et autres documents relatifs a la Nouvelle France*, 4 vols. (Quebec: 1883–85) (hereafter *CMNF*), 3:134–35; for an English translation, see *NYCD*, 9: 991; see also Lettre du R. P. Lauverjat Au R. P. de La Chasse, July 8, 1728, *CMNF*, 3:143–44.

55. December 22, 1725, *Journal of the House of Representatives of Massachusetts, 1715–1779*, 55 vols. (Boston, 1902–90) (hereafter *HJ*), 6:431–32.

56. *Conference with the Eastern Indians, at the Ratification of the Peace, held at Falmouth in Casco-Bay, in July and August, 1726* (Boston, 1726), 11; Seventeenth-Century Wabanaki to English Deeds Shown at the Casco Conference, August 3–4, 1726, *NET*, 316.

57. *The Conference with the Eastern Indians at the Further Ratification of the Peace, Held at Falmouth in Casco-Bay, in July 1727* (Boston, 1727), 12–13; *Conference* [1726], 13.

58. Ibid., 13.

59. Ibid., 12.

60. Seventeenth-Century Wabanaki to English deeds Shown at the Casco Conference, August 3–4, *NET,* 316.

61. The Madockawando sale is analyzed in Morrison, "Dawnland Decisions," 89–91; Bilodeau, "Economy of War," 280–91; Emerson W. Baker and John G. Reid, *The New England Knight: Sir William Phips, 1651–1695* (Toronto: University of Toronto Press, 1998), 167–72. The meeting was subsequently described by another Native witness to Capt. Claude Sebastian de Villieu. See John Clarence Webster, ed., *Acadia at the End of the Seventeenth Century, Letters, Journals, and Memoirs of Joseph Robineau de Villebon, Commandant in Acadia, 1690–1700, and Other Contemporary Documents* (St. John, NB, 1934). For the Madockawando cession to Phips, see *York Deeds*, 18 vols. (Portland, ME, 1887–1910), 10:237–38.

62. *Conference* [1726], 14–15, 22.

63. *HJ*, 1: 251; *George Town . . . 1717; Conference with the Eastern Indians, at the Ratification of the Peace, held at Falmouth in Casco-Bay, in July and August, 1726* (Boston, 1726), Evans Collection, ser. 1, no. 2571; *The Conference with the Eastern Indians at the Further Ratification of the Peace, Held at Falmouth in Casco-Bay, in July 1727* (Boston, 1727), Evans Collection, ser. 1, no. 2885.

64. *Conference* [1726], 13; proclamation repeated in *Conference* [1727], 12–13.

65. *Conference* [1726], Plymouth Company Records (hereafter PCR), MeHS, box 13, folder 3. On the first page is written "Belcher Noyes 1752/Josiah Little." Little's name is written in a different hand, in darker ink, indicating he acquired the treaty later.

66. *Conference* [1727], PCR, MeHS, box 14, folder 2. Henry Gibbs wrote his name, now faded, on the first page. The name of a later Pejepscot Proprietor, Josiah Little, is in newer, bolder ink lower on the page.

67. See, for example, *A Conference of His Excellency Jonathan Belcher with . . . Indian Tribes at Falmouth in Casco Bay, July 1732* (Boston, 1732), in PCR, MeHS, box 13, folder 3. This copy has Josiah Little's name written on the first page. Nathan Dane Papers, Massachusetts Historical Society, Boston (hereafter MHS), box 6, folder 4, book no. 1, "General Statement of the Title and Possession of the Kennebec Proprietors of the Kennebec Purchase, from the late Colony of New Plymouth[,] Nathan Dane," 16.

68. Deposition of John Gyles, June 7, 1754, PPP, MeHS, vol. 10, box 6, folder 2, pp. 4–5.

69. Testimony of Mary Varney, June 5, 1795, Sheepscot Manuscripts, Maine State Library, Augusta, vol. 2, p. 92b.

70. Belcher Noyes to Enoch Freeman, November 12, 1763, PPP, MeHS, vol. 5, box 3, folder 4, p. 77.

71. Pejepscot Proprietors Answer to North Yarmouth Petition to the General Court, July 1741 [draft by Adam Winthrop], PPP, MeHS, vol. 6, box 4, folder 12, pp. 352–53.

72. For Noyes, see *Conference with the Eastern Indians . . . , 1726,* PCR, MeHS, box 13, folder 3. Noyes highlighted passages on pages 6, 7, 9, 10, 11, 12, and 13; for Gibbs, see *Conference* [1727], PCR, MeHS, box 14, folder 2, pp. 9, 12.

73. The events in the following paragraph are treated in greater detail in Ian Saxine, "The Performance of Peace: Indians, Speculators, and the Politics of Property on the Maine Frontier, 1735–1737," *New England Quarterly* 87, no. 3 (September 2014): 379–411.

74. Report in *CSP*, 42: 375 ii f, http://www.british-history.ac.uk/report.aspx?compid=72849.

75. Muscongus Proprietor Elisha Cooke waged a rearguard action in favor of Waldo in the House, while Samuel Thaxter, Anthony Stoddard, and John Jeffries were the only three Muscongus Proprietors in the twenty-five-member Governor's Council. For Cooke's efforts, see *HJ*, 14:94; for membership of the council, see *HJ*, 14:7. For a list of the Muscongus Proprietors, see Lincolnshire Company Records, MHS, 14–24.

76. For Wabanaki complaints, see Belcher to Col. Thomas Westbrook [from Sec. Willard, draft], September 7, 1736, MAC, 52:542, and Conference with Polin & Indians of Presumpscot, August 10 & 13, 1739, *DHSM*, 23:257–62; Michael C. Batinski, *Jonathan Belcher, Colonial Governor* (Lexington: University Press of Kentucky, 1996), 71–72.

Part II

War, Revolution, Empires

Efficient and Effective

The Deceptive Success of British Strategy at Fort Stanwix during the Seven Years' War

James Coltrain

A first glance, little about the daily operations at Fort Stanwix would have suggested an administrative success. A dreary, frostbitten, hastily constructed assemblage of timber and earth at the least accessible point of a journey between colonial New York City and the Great Lakes, the eighteenth-century British fort paled in comparison to the stone defenses that French rivals had erected in the contest to control North America. Stanwix's stationed soldiers had endured every imaginable difficulty and setback in attempting to secure the isolated and unwieldy location. Hard labor and poor diets had kept men out of service with exhaustion and sickness, frequent desertions sapped manpower and morale, and tangled forest impeded even basic maintenance.

Fraught with such difficulties, the construction and operation of Fort Stanwix hardly seems emblematic of the growing power of the British Empire during the eighteenth century. Britain's eventual victory in the Seven Years' War would stem from the remarkable growth of a rapidly modernizing administrative state built on the sort of commerce that allowed many British subjects the flexibility and freedom to pursue their own interests while investing in those of the mother country. As public and private structures grew intertwined with one another, Britain's administrative, financial, and military capacities coalesced into a formidable Atlantic power that many of its own subjects still celebrated as more free than its neighbors. This powerful empire not only would seize control of North America but would do so by making the sort of calculated, practical decisions that produced the seemingly unremarkable Fort Stanwix.[1]

The experience of the soldiers and laborers at Fort Stanwix provides a window into the British imperial culture of efficiency and flexibility that gave even homely stations like Stanwix an advantage during the Seven Years' War. British commanders and engineers were able to build at such a far-flung location in part because they made better use of the Atlantic marketplace. Where French workers might wait weeks on shipments of tools from Europe, Stanwix's managers purchased manufactures like hammers, saws, and nails from Schenectady or Albany. This flexibility in markets extended to staffing, where commanders quickly employed private local carpenters, boatwrights, sutlers, and mill operators. Personnel decisions could quickly assign both provincial and regular troops, managing not only scouting and ranging but also careful and regular maintenance of the local environment and infrastructure, clearing roads, repairing bridges, and tending to earthworks. These improvements dovetailed with broader Native American policy in the area, facilitating and protecting local trade without added cultural and religious programming for local Iroquois tribes. British commanders also had the authority to delegate important responsibilities and move resources without hanging on the approval of the king or his ministers, further speeding the pace of frontier logistics. Taken as a whole, the routine administration of Fort Stanwix reveals a ruthlessly efficient and flexible British strategy that could swiftly allocate supplies, labor, and infrastructure across an unfriendly landscape, although often at the cost of soldiers' health and laborers' safety. Modest structures like Fort Stanwix could never rival their French counterparts for architectural sophistication, but Britain's careful and canny manipulation of resources would prove more effective for controlling central New York and achieving victory on the continent.[2]

The location where Fort Stanwix would stand was so remote that hardships were almost ensured. Traders and natives had traveled the thick woods and thin creeks around the site for decades, because the unassuming parcel of forest sat just between the two river systems that connected upstate New York to the Atlantic World. To the north of the fort, a provincial could make the passage from Wood Creek, into Lake Oneida, through the Oswego River into the Great Lake of Ontario, and even through Canada and out to sea on the St. Lawrence. To the south was the tip of the Mohawk River, which merged with the Hudson and flowed first by Albany and all the way into the New York harbor. Between these two important waterways were a few miles of dry land which locals called the Oneida Carrying Place, in reference to the practice of carrying canoes from one river to another. Just three to five miles across depending on the rains, the area served as the crucial land bridge between two great bodies of water. The possibility of fortifying the Carrying Place had obvious military value, but the site was so far from supply lines and clear roads or waterways that any plan to construct serious fortifications bordered on the foolhardy.[3]

Early in the Seven Years' War, British commanders in the American colonies began a series of convoluted and frustrating attempts to secure the Carrying Place against French threats. As major general of the North American forces, Massachusetts governor William Shirley worried over the security of the passage between Albany and Oswego, and he began planning a campaign to wrest the Great Lakes from French control. Shirley sent Capt. William Williams into Oneida country and instructed him to begin construction on a relatively modest fort structure at the Mohawk River landing called Fort Williams, which was followed with another fort on the landing at Wood Creek eventually called Fort Bull and nearly half a dozen smaller forts not far from the Carrying Place, each varying in sophistication. By French standards, however, none of these structures would have even represented a permanent construction. Frustrated by the inadequacies of these slapdash defenses, British agent Sir William Johnson fretted to the local commanders about their failure to properly supply Oswego, which soon fell to the French. Following the resulting British retreat to a German settlement further down the Mohawk River, British leaders ordered all the forts surrounding the Carrying Place to be destroyed.

A shift in leadership would lead the British to try building at the Carrying Place again, eventually culminating in the construction of Fort Stanwix. By 1758 the prospects for British victory in the American theater were improving rapidly. William Pitt had directed more resources to the war effort in the provinces, and the spectacular British victory at Louisbourg had already reverberated as far as the New York frontier. By midsummer Cdr. James Abercromby ordered Brig. John Stanwix to reestablish the British presence at the Carrying Place and once again connect Lake Ontario to the New York harbor through the construction of a new fort. Abercromby was clear the new building should transform the region, charging Stanwix that he must "annoy the Enemy, and remove all the Fears and Objections of the Five Nations." Abercromby's awareness of Native opinions was important, and through negotiations with the nearby Oneidas, William Johnson promised that the new fort would only be temporary. He stressed there would be increased trade to recompense the Oneidas for the commerce they had lost during the British withdrawal.[4]

British officials debated over whether the new fort should be cheap or foreboding. But in truth, by the standards of other empires, even the more expensive and formidable of the two designs was not terribly impressive. The modest initial plan came to the Carrying Place from Lt. Col. James Montressor and would have accommodated four hundred troops at highest capacity. Montressor instructed Stanwix and others onsite to aim for the simplest structure that would be adequate, even calling for the walls and accompanying buildings to be of "the Cheapest Form." Stanwix and his resident engineer, Capt. William Green, had other ideas. Working on intelligence about the size of artillery that the French in the area possessed, they called for a more sophisticated scientific design. Their structure would be of the preferred star shape, with adequate bastions to support serious firepower as well as outerworks like a ditch and glacis slope that could protect the Carrying Place in the event of a true frontier siege. Montressor and British leaders were not amused by the imagination of their colleagues and pressed hard on the construction of the inferior structure, which was to be finished in time for the coming winter.[5]

As well-informed as Engineer Green was about French capabilities, the prospect of building his more elaborate design on the difficult terrain of the Carrying Place seemed risky at best. He calculated that adequate curtain walls would need to be fourteen feet high, with an outer perimeter totaling hundreds of yards. This alone would require the logging of thousands of trees, and clearing adequate space for the long approach to the fort itself would mean thousands more. Such a labor would place dozens or even hundreds of workers out in undeveloped areas, constantly vulnerable to enemy attack. Most discouraging of all was the looming winter weather and the coming feet of snow that might obstruct the entire proceedings. Aware of all of these pitfalls, Green still lobbied for an advanced fort design. He understood there was little value in quickly finishing a shoddy structure, only to see it fall to the French. Eventually Abercromby's men relented, and the commander gave approval for a more advanced fort to be built.[6]

A 1757 plan shows the Green design which Abercromby had found outlandishly ambitious was in fact intensely practical. It called for a true fort rather than a simple palisade, but there was neither waste nor flourish to the proposal. The fort had adequate room for troops and officers, as well as space to shelter families, locals, and Native allies during a siege. Interior rooms behind the curtain walls certainly made the fort more expensive, but provided better shelter for a troop complement that could run into the thousands. The fort would also have the four standard bastions, conservatively proportioned, but capable of holding six large guns each. Green's design had presented his superiors with the bare minimum necessary to truly secure the Carrying Place without a gamble, and his argument had won the day.[7]

Designers would still add no architectural feature to Fort Stanwix unless it was absolutely necessary for immediate defense. Stanwix would be constructed only in timber and earth, but the inferior materials allowed for a breakneck pace. While elsewhere in North America, the Spanish and French constructed forts designed to reinforce imperial culture through architectural flourish, British frontier forts failed to aspire even to permanence, much less to grandeur. Beyond the British flag flying in the courtyard, there was no incorporation of imperial iconography like the decorative stonework common to French structures. Neither did the fort attempt to intimidate through its design or to plot out impressive approaches or gateways. Stanwix had only plain timber walls, its grand entrance little more than a post and lintel. While French designers used architectural features to commemorate imperial greatness, naming bastions, towers, and gates after prominent royals or noblemen, the British left each corner of Stanwix indistinguishable from another. Despite their place crowning the heights of the sizeable fort, even the guardhouses of Stanwix remained free from the considerable embellishment of French designs. Instead, the lookouts were built boxy, with about as much artistry as had been employed for the outhouse.[8]

Even the practical deign of Fort Stanwix proved difficult to build in such a far-flung location, as workers endured a host of setbacks and often fell behind schedule. Abercromby remained surprised by the rate at which troops fell ill in the damp, cold New York winter. The numbers were striking, with the commander writing that "from 5600 intend'd for the service this way that not 1500 left fit for duty." So many men fell sick that Stanwix ended up sending hundreds down the river in boat loads. Muster rolls are littered with a variety of maladies to stymie production. Some of these illnesses may have even resulted from the intense and dangerous construction process, as one letter requests a surgeon to deal with over fifty men suffering from gangrene. Given the limited military engagements for men stationed at Stanwix during the construction years, this suggests a frightening number of grisly workplace injuries, presumably to be followed with even more gruesome amputations. Numerous other times commanders detail large numbers of troops unfit for work, not only from simple exhaustion or injury but also from cases of smallpox that could endanger the entire operation.[9] Officers reported dozens with venereal disease, and the regularity of sickness at Stanwix prompted almost constant requests for leave, especially from provincial troops who could conceivably return to their homes to recover.[10] One general interpreted the morale of the men as relatively strong, but acknowledged that too many "are really worn out, work'd down & fairly jaded with Fatique."

Winter provided a host of challenges to the Stanwix project. With the frequent and heavy snowfall inside the Mohawk Valley, the moving and management of snow in the winter took considerable effort. Simply to ensure basic operation of the fort, nearly the entire grounds would need to be cleared following every fresh snowfall. Soldiers would need to clear the courtyard and bastion ramps to preserve space for drilling and lanes for cannon movement, along with keeping snow and ice off the guns themselves to preserve their readiness. Piling snow on the flat roof would put heavy stress on the hastily laid timbers and would have to be removed quickly. Any leftover accumulation was in danger of melting from heat from Stanwix's many hearths, only to refreeze as ice that could add even more weight and quickly erode the structure. While soldiers at Stanwix would appreciate the return of warm weather, the steady thaw of accumulated snow and ice could make the fort grounds a muddy, miserable mess, accelerating the natural rot of the untreated wood and impeding the movement of troops and artillery.[11]

The harsh New York weather also forced alterations to the construction schedule. Despite the considerable time saved by building in timber, workers could not avoid the necessity to provide adequate heat and so devoted significant energy to the forming and firing of bricks, presumably from local clay. Williams wrote in September that his men had "40,000 Bricks ready to Burn for the Chimneys & propose another Kiln of 100,000." Because the bomb-proof fort rooms could not be completed in time for winter, considerable time and effort went into building small huts and houses for everyone stationed in the garrison. Because workers were not using plaster to seal outside walls, significant effort also went into cutting plank shingles, to keep small shelters dry, as well as to give the roof additional strength to hold despite heavy snows. These efforts sapped manpower from completing the fort walls and bastions more quickly, but a formidable fort was of little use if its garrison had been thinned out by exposure to the snowy freeze and related sicknesses. Nevertheless, the progress continued, as workers finished the ditch and glacis, an unenviable task that would have required tens of thousands of buckets of earth moved and then reformed, and only after the grounds had been cleared of large rocks and tree stumps had been pulled for hundreds of feet in every direction. Despite his troops' vulnerability and the impending winter, Engineer Williams was pleased with the progress, writing of his confidence that such a "fine spot" would become the "principle Fortification to dominate the nearby landscape.[12]

The persistent danger of enemy attacks amplified every frustrating setback that soldiers and laborers endured at Fort Stanwix. As parties ventured out into the forest to cut sod for earthworks, clear roads and rivers, conduct patrols, and finish every other chore, they did so with a persistent awareness of the threat of potential attacks. With parties of both French rangers and Native Americans allied with that empire roaming the woods, skirmishes were regular, and those on duty in small groups might be killed or taken prisoner. Rumors from Native Americans coming to trade and shelter near the fort further stoked fear at Stanwix, as whispers of troop movements and raiding parties made perilous assignments seem even riskier.

While modest in comparison to some of the better connected French masonry forts on large rivers in the Great Lakes, Fort Stanwix was an impressive accomplishment for such a remote location. Nevertheless, like many of the British fortifications in the region, the completed Fort Stanwix was a makeshift shanty compared with many of the sophisticated French fortifications to the north. Built with cheap, easily decaying materials, during a construction that lurched forward in fits and starts, carried on by sickly, freezing men, Stanwix remained a primitive, plain structure. And yet, within the same context, Stanwix was a major achievement and an important example of British imperial culture. It embodied a practical and efficient mind-set that drew power from speed and flexibility to adapt quickly the constantly changing landscape of war. Drawing strength from a mastery of infrastructure, logistics, personnel management, and commercial networks, Stanwix fit perfectly into a system designed to hold territory and nothing else and to do it without spending a single pound more than was necessary.

Fort Stanwix was just one part of a larger infrastructure program to control the landscape surrounding the Carrying Place and through the greater Mohawk Valley. This program of targeted building provided the backbone for a sprawling logistical network. Through carefully measured spending on infrastructure, British agents laid the groundwork for moving men and materials across difficult terrain. The rapid construction and maintenance of passable roads was just as important and as technically challenging as building Stanwix itself. Additionally, the management of the landscape provided another diplomatic tool for dealing with the Oneida and other Iroquois tribes in the region, who had been negotiating infrastructure improvements with the British for half a century. This work would begin with surveying parties, who would venture out to take measurements and gather estimates on the necessary supplies and labor needed.[13] On difficult, uneven terrain surrounded by thick forest and winding between meandering creeks, British laborers worked to clear paths over the Carrying Place to Fort Herkimer and to Fort Bull, among other locations.[14] Soldiers also completed bridges, which required regular maintenance to remain steady through months of water flow, freezing and thawing, and shifting mud.[15] The cleared roads allowed for convoys that would have been impossible only months earlier. Commanders ordered livestock moved over the difficult terrain, teams of oxen from Albany to help clear woods more quickly, and herds of sheep to provide fresh meat.

British commanders manipulated local waterways for maximum efficiency as well. Rivers and creeks provided much speedier avenues for transport, but strategic decisions could quickly shift which streams were most important. So far into the woods, with shifting water table levels and falling brush, a creek could become impassable in only a few weeks. Officers sent laborers regularly to clear rivers for passing bateaus, to divert streams to power sawmills, and engineers to build dams to help keep water levels high.[16] Dam construction could involve sophisticated and even dangerous methods of construction. One crew was able to dam the Canada Creek in under ten days, but still had to deal with large boulders that could potentially obstruct bateau convoys. To solve the problem, an officer reported the use of explosive charges to blast the rocks completely out of the water.[17] A 1756 map showing the British "PLAN OF FORTS" details some of the infrastructure British agents brought to the forested trail at the Carrying Place.[18] At the site of the Wood Creek fort, which had fallen to French raiders, workers dammed the water and then installed a functioning flood gate to provide a modest reservoir of fresh water for stationed troops without risk of flooding during heavy rains. The reservoir also functioned as a loch, providing enough water for batteaus to be loaded near the fort before continuing on the float to the Great Lakes. The map shows how their efforts swelled into an artificial pond hundreds of yards across, an impressive alteration of a very remote landscape.

Along with transportation infrastructure were other individual building projects that supported Britain's network of frontier fortifications. Just in the area surrounding Fort Stanwix, British laborers threw up the supporting structures necessary to speed construction at a remote location. To save on transporting heavy bricks across difficult terrain, British agents completed an entire brick kiln near the Mohawk River. New York's cold winters necessitated wood burning for warmth, but the timber structures built in the area also posed constant fire hazards. Brick hearths and chimneys provided the means for safe heating, and so British agents began firing the kiln to produce new bricks on-site, which would have been prohibitively heavy to transport en masse. Not merely content to use roughhewn round logs in construction, British workers also built a sawpit to transform local round timber into proper, reliable planks. They also put up a forge and smithy to hammer out or repair metal goods for each fort in the line along the Carrying Place. British laborers even helped facilitate private contracting by building a store for use by approved sutlers.[19] And of course, Stanwix was only one of a handful of

British fortifications in the region. Each one featured a similarly plain design and inexpensive materials, but by building cheap and fast, British commanders spread their risk broadly across the landscape while retaining resources and flexibility to reinforce or abandon a certain site as the strategic landscape evolved.

The efficiency and scope of Britain's command network extended to its personnel decisions, as it quickly recruited, assigned, and transported labor for projects like Fort Stanwix. For simple labor, commanders preferred their own soldiers, who came at no extra cost and were already on-site. These could include British regulars as well as New York militiamen or other provincial volunteers. Most of the labor did not merit these men additional pay, but was simply considered part of their regular duties. The required labor occasionally produced tension among the troops, and General Stanwix wisely warned against potential changes to the construction plan that would render thousands of hours of backbreaking service irrelevant. The variety of available forces also had the potential to create problems. Much of Abercromby's continuing pressure to have Williams finish the fort in time was based on the mistaken assumption that colonial militiamen from the surrounding area were experienced woodsmen and as a result skilled as carpenters. In fact, few in the camp had any experience with large-scale, precise construction and had to learn on the job. For jobs requiring skills beyond those of average soldiers, British officers recruited craftsmen from the surrounding countryside, preferring to quickly contract available talent rather than take time to train their own men on-site. When no talent was available locally, commanders at Stanwix could petition other fort sites and nearby towns to send appropriately trained men.[20]

British personnel management ruthlessly exploited the strengths and weaknesses of the available workforce, often stirring resentment within the ranks. At Fort Stanwix, the case of a provincial regiment from Rhode Island assigned to duty at the fort provides a useful example. With less experience than the British regulars who had made a transatlantic journey to serve in the North American theater of the Seven Years' War, provincial units suffered from the reputation, sometimes deserved, that they were undisciplined and less effective in battle. To avoid such a liability, a colonel at Stanwix hand-picked dozens of soldiers from the Rhode Island regiment to labor exclusively on fort construction during the winter, freeing more experienced troops to serve on ranging expeditions or to transfer wherever fighting grew fierce.

Slave labor does not appear to have been a large part of the construction force. There were the numbers of African American slaves at Stanwix that would accompany any large British military engagement, and there are suggestive references in some of the musters rolls, such as individuals recorded without rank or surname, under common single slave monikers such as "Jack." These records may be evidence of slaves accompanying their masters on militia duty, or of freed blacks, either impressed or serving as volunteers.

British agents were able to manage resources and manpower efficiently in part because of an imperial culture with the confidence to delegate authority. Many of France's major building decisions required extensive input from royal councilors overseas, putting a major drag on the empire's ability to fortify the landscape. In the British case, however, many significant decisions did not even rise to the level of the commander of the North American forces, let along the Crown. While each step in the chain of command remained responsible to higher leadership, the ability of officers on the scene to make snap judgments on how to allocate resources helped the British imperial machine move faster and more effectively in its attempts to control the landscape. The small administrative footprint of constructions like Stanwix also meant that such outposts would not overshadow the existing diplomatic policies of current British Indian agents.

Market access also benefited Fort Stanwix because British officials in New York so rarely had to worry about funding. Frequently the projects of other North America empires struggled to maintain transatlantic financial support, but the Stanwix construction never stalled for lack of imperial coin. Britain's sophisticated financial network meant that suppliers had reasonable confidence in the Crown's purse, and Pitt had made North America enough of a priority that aside from calls for prudent use and eliminating waste, the availability of cash rarely posed a problem.

British commanders could also streamline their operation by buying from private suppliers. Officers could search for lower prices among merchants and could be more flexible in decisions about where to quarter troops. The ability to purchase manufactured goods, like tools and hardware, was especially advantageous. Thus while French smiths were beating shipments of pig iron into tools before work could even begin, British commanders were simply sending supply orders to Albany or Schenectady to buy the same supplies ready-made.[21] Local markets filled British needs so thoroughly that one British official even purchased precut firewood rather than commit laborers to gathering it themselves.[22] Such expenditures were not to purchase luxury but the speed and flexibility to adapt to unforeseen circumstances. If winter snows rose unusually high, British leaders could buy more snowshoes, and if soldiers became available to clear brush, then the British could buy axes. In one case, commanders found themselves with an unexpected cache of butchered pork, so they quickly bought salt to preserve the provisions for later.[23] The advantages of British markets are also apparent in the case of Stanwix's chimneys. Lime burning had consumed years of labor in French and Spanish fort projects, as workers processed gathered shells or cut stone in huge kilns. Records show little evidence that lime burning of any kind took place at the Stanwix site, meaning that engineers were simply able to purchase and transport barrels of lime from elsewhere in the empire, saving time and manpower in mixing the mortar for the fort's crucial hearths.[24]

The strength of British commerce allowed commanders to place regular soldiers into the market as well. Recalling the Carrying Place's early function as a trading post, officers commissioned sutlers' stores to sell directly to troops. While French fortifications often securely housed and carefully distributed many community resources, British officials allowed for the construction of a sutler's house nearby on the glacis, where private business could sell goods and supplies to individual soldiers. Stationed men and traders at Stanwix bought and traded a host of commercial goods, including imported manufactures. These included items of clothing, belts and shoes, cutlery, ceramics, tools large and small, even small luxuries like tea, wine, spirits, and especially tobacco, as shown by the thousands of pipes recovered by modern archaeological surveys onsite.[25]

British alcohol policy further demonstrates the flexibility commanders had by using private suppliers. Officers on-site sought out shipments of rum to boost morale among troops, especially during the hard work of clearing the woods surrounding the fort.[26] But the sale of alcohol in the region complicated relationships with Native Americans. Fearing erratic behavior, British officials banned settlers on-site from selling to local Indians, but prohibition complicated matters further when members of a local tribe broke into the store to take it for themselves.[27] Eventually British commanders became frustrated with their own men's lack of control, as some soldiers became so intoxicated they were unfit for service. Ranking officers began to reject shipments of rum and molasses if their superiors had not already prohibited them, but none would go to waste.[28] Instead, a colonel had them shipped to Carolina, a part of the imperial network far enough from the action to safely enjoy a drink.[29]

The British also manipulated the value of the fort's protection to shore up support from the surrounding communities. Early in the conflict, groups like the German community living in a settlement called the Flatts had hoped to remain neutral, declining to join as British subjects and even promising the French to remain outside of the conflict. After a series of bloody raids in the area by both French soldiers and allied Native Americans, however, all those living in the region came to see Fort Stanwix as a potential source of safety. Residents of New York depended just as dearly on a stable British presence to preserve the security of the local economy. Local fur traders, who were suffering from interruptions of commerce as well as the threat of violence, also became more likely to offer their services in exchange for protection. The availability of British defenses also put particular strain of British relations with the Iroquois leaders, who worried that flexible ebb and flow of British presence might leave their territories exposed to the French and their native allies. Diplomatic efforts ultimately smoothed over the long held alliance between the Iroquois and the British, but the need for colonial agents to use infrastructure and architecture at the Carrying Place remained a pressing concern.[30]

Finally, Fort Stanwix succeeded in part by eschewing the cultural programming and ceremony that the French found so important in their own settlements. Unlike her rival empires, many of Britain's forts like Stanwix lacked any attempt at reinforcing a broader cultural program. Fort Stanwix was a center for local residents to interact with and understand imperial presence, but the fort's design made few attempts at controlling and influencing these interactions. Trade in fur and other items was one of the underlying justifications for building the fort, but the designers had included no great storerooms to protect goods, no quarters for merchants, no attempts to limit and control trade. Stanwix at times provided shelter for local families from enemy raiding, and British officials at times used the fort's presence to communicate strength to potential Native American allies, but its design had no flourish intended to enhance its stateliness. Although the fort's resident troops fought enemies that they at times derided as Catholics and members of a popish conspiracy, the fort's design was wholly secular. Even when missionaries quartered there for brief stays, there was no chapel, no school, no space sacralized or even made especially available for Christian practice or instruction

Fort Stanwix's plain, functional design shows that Britain's imperial culture could allow for the coexistence of private enterprises within an important public zone. Soldiers stationed at Fort Stanwix had both greater economic freedom and a more sophisticated stake in the market economy.[31] In the same way, the clearest instances of nationalist ceremony and art at Fort Stanwix were often found in privately owned items. Efficient British managers could hardly be troubled to do more than fly the proper colors above the southwest bastion, but individual soldiers often expressed both their own patriotism as well as their virulence for the French opposition in individual goods purchased or personally crafted. There were bayonets cast with the British lion as an insignia, belt buckles with royal symbols, even a China cup celebrating Britain's alliance with Prussia in the European theater. British soldiers also appropriated the symbols of their rivals, refashioning the coins of rival empires into buttons and other trinkets. Like commerce and religious practice, British leadership expended few resources to promote nationalist sentiment, despite the possible community benefits of doing so.[32]

As Fort Stanwix neared completion, it revealed the character and priorities of a distinct British imperial culture operating on the New York frontier. In projects like Stanwix, the overarching objective was simple and clear, to maintain control of British territory. The design of Stanwix was neither comprehensive nor forward-looking, as it did not value permanence, inclusiveness, or versatility. British agents were not using elements of architecture to solidify the surrounding region into a frontier community, nor did they design their structure to rigidly reinforce national or religious values. Time after time, Britain's agents of empire in the Mohawk Valley prized only designs that could extend the greatest control over territory in the shortest amount of time. The empire's unique capabilities to deploy troops and resources, to delegate authority, and to access local market chains meant the British could extend and sustain the empire not by persuasion or culture but by simple and transformative force.

After the war concluded, British maintenance and attention to Stanwix waned and withered as quickly as its strategic significance on the new landscape. With the fort no longer providing a crucial defense, salary payments came late and supply lines slowed. Frustrated with delays, one officer gave his subordinates cash advances from his own funds, but then had to pester the empire for his own reimbursement.[33] The troop complement plummeted, as did the morale of those few who remained. Desertions jumped significantly, leaving the leftover command to chase absentees through the thick forest. In one incident, nearly two hundred men fled their posts, no doubt many feeling the uselessness of their continued service with the French now expelled from the continent. Desertions were particularly common in the Rhode Island regiment, which had for months worked primarily in the burdensome work of constructing and maintaining the fort itself.[34] Six men from that regiment claimed their service had expired before they deserted, but they were returned to building maintenance after their apprehension. Records from those months show that many of those who returned received pardons, suggesting a desperation among officers trying by any means simply to keep the operation going.[35] Others obtained exemptions from their service on account of infirmity due to persistent sickness or old age. At one point the prospects for the structure grew so bleak that a commander wrote to his superior with a proposal that grain be grown on-site and the post be converted into a brewery.

Viewed only as a fortification, the midcentury career of Fort Stanwix is hardly impressive. Its walls of timber and earth, already rotting by 1763, fell far short of the architectural accomplishments of France's stone forts in the Great Lakes region, to say nothing of the massive and sophisticated fortified towns at Louisburg and Quebec. Troops at Fort Stanwix were often sickly and disgruntled, the fort's construction often slowed in response to brutal weather, and by the war's end Stanwix had become a dilapidated mess ready to be retaken by the surrounding forest. But British officials had not set out to construct an architectural gem. They had only wanted to maintain control over the Mohawk Valley, and for that goal Stanwix was exactly what it needed to be.

Fort Stanwix embodied the larger strategy of the British forces during the Seven Years' War and the character of the British Empire during the eighteenth century. By leaning on infrastructure, logistics, and commerce in place of architectural sophistication and cultural programming, British officials had achieved an effective control of the landscape with maximum efficiency. In addition to saving money, the austere designs of British structures in the region allowed British commanders to build with unparalleled speed. Even the seemingly inconsistent and frequently interrupted construction of Fort Stanwix had been lightning fast when compared with the decades-long building programs that accompanied French fortifications. By refusing to indulge in anything but the most necessary expenditures in Stanwix's design, construction, and management, British commanders ensured the empire would maximize its flexibility as the war progressed. Fort Stanwix lapsed into neglect nearly as quickly as it was built, but it served precisely the function its designers had intended. And in view of the wider conflict, such targeted, pragmatic, and noncommittal expenditures proved perfectly adequate for preserving control over a crucial piece of territory. Moreover, Fort Stanwix's defense of British rule had created a unique sort of imperial power that exerted precise control over territory without needing to permanently remake the landscape or impose its culture on local populations. Stanwix could inspire recognition without significantly disrupting the imperial status quo among local farmers, traders, and the Iroquois powers in the broader region. Thus, by neglecting architectural flourish and imperialistic pageantry for the pragmatism of its efficient logistics, the British Empire of the eighteenth century had done very little to make the ordinary people living in and near Fort Stanwix feel British, but it had also ensured they would not have the opportunity to feel French.

Notes

1. Numerous historians have examined the growth and nature of the British Empire during the eighteenth century. See David Armitage and Michael J. Braddick, *The British Atlantic World, 1500–1800* (New York, 2002); John Brewer, *The Sinews of Power: War, Money, and the English State, 1688–1783* (Cambridge, MA, 1990); Linda Colley, *Britons: Forging the Nation, 1707–1837* (New Haven, CT, 2009); Anthony Pagden, *Lords of All the World: Ideologies of Empire in Spain, Britain, and France c.1500–c.1800* (New Haven, CT, 1998).

2. For general treatments of the Seven Years' War in America and the British Empire on the frontier, see Fred Anderson, *Crucible of War: The Seven Years' War and the Fate of Empire in British North America, 1754–1766* (New York, 2001); Francis Jennings, *Empire of Fortune: Crowns, Colonies, and Tribes in the Seven Years' War in America* (New York, 1990); Eric Hinderaker, *Elusive Empires: Constructing Colonialism in the Ohio Valley, 1673–1800* (New York, 1999); Peter Silver, *Our Savage Neighbors: How Indian War Transformed Early America* (New York, 2009); Patrick Griffin, *American Leviathan: Empire, Nation, and Revolutionary Frontier* (New York, 2008); Alan Taylor, *The Divided Ground: Indians, Settlers, and the Northern Borderland of the American Revolution* (New York, 2006).

3. Major correspondence for the construction and early administration of Fort Stanwix is found in The National Archives (TNA), in the War Office collection "Correspondence between Commander-in-Chief and officers and Fort Stanwix," WO 34/53, Kew, United Kingdom. Many other letters from the same archive are scattered elsewhere in the Colonial Office. Many major letters are also reproduced in Edmund B. O'Callaghan, ed., *Documents Relating to the Colonial History of the State of New York*, 15 vols. (Albany, NY, 1854) (hereafter *DNY*). A descriptive history of the construction and defense of the fort is found in the Parks Service Historic Structure Report by John Luzader, *The Construction and Military History of Fort Stanwix* (Office of Park Historic Preservation, 1969). *DNY*, 4:979, 981, 5:726, 6:858, quoted in Luzader, 7–11.

4. Abercromby to Pitt, July 12 1758, TNA; *DNY*, 7:378; Luzader, *Construction*, 25.

5. "Green Plan," TNA; *DNY*, 4:525–26; "Plan of Fort Stanwix Built at Oneida Carrying Place," British Museum, Crown Collection, CXXI, 100; reproduced in Luzader, *Construction*, 186; "Captain's Green's Observations on Col. Montressor's Plan for a Post at the Oneida Carrying Place," James Abercromby Papers, Huntington Library, quoted in Luzader, *Construction*, 20.

6. "Green Plan", TNA; *DNY*, 4:525–26.

7. "Plan of Fort Stanwix Built at Oneida Carrying Place," British Museum, Crown Collection CXXI, 100, reproduced in Luzader, *Construction*, 186.

8. "Plan of Forts at the Oneida or Great Carrying Place," TNA. For coverage of French fort construction in America, see Bruce W. Fry, *"An Appearance of Strength": The Fortifications of Louisbourg* (Ottawa, 1984); Andre Yvon Desloges and Marc LaFrance Charbonneau, *Quebec the Fortified City: From the 17th to the 19th Century* (Parks Canada, 1982). For Spanish styles, see Verne E. Chatelain, *The Defenses of Spanish Florida, 1565 to 1763*, Carnegie Institution of Washington Publication 511 (Carnegie Institution, 1941); Luis R.

Arana, *The Building of Castillo de San Marcos* (published by Eastern National Park and Monument Association for Castillo de San Marcos National Monument, 1977); National Park Service, *Forts of Old San Juan: San Juan National Historic Site, Puerto Rico*, ed. Raymond Baker (Washington, DC, 1997); Alejandro de Quesada, *Spanish Colonial Fortifications in North America, 1565–1822* (Oxford, 2010).

9. Letter, August 7, 1760, TNA.

10. Letter, November 1, 1763, TNA; Letter from Thomas Baugh, January 10, 1763, TNA; Letter to John Campbell, November 2, 1763, TNA.

11. "Green Plan," "Montressor Plan," "Plan of Fort Stanwix," TNA.

12. John Stanwix to James Abercromby, September 5 and 7, 1758; quoted in Luzader, *Construction*, 27.

13. Jeffrey Amherst to Ensigns Raster and Rivers, May 23, 1759, TNA.

14. Letter, May 25, 1760, TNA; Letter, June 6, 1760, TNA.

15. Letter to John Campbell, October 29, 1763, TNA.

16. Letter, May 13, 1760, TNA.

17. Letter, January 17, 1760, TNA.

18. "PLAN OF FORTS," British Museum, Crown Collection, no. XXX, Copy in the Map Division, Library of Congress, reproduced in Luzader, *Construction*, map appendix.

19. Letter, May 22, 1760, TNA.

20. Ibid.; Letter, May 24, 1760, TNA; Letter from John Darby to Jeffrey Amherst, October 24, 1760, TNA.

21. Stanwix supply lists, Letter, October 16, 1760, TNA; Letter, December 1759, TNA; December, 1759, TNA; Jeffrey Amherst to Captain Fry, July 18, 1761, TNA.

22. Letter to Colonel Massey, February 16, 1761, TNA.

23. Letter to Colonel Massey, May 26, 1760, TNA.

24. Stanwix still occasionally struggled to provide enough rations for stationed troops, but that was more a problem of transportation than access to markets or the funds necessary for such purchases.

25. See David R. Starbuck, *Excavating the Sutlers' House: Artifacts of the British Armies in Fort Edward and Lake George* (UPNE, 2010).

26. Letter, June 6, 1760, TNA; June 9, 1760, TNA.

27. October 16, 1760, TNA; Letter to Thomas Baugh, August 1, 1762, TNA; Letter from Thomas Baugh, July 20, 1762, TNA.

28. Letter to Colonel Massey, June 11, 1760, TNA; John Christopher Hartwick to Jeffrey Amherst, November 7, 1759, TNA.

29. Letter from Colonel Massey, April 4, 1761, TNA.

30. Luzader, *Construction*, 21.

31. CHS Crown Collection, CXXI, 103, "A Sketch of Fort Stanwix," 1764; reproduced in Luzader; "Green Plan," TNA.

32. Lee Hanson and Dick Pick Hsu, *Casemates and Cannonballs: Archeological Investigations of Fort Stanwix, Rome, New York* (Department of the Interior, 1975).

33. Letter from John Campbell, April 12, 1763, TNA.

34. Letter to Thomas Baugh, May 16, 1762, TNA.

35. Letter from John Campbell, August 12, 1763, TNA.

Rethinking Failure

The French Empire in the Age of John Law

CHRISTOPHER HODSON

For over two centuries, failure has haunted the history of France's early modern Atlantic empire. The evidence appears damning. Overwhelmed by the resourcefulness of rivals and hamstrung by constitutional defects, historians have told us, the Bourbon kings and their subjects overseas never pulled a proper imperial system together. Their colonies remained stunted and scattered, their migrants too few in number, their gazes too fixed on events in continental Europe or the all-consuming yet unproductive notion of *la gloire*. And in the end, they lost the Seven Years' War and any pretension to a New World empire that really mattered.

Dip in at any moment since 1763 and you will probably find some version of the same explanation for these events. "The French genius," wrote Alexis de Tocqueville in 1833, "does not appear very favorable to colonization." The American orator Edward Everett said as much in 1853 ("The French, though excelling in the art of communicating for temporary purposes with savage tribes, seem . . . to be destitute of the august skill of founding States"), as did Victor Hugo, Francis Parkman, and a host of twentieth-century scholars on both sides of the Atlantic.[1] The Bourbons possessed "little worth the name" of empire, wrote James Pritchard in 2004, declaring French policy "ineffective, or at best ambiguous and wasteful."[2] In the dysfunctional family of European empire builders, the French come off as well-intentioned ne'er-do-wells: Fredo among the Corleones.[3]

Atlantic history, however, has changed things—not by elevating the French but by cutting other Europeans down to size. Emphasizing indigenous power and a host of contingencies at the expense of metropolitan designs, this sort of history treats empires less like structures and more like organisms. Fragile European regimes abroad evolved as environments and peoples pressed adaptations on thousands upon thousands of baffled, tongue-tied, but opportunistic colonists.[4] In effect, empires are all Fredos now.

Take the British, whose overseas expansion dominates not just this volume but Atlantic history in general. As David Armitage has argued, the very notion of a British Empire only really gained currency in the second quarter of the eighteenth century, as figures on its Irish, Scottish, American, and Caribbean margins imagined themselves as part of a transatlantic community of commerce-minded, liberty-loving Protestants.[5] In many respects, this vision of empire functioned as an anchor, steadying such peripheral people as they bobbed, rudderless, in a sea of ill-fated schemes and botched maneuvers. The correspondence of eighteenth-century provincial governors in North America, for instance, reads like a chronicle of impotence. Menaced by French and Spanish enemies, neighboring Native Americans, African slaves, and their own ethnically diverse and religiously combative subjects, they lived in a state of permanent crisis.[6] To the south, things were no better. Maroons and smugglers always had the drop on Anglo-Caribbean authorities, and savvy observers knew that production in the booming French colonies of Martinique, Guadeloupe, and Saint-Domingue was poised to outstrip that of the British West Indies.[7] By the 1740s, sharp-eyed British thinkers actually advocated emulating the French Empire, whose absolutist political culture struck them as the perfect antidote to the disorder then afflicting their own.[8] And of course, no sooner had the British defeated the French in the Seven Years' War than the empire collapsed into a transatlantic civil war so devastating that George III nearly abdicated after his side lost. Failure? Britain's empire had it in spades.

And yet empire became *the* political and cultural touchstone for British subjects in the Americas, infiltrating the most remote corners of provincial life even as the empire itself teetered on the brink of disaster. This seeming paradox lies at the heart of whatever tension exists between Atlantic and imperial history. The key question it raises is indeed a thorny one: if plans hatched in European staterooms rarely panned out as their authors intended, what effect did they have?

A closer look at the French Empire of the 1720s—a decade of dashed hopes and embarrassment often associated with the disgraced Scottish financier John Law—can help here, affording some remarkable views of European imperialism in a pan-oceanic context. For in those years, the French tried to build a transatlantic polity like no other. Armed with state-of-the-art monetary policies and outsized ambitions, the monarchy's officials aimed to create an empire in which settlement, commerce, and defense marched in lockstep to a single, unwavering beat emanating from the kingdom's heart. The punch line is a predictable one: it did not work.

But instead of waxing autopsical, probing the limp corpse of yet another French overseas scheme for the deficiencies that caused its death, we might instead ask what it did while it lived.[9] The answer, I think, shows the interpretive inutility of Parkman's old but resilient charge that France's empire was stymied by its "barren absolutism," an ideology that allegedly yielded the worst of all possible worlds: colonies at once too strong (that is, overmanaged by detached, arbitrary authorities) and too weak (that is, underpopulated and neglected by a king absorbed in European affairs).[10] It demonstrates that the early eighteenth-century struggle—and it was a struggle—to root the French Empire deep within the sinews of indigenous societies worldwide should not be read merely as evidence of that empire's failure. Rather, the struggle *was* empire. Indeed, if we broaden our angle of vision, taking in the lived experience of ordinary people and crown officials from the Sénégal Valley to the streets of Paris itself, the weaknesses we too often associate with failure emerge as precisely those traits that made the Law era's brand of imperialism—and the later imperialisms it prefigured—so influential in so many places.

A tour through John Law's empire and a closer look at the mechanisms that made it run might best begin at its creator's home: a fine apartment on Paris's exclusive Place Vendôme in September 1720.

Law peered from behind the curtains, catching only glimpses of the neighborhood boys keeping watch over his every move. Their spying had already produced results. A few days earlier, the Scot's wife and young daughter had taken a carriage ride through the city. Upon reaching a busy intersection, the pair and their coachman were surrounded by a crowd of lackeys. "It's the livery of that wretched bugger!" they shouted, overturning the carriage and injuring the little girl badly.[11] Once renowned for his good fortune, Law had become, in the words of a Parisian song, an "execrable tyrant."[12]

As his critics told it, the story of Law's crimes against the people of France had begun five years earlier. After nearly seven decades on the throne, Louis XIV died on September 1, 1715, leaving his kingdom's finances in disarray. After the royal funeral, ministers discovered how grave the problems really were. In 1715 Versailles collected 69 million livres while spending 146 million, saddling the monarchy with a deficit of 77 million livres for that year alone. France's total debt added up to over two billion livres, the interest on which required annual payments of at least 90 million livres.[13]

Into the post–Sun King gloom stepped John Law. Once condemned to death in England for killing a rival in a duel, Law had bounced from the Netherlands to Italy to France, amassing a fortune as a high-stakes bookmaker while honing his economic theories. His plan to reform Louis XV's finances was nothing if not ironic. Born into a family of Edinburgh goldsmiths and eager to craft policy for kings known to put gold leaf on anything, Law intended to disconnect France from gold altogether, creating Europe's first paper-based monetary system. After winning the confidence of Philippe, duc d'Orléans, then acting as regent for the toddler-king, Law set to work in 1716.

First, he set up a private bank modeled on the Bank of England capable of issuing notes that functioned as legal currency. As business picked up, Law secured Orléans's backing for the Company of the West, a joint-stock company intended to promote the settlement of Louisiana and the upper Mississippi Valley. Both projects soon turned profits, prompting Law to think bigger. By August 1719 his bank had become France's state bank, acquiring exclusive rights to print money, collect royal taxes, and reimburse the monarchy's debt. With the regent's support, the Company of the West swallowed up colonial companies focused on the Caribbean, the East Indies, China, and West Africa, effectively placing all of the kingdom's overseas trade under Law's control. Law merged the new joint-stock company with the state bank in January 1720, creating the mammoth Mississippi Company. Weeks later, Orléans named him controller-general of finances. Now fully realized, Law's plan revolutionized French finances, expanding the king's power in ways that would have made Louis XIV envious.[14]

Initially, the "Mississippi system" worked like a charm. Between May 1719 and March 1720, the price of a share in Law's enterprise shot up from 500 livres to 10,000, causing Parisians to coin a new word for those who made fortunes in the stock boom: *millionaires*. Law became a celebrity. "All the people of quality in France are on foot, in hundreds, before his door in the Place Vendôme," wrote one onlooker caught in the throng of investors.[15] Six "women of quality" went so far as to detain Law in the street for hours as they pumped him for information on investments, at last prompting him to declare that "if you don't let me go, I'm going to burst, for such is my need to take a piss."[16]

As popular as Law was, shares of his company were the real attraction. On the rue Quincampoix in Paris, traders set up an open-air stock market, forcing the police to build gates and mount patrols to keep crowds in line.[17] "From early in the morning to late at night," marveled one visitor, the street was packed with "princes and princesses, dukes and peers and duchesses . . . in a word, all that is great in France."[18] The company's fortunes, however, rested mainly on the 200,000 to 350,000 people who flooded into Paris in 1719 and 1720, hell-bent on catching the Mississippi wave.[19] "The reason of the sudden rise of the stock here is the great number of people come from the provinces who arrived all at once in the rue Quincampoix," explained one British official.[20] Such people "[sold] estates and pawn[ed] jewels to purchase Mississippi," exchanging old, established forms of wealth for paper shares.[21]

To the budding *philosophe* Voltaire, all of Paris had simply gone crazy. Perhaps, but there is a more elegant explanation for such behavior. Throwing its weight behind Law's paper-based economy, the monarchy transformed the way French people perceived value. Dutch critics thought as much. The frontispiece of Pieter Langendijk's 1720 play *The Harlequin Share Trader,* for example, depicts a scene of mass financial confusion on the rue Quincampoix, complete with what we might describe as didactic flatulence (fig. 1). The owl clutching the play's title emits two word-bubbles of gas: "The company is full," declares the first, while the second reads, "Last one in picks up the tab." From his own aft orifice, a man doubled over in the foreground blurts out "Miss," for Mississippi. Such images referenced the well-worn Dutch joke that trading in Law's shares was no different than trading in wind. From a platform above the crowd, three Mississippi Company officials drive the point home. One announces a new "project," while another forces gold nuggets through a funnel and into the mouth of a third, who defecates stock certificates marked "Law" into the crowd. This arresting image of reverse alchemy captured what others had only written: that Law's company had "upset conditions, corrupted morals, and changed the national character," burying the right order of society under an amoral avalanche of shares and banknotes.[22]

And, as Philippe d'Orléans's foul-mouthed mother would declare, those shares and banknotes would soon be useful only as "arse wipes."[23] In the spring of 1720, the overheating economy triggered severe inflation. Investors panicked. Some began converting stock back into specie, causing the price of shares to plummet. Worse, word from Louisiana, the settlement of which was crucial to Law's plans, was not good. Of the five thousand Europeans sent to the colony since 1718, two thousand had fled back to France, while the rest fought to survive a terrible famine.[24] The bubble burst that summer. Law's bank ran out of specie, saddling hundreds of thousands of French subjects with worthless currency. Perhaps 10 percent of the kingdom's population took direct losses before December 1720, when the stock price finally hit zero.[25] Conspiracy theories abounded. "It is very simple now to divine the goal and end of [Law's] system," the diarist Edmond Barbier wrote after watching his 60,000 *livre* investment in the Law's shares dwindle to nothing: "It was a shell

UITLEGGINGE

DER

TYTELPLAAT,

VOOR

ARLEQUYN ACTIONIST.

Ziet hoe dat deeze Actiebaazen,
  Agter het tooneelgordyn,
Door elkaâr met bubbels raazen,
Uitgelagt als regte dwaazen
  Van Scaramoes en Arlequyn.

Voor papier, brengt elk met hoopen
  Hier zyn gelt Kakkario,
Om diens windt dan te verkoopen
En zyns naaftens beurs te ftroopen
  Voor Kool van Bombario,

Die met lift hier weet te fteelen,
  Te befchyten met gewelt;
Kan met Aap en Jakhals deelen,
Afgeregt op dopjes fpeelen,
  Die fteeds roven fchat en gelt.

En Merkuur; die 't kwaat wil ftuiten
  Ziet Mejonker in de kouw,
Die de waarheit zal ontfluiten,
Na hy woekraars, dieven, guiten
  Heeft ontdekt aan 't naberouw.

Zulke die hun fchatten wagen
  Op bedrog of eigenbaat,
Moogen meê van rampen klagen;
Maar die voelen flingfche flagen,
  Zyn in meer beklagens ftaat.

Vrienden; hy die 't heeft gebrouwen,
  Krygt ligt andermaal u beet.
Wilt geen flang in 't gras vertrouwen?
Laat ons naar de Schrift, uitfpouwen
  't Walglyk tuffchen kou ten heet'.

FIG. 1. John Law's Mississippi Company through the eyes of its Dutch critics: the frontispiece of Pieter Langendijk's *The Harlequin Share Trader* (1720). (Courtesy of the Lewis Walpole Library, Yale University)

game that lasted two years and that pulled all of the kingdom's money into the Regent's coffers."[26]

The Law regime's impact, however, was hardly so clear-cut. The prince de Conti, a relative of Louis XV who had poured millions into Law's bank in 1717, contributed much to—and benefited much from—its collapse. Tipped off early to the trouble in Louisiana, he cashed in his stocks for three servant-drawn carts of gold early in 1720, panicking the crowds on the rue Quincampoix. Well-heeled investors like Conti made out like bandits, plowing profits back into their estates and contributing much to France's economic boom in the 1730s. Indebted peasants also benefited from Law's rise and fall. The devaluation of French currency that followed the Mississippi Company's collapse allowed them to pay back creditors quickly, contributing to a spike in rural consumption in the first years after Law's ouster.[27] As for the provincials who flocked to the capital at the height of Mississippi fever, some skulked home sadder if not wiser. Others, however, stayed in Paris, swelling the ranks of the urban poor. Early in 1720, the crown formed a posse of guardsmen to round them up, offering a bounty of ten livres for each arrest. As the city's prisons filled up, "twenty to thirty thousand poor people and do-nothings" fled for nearby towns to torment authorities there.[28]

Something, of course, is missing from this retelling of the rise and fall of Law's system. Although France's Atlantic empire was central to his plans (even contributing his company's name-turned-byword), it rarely figures prominently in accounts of Law's day. French historians usually limit themselves to a brief mention of the founding of New Orléans, Law's much-ballyhooed city that one 1721 visitor described as little more than "a wild and deserted place that canes and trees still cover." Scholars of Louisiana mirror them, hustling past the Mississippi Company itself to focus on the repercussions of France's post-Law "abandonment" of the colony.[29] There is, however, a better way of integrating the Parisian and imperial elements of this story. Indeed, the rule of Law takes on a new meaning when cast not as a financial sham but as an attempt by the monarchy to extend its influence over a worrisome indigenous people: the French.

For in addition to filling the treasury, the Mississippi Company was also built to bypass older ways of generating loyalty to the king's government. The absolutist regime of Louis XIV had tried to do so by whipsawing between careful negotiation with and outright bullying of the kingdom's powerful *corps*, the privileged bodies that had long fancied themselves bulwarks against monarchical power grabs. Chief among these were the *parlements*, and chief among these was the parlement of Paris, the court that claimed to be a "necessary bond between the sovereign and his subjects" and the "only channel through which the voice of the people can reach [the king]."[30] Louis tried to bypass parlement's "channel" via the public elaboration of the cult of the Sun King, a massive image-making program that ranged from architecture to histories to statuary to painting and that aimed to convince subjects of his divine right to their loyalty.[31]

But with the Sun King dead and the regency of Louis XV still in its infancy, Law hoped to achieve what he described as the "union of all opposing interests" by linking the monarch directly to his people through monetized paper.[32] The bills in their pockets or the stock certificates in their safes, he believed, would implicate millions of Frenchmen in "that unity which creates wealth as well as power." As Montesquieu would later argue, the "chimerical repayments" so fundamental to Law's system had been devised to allow the regency to buy off and restructure France's "constitution," forging good subjects in a royal crucible of buying, selling, and accumulating.[33]

Montesquieu, then, saw Law's financial maneuvering as little more than dressed-up "despotism." Nearly three hundred years on, however, we might more fruitfully see it as stripped-down imperialism. Indeed, Law built his system to do work at home we often associate with empire abroad—fabricating indigenous allegiance by manipulating and, in the end, cornering markets that nourished both the intimate habits and public ambitions of the king's would-be subjects. As far as state-building intent is concerned, the Mississippi Company's strange history validates Frederick Cooper's observation that the French Empire, including and especially metropolitan France itself, constituted a space "that was neither sharply differentiated nor wholly unitary."[34]

Figuring Law-era Paris as one part of an ocean-spanning circuit of interventions, reversals, and adaptations allows us to see beyond not only the persistent divide between France's domestic and colonial histories but also the false binary of imperial success and failure. For while the Law system surely failed to deliver what it promised, it nonetheless stamped old régime society with the monarchy's imprint in new and consequential ways. The company's office on the rue Quincampoix functioned like a magnet, attracting tens of thousands of migrants whose displacement altered the demography of Paris and its surroundings for years to come. Driving this mass movement was a change in symbolic comprehension in which the crown's paper currency trumped land or gold as *the* marker of wealth and status. On the Parisian street, people knew Law was unsuccessful; they also knew that his power, derived from the child-king whose image graced his notes, had been utterly transformative.

Far from the rue Quincampoix, equally imperfect applications of French power produced analogous results. On December 9, 1716, a few months after Law laid out his ambitious plan to repair the king's finances, André Brue sat down to write a plan of his own. From Saint-Louis, the little French town at the mouth of the Sénégal River, Brue's task appeared no less Herculean than Law's. For twenty years, Brue had directed the Sénégal Company's activities in West Africa, dealing with an inland mosaic of native peoples while fending off British, Portuguese, and Dutch rivals on the coast. Now, however, he hoped to make a move in the African interior that would not only enrich his company but secure for France a boundless source of wealth and labor for its Atlantic empire.

It would not be easy. Since the early seventeenth century, the French had pushed up the Sénégal River into a cockpit of warring African states. The potential payoff seemed to warrant the risk. Somewhere beyond the falls of Félu, the point five hundred miles inland from Saint-Louis where the river became impassable, lay Timbuktu, the legendary city at the edge of the Sahara reputed to be the lynchpin to trade networks stretching to the Nile. Promising too were the gold fields south of the falls in Bambouk, where visitors reported that the precious metal was "practically found on the surface, requiring nothing else . . . but to soak the ground to separate it from the dirt."[35] Less awe-inspiring but still profitable were the groves of acacia trees growing along the Sénégal's banks. Their trunks swelled in the wet summer and contracted in the dry winter, causing a hard, sugary resin to extrude from the shrinking bark. Called gum Arabic by the British and *gomme sénégal* by the French, the resin was used as a stabilizer in candy, textiles, and paints.[36] Finally, the river valley's inhabitants captured and sold slaves. The French had been buying them for decades, dealing with African merchants at inland outposts or in Saint-Louis. But the Sénégal Company wanted more.

So Brue penned thirty-two instructions for Jean-Baptiste Collé, a fellow company man recently picked to become the commander at Fort Saint-Joseph. Two hundred miles upriver in a kingdom known as Galam, the fort was a small, squarish building ringed by buggy ditches and perpetually short on men and guns. Brue expected Collé to do crucial work there. Unlike the previous commander, who had stolen money and alienated locals, Collé was to "fulfill has duty like an honest man, serving the Company with faithfulness and zeal, keeping his employees happy . . . and satisfying all of the Nobles and merchants of the country."[37] This last point was key, as Brue saw Galam as essential to the Sénégal Company's designs on continental African trade, which were in turn essential to French designs throughout the New World.

Upon reaching Fort Saint-Joseph, Collé was to assemble the ministers of Tonca Niamé, king of Galam, the kingdom's *baqueris*, or noblemen, and African merchants of other nations who might be nearby. Addressing this diverse audience, Collé was to swear that "in the future trade will be conducted faithfully, with much friendship, gentleness, and loyalty." The French would respect tax agreements made with Galam's rulers, ensuring that "not even the smallest thing will be taken from them." Still, Brue wanted Collé to match public penitence with private persuasion. The mind of Tonca Niamé, he wrote, must be "treated carefully," instructing Collé to remind the African king that through the French "he will have his profit, whereas he will have nothing if he distresses us." It also never hurt to grease the wheels. Brue sent a locked chest with Collé, ordering him to give the key to Tonca Niamé's ambassador after receiving a promise that the king alone would be allowed to open it and receive his customary bribe.[38]

Other Africans got similar treatment. Merchants who came north to Fort Saint-Joseph from Guianca country, for example, were to be indulged. Above all else, Collé was never to "grab them by the beard, threaten or beat them." He was instead to offer friendship, reestablishing "not just the trade in Captives, but also that in gold, both of which will doubtless surpass anything that has been done until now." In the same spirit, Brue gifted a handsome rifle to the "master" of the village of Cainoura, a slave-trading hub on one of the Sénégal River's southern tributaries. The company likewise demanded that Collé maintain good ties with the rulers of gold-rich Bambouk and strategic Bundu, both of which stretched off to the south from Fort Saint-Joseph. These "two great men of the country," Brue wrote, "could render us good service." By contrast, the Muslim peoples north of the Sénégal River were to be kept at arm's length. "Never give them gunpowder, gold, or livestock," Brue warned, "lest they be used against us."[39]

So much diplomatic maneuvering, Brue explained, was rooted in a single harsh fact of West African politics: "When one is in a place where one is not the strongest, the Fox's bearing is . . . better than the Lion's." Located where the Sénégal River's existing commerce met France's outsized hopes for the interior, Galam was such a place. If Fort Saint-Joseph was to benefit the French, Collé had to tread lightly around indigenous power, cementing trade alliances while gathering information about the mysterious east. Indeed, after attending to diplomatic matters in Galam, Collé was to hire, cajole, or threaten some white employee into undertaking a voyage up the Sénégal, pushing past the falls of Félou "as far as he can go, in order to know the peoples who frequent it, the commerce that takes place . . . and where Timbuktu is."[40]

Brue, then, was searching for riches. But he was also building a bulwark. For running parallel to the Sénégal and emptying into the Atlantic two hundred miles to the south of Saint-Louis was the Gambia River, the centerpiece of British ambitions in West Africa. Unlike the Sénégal, the upper reaches of which became unnavigable during the dry months between November and July, the Gambia's deep channel allowed British ships deep into the continent year-round. The result was a steady westward flow of gold, ivory, and especially slaves. James Fort sat at the Gambia's mouth, and although the outpost suffered pirate attacks and naval assaults early in the eighteenth century, it continued to funnel cargoes of captive laborers to Britain's Caribbean and North American colonies. Brue guessed that "the Gambia River furnishes more than 2,000 slaves each year," a figure that matches modern estimates of 20,000 Africans exported via the Gambia by the British between 1711 and 1720.[41]

Although the Sénégal Company kept its own post, Albréda, across the river from James Fort, it could scarcely block the flood of British captives before it reached the sea. Fort Saint-Joseph's network of trade partners, however, might do so at the source. Where the corruption of earlier administrations had pushed African traders to "take the Gambia road instead of selling us their wares in Galam," Collé's gentle tone and the company's well-stocked warehouses would inspire merchants to skip the long voyage south. Indeed, Brue's goal was to "make the Negroes forget the way to Gambia, and to make the British lose all hope of stealing any commerce from our lands."[42] Even if the French paid less for slaves than the British did, Galam's convenience would make trading there cost-effective for African merchants. "All caravans will stop [at Fort Saint-Joseph]," one company official later proclaimed, "to trade for the same goods that they would otherwise be obliged to seek four hundred miles away at the risk of losing their slaves to disease, or of being pillaged by Negro governors and princes whose countries they cross."[43]

Although he trafficked in the minute details of West African politics, culture, and trade, Brue did so in the service of something bigger. To be sure, there was the Sénégal Company, whose investors (a group of merchants and ship owners headquartered in the Seine River town of Rouen) wanted returns.[44] But that company had been sanctioned by a French monarchy increasingly willing to experiment with novel ways of integrating its overseas possessions into a coherent system. Brue's drive to unite the slave-, gold-, and ivory-trading economy of the upper Sénégal River valley with French interests in Saint Louis was part of a broader trend aimed at turning local affairs toward Atlantic ends.

Not surprisingly, Brue celebrated in 1719 when he got word from Paris that

John Law had succeeded in unifying all of France's colonial companies. The Mississippi plan, he exulted, had created "the strongest and most powerful company in the world." It promised not only to enrich Law's shareholders but to ensure that the "neglect" suffered by French West Africa at the hands of the Sénégal Company would be "repaid with interest" via the Parisian boom. "Because we will never want for money," Brue wrote, new projects could be undertaken, including a full-scale exploration of the "kingdom of Timbuktu," an expedition to the source of the Niger River, and mining probes in Bambouk. Through these efforts, "the regular trade of Galam will triple," sending ever-larger shipments of captives and commodities downriver to Saint Louis, and from there to France's sugar islands and the fledgling plantations of Louisiana.[45]

Like John Law, however, Brue and the other Frenchmen on the Sénégal River found out how complicated integration really was. The piles of money Brue believed to be destined for Saint-Louis disappeared with the collapse of Law's system, and French diplomacy at Fort Saint-Joseph never quite lived up to expectations. Indeed, the Sénégal Company's instructions for commanders at Fort Saint-Joseph during the 1720s bore a striking resemblance to those Brue sent with Jean-Baptiste Collé in 1716. French hopes and West Africa's capacity to dash them were equally persistent.

In 1723, for example, as Jean Levens de la Rouquette prepared to head upriver, he got a stern reminder of the task ahead. Fort Saint-Joseph, the company directors told him, had been established "uniquely in order to penetrate deeper into the country, and to seize a greater share of its trade in gold, ivory, and other merchandise." His charge was to snap up the caravan trade that fanned out from the headwaters of the Niger, Gambia, and Sénégal Rivers, sending goods and captives toward the French Atlantic and picking up precious clues about Timbuktu.[46] But like Collé before him, Levens failed. By 1724 his letters to Saint-Louis read like deliberate attempts to bring high hopes down to base realities. "I suffer from a fever nearly every day, and am now built like a skeleton," he wrote, complaining that the lack of wine at Fort Saint-Joseph made his stomach "so weak that I often vomit what I eat." "If God grants me the grace to live until next year," he vowed, "I swear to you that I will not spend it in Galam."[47]

Although he thought mostly of his own malfunctioning gut, Levens expressed a widely shared sense of why Sénégal did not work. From Galam to the river's mouth, the French were subject to deadly illnesses and uncertain navigation. In 1722 the company surgeon possessed "neither medicine nor so much as a lancet or razor" to care for the scores of sick and dying—both

Frenchmen and slaves awaiting transport—who languished inside Fort Saint-Joseph. After detailing his own bad health late in 1724, Levens revealed that he had sent the *Fidele* downriver from Fort Saint-Joseph with just 29 slaves on board, even though the same vessel had shipped as many as 120 slaves on previous voyages. He had been waiting for a "good cargo rumored to be on its way" from Bambara country, but the dwindling flow of the Sénégal forced his hand: early in the dry season a few years earlier, the crew of the *Curieuse* had been forced to "put its slaves in the water to push" for several miles near the fort, a mistake Levens did not want to repeat.[48] Although officials in Saint-Louis styled Galam the "most precious part" of Sénégal, a hostile environment ensured that Fort Saint-Joseph's existence remained tenuous.[49]

More troubling, however, were the tough-minded tactics of the fort's neighbors. African monarchs and merchants alike simply outmuscled their European guests, subordinating French designs to their own. For his part, Julien du Bellay knew there was little he could do about it. Writing to his bosses in France from Saint-Louis, du Bellay touted his "singular attention" to maintaining good relations with rulers along the Sénégal, swearing that any company employee who jeopardized relations would "feel the pain." He later confessed, however, that he could not make the king of Galam pay his debts to the company without provoking "the interruption of all commerce on the river."[50]

It was no idle threat, and the king of Galam was not alone in making it. In 1722 a man named Diagou, described as the "absolute master of all the merchants," began charging higher prices for slaves at Fort Saint-Joseph as the dry season set in. When the French balked, Diagou threatened to pull his captives from the market altogether. After huddling with his officers, the fort's commander caved in to the African's demand for fear of missing his last chance to float slaves downriver or of being obliged to "abandon the country." Diagou and several other local kings, the commander confessed, "were really starting to bother me," arriving unannounced and demanding food, drink, and presents. African kings "tyrannize me every day," the Frenchman let slip, inadvertently revealing his place in Galam's order of things.[51]

But even as they manipulated prices and intimidated officials at Fort Saint-Joseph, the Africans of the upper Sénégal Valley witnessed dramatic changes caused directly by France's presence. Some they could hear. In Galam, trade and diplomacy (as well as arguments, storytelling, and order-giving) took place in a mixture of French and Wolof that served as a *lingua franca* among Africans.[52]

Others they could see. The acacia forests north of the river grew crowded during the 1720s. Gangs of slaves owned by Islamic traders from the Sahara extracted the gum and hauled it to markets along the river, chewing balls of the resin to sustain themselves on the journey. The French had taken pains to reorient this lucrative commerce toward the Sénégal. In 1717 Brue signed a treaty with Alichandora, the Muslim ruler of Trarza in modern Mauritania, giving the French a monopoly over the gum trade. Alichandora paid a high price for the alliance. By 1720 his Islamic neighbors to the north, the Ulad Dellim, had driven him from power, eager to pursue their own designs on West Africa. Brue and his successors, however, kept pressing. They sent ships to patrol Trarza's Atlantic coast for interloping British and Dutch traders while ensuring supplies of iron and dyed cloth at French posts along the river, drawing desert-based gum merchants south. One Muslim leader arrived at Saint-Louis in 1720 with gifts of gold, petitioning the French to trade at his Saharan outpost, where he kept a buried stock of the previous year's gum as well as a recent bumper crop.[53]

Agriculture too fell under French influence. Put simply, the slave trade demanded a great deal of food. Captives had to be fed on the trip from Galam to the coast (and kept alive while awaiting transport to the Americas at Saint-Louis) if the Sénégal Company or their African suppliers were to turn a profit. This brutal calculus led to the expansion of slaveholding on the Sénégal River. Michel Jajolet de la Courbe, a commander at Saint-Louis during the 1680s, encountered one slaveholder in a millet field who, as six drums pounded out time, waved a sword and "encouraged his people in their work." Numbering about sixty, the naked slaves weeded and broke up clods with iron hoes, producing grain that would nourish those headed for the Atlantic. This sort of slave-based agriculture grew as the slave trade did, reshaping the market for labor as it expanded. Warriors along the river, for instance, grew to favor slaves from the distant Gambia or Niger rivers for their millet farms. Captives taken more locally (who, according to one observer, "were too near the confines of their own country to let any opportunity of recovering their liberty escape them") ended up on French ships bound for the Caribbean.[54] Although slaves in Sénégal experienced a wider range of conditions than their counterparts on Caribbean plantations, their bondage was likewise a local manifestation of France's Atlantic economy.

Rickety though it was, Fort Saint-Joseph helped shape the political landscape of the upper Sénégal as well. In the summer of 1724, for instance, Africans near Galam found themselves on edge. Five thousand Muslim warriors led by the sultan of Morocco had spent the past two years stomping through their lands, interrupting gum harvests and intervening in succession disputes in an effort to horn in on French commerce. In the chaos, Samba Gelaajo Jeggi, a member of the royal family of Futa Toro, a kingdom just to the west of Galam along the river's southern bank, parlayed divisions among the Moroccans into an agreement that netted him the throne. Back in 1719, the commander at Fort Saint-Joseph had given Samba asylum during a moment of civil war, reasoning that "his father had always numbered among our friends." Once in power, the ruler of Futa Toro seemed keen to repay the French.[55] Samba announced that the Moroccans "would no longer visit his country," promising to deliver one hundred slaves to Saint-Louis in exchange for powder and shot for the protection of French riverboats. And protect he did, fighting off Muslims who attacked a company shallop in July 1725 and warning the French of a Moroccan ambush the next year. He also begged for a French fort in his kingdom, showing the commander of Fort Saint-Joseph "marks of friendship on every occasion."[56]

To be sure, Samba had an agenda. Wedged between Saint-Louis and Fort Saint-Joseph, Futa Toro's alliance with the French seemed like a natural fit. Samba also faced a Moroccan threat, with many of his own noblemen siding with the northern Muslims to destroy his regime from the inside. In short, he used the French for his own ends, skillfully building relations that allowed him to fend off rivals in Futa Toro well into the 1730s.[57] But perhaps more to the point, Samba's choices funneled him down channels carved out in large part by the multigenerational flow of French power in the Sénégal River valley. He was not unique. Whether millet farmers, gum merchants, or gold traders, Africans across Senegambia fashioned and refashioned their lives while taking the measure of France's Atlantic system—a system that was itself groping to adjust to their shifting behavior.

Some Africans, of course, had their lives fashioned and refashioned against their will. Indeed, for all of the maddening inefficiency and local peculiarity that plagued Fort Saint-Joseph, Senegambians knew well that the sight of a Frenchman could signal the beginning of a terrible journey. Over 13,000 slaves sailed into the Atlantic from France's West African ports during the 1720s alone—including the 290 adults and 25 children who stepped aboard the *Pontchartrain* on September 4, 1722.[58] They had been captured in the interior, sold or gifted to the French in Galam, and transported (probably via Saint-Louis) to Gorée, a fortified island two hundred miles to the south.

Signs of the captives' hard times appeared in the ship's manifest, which recorded every slave by name along with their "defects." Jasmin, 26, and Kiacou, 22, caught the captain's attention for having an eye gouged out. Nolo, 24, was one of nine men with "horse balls," the distended testicles that accompanied elephantitis, a devastating parasitic disease spread by West African mosquitos. Twelve-year-old Cristine had a less obvious defect: she was a Christian.[59] Together in the *Pontchartrain*'s squalid hull, they sailed toward the port of Léogane in Saint-Domingue, where a short life of hard labor awaited.

Jasmin, Kiacou, Nolo, and Cristine would have been hard-pressed indeed to label the French Empire in West Africa a failure—except, no doubt, in a moral sense. But the description persisted, and not without reason. African kings and merchants continued to ride roughshod over French designs, reducing whatever luckless officer Brue sent upriver to a diseased mass of excuses. The British continued to funnel much of the slave trade toward the Gambia, the gold fields of Bambouk remained unexploited, and Timbuktu was as mysterious as ever. In the 1790s the geographer Sylvain-Meinrad-Xavier de Golbéry would complain bitterly that "we have possessed the Sénégal more than a century; this stream receives near Galam, the river of Felema, which forms the western limits of the country of Bambouk, and yet notwithstanding these advantages, we possess very few certain facts relating to this curious and interesting country."[60] And yet for much of the eighteenth century, for every Jean Levens de la Rouquette bemoaning his impotence from places like Fort Saint-Joseph, there were dozens of African gum merchants, slave traders, and regional lords who scrambled to adapt to the outcomes generated by power wielded from places like Fort Saint-Joseph by men like Jean Levens de la Rouquette.

Likewise, the success or failure of Law's system in France was very much in the eye of the beholder. In the wake of its collapse, no one would have argued publicly that the Mississippi Company had met its sky-high expectations—although peasants liberated from old debts and profit-taking noblemen like the prince de Conti must have chuckled to themselves as swindled investors cursed Law's name. The Scot did, however, cast a long shadow over French political culture. Oppositional forces associated with the parlements seized on the Mississippi fiasco to stitch financial reform into a comprehensive narrative of monarchical tyranny, making any kingly attempt to restructure credit markets a sign of still more nefarious intentions. Now gun-shy, the regent and Louis XV abandoned these ambitions, retreating to a *status quo ante*—Law dominated by the power-brokering clans of financiers who had funded the monarchy and serviced its debts before 1715.

No less momentously, Law's system generated a deep public tension between the king and his ordinary subjects—notably the people of Paris.

Spurred by the growing market in illicit pamphlets, they argued over the monarchy's role in their economic and political lives with fresh urgency, passing hard-to-ignore judgments on Louis's power and the capacity of currencies to express it. With his paper instruments, Law had tried to colonize such people, worming the imperatives of Versailles into their workaday lives. Ironically, the system's crash did the trick better (if differently) than he hoped, planting a new image of the monarch on Parisian paper and in Parisian heads for years to come.[61]

Edging away from success and failure in the age of Law, we might instead map out the gravitational effects that surrounded each node of French power. These uneven, multidirectional, and expansive forces did not simply respond to the dictates of men like Law. Rather, they emanated from the mass of insecurity and anxiety that was the French monarchy. Desperate for subjects and allies, its interventions triggered far-reaching changes: provincials flooded the streets of Paris, West African merchants trudged toward Fort Saint-Joseph, the French went briefly paper-crazy, and millet farmers along the Sénégal responded to French demand with an extra measure of brutality. From the Seine to the Sénégal, the French Empire was not influential in spite of its weakness. It was influential because of it.

If nothing else, then, John Law was exceptionally good at thinking both big and small: big, in his visionary coupling of metropolitan France to its Atlantic empire; small, in his attention to the economic routines and symbolic markets that promised to knit the king and his people together. But his approach was hardly original. Indeed, France and its overseas empire had been integrated long before Law's day, entangled in a history of state building that yoked France to the Atlantic. And small means—the introduction of new currencies, whether paper, weapons, or captives—had long been the mechanisms by which that integration was to take place. In the end, Law was less creator than creature, less a source of new energies than a subject of old ones. True, he founded New Orleans and pumped a little capital into imperial settlements elsewhere. But in reality Law had leapt without looking into a vast, ancient ocean whose tides and currents were attuned to the choppy, discordant rhythms of imperial power and indigenous engagement.

Notes

1. Alexis de Tocqueville, "Some Ideas about What Prevents the French from Having Good Colonies," in Alexis de Tocqueville, *Writings on Empire and Slavery*, ed. and trans. Jennifer Pitts (Baltimore, 2001), 1; Edward Everett, *Orations and Speeches on Various Occasions* (Boston, 1870), 3:205; Victor Hugo, *Le Rhin* (Paris, 1842), 2:280; on Parkman, see

W. J. Eccles, "The History of New France according to Francis Parkman," *William and Mary Quarterly*, 3rd ser., 18 (April 1961): 163–75. For more recent historiography on French imperialism, see Christopher Hodson and Brett Rushforth, "Absolutely Atlantic: Colonialism and the Early Modern French State in Recent Historiography," *History Compass* 7 (2009): 1–17.

2. James Pritchard, *In Search of Empire: The French in the Americas, 1670–1730* (New York, 2004).

3. Note here the common (to my generation, anyway, which loved *The Godfather*) usage of "Fredo" to mean one who is a screw-up or failure. For newer and more disturbing definitions, consult *www.urbandictionary.com* at your own peril.

4. On definitions of empire, see Eric Hinderaker, *Elusive Empires: Constructing Colonialism in the Ohio Valley, 1673–1800* (New York, 1997), xi–xii; Bernard Bailyn, *Atlantic History: Concepts and Contours* (Cambridge, MA, 2005), 61; Nicholas Canny, "Writing Atlantic History; or, Reconfiguring the History of Colonial British America," *Journal of American History* 86, no. 3 (December 1999): 1107. On indigenous agency and empire, see Richard White, *The Middle Ground: Indians, Empires, and Republics in the Great Lakes Region, 1650–1815* (New York, 1991); Kathleen Duval, *The Native Ground: Indians and Colonists in the Heart of the Continent* (Philadelphia: University of Pennsylvania Press, 2004); Juliana Barr, "Geographies of Power: Mapping Indian Borders in the 'Borderlands' of the Early Southwest," *William and Mary Quarterly* 68, no. 1 (January 2011): 5–46.

5. See Armitage, *The Ideological Origins of the British Empire* (New York, 2000).

6. See, for instance, Joshua Piker, "Lying Together: The Imperial Implications of Cross-Cultural Untruths," *American Historical Review* 116, no. 4 (October 2011): 964–86. Piker's fine microhistorical account of South Carolina governor James Glen's relationship with the supposedly powerful Creek headman Acorn Whistler suggests that instead of wrangling over whether Indians or imperialists held power, we might recognize that in most colonial contexts, neither did.

7. On the French Caribbean economy, see Pritchard, *In Search of Empire*; Jean Tarrade, *Le commerce colonial de la France à la fin de l'Ancien Régime: L'évolution du régime de l'exclusif de 1763 à 1789*, 2 vols. (Paris, 1972); John Garrigus, *Before Haiti: Race and Citizenship in French Saint-Domingue* (New York, 2006).

8. See Brendan McConville, *The King's Three Faces: The Rise and Fall of Royal America, 1688–1776* (Chapel Hill, NC, 2006), 223–26; Timothy Shannon, *Indians and Colonists at the Crossroads of Empire: The Albany Congress of 1754* (Ithaca, NY, 2000), 65–68.

9. Perhaps the best recent statement to this effect is Robert Michael Morrissey, *Empire by Collaboration: Indians, Colonists, and Governments in Colonial Illinois Country* (Philadelphia, 2015), 5.

10. Francis Parkman, *Montcalm and Wolfe: France and England in North America* (Boston, 1922), 1:38.

11. Edmond-François Barbier, *Chronique de la régence et du régne de Louis XV* (Paris, 1857), 1:66.

12. Thomas Kaiser, "Money, Despotism, and Public Opinion in Early Eighteenth-Century France: John Law and the Debate on Royal Credit," *Journal of Modern History* 63, no. 1 (March 1991): 20.

13. Antoin E. Murphy, *John Law: Economic Theorist and Policy-Maker* (New York, 1997), 128.

14. See Colin Jones, *The Great Nation: France from Louis XV to Napoleon* (London, 2003), 62–65.

15. Murphy, *John Law*, 205.

16. M. G. Brunet, ed., *Correspondance complète de Madame Duchesse d'Orléans* (Paris, 1857): 2:191–92.

17. Jones, *The Great Nation*, 66.

18. Murphy, *John Law*, 205.

19. Jones, *The Great Nation*, 66.

20. Murphy, *John Law*, 206.

21. Kaiser, "Money, Despotism, and Public Opinion," 22.

22. Charles Pinot Duclos, *Secret Memoirs of the Regency*, trans. E. Jules Meras (New York, 1910), 27. On *The Harlequin Share Trader* (*Arlequyn actionist*), itself part of a larger 1720 collection of Dutch writings and images on the Law system entitled *The Great Mirror of Folly* (*Het groote tafereel der dwaasheid*), see William N. Goetzmann, Catherine Labio, K. Geert Rouwenhorst, and Timothy G. Young, eds., *The Great Mirror of Folly: Finance, Culture, and the Crash of 1720* (New Haven, CT, 2013). For a literary interpretation of the Law moment, see Julia V. Douthwaite, "How Bad Economic Memories Are Made: John Law's System in *Les Lettres Persanes, Manon Lescaut*, and 'The Great Mirror of Folly,'" *L'Esprit Créateur* 55, no. 3 (Fall 2015): 43–58.

23. Jones, *The Great Nation*, 69.

24. See Jennifer Spear, *Race, Sex, and Social Order in Early New Orleans* (Baltimore, 2009), 44.

25. Jones, *The Great Nation*, 70.

26. Barbier, *Chronique de la régence*, 1:75.

27. Ibid., 1:70–71, 158. On the French economic boom after the downfall of Law's system, see James B. Collins, *The State in Early Modern France* (New York, 2009), 242.

28. Robert M. Schwartz, *Policing the Poor in Eighteenth-Century France* (Chapel Hill, NC, 1988), 31–32.

29. Pierre-François-Xavier de Charlevoix, quoted in Shannon Lee Dawdy, *Building the Devil's Empire: French Colonial New Orleans* (Chicago, 2008), 66.

30. Ibid., 13.

31. See, for instance, Peter Burke, *The Fabrication of Louis XIV* (New Haven, CT, 1992).

32. Prior to the advent of Law's system, paper currencies were used only by a tiny community of wealthy financiers. See Robert Minton, *John Law: The Father of Paper Money* (New York, 1975), 13.

33. Kaiser, "Money, Despotism, and Public Opinion," 23.

34. Frederick Cooper, "Provincializing France," in Ann Laura Stoler, Carole McGranahan, and Peter Perdue, eds., *Imperial Formations* (Santa Fe, 2007), 354.

35. "Instructions pour le sieur Levance, directeur et commandant pour la Compagnie des Indes au Fort Saint-Joseph," October 24, 1723, ANOM, AC, série C6, vol. 7, n.p. On the Bambouk gold fields, see Philip Curtin, *Economic Change in Precolonial Africa: Senegambia in the Era of the Slave Trade* (Madison, WI, 1975), 198–202.

36. See Curtin, *Economic Change in Precolonial Africa*, 215–16.

37. André Brue, "Instruction pour Mr. Jean-Baptiste Collé, directeur et commandant du Fort Saint-Joseph," December 9, 1716, ANOM, AC, série C6, vol. 5, n.p.

38. Ibid.

39. Ibid.

40. Ibid.

41. "Instructions pour le sieur Levance, directeur et commandant pour la Compagnie des Indes au Fort Saint-Joseph," October 24, 1723, ANOM, AC, série C6, vol. 7, n.p.; Boubacar Barry, *Senegambia and the Atlantic Slave Trade* (New York, 1998), 62–63.

42. Brue to Violane, April 30, 1720, ANOM, AC, série C6, vol. 6, n.p.

43. "Instructions pour le sieur Levance."

44. On the history of the Sénégal Company, see André Delcourt, *La France et les établissements français au Sénégal entre 1713 et 1763* (Paris, 1952), 63.

45. Brue to Violane, April 30, 1720. For explicit instructions to send captives from Galam to Louisiana, see "Instructions pour le Sr. Nicolas Despres de St. Robert, directeur general a la concession du Sénégal," 1720, ANOM, AC, C6, vol. 6, n.d.

46. "Instructions pour le sieur Levance.

47. Levens to du Bellay, October 22, 1724, ANOM, AC, série C6, vol. 8, n.p.

48. Charpentier to Saint-Robert, October 12, 1722, ANOM, AC, série C6, vol. 7, n.p.; Violane to Saint-Robert, n.d., ANOM, AC, série C6, vol. 6, n.p.

49. Du Bellay to Directeurs de la Compagnie, May 3, 1722, ANOM, AC, série C6, vol. 7, n.p.

50. Ibid.

51. Charpentier to Saint-Robert, October 12, 1722, ANOM, AC, série C6, vol. 7, n.p.

52. James F. Searing, *West African Slavery and Atlantic Commerce: The Senegal River Valley, 1700–1860* (New York, 1993), 60.

53. Saint-Robert to Compagnie du Sénégal, August 27, 1720, ANOM, AC, série C6, vol. 6, n.p. See also Delcourt, *La France*, 149.

54. Searing, *West African Slavery and Atlantic Commerce*, 54–56.

55. Saint-Robert to Directors, May 4, 1720, ANOM, AC, série C6, vol. 6, n.p.

56. Oumar Kane, "Les Maures et le Futa-Toro au XVIIIe siècle," *Cahiers d'Etudes Africaines* 14, no. 54 (1974): 245–46.

57. Barry, *Senegambia and the Atlantic Slave Trade*, 90–91.

58. Ibid., 63.

59. "Facture des captifs et captives," ANOM, AC, série C6, vol. 7, n.p.

60. Sylvain-Meinrad-Xavier de Golbéry, *Travels in Africa, performed during the years 1785, 1786, and 1787* (London, 1803), 317.

61. See Jones, *The Great Nation*, 71–73.

John Almon's Web

Networks of Print, Politics, and Place in Revolutionary London, 1760–1780

Michael Guenther

Genuinely democratic revolutions—of the kind that originate from the "bottom-up"—pose something of an interpretive challenge to historians. How do we explain the fact that ordinary people, in certain times and places, are capable of generating such extraordinary transformations, breaking the rhythms of everyday life to create moments of radical change? Typically historians have tended to explore why this occurs, searching for the shared ideas, interests, or grievances that can explain why people became so profoundly alienated from the status quo. For historians of early America, telling the story of how colonists got from 1763 to 1776 (and ultimately to 1787) involves explaining why the bulk of colonists came suddenly to reject the shared fabric of British imperialism, nationalism, and monarchical ties that had knitted together the Anglo-American world so successfully in the previous decades. But it is also crucial for historians to explore how such movements become possible. How is it that, in certain contexts, men and women have been able to translate their shared ideas or grievances into the kind of coordinated action that can alter the course of history? After all, revolutions depend as much upon new forms of mobilization and collective action as they do on new sources of disaffection or dissent. So if we want to understand the path that led from a dispute over imperial governance to a genuine revolution, we need to appreciate how contemporaries developed new forms of political engagement, new networks of political cooperation, and new capacities for coordinated action in the decades leading up to 1776.[1] And we might do well to examine these currents of politicization at the center as well as the periphery of empire.

This essay, in particular, uses the rich documentary record of London to begin tracing out such dynamics by focusing on the extensive networks of John Almon, an English printer and political operative, whose Piccadilly bookshop served as a critical locus of radical ideas and politics in the era of the American Revolution.[2] By reconstructing his tangible world of print shops and distribution routes, political clubs and coffeehouses, informants and intelligence networks, I aim to shed light on the broader cast of characters and spaces that defined the contours of popular politics in places like London as well as Boston or Philadelphia during this transformative era. Although Almon's name may be familiar to some historians of the period—given his prominent role in opposition politics, particularly the Wilkesite movement—I use his extant correspondence and papers to trace out the webs of intellectual, commercial, and political networking that allowed him to become such an effective operative and, more important, helped expand the capacities for radical political action among disaffected groups on both sides of the Atlantic.[3]

By focusing on Almon's wide-ranging activities, we can begin to appreciate the considerable work, skill, and relationship building that drove the expanding political culture of this period. In ways that might surprise us, success in both publishing and politics depended on mobilizing a vast array of "allies" or collaborators, ranging from porters to postal carriers, lawyers to tavern owners, newspapermen to aldermen. To immerse oneself in Almon's day-to-day routines, then, is to get an important glimpse into the way political life operated like a kind of ecosystem, a dense and interconnected web of human relationships bound together by the flows of information, cooperation, and exchange. As a conceptual metaphor, this "ecological" view of political life has the benefit of drawing attention to the wide range of people, places, and interactions that shaped the political landscape of London, not least by expanding the boundaries of what ordinary people could accomplish through political engagement and mobilization.

Such an approach charts out key sites and networks of everyday political engagement that fall outside of the twin focal points of scholars studying popular politics during this period. There has been considerable work, on the one hand, analyzing the emerging "public sphere" of the eighteenth century, which empowered ordinary citizens to take a more active role in scrutinizing and debating political matters through the expanding realm of print.[4] On the other hand, scholars have explored the political activism of "crowds" and public demonstrations, revealing how these visible forms of politics out-of-doors gave voice to large segments of Georgian society who could not vote or participate in the formal arenas of politics.[5] As a result, we know a lot about the political role ordinary people played as either *spectators* or as *spectacle*. But this essay uses Almon's political and publishing networks to shed light on the ways in which diverse groups contributed to the day-to-day operations of politics, not as consumers of information, or as members of a crowd, but as collaborative participants whose skill, connections, and ideas were needed on a daily basis to make the political system function. Even in the elite world of opposition politics, where ministers, MPs, and aristocrats competed in the high stakes and often cynical game for the reins of power, Almon's activities reveal the significant role that ordinary people had in shaping the political strategies and conversations of the moment. It was from such quarters, ironically enough, that new forms of British radicalism would emerge during the era of the American Revolution, as Almon and his associates fed off of colonial conversations about natural rights, equality, consent, and popular sovereignty to articulate new demands for fundamental reforms of the parliamentary system at home.[6] Revolutionary politics spanned the empire, creating a new landscape of political possibilities and shared interests connecting places like London, Dublin, Charleston, or Philadelphia. As a kind of "micro-history," then, Almon's web is a good place to begin examining this much larger story of how people, places, and ideas converged to create the capacities for revolutionary change.

The Printer's Web: Social Networks and Political Intelligence

Orphaned as a young child, and having received only a modest education and apprenticeship in Liverpool, John Almon had managed to transform himself by the age of twenty-eight into a prominent bookseller, publisher, and key player in the high-flying game of national politics.[7] By the summer of 1765, as the ministry in power fell from office, newspapers were already speculating on Almon's possible role within the new administration, and even the king, it was whispered, closely followed Almon's activities "out-of-doors."[8] For nearly two decades (1763–80), Almon's bookshop and publishing business were at the heart of the political campaigns to topple the unpopular ministries of Lord Bute and his successors, whom the opposition Whigs (led by figures such as John Wilkes, William Pitt, Lord Temple, or Lord Rockingham) believed were attempting to subvert England's constitutional system.[9] In an age when the "power of the press" was making itself felt throughout society, an effective publisher like John Almon could serve as an indispensable ally in the political battles being waged.

It would be a mistake, however, to assume that Almon's role in the political system, or his activities as a political publisher, were straightforward or predetermined. Most eighteenth-century printers, in fact, had carefully avoided being closely associated with particular factions or parties because it could be disastrous for their business. Far from embracing an active political role, as historians have shown, printers often wrapped themselves in the mantle of being "mere mechanics," workmen who simply produced a product without taking an interest in the content.[10] Almon, by contrast, was part of a rising generation of printers who charted a new career path in the 1760s and 1770s by consciously fusing party politics and the world of publishing. As his obituary in the *Gentleman's Magazine* later explained: "This was at the period when 'Wilkes and Liberty' was the predominant cry, [and] political discussion almost exclusively engrossed every man's attention; and publications were circulated, which printers and booksellers of established reputation would not venture to print or vend. The matchless intrepidity of Mr. Almon rendered him of all men the fittest to be thus employed."[11] Charting out this new landscape of commercial and political possibilities certainly required an "intrepid" sense of business savvy, political acumen, and extensive connections that came to define this new class of "political publishers," as the obituary put it. So rather than taking these dynamics as a given, Almon's remarkable career offers historians a chance to examine anew how everyday decisions and activities could forge new relationships in the realms of print, politics, and popular engagement.[12] In this section, I focus particularly on the pivotal role of social networks in explaining Almon's place within the evolving ecosystem of British politics.

We should begin with the concept of "intelligence" and its role in the world of eighteenth-century politics.[13] As we shall see, Almon literally made it his business to have one of the largest and most effective intelligence networks of the day, allowing him to access all kinds of political information that fed his newspapers, pamphlets, and working relationships with politicians in and out of office. As one observer declared, "Mr. Almon had information in streams from all quarters . . . at home and abroad, [which] was early, interesting, and authentic."[14] Indeed, contemporaries were consistently struck by his ability to report news or documents that no one else knew about. When the colonists sent the "Olive Branch Petition" to the king in 1775, Almon was distributing copies to the opposition almost before it had even made its way to the ministry, while on another occasion, the king was astonished to find that Almon had acquired and distributed his personal manuscript notes on army levels in Ireland.[15] Almon's reputation had become so legendary that when the Duke of Grafton was fielding questions in the House of Lords about the coercive policy in America in 1775 and was asked for specifics about the situation on the ground in the colonies, "the Duke replied that he did not know, but that those who wanted such information might probably obtain it by applying to Mr. Almon."[16] Beneath the sarcasm was a genuine recognition that Almon had become a chief broker of political intelligence in an age when such information served as a coveted form of political capital.

But how did an ordinary publisher like Almon become so central to this system? What activities and connections set him apart from other political operatives eager to trade in such vital intelligence? After all, it is not entirely clear why a "base-born bookseller" (as one sneering observer described Almon) would have more access to sensitive information than well-connected politicians like Temple, Pitt, or Rockingham.[17] We can begin to make sense of this puzzle, I would argue, by focusing on Almon's flourishing bookshop in London, where his day-to-day work reveals the kinds of robust networking needed to succeed in the realms of print, politics, and information gathering.[18] His well-preserved records offer a tantalizing glimpse into the complex web of people and relationships needed to mobilize information, ideas, texts, and political movements.[19]

Almon's bookshop, located in the genteel neighborhood of St. James, Westminster, was a place that catered to relationships as much as to consumption. Nestled among the fashionable residences of Whig grandees, politicians, and courtiers, Almon's shop served as a bustling haunt for opposition members who could rub shoulders while exchanging the latest gossip and political prints. The theme of "exchange" is important here. Some individuals came to Almon's shop, for example, not to buy texts but to solicit his services as a publisher, hoping to have their work printed as a pamphlet or inserted in a newspaper or periodical. As a result, Almon often assumed the responsibility of editing and financing a work, hiring a particular shop to print it, and then overseeing its distribution in bookstores.[20] Even customers who were simply looking to purchase a book were tapping into broader business networks that Almon had developed with printers and wholesalers throughout the city. In fact, Almon was able to assemble an impressive array of books, pamphlets, newspapers, magazines, and stationery supplies in his store—a stock valued at over £1,000—precisely because he had developed a dense web of working relationships with these vendors to acquire a mix of the most desirable titles.[21] Almon even offered to track down any book or magazine that his customers desired, training a group of shop assistants and porters who scoured London and Westminster to find these titles for his clients. As a result, Almon's work as a book dealer was more akin to being a personal *agent*—helping clients navigate the complex landscape of print—rather than a salesman conducting isolated transactions. Some contemporaries also relied upon Almon to handle their correspondence in London, having incoming mail directed to his shop or requesting to send items through his network of private couriers so as to avoid the postal system with its tendency to pry into sensitive material.[22]

It is crucial, in fact, to understand how the fortunes of Almon's publishing business hinged on his ability to mobilize these working relationships among customers so as to circulate texts and information more effectively. Because so much of the political class spent time away from London, Almon developed a set of robust partnerships with regional book dealers in Bath, Oxford, Cambridge, Tunbridge Wells, Salisbury, Winchester, Southampton, Norwich, and York who could help deliver printed material to clients.[23] Almon also created a complex network of private carriers to support his growing mail-order business, shielding his activities from the administration, which routinely directed its postmasters to inspect and copy sensitive correspondence from figures like Almon who they felt posed a threat to the government.[24] Yet even his political opponents had to admire the thriving distribution network Almon fashioned over time. "Almon has general orders from a great number of Members of Parliament to send them whatever comes out in the recess," the ministerial writer William Knox confessed. "He is an excellent fellow at circulating a work, and understands all the mystery of raising its character, and exciting purchasers."[25] The same dynamics played out overseas, where Almon spent a considerable amount of time and energy developing a network of colonial contacts, who rightly viewed Almon as a crucial conduit of political texts and news from London.[26] The Philadelphian Thomas Bradford, requested that Almon send the latest newspapers, the Parliamentary Debates, and "all other publications interesting to Americans." In return, he noted, "you may depend on my giving you from time to time, the best intelligence the country affords."[27]

Almon's surviving correspondence reveals how much these working relationships tended to revolve around the exchange of news and intelligence alongside orders for printed works. "You are very good in writing," the Rochester MP John Calcraft confessed. "You cannot do it too often, nor oblige me more." He was particularly grateful for the steady stream of news about the dealings of Parliament, the court, and the city, emphasizing his "many thanks to you for your correct and constant intelligence." Almost every letter asked for more: "Pray tell me, in confidence, what did Lord Temple's visits to St. James mean?" or "Write me all about the Remonstrances tonight," or "Pray send me the Report of the Lords of Trade . . . does Lord Hillsborough resign?"[28] For his part Calcraft reciprocated by sharing his intelligence gathered from Lord Shelburne's "intimates" or fresh news he obtained about changes in ministerial posts. Almon's surviving records, in fact, are filled with letters from contemporaries revealing the latest news on everything from government policy to naval intelligence to diplomatic negotiations that flowed next to orders for print.[29]

By diligently cultivating this extensive web of client-correspondents, Almon carved out an enviable position as one of the chief brokers of political intelligence in the British Isles and throughout the empire. Other politicians might be well connected within certain circles or within their local communities, but Almon's reach crossed many social and geographic boundaries.[30] His work depended upon cultivating a set of collaborative relationships with everyone from porters to lawyers, peddlers to MPs. It is telling, in this regard, that some people had trouble pinning down Almon's social identity, mistakenly presuming that he was Irish, for example, because he possessed such detailed intelligence about Irish politics. It was easier to imagine that this news came from deep family or social ties rather than from a network of carefully fostered contacts in Dublin.[31] A similar theme can be found in Lord Grafton's quip (mentioned earlier) about how members of Parliament should consult Almon, rather than the ministry, if they wanted to know about the current state of affairs in America. Many were no doubt bemused by the fact that this London bookseller managed to have a foothold in so many different spheres of society—a close confidant of aristocrats, tradesmen, politicians, and merchants throughout the empire.

Nowhere did this savvy networking come through more clearly than in Almon's bold campaign to systematically report the proceedings of Parliament. Accurate information about these debates was highly coveted and could play an important role in political mobilization out-of-doors. Yet printers were legally barred from publishing the speeches or votes of either House.[32] Determined to overcome these obstacles, Almon assembled a network of paid associates who memorized key points of speeches from the galleries, which were then corrected and enlarged by sympathetic MPs, who helped Almon reconstruct the day's debate in full. Finally, Almon put together a coalition of fellow publishers, lawyers, and city officials who teamed up to successfully block Parliament's ability to punish offending printers within London—effectively throwing open the doors to press coverage of its proceedings.[33] Meeting at houses throughout Westminster, Almon's team reconstructed not only the main speeches but also the "divisions" or votes of the House on important issues. "The expense" of this operation, Almon later admitted, "was more than the gain" in terms of additional revenues to his newspapers.[34] But the political dividends were quite large as the opposition movement learned to exploit these daily-published reports to shape popular sentiment out-of-doors. Almon even experimented with publishing cheap broadsides that identified where each MP stood on key votes concerning "the Rights and Liberties of the People," a kind of campaign flyer that functioned to draw sharper lines between the parties while at the same time diminishing the gap between politics in and out-of-doors.[35] There was nothing straightforward or simple, then, about the way political speeches or votes moved into the *public* realm. It took a surprisingly wide cast of characters, each bringing their own skills and agendas, in order to connect the high politics of Westminster to the growing worlds of print and popular engagement.

Thus the contributions of a political publisher ultimately rested upon the breadth and diversity of their working relationships. It is telling, in this regard, that one of Almon's principal successors in this field was his former porter, John Stockdale, a man who had no formal training in the printer's craft but instead had learned from Almon the art of networking and the importance of cultivating well-placed associates throughout the social and political landscape. Ideas and texts clearly mattered to men like Almon and Stockdale. But they also understood the extensive work (and networks) needed to make such material both accessible and politically germane.

The Politics of Place and the Geography of Opposition

Reconstructing the social mechanics of Almon's publishing business brings another set of important issues into focus involving the spatial dimensions of eighteenth-century politics. If one traces out Almon's web of activities or associates, it becomes clear that his interests tended to concentrate in very specific parts of London—particular coffeehouses, taverns, and coaching inns—that were central to the cultural landscape of the opposition. Contemporaries, in fact, were quick to recognize these spatial patterns, describing how certain cultural venues fostered distinct kinds of activities, relationships, and identities.[36] In this section, I survey the political geography of the opposition movement in the 1760s and 1770s, examining how particular sites allowed groups to coordinate their campaigns more effectively and to mobilize broader support out-of-doors. I am also interested in exploring how this political geography intersected with the geography of print. What roles, for instance, did printed materials play in such settings? Did their use, or access, change notably across different venues? And conversely, how did these sites provide more information, contacts, or opportunities to those engaged in the field of political publishing?[37] By reconstructing these spatial patterns, and the way Almon navigated them, we can develop a better understanding of how the dynamics of place shaped the capacities of ordinary people to engage in new forms of collective action and collective imagination during this revolutionary age.

Eighteenth-century printers were keenly aware of the role that geography could play in their professional lives. In addition to seeking out locations with easy access to supplies, supplemental services (such as bookbinders or engravers), and a steady clientele, printers were mindful that jurisdictional boundaries could prove decisive when libel suits or other prosecutions invariably occurred.[38] Almon's decision to settle in the Liberty of Westminster, as opposed to the City of London, placed his operation in a political environment where Crown prosecutors, judges, and juries were far more likely to convict in matters of libel or seditious writing, and where Parliament's authority was unchecked.[39] In fact, we might wonder why one of London's most radical printers would choose to set up shop in St. James, literally steps away from the seat of royal power, when he could have chosen to ply his trade from other well-established enclaves of the book trade such as Paternoster Row, Fleet Street, the Strand, or Covent Garden (fig. 1).

Yet Almon's choice of location reflected the powerful political currents driving his business. As one of the new breed of political publishers, Almon wanted to be as close as possible to the opposition's meeting grounds, most of whom were drawn to St. James because of court life and the accompanying array of aristocratic residences, assembly rooms, coffeehouses, inns, and theaters that sprang up here. By the early eighteenth century, the area became a premier site for political consorting, with different factions each staking out convivial haunts along Pall Mall or St. James Street where they could discuss the latest news or political tactics with like-minded associates.[40] At times, the link between particular groups and their meeting sites was so tight that "whoever wished to find a gentleman commonly asked, not where he resided, but which coffee-house he frequented."[41] If these public spaces were buzzing with activity in the afternoon and evening, the morning often revolved around the more intimate receptions or *levées* that took place at the court as well as the nearby homes of key aristocratic leaders. John Almon first met his chief patron, the Earl of Temple, when he was invited to attend one of these receptions at the earl's Pall Mall residence in 1762. Impressed by the young printer, Temple invited him to return frequently, introducing him to other prominent leaders of the emerging opposition who frequently attended. Almon boasted that he visited at least once a week "to pay my *devoirs*, and was always admitted" to these cozy gatherings where sociability and politics went hand in hand.[42] With Temple's backing, Almon secured a lease on a prime

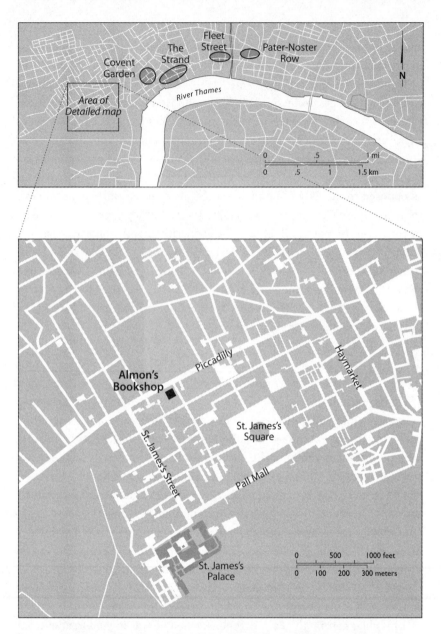

FIG. 1.   The geography of print in eighteenth-century London. Enlarged map of
St. James's parish, Westminster, indicating Almon's bookshop on Piccadilly, just a few
blocks from St. James's Palace, the official home of the monarch's Court. The circled
areas on the comprehensive map of London indicate some of the traditional enclaves
of the London print trade. (Map by Bill Nelson, after John Rocque's *A Plan of the
Cities of London and Westminster and Borough of Southwark* [London, 1746])

spot around the corner on Piccadilly, directly across the street from Burlington House, where the opposition Dukes of Devonshire and Portland resided.[43]

Almon's bookstore became an important political hub for the opposition—a place where one could access political prints as well as the latest news and intelligence.[44] During this period, in fact, bookstores and print shops often provided a conducive setting for day-to-day politicking, as groups used these spaces to hold meetings, strategize, and even recruit sympathetic customers. The colonial printer Isaiah Thomas, for example, remembered how certain print shops in Boston had served as key meeting sites for organizing the resistance to British taxation in Massachusetts.[45] Given this environment, and the number of opposition figures who mingled in Almon's shop, it is not surprising that the ministry tried to keep tabs on what was happening there. We know from court depositions, for instance, that the Treasury office had paid staffers who frequented Almon's shop to "buy all political daily publications . . . [and] pamphlets" so that the administration was up to speed on the activities of the minority out-of-doors.[46] There is also evidence that the government employed spies to monitor the conversations and gatherings that took place in Almon's store. The American agent Thomas Digges wrote to Benjamin Franklin warning about the web of government informants trying to infiltrate these sites where opposition figures and American supporters tended to mingle. He spotted one of this "race of Sad Dogs . . . [who] loung'd pretty much about Almons & tryd to put himself into the Company of our friends." The spy was eager to converse with the clientele about his plans "to publish some secrets, relative to underhand offers made to the Court of France by Lord M——s——d and other great men here, if they would give up America."[47] The incident suggests how gossip, intelligence, political networking, and print could feed off each other in sites like Almon's bookstore. Indeed, the government agent's attempt to insinuate himself within these circles by touting a made-up scheme to publish secret intelligence mimicked exactly the kind of behavior that such venues encouraged in the eyes of contemporaries. It is little wonder, then, that some politicians might find it desirable to live as close as possible to such locations. Both John Adams and Henry Laurens, for example, rented space directly above Stockdale's Piccadilly bookshop, just two doors down from Almon's address.[48]

Part of what made Almon's bookstore such a thriving *locus* of political intelligence was its close proximity to the rich transportation links of St. James, particularly its bustling array of coaching inns that served as prime conduits for the flow of information and people. Because Piccadilly had evolved into one of London's key thoroughfares, as well as a popular destination point for genteel travelers, it became a central hub for stagecoaches linking the growing metropolis to different parts of England.[49] Fortuitously, Almon's bookshop was located just around the corner from important sites like the White Horse Inn Yard, the White Bear, Dourant's Hotel, the New White Horse Cellar, and the Gloucester Coffee-House—all of which served as key points of exchange for passengers and communications traveling in and out of London (fig. 2). This steady flow certainly helped enliven the conversations within establishments like Almon's or the many taverns and coffeehouses ringing the neighborhood. It took only seconds, for example, for one disgruntled office holder from Ireland to make his way from the coach-yard to Almack's tavern, where he disclosed "his knowledge of the secrets of the two great Vice Kings [ministers]" that he was sure would be of "considerable consequence to the anti-ministerial party"—an episode that was eagerly published in sympathetic newspapers to complete the intelligence circuit.[50] But just as importantly, these stagecoaches proved crucial to those who needed a fast, reliable, and discreet way to communicate outside of the official post system, where the government frequently opened mail it deemed suspicious or subversive.[51] Almon's correspondence, in fact, is filled with repeated discussions about the need to send confidential letters and materials through these private channels in order to avoid the prying eyes of officialdom.[52] The situation was particularly dire during the "off-season," when London's political classes dispersed at the recess of Parliament and the court. Trying to coordinate a political movement in such circumstances was no easy task, but from his well-positioned hub in St. James, Almon was able to do better than expected in keeping distant members apprised of the latest political news and intelligence.[53]

During the prime political "season" between January and May, the opposition carved out a series of highly symbolic sites where members could gather to develop strategy and show their support for the cause. In some ways this built upon a tradition in British politics of the "reversionary" court, in which the political minority often flocked to the monarch-in-waiting, setting up a kind of "shadow" regime. George III's own father, Frederick, Prince of Wales, had set up one of the most effective opposition courts at Leicester House on the outskirts of St. James's parish, where disgruntled elements of the political spectrum could gather to form a more effective coalition.[54] Perhaps it is fitting, then, that George III's reign would see a similar dynamic unfold as the opposition movement sought to carve out highly symbolic spaces from which to coordinate their political operations while presenting a unified face to the public.[55] One of the early and most interesting examples was the establishment of a club at Wildman's, on Albermarle-Street, in the spring of 1763.

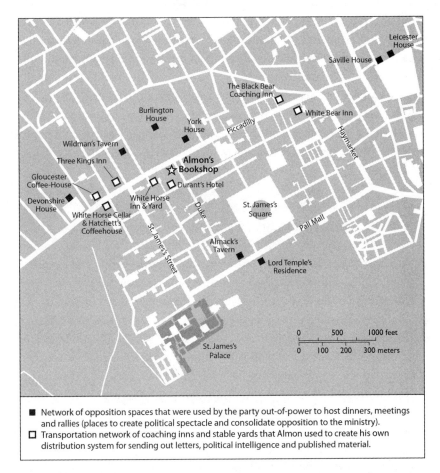

FIG. 2.   The political geography of opposition. (Map by Bill Nelson, after John Rocque's *A Plan of the Cities of London and Westminster and Borough of Southwark* [London, 1746])

Thomas Wildman was a provincial lawyer and aspiring politician who opened a posh tavern at this Albemarle address, which had long been the residence of Lord Waldegrave, a prominent opponent of Lord Bute.[56] Appropriating this symbolic space, the opposition set up a subscription club whereby paying members would meet regularly to dine, drink, and socialize. The club became known as the Coterie, and for a year it was one of the most talked about aspects of London politics. What made the Coterie so interesting was the way it helped solidify the unsure transition from scattered cliques of disaffected politicians to a cohesive party of opposition, as members used this unique space to build loyalty, articulate a shared platform, and to project a public image of the newly-minted "minority." The Coterie appointed Almon to be its official printer and publisher, a move that signaled the important role that newspaper coverage and political print, more broadly, would play at Wildman's. While the choice of Almon was not surprising, it was highly unusual for a political club to work so closely with a printer on such matters, and it may help explain the impressive newspaper coverage and pamphlet wars generated by this out-of-doors experiment. This vibrant fusion of politics and print caught the attention of one satirical writer who pretended to be a member:

> I am extremely rejoiced to find that you have so exactly followed [my] advice of inserting inflammatory letters and paragraphs in the news papers, and printing and distributing *gratis* in all coffee-houses, &c. incendiary papers and hand-bills. You must keep the bellows for ever in your hand to blow the coals of opposition. . . . I perused the *printed lists* [of voting divisions] with a most singular pleasure. . . . Your information that these lists lie in heaps, along with the Two Volumes of the North Briton, the *Royal Register,* and Gazetter, upon the tables at Wildman's, gives me great pleasure; as well as the resolutions lately made there to subscribe for Pamphlets, and to suffer dinner to come upon the table till both Houses break up. Cultivate Wildman's. Such a *Coterie* is of infinite importance.[57]

The evocative description highlights the central role that texts played in this setting, where the sociability of dinner was combined with voting lists to build political solidarities, or where pamphlets and conversations merged to generate new political convictions. In one case, for example, Almon revealed how a key pamphlet laying out the essential "creed of the minority" had been dictated by various members at Wildman's, suggesting the intriguing ways in which this space might have fostered new kinds of collaborative discussion, authorship, and political thinking.[58] And while the Coterie would eventually dissolve, the opposition continued to experiment with similar associations and meeting spots that could serve as a tangible focal point for the movement. Whether they met at Almack's or Leicester Square or Lord Temple's home, the minority "out-of-doors" knew that an important part of coordinating a political and ideological movement revolved around sustaining these prime sites of opposition.

Almon's activities highlight other important political venues that catered to less elite constituencies. He took a leading role, for example, in a political "association or club" that met regularly at the Standard Tavern in Leicester Square, composed of "respectable tradesmen. There [being] no gentleman of fashion or rank amongst them," he later recalled.[59] Such meetings provided a conducive atmosphere in which people of middling rank could discuss the latest political news. We know from Almon's correspondence that he frequently took manuscripts, letters, and political texts to the Standard to hear what his colleagues thought of them, and conversely, he sent their reactions and sentiments to associates in places as far away as Dublin.[60] In other words, this clubbable space became an effective node in the networks of political intelligence channeling ideas and debate throughout the metropolis and beyond. The history of this group and its locale also reveals how ordinary associations could generate extraordinary events. In the wake of the controversial Middlesex elections in 1769, the merchants, tradesmen, and shopkeepers who met at the Standard decided to take their organizing a step further, launching a plan to coordinate a large public gathering in which fellow subjects could hear, debate, and sign a petition calling upon the king to dissolve Parliament for overriding the rights of the Middlesex electors. Almon no doubt played a key part in drafting the petition and circulating the advertisements and handbills that directed the inhabitants of Westminster to this public rally.[61] The location they chose, Westminster Hall, was particularly striking. "This was the first time that Westminster-Hall was used for a public assembly of the inhabitants," Almon pointed out with pride, adding that the event was particularly embarrassing to the government, since it unfolded "under the nose of the minsters, at the threshold of all the state offices, and in the face of all that part of the nobility and gentry who are enemies to petitions."[62] With nearly ten thousand people gathered in Westminster Hall, surrounded by well-organized stations that collected their personal signatures, the event demonstrated how these networks could not only mobilize political action in new ways but also shape new political convictions and constitutional ideas as thousands of people paused from their daily routines to consider the legitimate bounds of Parliament's authority, the duties of the king, and the collective rights of the people.

Such moments—and the ideas forged during them—cannot be understood without appreciating the web of distinct spaces that conditioned people's capacity for collective deliberation, engagement, and mobilization at these turbulent moments.[63] Themes of space and place, in fact, can help historians construct more "grounded" narratives of political change that reveal how large-scale political movements become possible through the concrete activities and decisions of ordinary people.

Coda: The View from Westminster

The Westminster petition marked a defining moment in Almon's career as well as in the evolution of political radicalism on both sides of the Atlantic. Not only did it serve as a model for ideas about the inviolable rights of British subjects, but it also inspired new forms of political agitation and mobilization as radicals seized upon the petitioning process to engage broader segments of the public. In the aftermath of these events, as one newspaper reported, "Private letters from almost every county in England remark, that there is no other language to be heard, from highest to lowest, but petition, petition, petition!" The sentiment quickly spread to the American colonies where it intersected with the boycott movement, leading to calls for the broader public to subscribe to the nonimportation agreements that were emerging as the centerpiece of colonial resistance to Parliament.[64] On both sides of the Atlantic, "patriots" experimented with new and increasingly radical articulations of natural rights and popular sovereignty, as groups sought to challenge the expansive powers of Parliament while defending these new forms of popular agitation out-of-doors.

In 1763 few observers would have imagined that Almon or his associates would become involved in such radical tactics and positions. Almon's publishing network, after all, grew out of the rather conservative realm of elite Whig politics, where opposition to the ministry would not have been confused with calls for sweeping transformations of the political order. Many opposition Whigs, in fact, found Almon's later brand of politics as distasteful and threatening as the Toryism they perceived in George III's ministers. Yet Almon's prominent role in the transatlantic radicalism of the 1770s only underscored how these expanding networks and sites of popular political engagement could generate new forms of collective deliberation and action that were beyond the control of political elites.

Looking back on these years, Almon was himself struck by the seemingly prosaic roots of these important political changes. "Perhaps there are few Instances, in the ordinary occurrences of life," he declared, "which so remarkably distinguish the attainment of a great and unexpected object, by a small and fortuitous beginning, as the petition from Westminster."[65] He found it striking that a handful of tradesmen meeting in a tavern, or that electors assembling to sign petitions, could eventually lead to sweeping change. Yet moments of profound change are often rooted in such "small and fortuitous beginnings" when ordinary people decide to mobilize the resources around them to transform the world as they know it. What is sometimes overlooked is the fact that Almon's generation could draw upon networks of communication, political intelligence, and collective action that had only recently emerged in the previous decades. Had the imperial crises unfolded earlier in the century—say, in the 1720s or the 1740s—the social networks and sites of political engagement would have been radically different, and there might well have been no revolution at all.

Notes

1. The central themes of this opening paragraph are rooted in Tim Breen's approach to history and the role that ordinary people play in making it. See especially T. H. Breen, "Making History: The Force of Public Opinion and the Last Years of Slavery in Revolutionary Massachusetts," in *Through a Glass Darkly: Reflections on Personal Identity in Early America*, ed. Ronald Hoffman, Mechal Sobel, and Fredrika J. Teute (Chapel Hill, NC, 1997), 67–95; Breen, *The Marketplace of Revolution: How Consumer Politics Shaped American Independence* (Oxford, 2004); Breen, "Where Have All the People Gone? Reflections on Popular Political Mobilization on the Eve of American Independence," in *War in an Age of Revolution, 1775–1815*, ed. Roger Chickering and Stig Förster (Cambridge, 2010), 263–84.

2. For the growing scholarly attention to social networks during this period, see Natasha Glaisyer, "Networking: Trade and Exchange in the Eighteenth-Century British Empire," *Historical Journal* 47 (2004): 451–76; William B. Warner, *Protocols of Liberty: Communication Innovation and the American Revolution* (Chicago, 2013); Nicholas Wrightson, "Franklin's Networks: Aspects of British Atlantic Print Culture, Science, and Communication c. 1730–60," PhD diss., University of Oxford, 2007.

3. See Deborah Rogers, *Bookseller as Rogue: John Almon and the Politics of Eighteenth-Century Publishing* (New York, 1986); Eric Stockdale, *'Tis Treason, My Good Man! Four Revolutionary Presidents and a Piccadilly Bookshop* (New Castle, DE, 2005); Robert Rea, *The English Press in Politics, 1760–1774* (Lincoln, NE, 1963); Lucyle Werkmeister, *The London Daily Press, 1772–1792* (Lincoln, NE, 1963).

4. Hannah Barker and Simon Burrows, eds., *Press, Politics, and the Public Sphere in Europe and North America, 1760–1820* (Cambridge, 2002); Michael Warner, *The Letters of the Republic: Publication and the Public Sphere in Eighteenth-Century America* (Cambridge, MA, 2009); Kathleen Wilson, "Citizenship, Empire, and Modernity in the English Provinces, c. 1720–1790," *Eighteenth-Century Studies* 29 (1995): 69–96.

5. Ian Christie, *Wilkes, Wyvill, and Reform: The Parliamentary Reform Movement in British Politics, 1760–1785* (London, 1962); George Rudé, *Wilkes and Liberty: A Social Study of 1763 to 1774* (Oxford, 1965); Nicholas Rogers, *Crowds, Culture, and Politics in Georgian Britain* (Oxford, 1998).

6. Arthur Sheps, "The American Revolution and the Transformation of English Republicanism," *Historical Reflections/Réflexions Historiques* (1975): 3–28; John Sainsbury, *Disaffected Patriots: London Supporters of Revolutionary America, 1769–1782* (Kingston, ON, 1987); Colin Bonwick, *English Radicals and the American Revolution* (Chapel Hill, NC, 1977); and T. H. Breen, *Lockean Moment: The Language of Rights on the Eve of the American Revolution* (Oxford, 2001).

7. [Anon.], *Memoirs of John Almon, Bookseller of Piccadilly* (London, 1790), 9–14.

8. *Public Advertiser,* 24 August 1765 (no. 9685). See also the inquiries made by "Querus" on this front, *Gazetteer and New Daily Advertiser,* 19 July 1765 (no. 11,342). On the king's interest in Almon, see *Memoirs of a Bookseller,* 47; Robert Morris, *A Letter to Sir Richard Aston* (London, 1770), 37–38.

9. Eric Stockdale provides the best account of Almon's relationship to Wilkes and the opposition in his *'Tis Treason, My Good Man!* while Solomon Lutnick's *The American Revolution and the British Press, 1775–1783* (Columbia, MO, 1967) and Robert Rea's *The English Press in Politics* continue to offer the best surveys of the opposition press in these years.

10. Stephen Botein, "'Meer Mechanics' and an Open Press: The Business and Political Strategies of Colonial American Printers," *Perspectives in American History* 9 (1975): 127–225.

11. *Gentleman's Magazine* 75 (December 1805): 1179.

12. The recent historiography on print culture has tended to move in the direction of historicizing and problematizing the dynamics of print culture. See Adrian Johns, *The Nature of the Book: Print and Knowledge in the Making* (Chicago, 1998); James Raven, "New Reading Histories, Print Culture, and the Identification of Change: The Case of Eighteenth-Century England," *Social History* 23 (1998): 268–87; Trish Loughran, "Disseminating *Common Sense*: Thomas Paine and the Problem of the Early National Bestseller," *American Literature* 78 (2006): 1–28; Loughran, *The Republic in Print: Print Culture in the Age of U.S. Nation Building, 1770–1870* (New York, 2007); and the essays in *The Atlantic World of Print in the Age of Franklin,* a special edition of *Early American Studies* 8, no. 1 (Winter 2010).

13. My analysis of "political intelligence" draws some inspiration from the following works: Robert Darnton's *Poetry and the Police: Communication Networks in Eighteenth-Century Paris* (Cambridge, MA, 2010); Darnton, "An Early Information Society: News and the Media in Eighteenth-Century Paris," *American Historical Review* 105 (2000): 1–35; C. A. Bayly, *Empire and Information: Intelligence Gathering and Social Communication in India, 1780–1870* (Cambridge, 1996); and Joanne Freeman, "Slander, Poison, Whispers, and Fame: Jefferson's 'Anas' and Political Gossip in the Early Republic," *Journal of the Early Republic* 15 (1995): 25–57.

14. *Memoirs of a Bookseller,* 142, 93.

15. Ibid., 93, 47.

16. Ibid., 93.

17. For the derogatory comment by the Norfolk MP Thomas De Grey, see *Gentleman's Magazine* (August 1770): 457, and *Memoirs of a Bookseller,* 55–56.

18. My analysis of Almon's records is informed by some of the rich literature exploring the material and social dimensions of the book trade, particularly William L. Joyce, David D. Hall, and Richard D. Brown, eds., *Printing and Society in Early America* (Worcester, MA, 1983); W. C. Ford, "Henry Knox and the London Book Store in Boston, 1771–1774," *Proceedings of the Massachusetts Historical Society* 61 (1928): 227–303; John Feather, *The Provincial Book Trade in Eighteenth-Century England* (Cambridge, 1985); James Raven, *London Booksellers and American Customers: Transatlantic Literary Community and the Charleston Library Society, 1748–1811* (Columbia, SC, 2002).

19. On the deeply personal and networked nature of eighteenth-century business, see David Hancock, "The Trouble with Networks: Managing the Scots' Early-Modern Ma-

deira Trade," *Business History Review* 79 (2005): 467–91, and his *Citizens of the World: London Merchants and the Integration of the British Atlantic Community, 1735–1785* (London, 1995).

20. *Memoirs of a Bookseller*, 14–16. See also "The Curious Dialogue between an Author and His Bookseller," attached to *A Letter to the Right Honourable the E— T—* (London, 1766), v–xvi, and William Knox's evaluation of Almon's publishing operation (see note 25 below).

21. In addition to several extant catalogues of Almon's stock, his insurance policies give some idea of the size/value of his collection. Sun Insurance Records, Guildhall (London), S277 418549 (1779: £1,000) and S293 444451 (1781: £1,400).

22. "A New Catalogue of Books and Pamphlets, Printed for J. Almon," appended to *Another Letter to Mr. Almon in Matter of Libel* (London, 1770), 16. The best sense of what these services entailed can be gleaned from John Stockdale, Almon's former porter, who continued these practices in his own bookstore. See E. Stockdale, *'Tis Treason, My Good Man!* chapter 8.

23. *London Evening Post*, 6 December 1764 (no. 5788); Robin Myers and Michael Harris, *Spreading the Word: The Distribution Networks of Print, 1550–1850* (Detroit, 1990), and Christine Ferdinand, *Benjamin Collins and the Provincial Newspaper Trade in the Eighteenth Century* (Oxford, 1997), chapter 2.

24. See Kenneth Ellis, *The Post Office in the Eighteenth Century: A Study in Administrative History* (Oxford, 1958).

25. Knox to George Grenville, 4 October 1768, in *The Grenville Papers*, ed. William James Smith, 4 vols. (London, 1852), 4:368–69.

26. John Almon Correspondence, 1766–1805, Add MS 20733, f. 55–9, f. 65–78, f. 138, 140–43, and 145, British Library, London; Benjamin Franklin to Thomas Digges, 30 May 1779, *Papers of Benjamin Franklin*, 29:576.

27. Letter reprinted in *Memoirs of a Bookseller*, 112.

28. Ibid., 82–84.

29. John Almon Correspondence, ff. 8, 10, 57, 59, 71–2, 138–40, British Library.

30. Social network theorists have long recognized the pivotal role of brokers who link otherwise disconnected circles. See Mark S. Granovetter's classic paper, "The Strength of Weak Ties," *American Journal of Sociology* 78, no. 6 (May 1973): 1360–80, and a historical application of these insights to revolutionary mobilization in Boston in Shin-Kap Han's "The Other Ride of Paul Revere: The Brokerage Role in the Making of the American Revolution," *Mobilization: An International Quarterly* 14, no. 2 (June 2009): 143–62.

31. Lord Camden to Almon, 13 April 1778, John Almon Correspondence, f. 29., British Library.

32. P. D. G. Thomas, "The Beginning of Parliamentary Reporting in Newspapers, 1768–1774," *English Historical Review* 74 (1959): 623–36; Karl Schweizer, "Newspapers, Politics, and Public Opinion in the Later Hanoverian Era," *Parliamentary History* 25 (2006): 32–48; and Patrick Bullard, "Parliamentary Rhetoric, Enlightenment, and the Politics of Secrecy: The Printers' Crisis of March 1771," *History of European Ideas* 31 (2005): 313–25.

33. *Memoirs of a Bookseller*, 118–20. Other details about Almon's network are discussed in Thomas, "The Beginning of Parliamentary Reporting," and Bullard, "Parliamentary Rhetoric Enlightenment, and the Politics of Secrecy."

34. *Memoirs of a Bookseller*, 118.

35. *A Correct List of the . . . Votes in Certain Late Public Questions, in which the Rights and Liberties of the People Were Essentially Concerned* (broadside), preserved in the Bowood Papers (Lord Shelburne), Add MS 88906/7/5 f. 8, British Library, London.

36. *Spectator*, no. 403; Ann C. Dean, *The Talk of the Town: Figurative Publics in Eighteenth-Century Britain* (Lewisburg, PA, 2007); Miles Ogborn, *Spaces of Modernity: London's Geographies, 1680–1780* (New York, 1998).

37. On the spatial dimensions of print culture—a subject starting to attract more attention—see Charles W. J. Withers and Miles Ogborn, eds., *Geographies of the Book* (Surrey, UK, 2010), and James Raven, *Bookscape: Geographies of Printing and Publishing in London before 1800* (Chicago, 2014).

38. James Raven, "London and the Central Sites of the English Book Trade," in *Cambridge History of the Book*, vol. 5, ed. Michael F. Suarez and Michael L. Turner (Cambridge, 2009), 293–308.

39. *Memoirs of a Bookseller*, 144–46.

40. My discussion of the cultural geography of St. James draws upon the following accounts: John Mackey, *A Journey through England*, 3 vols. (London, 1722), 1:167–76; Walter Thornbury, *Old and New London: A Narrative of Its History, Its People, and Its Places*, 6 vols. (London, 1887–93), vol. 4, chapters 9–16; F. H. W. Sheppard, ed., *St James, Westminster, Part 1*, vols. 29 and 30 of *Survey of London*, 47 vols. (orig. publ., 1960), http://www .british-history.ac.uk/report.aspx?compid=40541, and Brewer, *Party Ideology and Popular Politics*, 147–51.

41. Quoted in John Timbs, *Clubs and Club Life in London* (London, 1908), 300.

42. The *Memoirs* describes these visits as "frequent and *notorious*"—a rather odd phrasing that hints at how much the chattering classes paid attention to these gatherings and who attended them. *Memoirs of a Bookseller*, 15.

43. Ibid., 16.

44. As a converted residence, Almon's ground-floor shop likely contained multiple rooms and meeting spaces reminiscent of the cozy setting immortalized in William Fettes Douglas's later painting, *The Bibliophilist's Haunt or Creech's Bookshop* (Edinburgh City Chambers, 1864).

45. Slauter, "Reading and Radicalization," 17–18.

46. These court proceedings are included in the lengthy appendix to Almon's *Memoirs of a Bookseller*, 173, 175.

47. Digges to Franklin, 6 September 1779, in *Papers of Benjamin Franklin*, 30:304–5. Almon also reported to Lord Temple about ministerial spies following him in his day-to-day activities. Almon to Temple, July 1763, *The Grenville Papers*, 2:67. See also the warnings in the *Public Advertiser*, 9 March 1765.

48. Stockdale, *'Tis Treason, My Good Man!* chapters 3–4 and 7.

49. See *The Shopkeeper's and Tradesman's Assistant: Being a new and correct Alphabetical List of all the Stage-coaches, Carriers, Coasting Vessels* (London, 1773, 1778, 1779); Thornbury, *Old and New London*, 4: 273–90; "Piccadilly, South Side" in Sheppard, ed., *St. James, Westminster*, 30:251–70. http://www.british-history.ac.uk/report.aspx?comp id=40571.

50. *St. James's Chronicle or the British Evening Post*, 12 June 1764 (no. 510). For another

interesting example, see Richard Rigby to the Duke of Bedford, 12 October 1761, in *Correspondence of John, Fourth Duke of Bedford*, 3 vols. (London, 1846), 3:51–54.

51. Ellis, *The Post Office in the Eighteenth Century*, chapter 6 (esp. 72); [House of Commons] *Report from the Secret Committee on the Post-Office* (London, 1844); "Government Interception of Letters from America and the Quest for Colonial Opinion in 1775," *William and Mary Quarterly* 58 (2001): 403–30.

52. See, for example, Almon's correspondence at the British Library with John Sykes (f. 128), John Kennion (ff. 61, 63), John Lloyd (ff. 67–79), Samuel Wharton (ff. 141, 143), and Ralph Izard (f. 55, ff. 59). In his correspondence with John Wilkes, nary a letter goes by without the two discussing how to avoid government monitoring.

53. See, for example, *The Grenville Papers*, 2:426–30, 460.

54. Archibald S. Foord, *His Majesty's Opposition, 1714–1830* (Oxford, 1964); Aubrey N. Newman, "Leicester House Politics, 1748–1751," *English Historical Review* 76 (1961): 577–89.

55. See the clever poem "The Modern Progress of Patriotism," which tracked these evolving sites of opposition as they moved across the landscape of Westminster, warning that they seemed to be heading in the direction of Tyburn. *St. James's Chronicle or the British Evening Post*, 21 July 1764.

56. John Almon, *The History of the Late Minority*, 3rd ed. (London, 1766), chapter 20; and Derek H. Watson, "The Rise of the Opposition at Wildman's Club," *Historical Research* 44 (1971): 55–77. On Waldegrave, see J. C. D. Clark's introduction to *The Memoirs and Speeches of James, 2nd Earl Waldegrave, 1742–1763* (Cambridge, 1988), esp. 72–101.

57. [Anon.], *A Letter to a Noble Member of the Club in Albemarle-Street* (London, 1764), 3 (italics in original).

58. The pamphlet in question was *A Letter from Albemarle-street to the Cocoa Tree* (1764). Almon, *Biographical, Literary, and Political Anecdotes*, 3 vols. (London, 1797), 2:37–38.

59. *Memoirs of a Bookseller*, 54.

60. See, for example, Lord Montmoreres to Almon, 14 January 1772 and 14 February 1772, John Almon Correspondence, ff. 96–99, British Library.

61. *Memoirs of a Bookseller*, 54–62; *Lloyd's Evening Post*, 14 August 1769 (no. 1889); *London Chronicle*, 19 August 1769 (no. 1978); *Public Advertiser*, 17 January 1770 (no. 10978).

62. *Memoirs of a Bookseller*, 56.

63. On this theme, see Benjamin Carp's *Rebels Rising: Cities and the American Revolution* (Oxford, 2007).

64. Quoted in Pauline Maier, *From Resistance to Revolution: Colonial Radicals and the Development of American Opposition to Britain, 1765–1776* (New York, 1972), 205.

65. *Memoirs of a Bookseller*, 54.

Part III

The Ghosts of Empire

Forgiving and Forgetting in Postrevolutionary America

DONALD F. JOHNSON

The conclusion of the Revolutionary War forced Americans who cooperated with the British army to grapple not only with the new realities of independence but also with their own complicity in the failed attempt to preserve imperial authority. It is not unusual at the end of a revolutionary struggle for collaborators to transform themselves into patriots. If so many people actively resisted their oppressors, one wonders how the old regime managed to exercise control for so long. But self-serving memories are a means of survival; cooperation and accommodation are best forgotten. The aftermath of the American Revolution was no exception. Those who had lived under British military rule came under particularly harsh scrutiny, and the potential consequences of their actions were serious. During the war, revolutionary governments routinely banished, imprisoned, and even executed those accused of aiding British forces, and at the end of the conflict some sixty thousand such people were forced into exile, along with fifteen thousand of their enslaved servants. Still, many more erstwhile British sympathizers remained in the new United States, living quietly alongside their neighbors who had supported the rebellion. And while many of the exiles blazed bright, bitter trails into the historical record, most of those who remained vanished into obscurity, becoming part of the fabric of a new nation they had once bitterly opposed.

They did not survive by accident. Rather, former collaborators developed sophisticated strategies to alter collective and personal memories of the Revolution. These people destroyed and secreted away evidence of their complicity with Great Britain, and many lied about their wartime activities for decades after the end of the conflict. Early historians aided these survivors by popularizing a new public memory of the event in which all but the worst of those who had supported British authority during the war could be forgiven. Many of these figures, like David Ramsay and Mercy Otis Warren, had both firsthand experience of military rule and a vested political interest in suppressing the ambiguous allegiances it had engendered. When survivors laid claim to this new narrative of forgiveness, their wartime actions faded into obscurity as they shed their British associations and integrated into the new republic. As they did so, they provided a model for the nation as a whole to erase its British imperial past and make the world anew.

Those who remained in America rewrote the narrative of their actions during the war to fit into a postrevolutionary reality that left little room for nuance. Americans who had signed loyalty oaths to the king, formed relationships with British soldiers, and even held offices in the occupation regimes either had to explain away or hide the evidence of their actions in a new society built, in many ways, on the exclusion of those who had remained loyal to the Crown. As a result, in the decades after 1783, civilians who had lived under military rule became adept at hiding or explaining away their wartime actions. As many had done during the war, survivors cultivated familial and social networks and crafted new narratives to survive and begin their lives again in the new republic. As these people worked to forget their experiences, their neighbors and leaders proved willing to forgive their actions in the interest of forging a new American nationalism in the place of British imperial identity.

Indeed, these acts of forgiving and forgetting took place in the context of a larger reframing of the Revolution that occurred after 1783, one concerned with shedding all traces of British imperial heritage and thus sympathetic to those trying to erase their wartime sympathies. From the 1780s until the Revolutionary generation passed on, historians, politicians, clergymen, novelists, and others crafted polemic, nationalistic narratives of the war to which Americans seeking to reinvent their wartime experiences could cling. These historians, like many who came later, stressed a total break with Britain rather than the continuity of social relationships, demographics, and trade connections that many observed. This newly imagined war narrative elided the ambiguities and contradictions inherent in the often chaotic revolutionary experience. Because of their selective memory, American society proved willing, in the interests of renewed economic prosperity and the maintenance of a fragile new social order, to overlook the offenses of all but the worst of those who had sided with the British army during the war. So long as survivors of occupation could forget the troublesome elements of their wartime experiences and embrace the new narratives provided by patriot historians, they could claim their place in the republic alongside those who had fought against the Crown from the beginning. Indeed, such forgiveness proved essential for the emergence of a new vision of republican empire that was to encompass not only the thirteen former colonies but, by the early nineteenth century, the entire continent of North America.

The decision whether or not to remain in those thirteen former colonies marked the first time many survivors of military rule had to make sense of their experiences in the face of new realities. As the fighting between the British and Continental armies largely ceased in 1782 and peace approached the next year, occupied zones became clearinghouses for those fleeing the new republican regime. Between July and November 1782, some 2,165 civilians, along with 3,340 enslaved men and women belonging to them, arrived in New York City.[1] Although occupied New York had become a center for distressed refugees, these people were different. They came not from rebel-held areas but from British-occupied Savannah and Charleston and represented the first trickle of what would become a flood of refugees as the British army evacuated its southern strongholds in preparation for the impending peace. In August of that year, as many as 3,000 white Georgians and between 3,000 and 5,000 slaves left the province as British forces abandoned Savannah. Most settled not in New York but in Florida and the West Indies. When the last British troops left Charleston in December, 3,794 white South Carolinians, along with 5,333 slaves, went with them, again mostly bound for the Caribbean.[2] These southern refugees and their slaves were forerunners of the even greater exodus that occurred when the British army withdrew from New York in November 1783. All told, around 60,000 free people, along with as many as 15,000 slaves, left occupied America, dispersing to various British possessions across the globe.[3]

Those who left did so for a variety of reasons. A few had taken the king's side early in the conflict and had been exiled from their communities as a consequence. Around 19,000 men had volunteered to fight alongside British regulars in loyalist regiments, and more had taken part in the vicious guerilla conflicts that raged in the backcountries of many of the rebelling colonies.[4] Many of these men took their wives and children with them when they fled. Other women had married or become the mistresses of British soldiers, and still others had become servants to officers. At least 3,000 of this exodus were escaped slaves who faced the terrifying prospect of a return to bondage should they remain.[5] Still more simply did not wish to live in the new American republic. The approximately 75,000 people who left did so for myriad reasons and represented a wide array of colonial American society.

Many more Americans who had sided at times with the king's forces remained and successfully reintegrated themselves into postrevolutionary

American society. Assuming that, as one historian has calculated, at least 500,000 white men and women became loyalists between 1775 and 1783, then the 60,000 who fled represent only around 12 percent of the total number.[6] Although the number of African Americans who fled was likely higher than those who became loyalists, many blacks almost certainly remained in America after the war.[7] And although a disproportionate number of those who fled did reside in the occupied territories at one time or another, most residents of cities under military rule also remained in the new United States.

While many have assumed that those who left constituted the bulk of those who collaborated with the British, those who remained were equally complicit in military rule. Almost all civilians who lived under British military rule collaborated with the occupation regimes in one way or another, be it actively joining a provincial corps, taking money or aid from the military government, housing and feeding soldiers, or simply engaging in social relationships with military personnel. Revolutionaries were not ignorant of this fact, and often they sought revenge against the Tories who populated occupied cities. In the later years of the war, the republican governments of New York, Georgia, South Carolina, and several other states passed acts of attainder against prominent citizens residing in the occupied territories, giving the revolutionaries legal basis to seize their property and threatening them with imprisonment, exile, or even death should they be found in rebel-held territory.[8] Such confiscations formed the backbone of revolutionary governments, providing funding and a common enemy for the people to rally around.[9] Further, denigration of loyalists within occupied cities played an important part in the revolutionary celebrations that leaders used to consolidate popular support for the republican cause. After the occupation of Philadelphia ended in mid-June 1778, two prominent loyalists were publicly executed for collaboration, and in a raucous Fourth of July celebration, crowds in the city dressed a prostitute in similar garb to those Philadelphians who participated in the Meschianza and proceeded to ridicule and abuse her.[10] After the war, the victorious national government continued to persecute loyalists, refusing to abide by the article of the Treaty of Paris, which required it to cease such activity and even urged the various states to make restitution.[11] Still, most survivors of the occupied territories escaped these repercussions and were able to reintegrate themselves into American society.

The fate of two members of the Brinley family, a clan of middling New England merchants, reflects this. Two occupation survivors were equally guilty of collaboration and yet had remarkably different fates. During the war, George Brinley used the position he managed to obtain in the British army's commissary department to aid his family in both occupied and rebel-held zones. In 1783 he left New York as the army evacuated the town. Like many who had served the occupation regimes, his complicity with the British military rule had made it impossible for him to remain in the city safely when it reverted to revolutionary rule. Indeed, in the months before his departure, Brinley seemed resigned to his fate, forlornly writing to his brother Francis in Newport, Rhode Island, that "I must suppose Nova Scotia abounds with good things" and requesting that his relatives in Rhode Island send provisions and "an assortment of seed for a Kitchen Garden" in his future home.[12] Francis Brinley remained in Newport after the British occupation ended and lived there with his family for the rest of his life. By any stretch of the imagination, Francis was just as complicit in British occupation as George. Before Newport was occupied, he had sent food to be smuggled into occupied Boston, and during the occupation Ezra Stiles, former minister of Newport's Second Congregational Church and future president of Yale University, ranked him among the town's "Principal and Active Tories."[13] The radically different fates of the two brothers begs a question that could be asked of thousands of Americans in the postwar decades: how did Francis Brinley and those like him successfully remain in America?

Philadelphia merchant Tench Coxe's postoccupation experience sheds light into how thousands of survivors, even those that collaborated with the British to a great extent, rebuilt their lives and avoided punishment and exile after occupation ended. Before and during the occupation of Philadelphia, Coxe had cooperated in almost all aspects of British military rule. As a young merchant, he had fled his native city for occupied New York in the winter of 1776 and had moved in the same social circles as prominent loyalist politicians and merchants. Under military rule, he had leveraged his social connections with British commanders, loyalist civil officials, and New York merchants into a lucrative trading business, obtaining valuable special permissions to ship goods to Europe and the West Indies and receive imports from Europe.[14] Like others within the occupied city, the young merchant also kept lines of communication open to family members and friends in the countryside, but for the most part Coxe played the part of a loyal subject and a vital player in occupied Philadelphia's social scene. However, numerous aspects of the experience of occupation grated on the young Coxe, and by its end, like thousands of other Americans, he had decided not to follow the British army back to New York but to become, as he wrote, "a perfect American" within the new state.[15]

While his conversion to the revolutionary cause may have been earnest, however, avoiding recriminations for his loyalism required deliberate action. The month before the British evacuated, Pennsylvania's executive council placed Coxe's name on a Proclamation of Attainder identifying those "adjudged guilty of High Treason."[16] A few days later, Coxe snuck out of occupied Philadelphia to sign of an oath of allegiance to the new state of Pennsylvania, although he later claimed to have no inkling of the planned British evacuation.[17] While not releasing him entirely from suspicion, the oath at least would allow him to claim loyalty to the revolutionary state and would entitle him to the protections of its laws.

In addition to swearing allegiance to the revolutionary state of Pennsylvania, in the weeks leading up to the British evacuation, the young merchant also took steps to eliminate written evidence of his complicity in British rule. After the British left Philadelphia, he urged his acquaintances in New York to "destroy all my letters, that I may not suffer from their being seen by either side," worrying that "both might perhaps blame me."[18] In addition to instructing his correspondents to eliminate evidence of his complicity, Coxe also made alterations in his company's letterbook, cutting out sections of letters sent to others to hide his actions. Coxe excised names of ships he owned shares in, people he dealt with, and some of the methods by which he obtained his licenses to trade. In one particularly egregious instance, Coxe ripped out almost all of a letter regarding a voyage to the Caribbean whose legality was dubious under both British and revolutionary law.[19] While the letterbook survives, little else from Coxe's occupation experience remains in an otherwise well stocked family archive of correspondence and business ephemera. By altering and destroying the physical records of his actions, Coxe was attempting to wipe out his complicity in British military rule forces and clear the path for a new start under the republican regime.

While perhaps most occupation survivors did not rise as spectacularly as Coxe. He eventually became a member of the Continental Congress and a delegate to the Albany Convention and served in a variety of official posts in both the Washington and Jefferson administrations. Thousands of other ex-collaborators used similar strategies to avoid recriminations and to adapt to postrevolutionary society. Mary Almy, a boardinghouse keeper who had sided against her revolutionary husband to remain in Newport during the occupation, also rehabilitated her reputation following the war, like Coxe using a combination of obfuscation and family connections. After the occupation ended, Almy escaped any suspicion for her politics. She continued to live in Newport and to operate her large boardinghouse on Thames Street (which, ironically, had been confiscated from another loyalist in 1776 and awarded to her husband, Benjamin, while a member of the council of the revolutionary state).[20] Likely, her connection with her husband facilitated this smooth transition to civilian life, as he was a Continental army captain and civil officer in Rhode Island's republican government with unassailable republican bona fides. Almy's rehabilitation went so far that, when George Washington visited the town in 1790, he boarded at the Almys' residence. The visit was so remarkable that the family saved the blanket he had slept in for decades after the fact.[21] When she died in 1808, Almy's loyalism had been so long forgotten that her husband, from whom she had been estranged during the war, was, according to her obituary "overwhelmed with sorrow" at "being deprived in an advanced age of so valuable an associate."[22]

Although Newport's evacuation occurred before the end of the fighting, survivors choosing to remain in New York at the end of the war were often able to rehabilitate themselves and remain in postrevolutionary society. Many of those who moved in prominent loyalist circles and who even served in the occupation regimes remained in town after the war, living out full lives with few, if any, repercussions from their wartime activities. William Seton, a Scottish immigrant who had held a variety of clerical posts in New York's occupation regime and who, during the war, counted loyalist judge William Smith and the British-sympathizing author Hector St. John de Crevecoeur as his friends, remained after the occupation ended, eventually becoming a cashier at the Bank of New York.[23] Jonathan Simpson, a refugee in New York in 1778 who later took a position in the British commissary department in Charleston, remained in the new United States and eventually died in Boston in 1802.[24] Even James Rivington, a prominent loyalist printer who published and even penned loyalist propaganda throughout the war, was able to remain, continuing to operate his press (albeit without much success) and dying in New York City in 1802. Rivington even acted as an intermediary between the incoming revolutionaries and at least one outgoing loyalist landowner in negotiations as the war came to an end.[25] Although only the records of the most prominent survive, if estimates that New York's population approached 25,000 in the closing years of the war hold, thousands more who participated in occupied society made similar transformations in the months and years after December 1783.

Because of the public nature of his collaboration with occupation authorities, Rivington's survival reveals the willingness of American society, despite hostile rhetoric and prosecution of loyalists who went into exile, to largely forgive the transgressions of those that remained in the new nation. The sheer numbers of Americans who remained and successfully rebuilt their lives suggests that early republican communities tended much more to forgive than to recriminate against former collaborators. After all, even with the most careful destruction or secreting of records and the most complete smoothing over of prosecutions by well-connected family members, these were still fairly small communities, and even if no written or oral evidence emerged to convict, neighbors well remembered one another's wartime actions. In the absence of official prosecution, one might expect, as in other historical instances, a multitude of informal acts of retaliation against those complicit in British rule. And indeed, in the closing years of the war, retaliatory violence had become endemic between bands of patriots and loyalists in the southern backcountry and no-man's lands in New York and New Jersey.[26] But while some such acts did continue after the war ended, the vast majority of former collaborators escaped even vigilante justice. That these people largely escaped such recriminations suggests that, by and large, Americans in the postwar years proved far more willing to forgive and forget wartime actions than to pursue vengeance.

This remarkable turnabout resulted from a much wider change in the public memory of the American Revolution that took place in the years following 1783. Beginning during the war and continuing for decades, Americans developed commemorative rituals, ceremonies, and myths designed to promote unity in the new nation. Politicians and civic leaders harnessed celebration and commemoration to unite diverse classes and races and create a sense of nationalism definite enough to cohere but vague enough that many different groups could claim in. While rhetoric against loyalism and symbolic punishment against loyalists played an important role in these fêtes, their architects worked hard to restrain the fury of the crowds and incorporate those former loyalists willing to resign themselves to the revolutionary cause.[27] These celebrations combined with other aspects of the emerging nationalist culture, including material culture, music, art, and countless other manifestations, to change public memories of the Revolution.[28] As Alfred Young has demonstrated in his study of George Robert Twelves Hewes, individual memories of events changed significantly in response to commemorative culture. In the case of Hewes, this meant that much of the complicated nature of his revolutionary experience had been smoothed over by the time he told his life story to biographers in the 1830s, and certain events had changed completely in nature in the intervening years.[29] For Hewes and thousands of Americans in the decades after the war, remembered events reshaped themselves to conform to the revised public memory of the war.

A similar process took place for the public and private memories of military occupation, in which public memory shifted to eliminate much of the ambiguity and compromise that living under military rule entailed. As a result, the experience of occupation lost much of its nuance, and a new narrative emerged of oppression under a brutal and inhuman British army. In this new version of events, the vast majority of those who endured occupation had been revolutionaries to begin with, had not compromised their republican values, and had actively resisted the brutality of British rule. Most of those who signed loyalty oaths never intended to collaborate, but did so because they feared for their lives and fortunes. Those who truly collaborated with the British army were hated former officials and backcountry ne'er-do-wells, who were vastly outnumbered by patriotic sufferers. The opportunities, compromises, and ambiguities that marked the experience of military rule disappeared entirely from the public memory of the event. As they did, so too did the new possibilities for social reorganization that occupation society had briefly opened. But by reshaping their memories to fit into this new public narrative, survivors and their countrymen who spent the war outside the lines could live alongside one another largely without the cycles of blame, recrimination, and violence that have marked the aftermath of many other historical instances of military occupation.

Occupation's treatment in early published histories of the Revolution demonstrates this shift in public memory. In the decades after the war, dozens of historians penned major works attempting to make sense of the event. Those who did so in America, or in sympathy with the republican cause, engaged in a deliberate nation-building project in tandem with the efforts of elites in the cultural sphere. They were typically either politicians, jurists, or intellectuals, and all were concerned with promoting American nationalism and establishing a rational, enlightened, and historical basis for the emerging patriotic consensus.[30] Their histories focused mainly on political events preceding the revolution, state-formation and diplomacy during the war, and the military campaigns, rarely touching on military rule. Where they did describe occupation, their interpretations reveal how larger American society had begun to sketch a narrative that wiped the history of much of its nuance and may even have contradicted their own personal experiences.

Two of the most important of these historians, at least, had firsthand experience of military rule during the war. David Ramsay, a Charleston physician before the war and later a congressman in the Confederation Congress, penned two of the most influential early works on the Revolution in 1785 and 1793. During the Revolution, he served as a surgeon in the Continental army and was caught up in the capture of Charleston, remaining in the occupied city several months on parole before suffering exile in St. Augustine with other prominent citizens suspected of aiding revolutionary forces.[31] Mercy Otis Warren, who in 1805 published her far-reaching *History of the Rise, Progress, and Termination of the American Revolution,* endured the occupation of Boston at the beginning of the war and, through her wide-ranging social connections, likely had friends and acquaintances who experienced military rule elsewhere in Philadelphia, Newport, and New York.[32] Despite their personal experiences with the ambiguous and often conflicted pulls of loyalty and survival that marked occupation, both Ramsay and Warren led the way in reinterpreting the experience of occupation to fit a new national narrative.

The early histories almost universally emphasized the brutality and oppression of British forces in occupied zones, using accounts of abuses and atrocities to underscore the oppression of military rule. Accounts of plunder far exceeding even the most liberal postwar estimates of losses became common in these historical accounts, wherever the British army traveled. David Ramsay wrote that once the evacuation of Boston had been ordered, a "licentious plundering took place; much was carried off, and more was wantonly destroyed."[33] Accounts of worse crimes also populated the pages of these histories, serving as proof of the British army's inhumanity and the righteousness of resisting it. Mercy Otis Warren related that, after the conquest of New York, the British army engaged in "the most wanton instances of rapine and bloodshed" during foraging expeditions to New Jersey, and "the licentiousness of their officers spread rape, misery, and despair, indiscriminately through every village."[34] Tellingly, neither author described the extent of plundering in areas they actually lived in, but rather relied on generalizations and secondhand accounts.

Historians who never saw the inside of an occupied town relished the plunder of the British army even more than those who had. In his *Annals of the American Revolution,* the Reverend Jedidiah Morse lambasted the British treatment of a young continental officer captured and executed on occupied Long Island, calling the British commander "as great a savage as ever disgraced humanity."[35] Historian and veteran of the southern campaign Alexander Garden claimed that the British army plundered the people of Charleston indiscriminately, simply labeling those from whom it stole revolutionaries: "the term *Rebel,* gave licence to plunder with impunity."[36] In his brief 1826 history intended for schoolchildren, Samuel Wilson wrote that during the southern campaign of 1779, "Negroes were seduced or forced from their masters; furniture and plate were seized without decency or authority; and the most infamous violations of every law of honour and honesty were openly perpetrated."[37] Even the Italian historian Carlo Botta, who wrote his history largely based on documentary and anecdotal evidence, stressed the inhumanity of the British in their plundering, writing hyperbolically of these crimes, "It was exclaimed every where, that the English government had revived in the new world the fury of the Goths, and the barbarity of the northern Hordes."[38]

These descriptions served a purpose beyond demonizing the British army. Ramsay credited the desire for plunder for the lack of an effective civil government in occupied territories. During the occupation of South Carolina, despite efforts of civil officials, Ramsay lamented, "The officers, privates, and followers of the royal army were generally more intent on amassing fortunes by plunder and rapine, than on promoting a re-union of the dissevered members of the empire."[39] In the new narrative, plundering became not just a facet of life under military rule but its defining factor and one that established the British army as an oppressive force to be resisted by patriotic Americans.

One particular narrative most of these historians took up was the brutality that British forces showed toward women, especially those of the upper classes. Mercy Otis Warren decried that, in the face of British plundering in New Jersey, "the army spared neither age or sex, youth, beauty, or innocence."[40] During the occupation of Charleston, Ramsay recounted the tale of "[t]wo young ladies, of most amiable characters and respectable connexions," thrown into the Provost jail and "crowded together with the sick, labouring under contagious diseases, with negroes, deserters, and women of infamous characters."[41] Botta included an anecdote from Connecticut in which a woman was murdered by "A furious soldier . . . a Hessian, as it is said," who "took aim at this unfortunate mother, and pierced her breast with an instantly mortal shot; her blood gushed upon all her tender orphans."[42] He probably picked up the tale from Warren, who credited the act to "a British barbarian" who "instantly shot her threw [sic] her lungs."[43] In the new narrative that these historians were crafting, violence against upper-class women became further proof of the inhumanity of the British army.

Racial and ethnic narratives also came into play in the public memory of the Revolution. Historians saw the British alliance with escaped slaves as further proof of the atrocities of the king's army. Many historians attempted to ignore the issue entirely. In his two-volume history of the Revolution, David Ramsay devoted only three sentences to the large black insurrection in South Carolina after the conquest of Charleston, lamenting "[t]he mischievous effects of slavery, in facilitating the conquest of the country."[44] While Ramsay attempted to side-step the issue, evidence of black participation on the British side presented by other authors often stressed the army's abrogation of America's racial hierarchy. In one story published by Alexander

Garden decades after the occupation of Charleston, an upper-class woman, engaged in a debate with a British officer over the United States' alliance with France, observed that "a *Negro*, trigged out in full *British* uniform, happened to pass [by]." The sharp-witted woman turned to the officer and remarked, "See, Major . . . one of *your allies*—bow with gratitude for the service received from such honourable associat[ion]."[45] Early historians did not reserve their repugnance for the British alliance with black slaves but castigated the use of Native Americans and mercenaries as well. In opposition to the politics of retaliation, Botta wrote that "the Americans should abhor to imitate their adversaries, or the allies they had subsidized, whether Germans, blacks, or savages."[46] Mercy Otis Warren repeatedly criticized the British army for using Native American auxiliaries, relating as early as 1776 that the "irruptions of the natives in various parts" of the country were "stimulated by their native fierceness, wrought up higher by British influence, and headed up by some American desparadoes [*sic*] in the service of Britain."[47] The violation of racial hierarchies, like atrocities committed against women, demonized the British forces in their conduct of military rule.

Early historians' invocation of plundering, abuse of women, and abrogation of racial hierarchies served not only to cast the British troops as oppressors but also to erase the positive opportunities these groups realized under occupation. In making plunder and violence, rather than restructuring of the civil order, the main feature of life under military rule, the historians attempted to eliminate from memory the real opportunities that occupation regimes offered previously disenfranchised citizens. By emphasizing brutality against women, these narratives elided the memories, likely still active in many minds, of the greater social freedoms that women had exercised under military rule. Similarly, focusing on the outrage many whites felt at the British army's offers of freedom for slaves and use of Native Americans as allies attempted to erase the memory of slave insurrection and disruption of the racial hierarchy. In doing so, they created a new narrative, unencumbered by aspects of the occupation experience potentially subversive to the new republican regime.

To further suppress the potential danger to social order implied by the occupation experience, they cast upper-class women not as independent actors but as virtuous symbols of resistance. The ladies of Charleston received particular acclamation from revolutionary historians. Alexander Garden claimed that there were "invitations to engage in scenes of gaiety and dissipation, indignantly rejected" by the ladies of the town, and that "[t]he dungeons of the Provost, the crowded holds of the prison-ships, were anxiously sought."[48] Ramsay made similar assertions, writing that "the ladies in a great measure retired from the public eye, wept over the distresses of their country, and gave every proof of the warmest attachment to its suffering cause."[49] While Ramsay kept his observations general, Garden elaborated on the bravery of these women, recounting in one instance the "contrivances adopted by the ladies, to carry from the British Garrison supplies to the gallant defenders of their country." The veteran claimed to personally recall "a horseman's helmet concealed by a well arranged head-dress, and epaulettes delivered from the folds of the simple cap of a matron."[50] As with many other aspects of the revisionist narrative, the trope was picked up beyond those with personal experience of the war. Botta asserted of Charleston's women that "[f]ar from being offended at the name of rebel ladies, they esteemed it a title of distinction and glory."[51] Forgotten were the romances between British soldiers and civilian women, the accommodations women made, and, above all, the social freedom they exercised under military rule. In their place these historians applied a much safer postrevolutionary narrative of resistance and patriotism.

Having established the brutality of the soldiers of the British army in occupied territories, its abrogation of social and racial hierarchies, and the heroic resistance of ladies of Charleston as an alternative to the social opportunities they exercised, historians of the Revolution went on to largely excuse the vast majority of civilians who had participated in military rule. This apologia came out particularly keenly in representations of Charleston, South Carolina, where the fact that thousands had signed loyalty oaths and submitted to the Crown could not be ignored. Still, the actions of survivors who cooperated and declared their loyalty to the British could be excused by their claiming to have sided with the British out of fear or having been coerced because of threats to their families. Garden stressed that the "liberty of working for the support of their starving families, was denied to all who refused to solicit protection" of the British army in Charleston, and worse, that "suits against them were encouraged" in the occupation regimes' courts, "but against their pleas, the doors of Justice, as well as of Mercy, were closed."[52] Given these dangers, Americans could be forgiven for signing loyalty oaths. Ramsay concluded in his early history of the war in South Carolina that "fear and interest," rather than ideology, "had brought many of their new subjects to the British standard."[53] Revising this thesis a few years later in his more general history of the Revolution, Ramsay wrote that "though the inhabitants, from motives of fear or convenience, had generally submitted, the greatest part of them retained an affection for their American brethren."[54] Stressing the brutality of the British army and their total victory in South Carolina, these historians could begin to forgive and potentially rehabilitate those who had, under necessity, renounced the Revolution.

The early historians' revisionist take on military rule and the wider reinterpretation of the revolutionary experience of which it was a part provided an opening for those who had participated in occupation to rehabilitate themselves by rewriting the history of their own lives to conform to the new narrative. A brief return to the postwar experiences of Tench Coxe demonstrate how one survivor, at least, retroactively molded his occupation experiences to escape potential consequences of their acts. Throughout his political career, Coxe's opponents periodically brought up his former loyalism to discredit his ambitions. In his defenses against these critiques, Coxe's arguments tracked remarkably well to the narrative set forth by Ramsay and the other historians. In one early instance, brought on by Coxe's potential appointment to Congress in 1788, the merchant-turned-politician cast his collaborator past as "one youthful indiscretion" and explained his loyalism as circumstantial. Coxe had rather been "*driven* by the violence and threats of a body of armed men, when a boy to the British army"—life under occupation had not been his choice—and while living in occupied Philadelphia had "in many instances [been] kind to the friends of the American cause." Finally, Coxe and his supporters appealed to "the necessity of moderation and conciliation" in the postwar era, in a ploy perfectly adapted to the sentiments of much of American society after the end of the revolution.[55] By adopting this carefully developed narrative in 1788 and again and again throughout his life, Coxe was able to successfully defend himself against accusations and rehabilitate himself in early republican society. Although Coxe's case is particularly well documented due to his eventual high standing, thousands of others followed more obscure routes to acceptance under the new republic.

By the first decade of the nineteenth century, then, American society proved ready and even eager to forget the ambiguities, compromises, and messiness of the revolutionary experience and to accept a much more clear-cut version of its memory, even if that new version allowed former collaborators to remain in American society. This public forgetting was not only deliberate on the part of historians and nation-builders but also vital to the survival of thousands of Americans who lived under military rule and whose experiences shaped the course of the event. But it came at a steep cost and one that remains with us today. Because of the revisionist narrative that survivors and historians crafted, much of the complexity and dynamism of the revolutionary experience has been washed from our memory of the event, and in its place we cling to a static narrative populated by virtuous patriots, misguided loyalists, and oppressive British soldiers.

Those who crafted this new narrative did not do so out of compassion for these survivors, and that makes revealing its fabrication all the more important, because it proved essential to visions of the new American state propagated by early patriot elites. With the worst loyalists safely labeled and exiled, and those remaining forgiven their trespasses or even, like Tench Coxe, incorporated into the ruling class, revolutionary leaders could go about the business of consolidating their authority in the new republic free from challenge by a large segment of the population whose experience of the Revolution had been quite different. Further, by rhetorically unifying Americans and pitting them against a despotic British Empire, nation-builders used revolutionary history to propagate visions of a new North American empire. For leaders such as Thomas Jefferson and Andrew Jackson, the version of the Revolution propagated by early historians became justification for American patriots to sweep aside Native Americans, continue to hold Africans in bondage, and deny women political rights in the name of protection. After all, most Native Americans and slaves had sided with the British, whose permissive societies had in turn failed to protect American women from their soldiers' depredations.[56] Further, the reintegration of these loyalists into the republic became a model by which Jeffersonians and others could imagine the Empire of Liberty extending not only to the new republic but across the North American continent, incorporating even those exiled loyalists in Canada who had actively resisted republicanism less than a generation earlier.[57] Only by forgiving and forgetting those in their own midst who had once supported the Crown could patriot elites contemplate a new American empire not only separate but also more virtuous and even more expansive than the British one that had preceded it.

Notes

1. "Return of Refugees, and Their Slaves Arrived from Georgia and South Carolina," Sir Guy Carleton Papers, British Public Records Office (PRO), #620. Unless otherwise noted, all references to sources in the PRO used in this dissertation were accessed on microfilm at the David Library of the American Revolution, the Library of Congress, or the South Carolina State Archives.

2. Jim Piecuch, *Three Peoples, One King: Loyalists, Indians, and Slaves in the Revolutionary South* (Columbia, SC, 2008), 290.

3. Maya Jasanoff, *Liberty's Exiles: American Loyalists in the Revolutionary World* (New York, 2011), 6.

4. Paul H. Smith, "The American Loyalists: Notes on Their Organizational and Numerical Strength," *William and Mary Quarterly* 25 (1968): 267.

5. Graham Hodges, ed., *The Black Loyalist Directory: African Americans in Exile after the American Revolution* (New York, 1996), xi.

6. Smith, "The American Loyalists," 269.

7. Silvia Frey estimates that "perhaps as much as two-thirds of Georgia's total prewar black population of approximately fifteenth thousand," and a similar proportion of blacks in South Carolina, left after the war, mostly destined for continued slavery in the West Indies, but several thousand others left as free people. This would leave approximately one-third remaining in bondage in the southern states. Silvia Frey, *Water from the Rock: Black Resistance in a Revolutionary Age* (Princeton, 1991), 174.

8. See Robert Calhoon, *The Loyalists in Revolutionary America, 1760–1781* (New York, 1965), 290–94, 409–14; Robert Lambert, *South Carolina Loyalists in the American Revolution* (Columbia, SC, 1987), 291–94; and Piecuch, *Three Peoples, One King,* 296.

9. For one example of this in revolutionary New York, see Howard Pashman, "The People's Property Law: A Step toward Building a New Legal Order in Revolutionary New York," *Law and History Review* 31 (2013): 587–626.

10. Lois Masur, *Rites of Execution: Capital Punishment and the Transformation of American Culture, 1776–1865* (New York, 1991), 74; see also David Waldstreicher, *In the Midst of Perpetual Fetes: The Making of American Nationalism, 1776–1820* (Chapel Hill, NC, 1997), 39.

11. Jasanoff, *Liberty's Exiles,* 91–92.

12. George Brinley to Francis Brinley, 24 August 1783, Malbone/Brinley Papers, Newport Historical Society.

13. For a full account the Brinleys' smuggling activities, see Donald Johnson, "Occupied America: Everyday Experience and the Failure of Imperial Authority in Revolutionary Cities under British Rule, 1775–1783," PhD diss., Northwestern University, 2015, 139–42. For Francis Brinley's reputation as a loyalist, see Ezra Stiles, *The Literary Diary of Ezra Stiles, DD, LLD,* ed. Franklin Dexter (March 1776–December 1781) (New York, 1901), 2:134.

14. Jacob Cooke, *Tench Coxe and the Early Republic* (Chapel Hill, NC, 1978), 20, 30–31, 34–36.

15. Tench Coxe to John Cox, 10 June 1778, Tench Coxe Letterbook, May–December 1778, Coxe Family Papers, Historical Society of Pennsylvania.

16. Quoted in Cooke, *Tench Coxe and the Early Republic,* 41.

17. John Knowles, Certification of Tench Coxe's subscription to the Oath of Allegiance and Fidelity, 23 May 1778, Coxe Papers; see also Cooke, *Tench Coxe and the Early Republic,* 41.

18. Tench Coxe to John Cox, 10 June 1778, Tench Coxe Letterbook, May-December 1778, Coxe Papers.

19. Tench Coxe to unknown, n.d. Coxe, Furman, and Coxe Letterbook, 1776–79, 141. The company's letterbook during this period is riddled with mutilations, which are not nearly so common in other sections. Coxe Papers.

20. Elizabeth Evans, ed., "Mary Gould Almy," in *Weathering the Storm: Women of the American Revolution* (New York, 1975), 249.

21. Ibid., 269.

22. Ibid., 270.

23. William Sabine, ed., *Historical Memoirs of William Smith, from 26 August 1778 to 12 November 1783* (New York, 1971), 133n.

24. George Atkinson Ward, ed., *Journal and Letters of the Late Samuel Curwin, Judge of the Admiralty, Etc., an American Refugee in England, from 1775 to 1784* (New York, 1842), 493.

25. James Rivington to James DeLancey, 20 December 1783, James DeLancey Papers, New-York Historical Society. For Rivington's fate, see Morton Pennypacker, *General Washington's Spies on Long Island and in New York* (Brooklyn, 1939), 7. Pennypacker and later authors such as Alexander Rose have identified Rivington as a member of the Culper Spy Ring for the Continental Army, which may explain his exemption from prosecution after the war. However, very little evidence exists to corroborate the printer's involvement, and it was certainly not a well-known idea until long after the war.

26. For the best recent account of this type of violence and the motivations behind it, see David Fowler, "'Loyalty Is Now Bleeding in New Jersey': Motivations of the Disaffected," in Joseph Tiedemann, Eugene Fingerhut, and Robert Venables, eds., *The Other Loyalists: Ordinary People, Royalism, and the Revolution in the Middle Colonies, 1763–1787* (Albany, NY, 2009), 45–77.

27. For more on this, see Waldstreicher, *In the Midst of Perpetual Fetes* and Benjamin Irvin, *Clothed in the Robes of Sovereignty: The Continental Congress and the People Out of Doors* (New York, 2011).

28. For material and other incarnations of this new American nationalism, see Kariann Yakota, *Unbecoming British: How America Became a Post-Colonial Nation* (New York, 2011).

29. See Alfred Young, *The Shoemaker and the Tea Party: Memory and the American Revolution* (Boston, 1999), esp. 12–13.

30. For more on this, see the introduction to Lester Cohen, *The Revolutionary Histories: Contemporary Narratives of the American Revolution* (Ithaca, NY, 1980) and chapter 1 of Arthur Shaffer, *The Politics of History: Writing the History of the American Revolution, 1783–1815*.

31. For biographical details on Ramsay, see Arthur Schaffer, *To Be an American: David Ramsay and the Making of the American Consciousness* (Columbia, SC, 1991), esp. 54–58.

32. For biographical details on Warren, see Rosemarie Zagarri, *A Woman's Dilemma: Mercy Otis Warren and the American Revolution*, 2nd ed. (Boston, 2015).

33. David Ramsay, *The History of the American Revolution* (London, 1793), 1:263.

34. Mercy Otis Warren, *History of the Rise, Progress, and Termination of the American Revolution, Interspersed with Biographical, Political, and Moral Observations* (Boston, 1805), 1:338–39.

35. Jedidiah Morse, *Annals of the American Revolution; or, A Record of the Causes and Events Which Produced, and Terminated in the Establishment and Independence of the American Republic* (Hartford, CT, 1824), 260.

36. Alexander Garden, *Anecdotes of the Revolutionary War in America, with Sketches of Character of Persons Most Distinguished, in the Southern States, for Civil and Military Services* (Charleston, SC, 1822), 258.

37. Samuel Wilson, *A History of the American Revolution: Intended as a Reading Book for Schools* (Stonington, CT, 1826), 127.

38. Charles [Carlo] Botta, *History of the War of the Independence of the United States*, trans. George Alexander Otis (Cooperstown, NY, 1845), 1:435.

39. Ramsay, *History of the American Revolution*, 2:165.

40. Warren, *History of the Rise, Progress, and Termination*, 1:339.

41. Ramsay, *History of the Revolution of South-Carolina* (Trenton, NJ, 1785), 2:265.

42. Botta, *History of the War of the Independence of the United States*, 2:255.

43. Warren, *History of the Rise, Progress, and Termination*, 2:203.

44. Ramsay, *History of the American Revolution*, 2:172. Ramsay does devote more space to the slave rebellion in his *History of the Revolution of South-Carolina* (2:374–79), but still discounts it as a nonfactor in the war as a whole.

45. Garden, *Anecdotes*, 237.

46. Botta, *History of the War of Independence*, 145

47. Warren, *History of the Rise, Progress, and Termination*, 1:341.

48. Garden, *Anecdotes*, 227.

49. Ramsay, *History of the American Revolution*, 2:172–73.

50. Garden, *Anecdotes*, 243.

51. Botta, *History of the War for Independence*, 2:261.

52. Garden, *Anecdotes*, 267.

53. Ramsay, *History of the Revolution of South Carolina*, 2:263.

54. Ramsay, *History of the American Revolution*, 2:161.

55. For the editorials during the 1788 congressional election, see the *Federal Gazette*, 22 November 1788, 2. For the charges of loyalism that came up throughout Coxe's political career, see Cooke, *Tench Coxe and the Early Republic*, 44–45.

56. For Jefferson's views on the memory of the Revolution and its justification of expansion and exploitation, see Peter Onuf, *Jefferson's Empire: The Language of American Nationhood* (Charlottesville, VA, 2000), 4–6, 21, 27.

57. For more on these visions of the incorporation of Canada, see Alan Taylor, *The Civil War of 1812: American Subjects, British Citizens, Irish Rebels, and Indian Allies* (New York, 2010), 5–6.

Abbe's Ghost

Negotiating Slavery in Paris, 1783–1784

DAVID N. GELLMAN

The servants sensed a ghostly presence, but their masters laughed. Abbe, a married slave woman from colonial New Jersey, had traveled to Madrid and then to Paris with the family of John Jay as he embarked on a diplomatic journey that ultimately secured independence for the fledgling United States. The slave woman had tended to her mistress, Sarah Jay, as the diplomat's wife endured three pregnancies while Abbe lived an ocean apart from her own husband. In France a falling out with Mrs. Jay prompted Abbe to run away to work for a nearby laundress. John Jay's fellow peace negotiator Benjamin Franklin helped Sarah Jay punish the slave by having her thrown in jail. In her cell, the unrepentant Abbe, who expressed her wish to return to America, caught the "violent Cold" that would kill her despite her distressed mistress's belated efforts at revival.[1] Abbe's spirit haunted her fellow servants, including the slave Benoit from Martinique, who sensed the injustice of this tragedy.

Although John Jay, kept abreast of the situation while he traveled in England, had puzzled over Abbe's motives, he knew a lot about slavery. Having enjoyed the fruits of the institution, the New Yorker already believed that slavery contradicted the spirit of the American Revolution. Even so, he had negotiated a treaty barring Britain from evacuating runaway slaves. In this diplomatic context, Abbe's personal protest underscored conflicts between ideology and interest, illustrating how inequalities of gender, class, race, and law enforcement shaped the Atlantic world at the very moment that white liberal revolutionaries achieved a seminal triumph. The burden of order and stability fell on the enslaved.

Abbe's death does far more than poignantly expose yet again the hypocrisy of the founders on the issue of slavery. This story is not merely a Jeffersonian tale without the sex and the denial-erasing DNA.[2] The episode conjoins the personal and the political to reveal how negotiations between masters and servants, between British and American diplomats, and between founders and their own consciences could produce callous cruelty while at the same time solidifying antislavery principles.[3] Abbe was one of the Revolutionary War's final casualties, with her own story to tell. Her ghost betokened unacknowledged guilt while also serving as a harbinger of liberating alternatives. For Abbe's master, John Jay, the public and private events that unfolded in Paris revealed that the coupling of paternal condescension and emancipatory commitment could produce morally uneven results. By closely examining stories on this shifting terrain, we gain a more intimate understanding of how this revolutionary age became a crossroads of slavery and freedom for so many founders, black and white.[4] As empires forged new boundaries, unsettling truths about liberty haunted participants high and low. The desire to consolidate sovereignty over vast territories and fractious polities restrained—when not mocking—the egalitarian intentions of revolutionary elites. In an imperial house united under a new flag, black voices struggled to be heard.

"I bought a very fine negroe Boy of 15 years old at Martinico," John Jay reported from Spain to his father in May 1780. On his way to Europe to try to gain support for the war effort, the thirty-four-year-old former president of the Continental Congress acquired a slave to attend to him just as his wife, Sarah Livingston Jay (known as Sally), had Abbe, a female slave who had previously served in the household of Sally's father.[5] For wealthy families like the Jays and the Livingstons, the personal service of slaves was one of the privileges of their position, though in truth it was quite common to find slaves in New York and New Jersey households of much less means.[6] If John and Sally Jay's first and only direct encounter with a plantation slavery society shocked their mid-Atlantic mainland slaveholding sensibilities, they left little indication. Sally relished her ten-day encounter with Martinique. Her first sight of the West Indian island from shipboard revealed "the most verdant, romantic country I ever beheld." The French she found to be good stewards of their colony, commenting, "The neatness that prevails here cannot be exceeded & I frankly confess I never saw it equal'd." The presence of slaves prompted only a mildly discordant note: as she reported to her father, patriot governor of New Jersey William Livingston, "every here and there the eye is supris'd [by] settlements aside & amid the hills belonging to the negros who are employed upon the plantations." But she immediately followed this sentence with the reassuring observation: "Then again a plain of small extent with genteel houses diversify the prospect." With the slave Benoit now part of their party, the Jays left their French Caribbean "friends of American Liberty" for Spain.[7] Slavery and the revolutionary mission seemed to go neatly together.

If Martinique offered exotic diversions, slavery helped the Jays maintain comforting connections to home amid personal and professional travail. While Spanish indifference stymied John's diplomatic mission, Sally gave birth to a daughter who died twenty-three days later. Having longtime Livingston-family slave Abbe with her proved invaluable to easing Sally's pain. Writing her mother Susannah French Livingston in devastation over the death of her child, Sally paused to note, "The attention and proofs of fidelity which we have receiv'd from Abbe, demand, & ever shall have my acknowledgments, you can hardly imagine how useful she is to us, for indeed her place cou'd not be supplied, at least not here." Self-described as "bewilder'd," Sally no doubt relied on Abbe all the more because at the time she wrote her mother, John had followed the Spanish royal court from Madrid to St. Ildefonso.[8] The seeming necessity of Abbe's service became magnified when, in February 1782, Sally gave birth to Maria, a girl who remained healthy even as the family relocated from Spain to the epicenter of American revolutionary diplomacy in Paris.[9]

The teenage slave Benoit from Martinique served to connect Sally Jay to her American home life as well. The Jays had left their young son, Peter Augustus, in America with Sally's parents. Sally promised her five-year-old, "When I return I'll bring you a clever little black boy that speaks french, & then if you can read & write english well, you may learn that language."[10] The lack of self-consciousness, the ease with which Mrs. Jay assumed her class and racial privilege would contribute to her own son's ascent to cosmopolitan achievement, conveys how perfectly normal slavery could seem to these revolutionary Americans.

Their slaves' vulnerabilities allowed Sally and John to imagine themselves as beneficent dispensers of favor. Abbe endured her own trying separations by coming to Europe, her status and personal circumstances making her displacement all the worse, a fact her mistress's cavalier commentary revealed. Sally noted in a postscript to her sister Kitty, "Abbe is well & would be glad to know if she is mistress of a husband still."[11] Abbe's service to Sally had strained a family bond. Separation provoked anxiety about her husband's faithfulness. But to receive assurances, Abbe had to ask her literate white mistress to make inquiries on her behalf. Relying on Sally, the cause of Abbe's removal, in this intimate matter could not have been pleasant. In any event, the cool irony with which Sally conveyed this request expressed a great deal about the inequalities of power at the core of Abbe's relationship to her. Sally wrote with patronizing freedom about the faithfulness of Abbe's "husband," whom Abbe wished to serve even at a distance of three thousand miles. As slave marriages had no legal meaning, their status as husband and wife was solely a matter of fidelity or at least personal devotion, leaving Abbe particularly vulnerable to circumstance and the fickleness of the human heart.

John Jay's European correspondence to his younger brother Frederick expressed his own sense of condescending mastery, blending an acceptance of the reality of slavery with a personal sense of responsibility and hints of an emerging antislavery sensibility.[12] During the war, Jay's family took refuge in Dutchess County, attempting to avoid the ravages inflicted by regular and irregular forces waging war on both sides in their home ground of Westchester County.[13] It fell to Frederick to manage a household that included their father, Peter, well past seventy, as well as some of his handicapped siblings, with only a few of the family's slaves in a position to lend much help. In April 1781 Frederick made no attempt to sugarcoat to his brother John what he regarded as a very bad situation in their "large and helpless Family." Frederick desperately wished to downsize, and reducing the white portion of the family was not what he had in mind.[14] Distance seemed to make John more sanguine about the family's ability to negotiate the challenges they faced and prompted the diplomat to be solicitous of the slaves' well-being. John wrote, "Tell all the servants that I remember them. The Trunk I sent from Bordeaux contained something for each of them." He regretted that it got lost in transit.[15] He wanted to play the role of benevolent patriarch, becoming fixated on the idea that providing the family slaves with a type of coarse cloth he had come across in Spain would be helpful to everyone concerned and would serve as a token of his esteem for the slaves.[16]

John clearly felt uncomfortable with Frederick's desire to cut the family loose of responsibility for unproductive slaves, mixing paternalism and moralism to justify a foot-dragging approach. He authorized Frederick to threaten one particularly mischievous servant by informing her that John would not protect her if she continued to behave badly. But John balked at disposing of the family's "old servants who have expended their Strength & youth for the family, they ought and must be taken good care of while we have the means of doing it. [C]ommon justice and I may say Gratitude demands it." John conceded that Frederick might dispose with "one or more" from a list that included Clarinda, Little Mary, Castor, and Peet, some or all of whom were relatively young, perhaps even children, but then immediately qualified that suggestion with the telling remark, "how far this may suit with your conscience I know not."[17]

Even as John, Sally, Abbe, and Benoit made the transition from Spain to France in the spring and summer of 1782, John continued to express concern for his family's slaves and former slaves in New York. In April 1782 Jay inquired of his brother, "How do all the old servants do?" and asked that Frederick "tell them I have not forgotten them, and that they would have been convinced of it, if the Enemy had not intercepted the things I have sent for them." News of his father's death deepened rather than dampened Jay's concern for the family's elderly former slaves.[18]

John's repeated expressions of protectiveness toward Plato, Zilpha, Mary, and other family slaves indicates that slavery weighed on his conscious and that he understood how the death of whites could have severe consequences for blacks. It is telling that John's continued insistence on caring for Zilpha paid no heed to the fact that his father had already freed her. At the same time, John's attitude toward Jay family slaves back in New York was psychologically convenient. He played the role of the protective and sympathetic master without having to do any of the work or make any of the hard decisions, a responsibility that he left to his hard-pressed younger brother. Still, John Jay's solicitude shows that the diplomat wished to weave a moral context for his actions with regard to African American servitude based on notions deeper and more humane than the chattel principle or racial contempt.[19]

By the time John Jay expressed his concerns for the well-being of the family's slaves and former slaves, this prominent patriot had already developed some profound moral concerns about the concept and the institution of slavery. Like so many of his fellow revolutionaries, Jay freely employed metaphors of enslavement to justify resistance to repressive British policies and then to defend the war for independence. In December 1776 Jay placed this theme on a theological and biblical plane: it was not, he asserted, God's plan to "suffer Slavery" in the newly independent land and therefore circumvent the future spread of the gospels across the continent.[20]

Jay was well aware that in the crucible of revolution, the distance from political metaphors of enslavement to taking measures against actual slavery had compressed. In the years immediately preceding his diplomatic service in Europe, he knew that some of his contemporaries had big plans, plans which he at least tacitly endorsed. Assessing the state's new 1777 Constitution in a letter to his friends and political collaborators Gouverneur Morris and Robert

Livingston, Jay commented: "I should also have been for a Clause against the Continuation of domestic Slavery."[21]

While president of the Continental Congress, Jay presided over deliberations for one of the most daring emancipation proposals of the war, known to history as the Laurens plan. The brainchild of John Laurens, son of influential South Carolina politician Henry Laurens, the plan called for the arming of thousands of that state's slaves in the patriot cause in exchange for their freedom. Two weeks prior to the Continental Congress's unanimous endorsement of the proposal, Jay received an enthusiastic letter from his fellow New Yorker and George Washington's aide-de-camp, Alexander Hamilton. Although Hamilton viewed the measure as a military expedient, long-term moral progress would also result. Hamilton wrote Jay that the prospect of a wider "emancipation . . . I confess, has no small weight in inducing me to wish the success of the project."[22] Although the Continental Congress approved the plan to raise three thousand black soldiers, including funding to buy the slaves' freedom from their masters, the plan foundered when the South Carolina legislature and George Washington balked at such daring.[23]

Attacks on slavery cropped up from an even more radical direction during Jay's presidency. In early 1779 John Jay heard directly from pioneering Quaker antislavery activist Anthony Benezet. Benezet wished Jay to read his pamphlet *Serious Considerations on several Important Subjects,* which included sections on war, slavery, and the dangers of alcohol. Benezet's cover letter focused exclusively on the first of these themes, war, explaining Quaker pacifism as a sincere commitment to the Friends' understanding of Christianity.[24] War constituted "impious rebellion and defiance against" the Lord. Meanwhile, Benezet's *Observations on Slavery* argued that immoral impulses governed "the minds of most Slave Holders" even in the current climate where "the rights and liberties of mankind have been" so frequently discussed. He asked pointedly, "Will not the Americans, amongst whom the establishment of religious as well as civil liberty is the present and great object of consideration and debate, be a witness against themselves, so long as they continue to keep their Fellow-Inhabitants in such grievous circumstances?" The only righteous path was the granting of freedom to all.[25]

Jay greeted the Quaker appeal to conscience with even-tempered courtesy, implicitly indicating agreement with Benezet's views on slavery. In a draft penned directly on the letter from Benezet, Jay praised Benezet's "Benevolence." The president of the Continental Congress attempting to win a war of independence could not "subscribe to all his opinions," but Jay endorsed the broad principle that "Civil and religious Liberty is a Blessing which I sincerely wish to all mankind" and expressed his "hope [that] it will ever be the policy of these States so to extend and secure it to all their citizens" who "may have Reason to complain of Partiality or oppression."[26] His self-conscious broadness, at once vague and inclusive, suggests Jay's assent that the liberating mission of the Revolution ought to include slaves.

By the time Jay arrived in Europe, he internalized the idea that slavery contradicted the principles of the revolution in terms that echoed Benezet. Writing from Spain in September 1780, Jay voiced his most complete and eloquent view on abolition to that date. Earlier that year Pennsylvania initiated gradual emancipation by promising full freedom at age twenty-eight to children subsequently born to enslaved women. Jay proclaimed to his good friend and New York political ally Egbert Benson: "Till America comes into this Measure her Prayers to Heaven for Liberty will be impious," this last word the same one Benezet had used to describe war. Jay continued:

> This is a strong Expression but it is just. Were I in your Legislature I would prepare a Bill for the Purpose with great Care, and I would never cease moving it till it became a Law or I ceased to be a member. I believe God governs this World, and I believe it to be a Maxim in his as in our Court that those who ask for Equity ought to do it.[27]

The ambitious New York lawyer shared crucial beliefs with the Pennsylvania educator and pamphleteer. Jay, like Benezet, expressed the conviction that morality required consistency, that the revolution stated one thing on slavery but did another, and that piety dictated honoring the natural rights of men. They also shared a belief that some form of gradualism answered this divine imperative.[28] Religious duty required a concrete application of the principles of American liberty to African American slaves. But "to do it"—to treat black people with equity—would prove no more straightforward for Jay residing in Europe than for his family members, his fellow New Yorkers, or his fellow Americans grappling with slavery at home.

If the moral link between revolution and slavery had become clear, John Jay's negotiations over slavery in Paris exposed the reality that slaves remained valuable property in which his countrymen retained a keen interest. As a delegate charged with formulating a formal peace treaty with the British, Jay found himself with a job to do—and that job included protecting the demands of slaveholders. Doing "equity" in this arena, then, meant something quite different than freeing slaves, regardless of what he had told Egbert Benson.

Because slaves had emphatically inserted themselves in the war, the disposition of slaves became a feature of the peace. The Laurens plan to arm South Carolina slaves had been an attempt to play catch-up. Even before independence the British had tried to induce the Virginia slaves of patriot masters to flee; offering freedom to those running away from rebellious owners subsequently became official continental British war policy. Thousands of slaves would take advantage of this opportunity to secure their own freedom on their own terms.[29] With the cessation of fighting after the British defeat at Yorktown, former slaves crowded behind loyalist lines, shielded for the time being from the claims of their once and would-be masters. Resolving the status of these African Americans and their potential evacuation eventually made its way onto the diplomatic agenda in Paris in ways that put the expressed antislavery inclinations of the four U.S. peace commissioners—Jay, along with John Adams, Benjamin Franklin, and Henry Laurens—to the test. As Jay and his colleagues implemented on this earth America's "Prayers to Heaven for Liberty," the necessity to do something about slavery yielded to realpolitik.

Slavery emerged late in the provisional treaty negotiations as a bargaining chip, though slavery fell well down the list of priorities, which from the U.S. perspective was headed by the need to secure British acknowledgment of U.S. independence and establishing the widest possible boundaries of postwar U.S. territory.[30] The impetus to take up the issue came from the Continental Congress, which in September 1782, on a motion by James Madison, instructed Secretary of Foreign Affairs Robert R. Livingston "to obtain as speedily as possible authentic returns of the Slaves and other property which have been carried off or destroyed in the course of this War by the Enemy" and forward that information to the U.S. negotiating team in France. Meanwhile, Livingston should apprise the U.S. representatives there "that many thousands of Slaves and other property . . . have been carried off" and that "the great loss of property which the Citizens of the United States have sustained by the Enemy will be considered by the several States as an insuperable bar" to compensating Americans who cast their lot with the Crown for property confiscated during the war.[31] Jay and Adams introduced congressional concerns into negotiations with their British counterparts.[32]

During the final day of negotiations of the Preliminary and Conditional Articles of Peace, language regarding slaves held by the British made its way into the treaty as part of a final bargain. Aided by newly arrived American peace commissioner Henry Laurens, the negotiators added the prohibition against "carrying away any Negroes, or other Property of the American Inhabitants" to the Seventh Article, which governed the terms of British evacuation from U.S. territory.[33]

The Americans had come into the session asking for even sterner and explicit language to demand "Compensation . . . for the Tobacco, Rice, Indigo and Negroes &c. seized and carried off" by the British in "the States of Virginia, North and South Carolina, and Georgia." Franklin assimilated southern grievances into the broader case he and his colleagues wished to make against holding Americans liable for debts to British merchants. The premise of selling Americans British imports on credit was that American planters would be able to pay off their debts "by the Labour of their Negroes and the Produce of that Labour." But the seizure of American property, including "even the Negroes," undermined the ability of American planters to pay their debts. While the Americans did not get their demand for compensation inserted in Article 5, they had made their point. On this final day of negotiation, the British acceded to American demands on the Newfoundland fisheries and allowed restrictions to be placed on the amount of time Loyalists would have to seek restitution for their lost property.[34]

The commissioners, including John Jay, expressed satisfaction with what they had accomplished together. Adams even specifically approved of Article 7's prohibition against evacuating slave refugees, while also singling out Jay's particularly excellent work during the course of the lengthy process.[35] Anticipating the next round of negotiations that would finalize the treaty, Jay himself wrote Livingston indicating that it was unlikely that the British would agree to "Compensation for Damages," but that in any case, "Our affairs have a very promising Aspect, and a little prudence will secure us all that we can reasonably wish [or] expect."[36] Reading between the lines, Jay accepted the principle that the British should not evacuate former slaves and other American property, though he did not regard making such issues an obstacle to concluding a permanent peace.

In the interim between the provisional and the final treaty, Jay and his fellow diplomats would receive pressure from home to take a more aggressive stance on the dispensation of American slaves sheltered by the British. Manhattan, which the British occupied while awaiting a final treaty, had become a haven of last resort for African Americans from up and down the east coast who had availed themselves of the British offer of freedom. British commander Guy Carleton intentionally thwarted both informal and formal efforts by American slave owners to retrieve slaves from Manhattan.[37]

Franklin, Adams, and Jay dutifully presented American grievances during the definitive treaty negotiations, but attempts to add language to that document that would financially account for the British evacuation of blacks and other American property failed.[38] British officials viewed Carleton's logic that the British must honor their promise of freedom to runaway slaves as "solid & founded in Equity," a word Jay may well have recognized from his own thoughts about slavery.[39]

Like the U.S. Constitution ratified six years later, the Peace of Paris wove the principle of slavery into the fabric of the nation's legal existence, even though all four U.S. negotiators had in other contexts become at least sometimes critical of slavery.[40] Property rights in man mattered to the newly sovereign nation. Prayers for future emancipation notwithstanding, the British did not have a right, the commissioners believed, to interfere in the sovereign domestic affairs of the new nation, even though the United States had limited leverage to prevent the British from doing so in actual practice.[41] With the definitive treaty concluded, Jay could join his fellow commissioners in taking pride that they had done what they could to secure the nation's independence and protect its interests. The irrepressible human will of slaves to seek freedom and the responsibility of moral men to advance that freedom could be work for John Jay and Benjamin Franklin to pursue some other time, perhaps they imagined, upon their return to American soil.

The final months of 1783 should have been a joyous time for the Jay household. Three weeks before the signing of the final treaty, Sally Jay gave birth to another daughter, Ann. Apparently believing that he had little to offer in the way of service to a new mother and young children, John departed for England to take care of some family business and to seek some rest and relaxation. But then Abbe, who had served Sally Jay in Europe without noted incident, shattered the household's equilibrium by running away, touching off a new round of negotiations over slavery that tested the principles of the founders directly. In Abbe's case, slavery wasn't an abstraction—a bargaining chip, a financial calculation, a matter of national pride. It was a personal test of wills between servant and master that exposed the unsteadiness of Jay's (and Franklin's) antislavery principles even more than the peace negotiations.

When Abbe ran away, she made a bid to communicate her objections to the life imposed upon her. The slave forced Sally Jay, John Jay, Peter Jay Munro, Benjamin Franklin, and Franklin's grandson William Temple Franklin to consider how a black female slave viewed her situation, what frustrations and anxieties motivated her, and how best to respond. As Abbe revealed her resentment and even her sense of desperation, whites accustomed to exercising their command over her and people like her demonstrated how partially they understood Abbe, a person from whom they expected self-abnegating service, not self-assertion. Abbe's tale, then, is one of resistance and the life-threatening limits of paternalistic benevolence and antislavery convictions, the moral drama of American slavery played out in the unlikely setting of early 1780s France.[42]

A difficult relationship with a French nurse named Louisson hired to take care of the Sally and John's two young daughters precipitated Abbe's departure.[43] Louisson took offense at Abbe's alleged incivility toward her, a problem that the Frenchwoman took up with Sally herself. Louisson, in Sally's telling of the story, wished that Abbe could be "dismiss[ed]" but promised to tolerate Abbe's rudeness and not quit her post because Sally even tolerated Abbe's "impertinent" behavior toward Sally herself. Tensions ran high, as Abbe even started to show displeasure with her mistress. For her part, Sally attributed Abbe's departure to "her extreme jealousy of Louisson" and "the inticements of an English washer-woman who promised to pay her if she would assist her in washing."

Lacking Abbe's own written account of her motives, we are left to guess how much credit to give to Sally's explanation. A personally difficult, even jealous, relationship with a rival French servant seems plausible, but this tension may have been exacerbated by the fact that Abbe observed a key difference between her and other female servants. Louisson and the English washerwoman received monetary compensation for their work and could choose to leave or turn down jobs if they desired. Abbe, on the other hand, was bound to her mistress. In the face of stress she felt, Abbe may have found the inducement of wages from the English washerwoman an appealing chance to show her disfavor *and* to try out another life role, humble to be sure, but still different from being someone's slave. Thus Abbe took her clothes and left the household.[44]

Under French law, Abbe may have been entitled to her freedom all along. Precedents dating back to the sixteenth century established France as free soil, and French West Indian slaves brought to Europe by their masters successfully petitioned for their freedom in the 1780s as well. French authorities, however, were far more interested in eliminating the presence of blacks in France than freeing slaves. Thus the 1770s brought new regulations attempting to quarantine colonial slaves in *depots* upon arriving in France with their Caribbean masters. The 1777 law explicitly banned "foreigners" from entering with blacks and imposed a fine for all violations. In addition, the law, which avoided the use of the word *slave* in order not to tread directly on free soil principles, indicated that the servants covered by the law retain the same status under which they arrived, in essence trying to forestall freedom suits. This "legal morass" still left enough ambiguity to allow some slaves to obtain their freedom by court petition. One way or another, the Jays' ownership of Abbe lacked legal legitimacy. But no one seemed concerned with the legal details in Abbe's case. She had violated American law and custom, blacks were to some extent illegal aliens under the law, and powerful whites wished to make sure that she understood that such transgressions would not be tolerated.[45] Negotiations of her fate were dramatically uneven.

Rather than wait for John Jay's direction, indeed wanting not to trouble John with a problem that could be solved locally, Benjamin Franklin himself intervened quickly to restore order. At Sally's prompting, the eminent elder American diplomat contacted a police lieutenant, who went to the English washerwoman's residence, seized Abbe, and placed her in jail. Franklin had been in France long enough to know that technically Abbe might have a stronger legal position than her masters, but Franklin was a prominent person who knew how to work the system far better than she.[46] Abbe's pique was no match for white people's power, influence, and authority.

Abbe's white masters struggled to determine an appropriate resolution beyond the intimidation of imprisonment, believing that identifying the cause of her grievances should shape in some way a resolution to the predicament. Abbe's resentments likely went deeper than a mere impulsive desire to vex her masters. She felt humiliated by her status as a slave among servants and had had enough of life far away from her American home. These motivations registered albeit dimly with the Jays. The attempt by John's teenage nephew Peter Jay Munro to act as an emissary shed some light on Abbe's state of mind without suggesting a satisfactory way forward. His first visit to prison found Abbe defiant. The teenager proposed that he play the role of peacemaker between his aunt and the slave, offering to ask Sally to let Abbe rejoin the household. To this she answered "that instead of desiring that, she would run-a-way again . . . & that she wd. remain where she was" until John returned from England or until "she might be sent to America instead of returning home to be laughed at & work too." This answer, as filtered through Peter and Sally, indicated that Abbe understood that John Jay alone possessed the authority to address her situation. Moreover, her life in France had exposed her to humiliation; a white servant without nearly as much connection to the family occupied a higher status and commanded more respect than she did.

Thus she also told Peter Jay Munro that she "hop'd" Sally "was then Content" allowing herself to be "intirely govern'd by Louisson." Subsequent attempts by Peter to broker a solution proved even more fruitless as "This increased her Ideas of her own importance" and she became increasingly "sullen."[47] Abbe was tapping deeply into a reservoir of resentments.

John and Sally Jay did not exhibit an inclination to peel back the layers of meaning behind Abbe's actions and assumed that a measured approach to discipline would return her to the family and to her senses. From London, learning of Abbe's revolt, John assumed that it "was not resolved upon in a sober moment," but was perhaps a product of drunken misjudgment. Otherwise, John wrote to Franklin's grandson, "I cannot conceive of a Motive." But, at least subconsciously, John did in fact discern a motive: Abbe's desire to be free. Thus John noted, "I had promised to manumit her on our Return to America, provided she behaved properly in the mean Time." He had, in other words, previously entered into a sort of negotiation with her, and what struck him as odd was the seemingly impulsive way in which she misplayed her far weaker hand. Jay presumed she would and should continue to endure her degradation calmly.

At some level Abbe understood John more clearly than he understood her. After all, she insisted to Peter Jay Munro that she wished to deal directly with John, perhaps sensing from his promise of freedom in America that he was on her side and was, in any case, the only one with the full authority to make her life better. In this she was not entirely wrong, for in John's letter to William Temple Franklin, he stated that "amidst her Faults, she has several good Qualities, & I wish to see her happy and contented on her own account as well as ours." John hoped to mend the rift, and even in light of it, he did not take the offer of eventual manumission off the table. Indeed, Jay's initial response was not especially vindictive, although it was certainly condescending in tone and blame-shifting in its implications, his feeling being that "she should be punished, tho' not vigorously." His parting verdict on Abbe's actions was "too much Indulgence & improper Company have injured her—it is a Pity."[48] Sally reached a similarly self-serving conclusion after Peter Jay Munro reported Abbe's sarcastic refusal of amnesty, writing that being underworked had "been of great dis-service to her," as opposed to her slavery or being dragged overseas in the first place.[49]

John and Sally agreed that lenience rather than labor had triggered the slave's recalcitrance, but their calculation of how much pressure should be applied to Abbe differed. John supported Franklin's recommendation that they simply ignore her imprisonment "for 15 or 20 days," with John assuming that if she is "separated from Wine and improper Company" but given "all the Necessaries of Life" she would in "Sobriety, Solitude and want of Employment" become "more obedient to Reason." Sally had her doubts from the start, writing John, "I'm so afraid of her suffering from the Cold" that she would dispatch their nephew to periodically check on Abbe's well-being.[50] As it turned out, Sally's fears were well placed. Her male counterparts' counsel that they outwait Abbe's alleged irrationality proved to be tragic in its results. The punishment that Franklin and Jay reasonably calculated proved to be a death sentence.

Abbe fell quite ill in prison, prompting Sally Jay to urgently contact William Franklin to assist in getting her out of prison. Even in writing in the formal third person, Sally's fear for Abbe's life was palpable: she wrote that her servant "is very ill & extremely desirous to return & Mrs. Jay fears a delay may be dangerous." Wanting to put a braver face on matters to her husband, she drafted a letter to John the same day reporting that Abbe had "beg'd" to return and "As I fear'd she would not receive benefit from the society she had [in prison], I granted her request, & am glad to find her penitent & desirous to efface by her future Conduct the reproach her late misstep has merited." Abbe probably was scared and lonely, feelings that could trigger a sincere expression of regret. But she was undoubtedly very sick, with a cold so severe that Sally insisted she stay in bed, with the "hope she'll recover in a week or two."[51] But instead of recovering, Abbe died.

Abbe's protest cost her life, which was surely not her intention. In a sense, then, John's puzzlement over why she would risk the freedom he meant to give her by running off was well placed. She had misplayed a weak hand badly. But she had behaved like a three-dimensional human being, when John and Sally each would have preferred two dimensions. John wished her to be rational, to be "obedient to Reason," and therefore to wait patiently in subservience for the gift of liberty he wished to bestow. Sally wished her to remain loyal, attached to the family, as Sally was attached to Abbe, a familiar and extremely helpful person who connected Sally to America. John and Sally knew full well that Abbe was a person, neither suggesting that her race made her less so. But master and mistress alike underestimated the fullness of their servant's personhood, the desire for respect, the desire not to be mocked, the need to have an outlet for emotions that, as a personal slave, she was expected to suppress. Abbe paid a high price for letting loose her feelings, desiring respect, and expressing what was, at root, a perfectly rational desire to be free or at least to go home.

Upon hearing of Abbe's death, John dwelt far more on comforting his wife for her emotional trauma than on the slave's fatal trauma. To be sure, he "lament[ed] Abbys Death" and remarked that "it would have given me great Pleasure to have restored her in Health to our own Country." But his paramount concern was for Sally. She had dealt not only with Abbe's illness but with the discomfort of their young daughters, for whom she recently provided inoculations. He wished her to take "Consolation" in having done the right thing by bringing Abbe home and tending to her in her illness. Knowing "the Variety as well as Degree of Emotions which you have lately experienced . . . makes me extremely anxious to be with you." In the meantime, he urged her to remain calm and to reflect "that People passing thro' this World are not to expect to have *all* the Way strewed with Roses." "[L]et us," he advised, "be grateful for Blessings & resigned to adverse Incidents." No guilt, no remorse should cloud Sally's thoughts about Abbe's life, marked as it was by thorns rather than rose petals. The dirt barely shoveled over a foreign grave, Sally should regard Abbe's death as an "adverse Incident" put into a larger frame.[52]

For the servants, including Benoit, who lived in the Jays' French household, Abbe's death was something more daunting, and they put the trauma into a different philosophical perspective. It was a genuinely frightening, deeply disorienting event. Peter Jay Munro reported the servants' response to John, the teenager's sneering callousness magnifying all the more how different ideas of justice and tragedy could be for servants and masters living under the same roof. Peter wrote to his uncle that Abbe had "never kept the Servants in such awe as since her Death." According to Peter, "her *Friend* Ben does not stir without a Candle," calling out in French, "*C'est elle!*" (It's her!) when hearing "the least noise." A female servant (possibly Louisson) "was terribly frightened at seeing herself in the Glass" to which Peter sniggered, "I think with reason." When snow fell off the roof, these servants had to be convinced that "it was not a Spirit." Peter added, "nightly some thing happens which frightens them, and sets us a laughing."[53]

The fear that Abbe's ghost haunted the household suggests a belief that Abbe's death was unnatural. Her soul was literally restless, her time on earth cut short by events gone morally awry, or at least before she had time to get her spiritual affairs in order. Benoit may have been trying subconsciously to communicate that someone in the household, Sally or the French servants, had wronged Abbe, with whom he may have forged a close bond over their years of travel and work together. Louisson, who had a tempestuous relationship with Abbe, may have expressed guilt through her reaction, fearing the sight of her own image, and sharing in Benoit's broader fear of Abbe's restless spirit. A milder interpretation of the servants' reaction would be that they saw in Abbe's sad fate a reminder of their own vulnerability to a potentially lethal combination of the unchecked emotions of servants, their master's discipline, and plain bad luck. In any case, the servants' reactions, which they did not attempt to keep secret from their masters, should not be dismissed as superstition without meaning. Abbe's tragic story reminded Benoit of his own vulnerability, his own inherently unsettled condition, part and parcel of his status as a slave. As Munro put it, she exercised more power as a dead person than as a living one, a fact that a more mature person might have found pathetic rather than humorous.[54]

Peter Jay Munro's depiction is suggestive of the racial and class divide in perceptions of Abbe's story in particular as well as master-servant relations more generally. We can safely attribute part of his response to his age and circumstance, an adolescent member of the master class with every reason to want to distinguish himself from the older but subordinate Benoit. He also may have needed to decisively suppress any guilt that might well up from his participation in this sad affair. Condescending laughter at ignorant superstition, as well as a mean-spirited jibe at the female servant's alleged ugliness, would have done the trick. Intriguingly, he refers to those laughing at the servants in the plural, suggesting that his Aunt Sally joined in the fun. Since he does not say so explicitly, and since we will never be able to hear what the laughter sounded like, we cannot know whether that laughter was anxious, nervous, or truly mocking. In any event, the dispossessed had tried to send a message about their own troubled response to the events surrounding Abbe's sad misfortune, a message which at least one youthful social superior refused to acknowledge. Whatever she felt about the fear of Abbe's ghost, Sally likely did not view the death as a laughing matter. But however much Sally or John Jay imagined they cared for Abbe's happiness or the well-being of servants back home, the Jays occupied but did not share the world of their servants, the corners of their minds sadly remote and obscured. John Jay's paternalistic and antislavery impulses failed to prepare him to make initial sense of the incident, his empathy focused on Sally's trauma rather than Abbe's suffering. His fellow peace commissioner, Benjamin Franklin, in the midst of his own journey toward abolitionism, had been no help at all.

Abbe's death may have had some impact all the same.[55] John Jay did not believe in ghosts, nor was he one to favor gratuitous jokes, particularly regarding a subject as serious as death. The lawyer-turned-diplomat also did not like loose ends or unfinished business, and he thought of himself as a pious person committed to justice. As he prepared to leave Europe, he sought to wrap up his personal affairs.[56] Among these was the future of his Martiniquan slave, Benoit. What Jay claimed he had promised Abbe verbally, freedom upon return to America, may have inadvertently contributed to her own self-destructive resistance. Three months after Abbe's death, John put the terms defining Benoit's future in writing. To what degree John and Benoit discussed the terms, whether Benoit initiated these discussions, or whether either of them understood their relationship to French law, Jay did not say.[57] In any event, the document entailed a negotiation. Master and slave would navigate their future through a legal bond—the slave's good behavior secured by a written promise of freedom in three years' time. If Benoit "continue[d] to serve me with a common & reasonable degree of fidelity," Jay would renounce "all my Right and Title" to Benoit, who would then "be as free to all Intents & Purposes as if he had never been a Slave." Unlike his expressions of responsibility for his family's aged and infirm slaves and former slaves back in New York, Jay did not claim to be acting out of benevolent obligation to the weak in this case. He was obligated, he wrote, to strike a deal with Benoit because justice demanded that he do so, demanded that he restore Benoit to his inborn human liberty after he had worked off his purchase price. As Jay wrote in the manumission document, "the Children of men are by nature equally free and cannot without Injustice be either reduced to or held in Slavery."[58] This particular injustice, rested on considerable social inequality, now carried an expiration date.

The decision to arrange the terms of Benoit's freedom did not occur in a vacuum. Jay acted upon his already stated desire to see slavery set on a course toward abolition. The statesman's actions also reflected his personal experiences during his years in Europe. Jay's diplomatic service provided him with on-the-job training in conducting negotiations in which he had to stand on principle, calculate interests, and make concessions. Ironically, it was in Europe, where he sought to secure the nation's liberty, that John Jay also encountered the paradoxes of human bondage in uncomfortably direct ways, particularly when Abbe turned Sally's life upside down, but also in his attempt to influence from afar the disposition of the many slaves in his family's New York household. Having lost control of Abbe, Jay constructed an orderly alternative.[59] Or so it seemed. Benoit slips out of the Jay archive silently, apparently not returning to the Americas with the Jays. No one in the Jay entourage recorded a falling out or running away or a sale.[60] His master, by contrast, came back to the United States with a sense of how slavery might be unwound over time.

John Jay's experience overseas during this period encapsulates one of the ironies of the founding, which combined the empowerment of slaveholders in the new republic with a strongly felt impulse to extend human liberty to slaves. Jay himself emerged from the war believing slavery to be wrong, but also believing that managing his obligations and interests as a slaveholder and a diplomat required cautious planning rather than dramatic action. Like Benoit and Abbe, white Americans had been born naturally free. After his fellow patriots fended off political enslavement on the battlefield, Jay bargained at the negotiating table to confirm the United States' independence and its citizens' property rights in slaves. Jay preferred to negotiate the terms of black freedom domestically as a matter of morally sanctioned long-range planning rather than as a product of revolutionary political and social disorder that blacks exploited on their own terms rather than his. Thus he helped to smooth the imperial transition by attempting to manage its deepest ambiguities.[61]

The varied fates of the Jay entourage that reversed course and sailed to Europe in the midst of the American Revolution illustrate the unresolved nature of the imperial settlement of 1783. Visitors not colonists, Abbe, Benoit, John Jay, and Sally Jay nonetheless sought to transplant certain cultural assumptions. But new environs and new ideas about freedom forced these men and women to negotiate with themselves and with one another. Of the four, John, of course, wielded the most public and private power. Yet even he struggled, not least to bring his emerging antislavery principles into line with his status as a slaveholder and representative of his nation's material interests. His Parisian slaves experienced much more severe constraints. And yet they too insisted on being heard. Abbe's fatal protest exposed the tragic limits of the founders' commitment to liberty. When his household servants, including the West Indian Benoit, revived Abbe as a ghost, they communicated just how badly the Jays and the Franklins had faltered. The new world of national independence would be haunted by the inequalities of the colonial past, testing whether men like John Jay could adapt political victory into a lasting legacy of liberty for all.

Notes

The author thanks Leslie James, Robert Gross, Paul Polgar, and Patrick Griffin for fostering the development of this essay.

1. Sarah Livingston Jay (hereafter SLJ) to John Jay (hereafter JJ), December 11, 1783, in *Selected Letters of John Jay and Sarah Livingston Jay: Correspondence by or to the First Chief Justice of the United States and His Wife,* ed. Landa M. Freeman, Louise V. North, and Janet M. Wedge (Jefferson, NC, 2005), 161.

2. Henry Wiencek, *Master of the Mountain: Thomas Jefferson and His Slaves* (New York, 2012), has recently weighed in on the Jefferson-Hemings relationship as part of an impassioned autopsy of Jefferson's woeful and deceitful record on slavery.

3. On the importance of master-slave negotiations, despite their profoundly asymmetrical nature, see Walter Johnson, *Soul by Soul: Life inside the Antebellum Slave Market* (Cambridge, MA, 1999).

4. The literature of slavery and abolition in the age of the American Revolution is enormous. Christopher Leslie Brown, *Moral Capital: Foundations of British Abolitionism* (Chapel Hill, NC, 2006) confirms anew David Brion Davis's argument in *The Problem of Slavery in the Age of Revolution, 1770–1823* (Ithaca, NY, 1975) that the late eighteenth century constituted a hinge in the history of slavery and antislavery. T. H. Breen, "Making History: The Force of Public Opinion and the Last Years of Slavery in Massachusetts," in *Through a Glass Darkly: Reflections on Personal Identity in Early America*, ed. Ronald Hoffman, Mechal Sobel, and Fredrika J. Teute (Chapel Hill, NC, 1997), 67–95, models how to bring black and white stories together to study revolutionary emancipation. Daniel C. Littlefield, "John Jay, the Revolutionary Generation, and Slavery," *New York History* (2000): 91–132, offers the most comprehensive reflection in print on Jay and slavery, an understudied topic in great need of a more narrative approach. See also Richard S. Newman and Roy E. Finkenbine, "Black Founders in the New Republic: Introduction," *William and Mary Quarterly*, 3d ser., 64 (January 2007): 83–94.

5. JJ to Peter Jay, May 23, 1780, in *Selected Letters*, 84.

6. Graham Russell Hodges, *Root & Branch: African Americans in New York and East Jersey, 1612–1863* (Chapel Hill, NC, 1999), and Shane White, *Somewhat More Independent: The End of Slavery in New York City, 1770–1810* (Athens, NY, 1991) are among those who have studied the subject; see also David N. Gellman, *Emancipating New York: The Politics of Slavery and Freedom, 1777–1827* (Baton Rouge, 2006), chapter 1.

7. SLJ to Susannah French Livingston, December 12–26, 1779; SLJ to William Livingston, December 30, 1779; SLJ to Peter Jay, January 9, 1780, in *Selected Letters*, 68, 71, 73.

8. SLJ to Susannah French Livingston, August 28, 1780, in *Selected Letters*, 91.

9. SLJ to William Livingston, January 31, 1782, October 14, 1782; SLJ to Peter Jay, April 29, 1782, in *Selected Letters*, 117, 118, 122.

10. SLJ to Peter Augustus Jay, July 25, 1781, copy of transcription from Papers of John Jay, Columbia University Manuscript Collection, John Jay Homestead, Katonah, NY.

11. SLJ to Kitty Livingston, May 18, 1781, in *Selected Letters*, 106.

12. See Walter Johnson, *Soul by Soul*, and Johnson's "rereading" of Eugene D. Genovese, *Roll, Jordan, Roll* (New York, 1976) in *Common-Place* 1 (2001), http://www.common-place.org/vol-01/no-04/reviews/johnson.shtml, for commentary on paternalism's limitations and ironies. Jay's paternalism was not a strategy for morally digging in on slavery, but instead was compatible with his emerging criticisms of the institution. See also Littlefield, "John Jay," 123–26.

13. Sung Bok Kim, "The Limits of Politicization in the American Revolution: The Experience of Westchester County, New York," *Journal of American History* 80 (1993): 868–89.

14. Frederick Jay (hereafter FJ) to JJ, April 10, 1781, The Papers of John Jay—Online Edition (hereafter PJJ), Doc. 6327, New York, NY, Columbia University Libraries.

15. JJ to FJ, March 15, 1781, PJJ, Doc. 6326.

16. FJ to JJ December 1, 1781; JJ to Richard Harrison (draft), May 28, 1781; JJ to Robert Morris (draft), May 29, 1781; JJ to FJ, March 15, 1781, November 19, 1781, PJJ, Docs. 6331, 8818, 9322, 6326, 6333.

17. JJ to FJ (draft), July 31, 1781, PJJ, Doc. 6328.

18. JJ to FJ, April 29, 1782, PJJ, Doc. 6336; JJ to Robert R. Livingston, August 13, 1782; JJ to Egbert Benson (draft), August 26, 1782, in *The Selected Papers of John Jay*, ed. Elizabeth M. Nuxoll (Charlottesville, VA, 2013), 3:64, 92; see also JJ to FJ (draft), October 3, 1782, in *Selected Papers*, 3:172.

19. Littlefield, "John Jay," 121, 123–24; Johnson, *Soul by Soul*.

20. [JJ], Address of the Convention of the Representatives of the State of New York to Their Constituents, December 23, 1776, in *Public Papers of John Jay*, 1:119. See also JJ, Letter to the "Oppressed Inhabitants of Canada," July 6, 1775, in *The Correspondence and Public Papers of John Jay*, ed. Henry P Johnston (1890; New York, 1970), 1:35; and Littlefield, "John Jay," 105.

21. JJ to Robert R. Livingston and Gouverneur Morris (draft), April 29, 1777, in *John Jay, The Making of a Revolutionary: Unpublished Papers, 1745–1780*, ed. Richard B. Morris (New York, 1975), 401; see also *Journals of the Provincial Congress, Provincial Convention, Committee of Safety and Council of Safety of the State of New-York, 1775–1776–1777* (Albany, NY, 1842), 1:887, 889, 897.

22. Alexander Hamilton to JJ, March 14, 1779, in *The Papers of Alexander Hamilton*, ed. Harold C. Syrett (New York, 1961), 2:17–18.

23. This entire episode is dissected in Henry Wiencek, *An Imperfect God: George Washington, His Slaves, and the Creation of America* (New York, 2003), 221–33; for a longer, lively look at the Laurens story, see Jack Rakove, *Revolutionaries: A New History of the Invention of America* (Boston, 2010), 198–241.

24. Antony Benezet to JJ, February 2, 1779, PJJ, Doc. 5485.

25. [Anthony Benezet], *Serious Considerations on several Important Subjects; viz. On War and its Inconsistency with the Gospel; Observations on Slavery, and Remarks on the Nature and bad Effects of Spiritous Liquors* (Philadelphia, 1778), 11, 28, 30–31, 37–40. For a thorough study of Benezet, see Maurice Jackson, *Let This Voice Be Heard: Anthony Benezet, Father of Atlantic Abolitionism* (Philadelphia, 2010).

26. JJ to Anthony Benezet, March 5, 1779, draft attached to letter from Benezet, PJJ, Doc. 5485; Jackson, *Let This Voice Be Heard*, 133.

27. JJ to Egbert Benson (draft), September 18, 1780, in *Making of a Revolutionary*, 823.

28. Jackson, *Let This Voice Be Heard*, 109, 129, 134, 212–15, 219, 346–47n34.

29. James W. St. G. Walker, "Blacks as American Loyalists: The Slaves' War for Independence," *Historical Reflections/Reflections Historiques* 2 (1976): 51–67, offers a superb account.

30. JJ to Richard Oswald (draft), September 10, 1782, in *The Emerging Nation: Foreign Relations of the United States, 1780–1789*, ed. Mary A. Giunta (National Historical Publications and Records Commission, 1996), 1:561. For overviews of the peace negotiations, Richard B. Morris, *Witnesses at the Creation: Hamilton, Madison, Jay, and the Constitution* (New York, 1985), 76–93, and Samuel Flagg Bemis, *The Diplomacy of the American Revolution* (1935; Bloomington, IN, 1957). Rakove, *Revolutionaries*, 254–89, offers a fresh telling including insights into Jay's vigorous efforts to establish a strong negotiating position.

31. Congressional Resolutions, September 10, 1782, in *Emerging Nation,* 1:560; Robert R. Livingston to Benjamin Franklin (draft), September 13, 1782, in *The Papers of Benjamin Franklin,* ed. Ellen R. Cohn (New Haven, CT, 2006), 38:102.

32. Richard Oswald to Thomas Townshend, November 15, 1782, *Emerging Nation,* 1:658–59; John Adams to Robert R. Livingston, November 11, 1782, *Emerging Nation,* 1:656.

33. "Preliminary Articles of Peace between the United States and Great Britain," in *Emerging Nation,* 1:700; John Adams's Journal, November 30, 1782, in *Emerging Nation,* 1:692. Henry Laurens to South Carolina Delegates, December 16, 1782, in *The Papers of Henry Laurens,* ed. David R. Chestnut and C. James Taylor (Columbia, SC, 2003), 16:79–80, 80n2. Bemis, *Diplomacy of the American Revolution,* 238, writes the whole episode off rather cavalierly as a bargain between "two old slave merchants."

34. *Papers of Benjamin Franklin,* 38:375–77, 382n.

35. Adams's Journal, November 30, 1782, in *Emerging Nation,* 1:692–94; see also Benjamin Franklin to Robert R. Livingston, December 5, 1782, in *Emerging Nation,* 1:708–9.

36. JJ to Robert R. Livingston, December 14, 1782, in *Emerging Nation,* 1:719.

37. Memorandum of a Conference between George Washington and Guy Carleton, May 6, 1783, Washington to Carleton, May 6, 1783, Carleton to Washington, May 12, 1783, in *Emerging Nation,* 1:848–50, 852, 856–57.

38. Livingston to Franklin, May 9, 1783, Peace Commissioners to Robert Hartley, July 17, 1783, Commissioners to Livingston, July 18, 1783, in *Emerging Nation,* 1:854, 881, 885–86; Benjamin Franklin to Henry Laurens, July 6, 1783, *Papers of Henry Laurens,* 16:231. Compare the Draft Definitive Treaty (c. August 6, 1783) and the Definitive Treaty ratified by Congress (January 14, 1784), in *Emerging Nation,* 1:906–13, 963–67.

39. Henry Laurens to American Peace Commissioners, August 9,1783; Charles James Fox to David Hartley, August 9, 1783; Hartley to Fox, August 20,1783, in *Emerging Nation,* 1:913–15, 915–17 (quotation), 922–23. Wiencek, *An Imperfect God,* 253–58, offers a succinct account of the controversy; see also Gellman, *Emancipating New York,* 38–39, which has further citations to relevant sources.

40. On slavery and the U.S. Constitution, see David Waldstreicher, *Slavery's Constitution: From Revolution to Ratification* (New York: Hill & Wang, 2010); and George William Van Cleve, *A Slaveholder's Union: Slavery, Politics, and the Constitution in the Early American Republic* (Chicago, 2011). On Franklin, see David Waldstreicher, *Runaway America: Benjamin Franklin, Slavery, and the American Revolution* (New York, 2004); on 221–22 Waldstreicher takes up slavery in the peace negotiations. On Laurens, see Rakove, *Revolutionaries,* 215–16; for hints of Adams's budding views, see *The Works of John Adams,* ed. Charles Francis Adams (Boston, 1850), 2:200, 280, 497–98; 3:280.

41. John Jay subsequently would discover as one of the nation's chief foreign policy officials that the departure of thousands of African Americans under British auspices in alleged violation of Article 7 would cause diplomatic headaches and provide a political wedge issue for years to come. See John Jay, Secretary of Foreign Affairs, October 13, 1786, *Secret Journals of the Acts and Proceedings of Congress, From the First Meeting Thereof to the Dissolution of the Confederation, By the Adoption of the Constitution of the United States* (Boston, 1821), 185–287; Gellman, *Emancipating New York,* 135–40; Littlefield, "John Jay," 109–10. James Oakes, *The Scorpion's Sting: Antislavery and the Coming of the Civil*

War (New York, 2014), 108–30, reviews the controversy that swirled around Article 7 with an eye toward legal precedent.

42. Jan Horton, "Listening for Clarinda," unpublished ms. report for John Jay Homestead Historic Site, 2000, introduction and 62–66, tells Abbe's narrative as part of a superb effort to uncover the narrative of all of John Jay's slaves; I draw great inspiration from her example and benefit from her detective work. Littlefield, "John Jay," 128–30, also writes with insight on this episode.

43. Abbe had played an important role in assisting Sally Jay with her children, early in the year helping with the weaning of one of the girls, though Abbe's health in France had not been good. See SLJ to Susannah French Livingston, April 15, 1783, in *Selected Letters*, 133; SLJ to Kitty Livingston (draft), June 11, 1783, in *Selected Letters*, 135.

44. SLJ to JJ, November 6, 1783, in *Selected Letters*, 147–48.

45. On French law and slavery, see Pierre H. Boulle, "Racial Purity or Legal Clarity? The Status of Black Residents in Eighteenth-Century France," *Journal of the Historical Society* 6 (March 2006): 19–46, quotations 29, 40; and Sue Peabody, *"There Are No Slaves in France": The Political Culture of Race and Slavery in the Ancien Régime* (New York, 1996); see also Wiencek, *Master of the Mountain*, 190.

46. SLJ to JJ, November 6, 1783, in *Selected Letters*, 147–48; this incident was not the first time that Franklin intervened with authorities to help someone recover a slave—see Waldstreicher, *Runaway America*, 222–24.

47. SLJ to JJ, November 6, 1783, Peter Jay Munro to JJ (draft), November 12, 1783, in *Selected Letters*, 148–49.

48. JJ to William Temple Franklin, November 11, 1783, in *Selected Papers*, 513.

49. SLJ to JJ, November 18, 1783, in *Selected Letters*, 151.

50. SLJ to JJ, November 6, 1783; JJ to SLJ, November 23, 1783, in *Selected Letters*, 148, 153.

51. SLJ to William Temple Franklin, December 7, 1783; SLJ to JJ, December 7, 1783, December 11, 1783; Peter Jay Munro to JJ (draft), December 7, 1783, in *Selected Papers*, 527, 528, 529, 532.

52. JJ to SLJ, December 26, 1783, *Selected Papers*, 537; see also 541n for Peter Jay Munro's observation that Sally dealt with tragedy with "accustomed fortitude" and with more equanimity than most other people would have.

53. Munro to JJ (draft), January 4, 1784, in *Selected Papers*, 541.

54. The general inspiration for this insight is James C. Scott, *Domination and the Arts of Resistance: Hidden Transcripts* (New Haven, CT, 1990), esp. chapter 6 on "the arts of political disguise," including "spirit possession" on 141–42. For a similarly suggestive incident from colonial American of a slave ghost haunting a house where he was murdered by his master, see William Moraley, *The Infortunate: The Voyage and Adventures of William Moraley, an Indentured Servant*, ed. Susan E. Klepp and Billy G. Smith (University Park, PA, 1992), 83; for another colonial ghost story, see Douglas L. Winiarski, "'Pale Blewish Lights' and Dead Man's Groans: Tales of the Supernatural from Eighteenth-Century Plymouth, Massachusetts," *William and Mary Quarterly*, 3d ser., 55 (1998): 497–530. The literature on witchcraft and demonic possession in New England is suggestive as well, esp. the psychologically rich John Demos, *Entertaining Satan: Witchcraft and the Culture in Early New England*, updated ed. (New York, 2004); and Carol F. Karlsen, *The Devil in the Shape of a Woman: Witchcraft in Colonial New England* (New York, 1987).

55. Littlefield, "John Jay," 128, 130.

56. JJ to William Carmichael, April 24, 1784, PJJ, Doc. 7721.

57. Peabody, *"There Are No Slaves in France,"* 135, intriguingly suggests a rise in French masters freeing their slaves in France.

58. JJ, manumission document for Benoit, March 21, 1784, PJJ, Doc. 7298.

59. Jay's most recent biographer, Walter Stahr, *John Jay: Founding Father* (New York, 2005), 190, 193, views the connection between Abbe's death and Benoit's manumission document as plausible; for Stahr's broader assessment of Jay and slavery, see 236–39. Littlefield, "John Jay," summarizes his "ambivalence" regarding Jay and slavery on 131–32. See also thoughtful remarks by Freeman, North, and Wedge on Jay and slavery also pairing Abbe's death and Benoit's manumission document in the appendix to *Selected Letters,* 296–99.

60. Horton, "Listening for Clarinda," 62; Freeman, North, and Wedge, *Selected Letters,* 298; Nuxoll, *Selected Papers,* 569n.

61. Littlefield, "John Jay," 107.

Seeing Like an Antiquarian

Popular Nostalgia and the Rise of a Modern Historical Subjectivity in the 1820s

SETH COTLAR

In his book *Seeing Like a State*, anthropologist James Scott delineated the historically specific subjectivity that animated the leaders of high modernist states—the ways of knowing that structured how they looked at and acted upon the societies over which they presided.[1] In a similar though more modest spirit, this essay explores a very different, historically specific subjectivity, one inhabited by a new sort of nostalgic American subject that emerged in the first decades of the nineteenth century. What, I ask, can we learn when we try to see like an 1820s antiquarian historian who avidly collected relics and stories about "the olden times"?[2] What perhaps previously hidden features of American cultural and intellectual history emerge when we view the early American republic through the eyes of a nostalgic informant like the prolific amateur historian John Fanning Watson?

Generations of American historians have offered a very simple answer to that question: very little. Scholars of early America have frequently mined Watson's 1830 tome, the *Annals of Philadelphia*, for quirky anecdotes, yet until recently, very few have taken Watson seriously as a historical subject in and of himself.[3] His relationship to his historical material seems too unsystematic to merit consideration, and his disconnected, anecdotal style bespeaks an unseemly, nostalgic affection for the past. We value him as a collector of raw materials, but not as a knower or thinker. Our easy dismissal of Watson is symptomatic of a larger trend. Even though historians have long noted that the years between 1820 and 1860 were "an age of widespread and ritualized nostalgia,"[4] scholars rarely write about those many nostalgic Americans with much sophistication or sympathy. The general tendency has been to regard nostalgia in pre–Civil War America as a timeless psychological tick that afflicted simpleminded escapists who fled into distorted fantasy worlds of the past to avoid coping with the changing world around them. When we modern historians encounter nostalgic informants in the archive, we too often dismiss them as predictable and untrustworthy—*nothing interesting here, they're merely being nostalgic,* we whisper to ourselves. And it is precisely in this manner that people like John Fanning Watson and his innumerable nostalgic contemporaries have suffered from the condescension of posterity.

Although early American historians have had little of substance to say about nostalgia, scholars such as European historian Peter Fritzche, sociologist Janelle Wilson, literary critic Svetlana Boym, philosopher Edward Carey, and political theorist Kimberly Smith have begun to reconstruct nostalgia's complicated social and cultural history.[5] This recent scholarship suggests that the emotion or state of mind that we now call "nostalgia" was largely inaccessible to people before the turn of the nineteenth century when, thanks to the French Revolution and the technological changes associated with the beginnings of the industrial revolution, people began to experience and conceive of time in less cyclical and more linear terms. Only once one expects that the future will be irreducibly different from the past and the present—only once one lives in a world marked by the discontinuity of the incessantly new—can one feel nostalgic for a past that can never return. Thus early nineteenth-century Americans like Watson were nostalgic not in spite of being modern but because they were modern. There is no sound methodological rationale for why we have been unable to sympathetically hear nostalgic voices from the past. Our deafness, our inclination to regard nostalgia as childish or maudlin, is largely an ideological effect of modernity itself. Forward-looking, modern subjects (including generations of self-described "modern" historians) have defined themselves, in large part, against a backward-looking, nostalgic other. Thus to understand the process and experience of modernization more fully, it is imperative that we pay closer attention to its devalued, nostalgic undercurrent.

Whereas the emerging modern sensibility of the early nineteenth century insistently interpreted change as progress, nostalgic subjects fixated on precisely those things that had been discarded, destroyed, or rendered obsolete by the passage of time. The forms nostalgia took and the objects it fixed upon were not randomly determined by individual psychology but were patterned in ways that invite historical analysis. Open hearth fireplaces became objects of nostalgic reverie in the 1840s at precisely the moment when cast-iron stoves were becoming the norm in American households. The spinning wheel, the butter churn, and work parties among the sugar maples took on their appealing, nostalgic sheen in the same years that the expansion of the market economy made cheap cloth, butter, and sugar available to most families. Nietzsche's observation that "memory depends upon the pain of a still open sore" urges us to resist dismissing nostalgic cultural expressions as always cynical or reactionary distortions of the past.[6] Nostalgic longings frequently gave voice to the real personal and political harms inflicted by modernization, thus articulating oblique yet trenchant critiques of the present. Viewed in this light, we can reconceptualize the culture of nostalgia as the bittersweet counterpoint to modernity's boisterous and celebratory symphony.

The optimistic, modernizing voices from the early republic—the westward-looking pioneers, the plucky entrepreneurs and inventors, the visionary improvers, the millennialist reformers—have tended to be the ones at the center of our cultural histories of that era while the more ambivalent, nostalgic voices like John Fanning Watson's have either been ignored or treated as quirky sidebars to the real story. This essay starts from the more neutral premise that Americans in the early republic thought about their nation's past, present, and future in many different registers. The goal here is to loosen modernity's ideological hold on our historical imaginations in order to reassess the place of the nostalgic register in the broader landscape of American culture.

This essay focuses on one specific feature of the nostalgic sensibility, the way it fostered surprisingly sophisticated, even "modern" forms of historical thinking. Historian Dorothy Ross has argued that modern historicism emerged in early nineteenth-century Europe, but did not become common in America for several decades.[7] As indicated by their providential, Whiggish conception of the American past, most American historians of the pre–Civil War era regarded the past primarily as a justificatory prologue for the present. In George Bancroft's histories, for example, the heroic figures from the past were those who aspired to embrace Bancroft's Jacksonian values, while his villains were those who clung to old-fashioned and soon-to-be outdated ideas about aristocracy, monarchy, or religious establishments. Likewise, when modern Whiggish historians like Bancroft looked ahead, they could only imagine a future that extended and elaborated upon what already existed. Thus Ross argues that the modes of thinking we usually associate with a historicist sensibility—an attention to the unintended consequences of human action, a recognition of the historically constructed nature of human subjectivity, an appreciation for the radical unpredictability of the future and the irreducible differentness of the past—were all notably absent in pre–Civil War America.

While Ross's research focuses only on the historical consciousness of professional historians, her claims about the nonhistoricist nature of nineteenth-century American culture resonate with how most historians have depicted the broader cultural contours of that era. We generally assume that before the Civil War, Americans cared little for the past because they were so fixated on producing what they assumed would be an ever freer and more prosperous future.[8] They ripped down old, historically significant buildings as swiftly and eagerly as the American revolutionaries had rejected the deeply rooted habits of social deference and political exclusion that marked their colonial past. When Americans in the new nation looked back to the past, they did so in the spirit of simplistic hero worship rather than out of any earnest desire to engage with the past on its own terms. In the words of Jacksonian historian Daniel Feller, the Americans of the 1820s thought of themselves as perched "between a receding heroic past and a wonderful future just beginning to unfold."[9] In the rare moments when those Americans thought about the past at all, it simply made them feel good about their nation's benign origins and its easily imaginable and ever-happier future.[10]

The nostalgic writings of people like John Fanning Watson, however, establish a much more complicated and vexed relationship between the new nation's past and its future. Nostalgia speaks, usually in mournful tones, of discontinuity rather than continuity. The object of nostalgic desire is by definition unattainable—forever lost because it resides in a past from which the nostalgic subject has been permanently exiled. When viewed through nostalgic eyes, the forward progression of time does not lead smoothly and beneficently toward an ever better future; rather, it leaves one stranded in a present that is lacking in important ways. It is precisely this sense of rupture and dislocation that more and more Americans in the 1820s and '30s were beginning to sense and articulate. Nostalgia emerged, in other words, as a new, even modern way of telling and reckoning with time in a material and social world that was beginning to change at an ever faster rate. Although nostalgic Americans like Watson were usually conflicted about how to interpret and express such disruptive, even heretical feelings, the uneasy fit between their nostalgic longings and the dominant culture of optimistic boosterism tells us much about the dynamic ambivalences that structured American culture in the antebellum era.

Nothing in Watson's first thirty years foreshadowed the eccentric antiquarian historian he would become. Like so many other middling men of his era, he spent his young adulthood pursuing a range of economic opportunities— peddling fans in the stifling summer of 1798, working as a clerk in the Federal War Department, shepherding a few hundred barrels of flour on their trip down the Mississippi River to market, and running a bookstore in Philadelphia. By his own account, Watson was a diligent worker, yet he met with little lasting success.[11] In 1814, at the age of thirty-four, he found himself with a growing family, a failing bookselling business, and very little capital to his name. So he took on steady but uninspiring work as a cashier for the Bank of Germantown. Having exchanged his dreams of independent proprietorship for a respectable salary of $1,000 a year, Watson moved into a house owned by the bank on the outskirts of Philadelphia where he would spend the remainder of his life. Between 1820 and 1860 Watson produced thousands of pages of manuscripts that contain not a single positive mention of the work he did for pay. Much to the chagrin of his boss at the bank, Watson devoted the last half of his life to his new vocation as a self-described annalist whose calling was to collect stories and relics from "the olden times."[12]

The upstairs bedroom in which he spent the last weeks of his life speaks volumes about the nature of Watson's historical pursuits. He asked his daughter to place next to his bed the desk at which he had written his *Annals of Philadelphia*. Beside the desk sat a chair that had belonged to William Penn and that had subsequently been graced by the backsides of Prince William and Lafayette. In the corner of the room sat a clock case that had also belonged to Penn and that now contained a "tray holding seven canes of relic wood." Crowding the walls were "pictures of ancient houses, scenes, etc., all framed from some portion of the woods represented; and from two windows were suspended cannonballs." One was from the battle of Germantown, and the other bore a label Watson had written for it twenty-four years earlier: "This Ball is a curiosity.—It is older than Philadelphia;—was found imbedded in the root of a large tree-stump, in a house of Budd's long row."[13] From the perspective of the nineteenth-century antiquarian, this was probably the best death imaginable.

The most predictable objects in this bedroom of curiosities were those that derived historical meaning from their association with great men. Objects owned or merely touched by figures like William Penn comforted Watson, giving him a deep sense of connection to the vanished past and the virtuous men who inhabited it. While collecting objects associated with famous leaders was standard for antiquarians like Watson, the other objects in his collection were a bit more unusual. The "pictures of ancient houses, scenes, etc." depicted fairly quotidian aspects of the past—houses that once served as an artisan's shop or a tavern and street scenes depicting the residences of the city's more humble occupants. The emotional pull of these images lay in their ordinariness rather than in their connection to a famous and exceptional historical figure. In contrast to the more canonical, great-man conception of history implied by Watson's treasured William Penn relics, his interest in

buildings from the "olden times" and the lifeways of the people who inhabited them reflected a much more inclusive and populist concept of history.
Watson cherished stories about the nation's honored leaders, but he spent far
more time inquiring and writing about the experiences of ordinary men and
women—their leisure pursuits, the clothes they wore, the food they ate, the
design of their houses, the modes of transportation they used, their opinions
about changing hairstyles, and a host of other topics that today we would
associate with social or cultural history. Although at the time most "serious"
historians considered such topics frivolous, Watson found the history of the
daily and quotidian facets of ordinary life to be the most compelling aspect
of his work. He had sketched most of those obscure old buildings himself and
had built their relic wood frames as well. While a piece of famous furniture
was acquired in a moment and then passively admired, the framed drawings
of now-vanished buildings were the products of days of unremunerated, lov-
ingly bestowed labor.[14]

Perhaps most revelatory of Watson's historical inclinations, however, is the
mysterious cannonball that was supposedly older than Philadelphia. Watson
cherished such objects that simply did not fit with what he and his contemporaries thought they knew. How could a cannonball predate the arrival of
Europeans in Philadelphia? How did it get there? Who made it? The ancient
provenance of the cannonball is dubious at best, but what matters is Watson's fascination with it. He never figured out what that object meant, yet as
he lay dying he refused to banish it as an inconvenient fact to be buried or
forgotten. He wanted it close by so he could continue to contemplate it. In all
of his collecting and writing, Watson had a keen eye for the detail that would
surprise and at times even unsettle his contemporaries. Such details brought
him pleasure, I would suggest, because they spoke of a mysterious past replete
with the unknown and the forgotten—a past so foreign and intricately different from the present that it could only be apprehended by applying a lively
historical imagination to the fragmented relics that remained.

Watson never offered an account of when or why he embarked on his
new career as an annalist. Nothing in his pre-1820 letters and manuscripts
indicates a uniquely historical or nostalgic cast of mind. Yet by 1823 he had
produced an enormous handwritten manuscript that would serve as the first
draft of his nine hundred–page *Annals of Philadelphia* published seven years
later. After settling in Germantown, Watson quickly found a large community
of like-minded people who happily listened to his tales of the "olden times"
and offered to serve as his research assistants. His *Annals* circulated widely
among Philadelphia's elite, and this generated even more unsolicited letters

of support and assistance. To capitalize on his newfound popularity, Watson produced a long list of questions that he distributed among his friends so that if they encountered one of the city's "ancient inhabitants," they could pump them for stories about hairstyles, porches, pirates, pigeons, Indians, or African American dances at Potter's Field.[15] Watson himself tracked down as many elderly people as possible so he could collect their stories. His daughter Lavinia remembers that "he once took me to see a man a hundred and ten years old,—who was very communicative . . . and tried to impress me with the thought that I might never again see so old a person;—Look at him! Touch him! Remember him!"[16] Watson also established intimate friendships with several descendants of Philadelphia's colonial elite. In return for flattering stories about their ancestors, these people granted Watson access to family heirlooms and chests stuffed with old letters that he could mine for additional information.

Watson and his new antiquarian friends derived much mutual pleasure from their frequent gatherings where they communed with objects from and memories of the "olden times." Deborah Norris Logan's diary records dozens of evenings when Watson and friends would come to her house to peruse her extensive collection of historical manuscripts and newspapers. At such gatherings "The 'Olden time' and its pleasant associations, and worthy characters, [were] our untiring theme."[17] Logan described one particularly enjoyable evening thus: "there, in the twilight by the fire side we discussed Characters and times by-past, and raked up from oblivion old anecdotes and things. What is the proper colour of Antiquarianism. I do not know. Grey I suppose. 'Grey with the Rust of years.' We were Grey enough then for we were deep in Antiquaries, but we were not Blue nor any approach of it."[18] That same year, 1827, Watson initiated an especially intense relationship, verging on the erotic, with a young, aspiring antiquarian, John J. Smith of Philadelphia. Upon returning home from an evening of shared contemplation of the past, Watson wrote Smith a brief letter reflecting on "how very much our intellectual pleasures surpass those of sense. How our souls coalesced, & what friendship it inspired, because we were mutually prompted by an intellectual passion, as moving & affecting to the imagination as Poetry itself! But I am saying too much!"[19] Exploring the "olden days" felt excitingly fresh and new for Watson and his antiquarian friends.

The emotional power of these relationships derived in part from a shared sense that lovers of the olden times were largely unappreciated, even looked down upon by many of their contemporaries. John Smith commiserated with Watson about "the *want of soul* of one half the world who seem to think . . .

that antiquarians remember only those things which other people ought to forget."[20] The historical data that so powerfully fired the imaginations of Watson and his friends seemed utterly irrelevant, dry as dust, to most of their contemporaries. Such popular disinterest did not deter Watson, and as he became ever more enchanted with his growing collection of historical information, he contacted historians across the country seeking their assistance in his pursuit and encouraging them to engage in similar projects in their own localities. Such inquiries adopted a decidedly modest, almost apologetic tone: "My scheme enables you to detail much of that which would not suit the gravity and dignity of common history; indeed, I rather aim to notice just such incidents as that omits."[21] Recognizing that others would regard his approach to history as insufficiently weighty and dignified, Watson pushed on nonetheless, hoping that someday others would derive as much pleasure and meaning from his collection as he and his friends did.

Indeed, Watson opened the first draft of his *Annals* with a confident justification for his polymorphously perverse urge to gather and record anything and everything associated with the past. "The object of the present pages might appear supremely ridiculous to some. Men of obtuse and boetian minds, who have no sense of the moral pleasures, which it is the province of *History* to impart, may scout as idle and puerile, the enterprise which institutes enquiries to revive the recollections of the changes & improvements of a great city." Like his more Whiggish contemporaries, Watson expressed pride and wonder at Philadelphia's rapid growth and rising prosperity, but his book made little effort to explain or justify those changes. Watson's account of America's political transition from colony to nation, for example, occupies only twenty-one pages and is sandwiched between a chapter detailing the presence of wolves and bears on the streets of eighteenth-century Philadelphia and a chapter on the rural retreats of the city's pre- and postrevolutionary gentry. Watson acknowledged, "If I had rewritten my work I should have presented it more compact & connected: but it would not have been half so grateful to men of antiquarian minds, whom I am most sedulous to please."

Eschewing a narrative form that would tie the past to the present in a celebratory manner, Watson's text functioned as a cabinet of curious stories that preserved a past that was rapidly disappearing from view and thus losing its ability to inform the imaginations of future generations: "We have now communication with the inhabitants of the middle of the past Century; if we would be faithful reporters to the generation which is to succeed us, . . . we must begin to make our collections of facts before the waning generation make their everlasting exit. It is not romantic to presume that a day is coming in which the *memorabilia* of Philadelphia & its primitive inhabitants (so different from the present) will be highly appreciated." Watson's nostalgia sutured Philadelphia's nineteenth-century present to its eighteenth-century past in numerous ways—pointing out the current (as of 1830) houses in which British officers lived when they occupied the city, noting current "ruins" that were once important buildings in the city's past, populating the streets of Philadelphia's present with engaging stories about scores of figures from the city's past who were now departed. Watson's *Annals* notes the continuities of the city's colonial, revolutionary, and postcolonial history, while also acknowledging the irreversible ruptures that had occurred. Many of his fellow citizens and the leading historical writers of his day may have had little use for Watson's massive collection of disconnected anecdotes, but he held out hope that future generations of fiction writers might "lend [their] genius, to *amplify* & consecrate *Facts*."[22] Such imaginative *"Tales of Ancient Philadelphia"* would enable the city's future residents to derive pleasure and insight from contemplating a past that was simultaneously different, desirable, *and* disappearing.

There were abundant signs in the 1820s that many of Watson's fellow Americans were beginning to share his nostalgic affection for the past. The recent popularity of Sir Walter Scott's novels—with their sympathetic depiction of the tangled kin and neighborhood ties that made premodern society function—gave Watson and his friends hope that American imitators would soon emerge. James Fenimore Cooper, many miles away in upstate New York, took up that work at precisely the same time that Watson was writing the first draft of his *Annals*.[23] In the 1820s Americans founded fifteen new historical societies across the country—more than in the previous three decades combined. That same decade witnessed the invention of a popular new genre of newspaper and magazine writing, the chronicle of the "olden times."[24] President James Monroe tried to keep the revolutionary past alive by making public appearances in the self-consciously anachronistic uniform of the founders—powdered wig and knee breeches. Meanwhile, the combination of Lafayette's 1824 visit and the implementation of the Pension Act in 1820 fostered much public reflection on the American Revolution and the passing generation of men who had fought in it.[25]

The case of the veterans' pensions illustrates how the pleasures of contemplating the American yet foreign past, with its "old-fashioned" clothes and people, was often tinged with a sense of loss. While much of the public conversation about and commemorations of the revolutionary war veterans in the 1820s had a positive valence—emphasizing the gratitude of the present generation and the glorious achievements of the veterans—the actual imentation of the Pension Act led to the enactment of melancholy scenes in scores of towns across the nation. Only veterans who could "prove their poverty" were eligible for pensions. Hence when government officials arrived in a town to register the veterans' claims, it created a massive public display of suffering. One newspaper account described a representative collection of veterans, "some with the entire loss of the use of all their limbs, bowed down with age and worn out with the labors of life."[26] Much of the private conversation among the decrepit and impoverished men undoubtedly revolved around youthful dreams of personal independence that somehow never came to pass. To those viewing these processions, the old fraying uniforms draped over time-ravaged bodies told a story in which the passage of time did not lead toward ever greater glory, but instead left in its wake a body of depleted and anachronistic people who had remained dispersed and culturally invisible until called together to make their claim on the present generation. While the public transcript of these gatherings was often upbeat, the multiple private (or hidden) transcripts produced by the participants had a more bittersweet valence, amplifying the destructive elements of the early republic over the creative ones.

A comparison of Watson's public and private historical writing reveals a similar tension between a more upbeat, public form of nostalgia and more melancholic, private manifestations of it. On an 1827 trip to Niagara Falls, Watson passed through the town where he had lived in his late teens. He lamented in his travel journal that "the *emotions* which the Scenery & surrounding objects *then* afforded, can *now* but feebly stir." At the time "it was then a *world* of pleasure to me," but "since then other scenes have worn off the charm." As he frequently did in these journals, Watson turned to a contemporary poet—in this case British romantic Thomas Hood—to help him articulate his feelings:

> All things I lov'd *are altered* so,
> Nor does it ease my heart to know
> That change resides in me.[27]

Such wistful commentary on the changes that time had wrought on a familiar landscape and within his own mind appeared in almost every one of his travel journals. Traveling over the same route six years later tson this hastily noted: "Thought much as we rode onward of my boyhood m is all road was so familiar to me. Feel sorry that time passes—the m onward—running off our reel!"[28]

Such reflections upon mortality, aging, and the galloping rapidity of time's passage, clichéd as they were, reflect something important about Watson's historical sensibility. While phrases like "running off our reel" and poems like Hood's referred solely to a personal register of time—the lifetime of one human being—Watson applied the melancholy lessons of these clichés to more public national registers of time as well. In 1835, as Watson began his tenth travel journal, he noted that on his trip to Harrisburg he would indulge his "usual habit of comparing olden time events, with the present extensive improvement." Watson himself was aware that this was a distinctive and fairly uncommon way of narrating an excursion: "It is usual with *me* to draw a secret unenvied pleasure from a thousand incidents overlooked by other men."[29] Whereas most of his contemporaries noted the best places to eat and sleep and the occasional natural or historical sights their friends should see, Watson gazed upon new scenery with an archaeologist's eye. Ever "studious of change," he sought out elderly locals to interview and used his substantial historical knowledge to try to identify remnants of the vanishing past.[30] Most important, where his contemporaries almost always viewed modern improvements as unquestionably good, Watson expressed more ambivalence about the direction of change.

Take, for example, one of those unusual things which Watson had an eye for on his travels—the front porch. On a trip through Reading, Pennsylvania, in 1825, he happily "noticed a great many families sitting in Porches at their Doors & filled with talkers—a good old practice of Philadelphia now disused there." Two years earlier, in the first draft of his *Annals*, he had lamented that porches had been systematically removed from Philadelphia's houses "within the last 30 to 25 years" and that "such an easy access to the inhabitants made the population much more social than now."[31] Traveling to the region's smaller towns felt to Watson like traveling back in time because the material and social fabric of daily life there reminded him of the Philadelphia of his youth. This pleased Watson, yet he also could not "avoid estimating in my mind how very different will be the most of the present scenes in 20 yrs ahead."[32] Charmed as he was, his historical sensibilities told him that some future Watson would be walking through these same Reading streets in twenty years lamenting the demise of that "olden time" sociability.

While the sight of porches in Reading invoked nostalgic memories of his childhood in Philadelphia, traveling through the woods of Pennsylvania and New York conjured up similarly pleasing and melancholy visions of the Indians who had once called those woods home. "As I rode through the Tulpehocken I thought of the former Indian owners—

Whose hundred bands
Ranged freely o'er those shaded lands
Where now there's scarcely left a trace
To mind one of that tawny race.[33]

Two years later on a trip to Pottsville he found that he could not "forbear to think of the aborigines, once its sole lords, & at this season of the year once so busy in catching their shad &c!"[34] A few years later when touring the Jersey shore he wondered "at what *could* have been all the features of this place before Civilization & European eyes scanned this island. I peopled it in imagination with *Indians,* seeking here & finding a safe summer home for their unrestricted supply of fish."[35] Watson loved to sit beneath old trees "which the natives once claimed as their contemporaries & property,"[36] using them in the same way that he and Deborah Logan used their relics of Philadelphia's "olden days"—as a material wedge that could lift them out of the present and enable them to imaginatively share the subjective experience of temporally distant people. In her eulogy for her father, Lavinia Watson fondly remembered their frequent walks in the countryside during her childhood in the 1820s and 1830s when "he would try to picture to my young mind the Indians roaming over those same cultivated fields."[37]

Watson was hardly the only white American who was fascinated by vanishing Indians in the 1820s. As many scholars have pointed out, such affectionate tales of Native Americans were perfectly congruent with the cultural and political logic of Indian removal.[38] Watson's nostalgic identification with Indian history, however, is more complicated than this argument would suggest. In the late 1820s, when he started noticing the ghosts of Indians past on his travels, Watson became a supporter of the anti-removal movement. In 1829 Deborah Logan reported in her diary that Watson had stopped by to happily inform her that "the cause of the poor Indians gains ground and that he felt assured that a spirit was raising in their defense in the nation generally, which would insist upon Justice being done towards them and the measure of their removal prevented from going into effect."[39]

While no records exist that attest to the extent of Watson's participation in the anti-removal agitation, the prolonged national debate over the fate of the Creek and Cherokee peoples clearly shaped how he viewed his own region's history. On an 1835 trip to central Pennsylvania Watson visited an Indian mound on an island in the middle of the Susquehanna River. Watson thought it a "sacrilege" that local residents had dug hundreds of cartloads of human bones" out of the mound and "used as filling-in materials" for a dam that was part of the recently built canal.[40] On a trip up the Hudson Watson noted a spot where Hudson and his men "did some violence to the poor Indns whom they caught in some trifling thefts at the cabin windows . . . these violences were *blots* on the renown of the *Founders* whenever they occurd." Encountering the "long town of the Oneida Indians" on that same trip led Watson to ponder the relationship between the expansion of white civilization and Indian dispossession. "The sight of these Indians in this locality & the nature of the Country we have been travelling *this day*, forcibly reminds me of the very recent recovery of these regions from *their* Sovereignty or possession. . . . All the villages we pass seem, as a general rule, to be near water courses & at the foot of Hills. . . . As the Indians always located near Water, we may generally suppose, *we* generally occupy their towns."[41] While he did not explicitly draw the parallel himself, it seems as if his anger at the events in the contemporary southwest tinged his view of the rapidly "improving" landscape of upstate New York. As fellow travelers marveled at the rapid spread of civilization, Watson's understanding of recent history appears significantly more ambivalent.

In his published *Annals* Watson dealt more breezily with the history of Indian displacement in Pennsylvania, repeating the canonical stories about the kindness of William Penn and the other Quaker founders. But in his more unguarded reflections that he jotted down during his travels, Watson's nostalgic identification with historical Indians led him to comment more directly about the often violent process through which white civilization displaced the land's previous inhabitants.[42] The "improvements" that made his travels possible and the new towns that he visited had literally been built upon (and at times out of) the ruins of a past society. Unlike many of his contemporaries, Watson never tried to justify or explain away this process. His nostalgic urge to imagine himself in the place of past Indians was thus more than shallow sentimentality. It shaped the melancholy, tragic terms in which he understood the changes that had reshaped the American landscape in the previous centuries. Watson's nostalgic affection for vanished Indians fell far short of a meaningful antiracist critique of colonialism. It did, however, lead him to tell stories about the dispossession and suffering of Native Americans that most of his white contemporaries preferred to ignore.

Watson's attentiveness to the dislocation of Native Americans resulted, in part, from his own sense of being displaced by the passage of time. In an era when public reserve was increasingly expected from middle-class men, Watson had a childlike "simplicity" and "innocent faith and confidence in others" that led him to strike up conversations with just about every stranger he met. Occasionally his "olden time" sociability served him well, like on his trip along the Erie Canal when a Captain Dwight took a liking to him and offered up "a piece of the keel of Captn Cooks discovery Ship," or when another "old Gentlmn who was 7 yrs a Prisoner with the Indians" gladly shared with him "much information of things as they were in *auld lang Syne.*"[43] Such experiences, however, seemed to be the exception rather than the rule. His travel journals are filled with complaints about the "cold reserve" of many of his traveling companions who did not appreciate his ardent curiosity about the "olden times." His steamboat and railroad trips in the late 1820s and early 1830s particularly troubled him because he could hardly recognize any of the faces in the crowd.

> While crowded among so many persons of both sexes, I could, but consider how greatly Philada & Philada things had changed in a course of years—once I could have known, by sight, almost all faces I could meet; but among all these how very few could I name! A generation had risen up that knew not me or my Fathers—Even among themselves, but few seemed acquainted. A selfish reserve pervaded all; and a sense of melancholy & loneliness stole upon the mind to consider yourself so isolated in a crowd—This is one of the positive evils of our cherished overgrown population—It shows that we have already passed the maximum point of our happiness.[44]

To the lover of porches and the walking city that Philadelphia had been in his youth, the anonymity of the growing city made him feel like a stranger in his hometown. To make matters worse, Watson was a good enough historian to recognize that these dislocating, home-wrecking changes would only continue into the future and at an ever faster pace.

Watson's concerns about the present and future generations derived in part from his experiences with his own children. After his death Watson's children spoke endearingly of his historical pursuits, but during his life few of them found his frequent expostulations on the contrast between the olden times and the present so enthralling. In 1826 he took his two young daughters on a trip down the Delaware River. As he excitedly talked to them about the wonders of the ships, the new technology that made them work, and the rapidly expanding volume of trade, they seemed unable or unwilling to share his historian's sense of wonder at the scene. "They heard all with marked attention but made few Enquiries or answers—on the whole, there was less striking surprise than I had expected."[45] Nine years later Watson traveled on a recently built railroad with his twelve-year-old son, Baron, who, like his sisters, failed to share his father's enthusiasm. Baron sat in mortified silence as his fifty-four-year-old father looked out the windows and tried to count the fence posts whizzing by, regaling his son and whoever else would listen with stories about the old "flying stages" that used to take "*three days*" to travel this same route. Watson's journal from the outing ends with a laconic and slightly peeved description of his son: "In all these notices I have said little of my Son; I made him, however, partake of my feelings & remarks, so far as he was able; and perhaps he will remember this common visit, and our several conversations & remarks . . . in years to come."[46]

There is more going on here than some timeless sense of embarrassment that all children feel about their parents. The script of generational alienation that Watson and his children acted out was fairly new at the time.[47] The material world Watson grew up in did not differ significantly from that of his parents—as a young man he had engaged in the same sort of work as his father, and no significant technological or demographic changes had occurred in the intervening years to render the texture of his daily life significantly different from that of the previous generation. Watson's children, however, grew up in a world where the material and social world was changing far more rapidly. They did not share their father's historically specific sense of wonder because they felt more at home in Watson's strange new world. Watson tried desperately to "explain" and "contrast" the "wonder[ous]" changes he had seen in his lifetime for his son's benefit. He finally admitted, however, that "these novelties of invention" were "so common . . . to his [son's] every day observation, that he probably most admired, at the former state of dullness, & patient submission to olden-time necessities!"[48] Unlike their father, Watson's children had been effectively socialized as good moderns who had learned to show embarrassment about their father's nostalgic connection to the past. "Things change, who cares about those olden days," we can almost hear them saying. After his disappointing trip with his daughters, Watson glumly wondered to himself if "any of my children possess" the "family faculty" of closely remembering things from their childhoods. "I think not."[49]

It would be inappropriate to close this discussion of Watson on such a despondent note, for his outlook on the present and future was not nearly so curmudgeonly as those last stories suggest. Many of his travels on modern canals and railways filled him with "grateful emotion[s]" regarding the "progress of our country in the encrease of comforts," and he spent the last ten years of his life working as the secretary-treasurer of the Philadelphia, Germantown, and Norristown Railroad. When a practitioner of the cutting-edge science of phrenology came through Philadelphia in the 1840s, Watson jumped at the chance to have his and all of his children's craniums assessed. All the same, Watson's historical sensibilities enabled him to consider the changes of his day with a distinctly critical, measured eye. As Deborah Logan explained in 1829: "We have a way of thinking and talking of modern improvements that savours of our antiquarian taste. We can view things as we think Posterity will view them—but notwithstanding their acknowledged importance in many localities he agreed with me in thinking that Canals and Rail-roads were almost overdone."[50] The "antiquarian" cast of mind that Logan invokes here is, I would argue, what we today might call using good historical thinking to better understand the present. The many nostalgic tours Watson and his friends took into the irreducibly different past with its ever so foreign characters had made them keenly aware of the historically constructed nature of their present and the subjectivities of the people who inhabited it. They looked to the future not with the heedless optimism of the civic booster but with the chastened ambivalence of a nostalgic subject who recognized that change involved both gain and loss, the exciting emergence of the unexpected new, and the inevitable destruction of the oftentimes cherished old.

Watson's nostalgia did not simply hold him in thrall to a distorted, romanticized picture of an irrelevant past. I would argue instead that it partially liberated him (and his other nostalgic contemporaries) from the thralldom of the modernizing present, the insistent imperative that the only good American was the one who paddled gleefully along with the ever-quickening current of the times. It enabled him to see things that were invisible to his more dogmatically modern contemporaries—things that were obsolete, irreversibly superseded and thus unimportant, of only antiquarian interest. As modernity sought to cover its tracks with an ideology of inevitable and always beneficent progress, Watson's nostalgic instincts urged him to pull back that cover to expose what was underneath. This explains why Watson and other antiquarians were the historians of this era who painstakingly researched topics like the leisure-time pursuits and hairstyles of revolutionary-era Americans, the stage coach routes of the 1780s, or the Indian trails of the seventeenth century—the stuff of what we today call social history. It is why we should think twice before we regard antiquarians like Watson as epistemologically simplistic amateurs who were thankfully superseded by more sophisticated "professionals" like George Bancroft.

Although the nostalgic sensibility of the antebellum era emerged in critical tension with modernity, it never succeeded in articulating a clear alternative. Watson knew his antiquarian research was enjoyable and that it enriched his understanding of the present, but as the disconnected nature of his historical writing illustrates, he was never able to discern a nostalgic counternarrative that could challenge the powerful pull of the optimistic Whiggish story. He instinctively knew that disappearing porches and enormous new steam engines changed how people related to each other in significant, often atomizing ways, but these feelings never congealed into a fleshed-out critique of modernization. All the same, in an age when historicism had barely begun to emerge as a way of understanding the past, the nostalgia of Americans like Watson often functioned as a critical and at times creative idiom that enabled such people to locate themselves in time, name the costs of change, and, in some moments, imagine alternative paths into the future.

Notes

1. James C. Scott, *Seeing Like a State: How Certain Schemes to Improve the Human Condition Have Failed* (New Haven, CT, 1998).

2. The bigger project, of which this essay is a part, explores a range of other nostalgic subjects from the antebellum era—women on the western frontier, enslaved people who had been sold south and away from family and friends, Indian communities forcibly removed from their lands, Irish immigrants, and recent migrants from the countryside to the city.

3. A notable exception is the excellent analysis of Watson's work in Elisa Tamarkin, *Anglophilia: Deference, Devotion, and Antebellum America* (Chicago, 2008), 89–93, 127–31. I have also learned much from Lois Amorette Dietz, "John Fanning Watson: Looking Ahead with a Backwards Glance," MA thesis, University of Delaware, 2004, which the author generously shared with me. For a fuller biography of Watson, see Deborah Depondahl Waters, "Philadelphia's Boswell: John Fanning Watson," *Pennsylvania Magazine of History and Biography* 98 (January 1974): 3–52. The broader community of antebellum antiquarian historians, of which Watson was a part, has only recently begun to attract scholarly attention. See, for example, Whitney Martinko, "'So Majestic a Monument of Antiquity'; Landscape, Knowledge, and Authority in the Early National West," *Buildings & Landscapes* 16, no. 1 (Spring 2009): 29–61; Whitney Martinko, "Progress and Preservation: Representing History in Boston's Landscape of Urban Reform, 1820–1860," *New England Quarterly* 82, no. 2 (June 2009): 304–34; Alea Henle, "The Widow's Mite: Hannah Mather Crocker and the Mather Libraries," *Information & Culture: A Journal of History* 48, no. 3 (2013): 323–43; Francesca Morgan, "Lineage as Capital: Genealogy in Antebellum New England," *New England Quarterly* 83 (June 2010): 250–82; and Lindsay DiCuirci, "Reviving Puritan History: Evangelicalism, Antiquarianism, and Mather's 'Magnalia' in Antebellum America," *Early American Literature* 45, no. 3 (November 2010): 565–92.

4. Lewis Perry, *Boats against the Current* (New York, 1993), 58.

5. Peter Fritzche, "Specters of History: On Nostalgia, Exile, and Modernity," *American Historical Review* 106, no. 5 (December 2001): 1587–1618; Fritzsche, *Stranded in the Present: Modern Time and the Melancholy of History* (Cambridge, CT, 2004); Svetlana Boym, *The Future of Nostalgia* (New York, 2002); Edward Casey, "The World of Nostalgia," *Man*

and World 20 (1987): 361–84; Kimberly K. Smith, "Mere Nostalgia: Notes on a Progressive Paratheory," *Rhetoric & Public Affairs* 3, no. 4 (2000): 505–27; and Janelle Wilson, *Nostalgia: Sanctuary of Meaning* (Lewisburg, PA, 2005). For the only recent extended study of nostalgia in pre–Civil War America, see Susan J. Matt, *Homesickness: An American History* (New York, 2011).

6. Quoted in Thomas Laqueur, "Unquiet Bodies," *London Review of Books*, 6 April 2006.

7. Dorothy Ross, "Historical Consciousness in Nineteenth-Century America," *American Historical Review* 89 (October 1984): 909–28.

8. The exception here are those historians who study the "anxieties" expressed by many elites in the early republic who found the democratization of the era troubling. See, for example, Robert P. Sutton, "Nostalgia, Pessimism, and Malaise: The Doomed Aristocrat in Late-Jeffersonian Virginia," *Virginia Magazine of Biography and History* 76, no. 1 (January 1968): 41–55. Elitism and nostalgia were certainly compatible in this era, but historians have too easily assumed that elitism always provided the "real" force behind nostalgic conceptions of the past. Nostalgia was too widespread (and experienced and articulated by too many nonelites) to be treated in such a reductive manner.

9. Daniel Feller, *The Jacksonian Promise* (Baltimore, 1995), 4. For similar accounts of the Whiggish dimension of American popular culture in the early republic, see Joyce Appleby, *Inheriting the Revolution: The First Generation of Americans* (Cambridge, MA, 2001) and Gordon Wood, *Empire of Liberty* (New York, 2011).

10. The generalizations in this paragraph apply primarily to scholarship produced before 2009. A new generation of scholars has begun to pay closer, sympathetic attention to the backward-looking aspects of early nineteenth-century American culture. For example (and in addition to the scholarship cited in note 3), Aaron Sachs, *Arcadian America: The Death and Life of an Environmental Tradition* (New Haven, CT, 2013), excavates a modernist cultural tradition that was also profoundly ambivalent about progress, while Susan Matt explores the ubiquity of nostalgic homesickness in American culture in *Homesickness: An American Story.*

11. Scott Sandage, *Born Losers: A History of Failure in America* (Cambridge, MA, 2006). Sandage's book is a useful reminder that despite the numerous success stories of the early republic, a significant number of men (perhaps even the majority of white men of that era) shared Watson's frustration with never being able to realize their aspirations for independent proprietorship.

12. One of Watson's friends, Deborah Norris Logan, described Watson as a happy man with "a fountain of amusement in his love of antiquities." His only "uneasiness must spring from his fear that Sammy Harvey, who is entirely a matter of fact man, money-making and careful of the main-chance, and who by the way has become suspicious that Watson's antiquarian researches may engross too much of his time. . . . I once gave him a hint on this subject and advised him to be very careful to never let his favourite amusement encroach upon his hours of business in the least. . . . I did this from something which one of the monaters [*sic*] of the Bank let fall in my hearing. [Watson] thanked me very kindly . . . he was fully aware that his Principal had watched with a little Jealousy over his amusements and that he would not be inclined to be indulgent if he suspected these amusements encroached at all on the hours of business." Deborah Norris Logan, diary, 4 November 1827, Historical Society of Pennsylvania.

13. Watson's daughter, Lavinia F. Whitman, provided this description, which was then included in Benjamin Dorr, *Memoir of John Fanning Watson* (Philadelphia, 1861), 24.

14. I am grateful to Laura Keim, curator at Stenton (the historic home of George and Deborah Logan), who first alerted me to the relationship between antiquarian collecting and manual craft labor in Watson's life.

15. Watson composed several lists for friends. One such list, entitled "Queries of aged Persons of Philad," contains an illustrative sampling of the sort of historical information that intrigued Watson. Note the extent to which he is curious about past opinions or impressions of features of the past that had, by 1825, either disappeared or become common:

> 7. Opinions of Carriages.
>
> 9. Opinion of the use and advantages of Porches and Penthouses
>
> 10. What of Sociability in neighbourhoods. What hours of visiting—& what given as entertainment. What did the young then most do for pass time. Were not the young then more reserved.
>
> 13. Any remarkable houses now down.
>
> 16. What of furniture. Difference between Walnut and mahogany.
>
> 19. What stories of blackbeard & Pirates.
>
> 24. Were wild bird & game much more frequent & what prices.
>
> 25. Were Indians much more common in City, on the road, &c.
>
> 27. Did wigs seem natural. The first heads of *natural* hair, how did they seem?
>
> 28. Negro & dutch Servants & Irish much more numerous—of Dances of Negroes at Potters field.
>
> 29. How did you feel to see men & women whipped—[sent?] off—behind carts—what of wheelbarrow men? (Watson Family Papers, box 1, folder 2, Winterthur Library)

16. Quoted in Benjamin Dorr, *A Memoir of John Fanning Watson*, 29.

17. Logan, diary, 3 September 1827.

18. Logan, diary, 13 May 1827.

19. Watson to John J. Smith, 1 March 1827, Watson Letters, Historical Society of Pennsylvania. The pleasurable intensity of their connection is articulated even more forcefully in a letter Watson sent Smith a few months later (13 July 1827) as he embarked on a vacation with his wife: "There must be an interregnum in affairs in *our* mutual government. Try & keep *cool* till I can get back. I expect you feel now as *mercurial* & *sensitive* in this new scheme of happiness, as when you was *beginning* to be married!!!"

20. Smith to Watson, 3 March 1827, Watson Letters.

21. Letter to Edward Everett, 1825, Dorr, *Memoir of John Fanning Watson*, 29.

22. Introduction to manuscript version of the *Annals of Philadelphia*, Library Company of Philadelphia.

23. In 1833 Rufus Choate delivered an oration on "The Importance of Illustrating New England History by a Series of Romances Like the Waverly Novels" that articulated a vision of historical writing very similar to Watson's.

24. A title search in the American Periodicals Database turned up two hits for "olden times" in the years before 1820, and six thousand hits for the years between 1820 and 1860.

25. On Lafayette's visit to America, see Andrew Burstein, *America's Jubilee: A Genera-*

tion Remembers the Revolution after 50 Years of Independence (New York, 2002), chapter 1. On veterans, see John Resch, *Suffering Soldiers: Revolutionary War Veterans, Moral Sentiment, and Political Culture in the Early Republic* (Amherst, MA, 1999).

26. *Dedham Village Register*, 21 July 1820, quoted in Resch, *Suffering Soldiers*, 148. See also 88–99 and 148–50 for discussions of this wave of nostalgia surrounding veterans.

27. "Tour to Niagara," Watson Papers, Winterthur Library.

28. "Traveling Notes of J. F. Watson—Trip to Manahawkin July 1833," Watson Papers.

29. "Traveling Notes of J. F. Watson—To Harrisburgh &c in Jany 1835," Watson Papers.

30. Watson included the phrase "studious of change," taken from *The Task* by poet William Cowper, in almost every travel journal he kept.

31. "Trip to Reading, 1825," Watson Papers; ms. version of *Annals of Philadelphia*, Library Company of Philadelphia.

32. "Trip to Reading, 1825."

33. "Summer Tour 1829 to Maunck Chunk," Watson Papers.

34. "Summer Excursions of 1831," Watson Papers.

35. "Traveling Notes of J. F. Watson—Trip to Manahawkin July 1833."

36. "Trip to Reading, 1825." Ten years later on another trip to central Pennsylvania, Watson reports thinking often "of those Susquehannah Indians, which but 80 years ago, were still inhabiting these fine bottoms, as their *home*. Here thought I, 'it soothes to be where ye have been'—and I could not but consider that I had been seeing at least the same woods—including thousands of *the same trees* upon which they had looked, or under which they had been shadowed or sheltered!"

37. Quoted in Benjamin Dorr, *A Memoir of John Fanning Watson*, 24.

38. Philip Deloria, *Playing Indian* (New Haven, CT, 1998) and Jean M. O'Brien, *Firsting and Lasting: Writing Indians out of Existence in New England* (Minneapolis, 2010).

39. Logan, diary, 7 December 1829.

40. "Traveling Notes of J. F. Watson—Harrisburgh &c in Jany 1835."

41. "Niagara 1827," Watson Family Papers.

42. Watson's travel journals remained private until they were published as an appendix to the 1857 edition of the *Annals*, three years before Watson's death.

43. "Niagara 1827."

44. "Summer Excursions of Year 1831," Watson Papers.

45. "Trip to the Canal Leading from Delaware to Chesapeake, 1826," Watson Family Papers, Winterthur Library.

46. "Excursion to Trenton, 1835," Watson Papers.

47. This theme of nostalgia, modernization, and generational alienation is developed more fully in "'When I was your age . . .': Nostalgic Representations of the Recent Past in Antebellum Children's Literature," slated for inclusion in a collection of essays tentatively entitled "Home, School, Play, Work: The Visual and Textual Worlds of Children," edited by Pat Crain, Martin Bruckner, and Caroline Sloat.

48. "Excursion to Trenton, 1835."

49. Watson Family Papers, box 2, folder 3, Winterthur Library.

50. Logan, diary, 6 October 1829.

Conclusion

What Time Was the American Revolution?
Reflections on a Familiar Narrative

T. H. BREEN

Even to pose the question—What time was the American Revolution?—
seems slightly perverse, since in fact the temporal boundaries of the American Revolution from initial colonial grievance to the achievement of political
stability under the federal Constitution have been well established in our
shared historical memory for several centuries. However, the essays in this
collection, especially Patrick Griffin's provocative survey of the field, invite a
thorough rethinking of this familiar narrative.[1]

Although some scholars once traced the origins of the American Revolution back to the forests of ancient Germany and others have insisted that
the Revolution did not realize its full democratic potential until the Age of
Jackson, the story of our national origins most often begins with the 1760
coronation of George III and then, step by step, traces the growth of colonial
unrest from resistance to the Stamp Act through the Boston Massacre, the
Tea Party, the Battle of Bunker Hill, and then the drafting of the Declaration
of Independence. After this defining moment in 1776, the standard litany of
events loses clarity, and many historians have leapt with interpretive grace
from the Declaration all the way to the Constitution, pausing only briefly to
praise George Washington for keeping an army in the field until the British
finally negotiated peace. Of course, this traditional approach to time and narrative works best with intellectual history or the history of political thought,
since the development of abstract concepts such as virtue and liberty often does not concern itself with the changing social and political context of
events on the ground.[2]

A revolutionary narrative framed by the ascension of George III and the
ratification of the Constitution possesses a compelling logic. It allows us to
navigate a smooth path from national liberation to political stability. This traditional periodization, however, raises troublesome interpretive challenges.
The standard narrative suggests—often implicitly—a kind of inevitability, a

celebratory chronicle of the American people marching forward under the banner of rights and liberty to their well-deserved destiny as citizens of the new republic.

Not surprisingly, this story lends itself to organic, even providential metaphors—children growing up and demanding that the mother country grant them the right to govern themselves or colonies slowly maturing like political plants to the moment when they bring forth independence. From this perspective, the flow of crucial events acquires a causal aspect, becoming in the telling a coherent teleological tale in which one thing leads necessarily to another from beginning to end. This description of the nation's origins often takes on a self-congratulatory tone—one grounded on a belief in American exceptionalism. In this rendering there is not much incentive to engage in comparative analysis, in other words, to examine whether our revolutionary experience over time paralleled in interesting ways that of other nations throughout the world.[3]

What is at stake in posing a question about revolutionary time, therefore, is the possibility of developing a different, less teleological understanding of the relation between interpretation, periodization, and narrative.[4] The alternative conceptualization of revolutionary time advanced here divides what we now generally regard as a single, essentially monolithic block of time— roughly, from 1760 to 1788—into three discrete segments, with each possessing persuasive evidence for its own independent standing in the flow of time.

This revised perspective does not start with the assumption that history is moving toward a predestined goal such as greater democracy or more personal freedom. Rather, the argument begins with a bold assertion that the period most often associated with the run-up to revolution and independence, 1760 to 1773, was nothing of the sort. These years are more accurately defined as a general crisis of imperial rule throughout the Atlantic World. The relatively minor provincial risings in the American colonies—the Stamp Act protests, the Boston Massacre, and the destruction of the tea in Boston Harbor, for example—were mere tremors in an ongoing effort by an ambitious imperial power to make sense of the unprecedented challenge of governing peoples of different races and backgrounds over vast regions where communication remained slow and unreliable. France and Spain confronted many of the same problems in governing the New World as did Great Britain.

The second stage in a reconfigured story of revolutionary time begins in 1774 with the military occupation of Boston and ends with the peace treaty of 1783, a period during which a colonial rebellion transformed itself into a genuine political and social revolution. It involved the experience of armed resistance, of large numbers of ordinary people assuming meaningful authority for the first time in communities throughout America, and of social relations that no longer depended on aristocratic bloodlines. These developments promoted a strong sense of republican equality among white males that turned an initial armed protest against monarchical authority into a revolutionary situation that few colonists anticipated or desired before 1774.

And finally, in a revised narrative scheme, the years following the end of the war did not lead inevitably to the Constitution. Divorced from the traditional triumphal discourse, we should see this period as a postrevolutionary moment in which ordinary people came to terms with life under an experimental federal regime and, as they did so, sought to reabsorb into an uncertain civil society a large number of Americans who had recently sided with Great Britain. To depict the decade of the 1780s as the "Critical Period"—as did the nineteenth-century historian John Fiske—focuses unwarranted attention on elite fears of disorder and anarchy and, by so doing, turns an explosion of entrepreneurial energy among ordinary Americans into an alarming account of a revolution betrayed at the moment of its success.

By the same token, describing this period as postcolonial—as some have done—does not adequately address the issue of periodization, since after 1783 most Americans were eager to rid themselves of monarchical rule and all the aristocratic trappings that accompanied it. Outside a very small group of elite leaders, there was little nostalgia for a lost monarchical world. As Thomas Paine observed in *Rights of Man*, "If I ask a man in America if he wants a King, he retorts, and asks me if I take him for an idiot."[5]

A recasting of revolutionary chronology begins with the period before 1774. These years seem especially vulnerable to teleological interpretation. One can easily understand the temptation to anticipate the coming of revolution and independence. We know, of course, what was coming, and it appears only fair from our perspective to depict every protest over parliamentary regulations and taxation no matter how small as harbingers of the final break with Great Britain. But even armed with the clarity of hindsight, there is no reason to conclude that local complaints about imperial rule—even urban riots and threats of organized resistance—amounted to any more than what they were: highly limited urban protests that lost the potential for large-scale mobilization within days or months.

Such episodes hardly represented a serious breakdown of imperial authority. Throughout the eighteenth century, the British authorities showed remarkable ability to maintain order in England, Scotland, and Ireland. Negotiations usually involved a pragmatic mixture of carrots and sticks, and at the end of the day, even when lethal violence was employed, the negotiating process successfully contained or rechanneled local anger. For example, the bloody conclusion of the Massacre of St. George's Fields in London on May 10, 1768—at least seven people shot down by government troops—was not a sign that the British people were conspiring to launch a revolution.[6] Conditions in the North American colonies were not that different. The Boston Massacre of 1770 certainly did not lead inevitably to Bunker Hill or the Declaration of Independence. Instead, the event brought on three years of extraordinary peace within the empire that caused a frustrated Samuel Adams to despair of ever being able to mount sustained popular resistance to parliamentary regulations. He may have complained about the lack of revolutionary fervor, but as he could see for himself, ordinary Americans between 1771 and 1773 thought that the imperial crisis was over. And in recognition of the return of political normalcy, they purchased record amounts of British manufactured goods. The moments of mob protest in Boston were only small perturbations within an imperial regime. Moreover, they were not uniquely American. For comparison, we might consider the Irish situation where British authorities were able to deal easily with the likes of William Wood (author of an extremely unpopular scheme to produce a new coinage for Ireland) or Charles Lucas (a radical mid-eighteenth-century Dublin apothecary whose political ideas led to exile, but not to revolution).

No doubt, Parliament's attempts during the 1760s to raise revenue from stamps, sugar, and other consumer goods irritated colonial Americans, especially those who lived in port cities. And it is true that the members of the British cabinet at the time found the destruction of private property in Boston alarming. But the fact of the matter is that the Boston agitators even at the height of the Stamp Act crisis did not receive much support from ordinary people living in other parts of British America. Leaders of colonial assemblies wrote to their counterparts in other colonies; highly localized threats of coercion persuaded the collectors of the stamp fees to resign their posts.[7] That was about it. Even in Massachusetts, town meetings in the countryside showed little enthusiasm for the agenda of the Boston radicals. Efforts to organize boycotts of British imported manufactures sputtered, and American merchants seemed more worried that other American merchants were cheating than about parliamentary oppression. The imperial system muddled along; strategic retreats on regulatory policies quieted the urban protesters.

Success at limiting and controlling occasional controversy is precisely what one might have predicted at the time. After all, the American colonists viewed the victory of Great Britain over the French during the Seven Years'

War as incontrovertible evidence of their loyalty to the empire. By their own lights, they were now full partners in a powerful, expanding imperial regime. In so much as the Americans experienced a growing sense of nationalism after the war, they expressed an almost reflexive emotional attachment with Great Britain, a bond sometimes described as colonial nationalism. Like other people throughout the British Empire, they insisted that the relationship with the mother country was the source of basic constitutional rights, the driving engine of Atlantic commerce, and the guarantor of the Protestant faith against Catholic rivals.[8] As Michael Guenther argues in his essay, a new, ambitious press carried cultural and commercial information from the center of the empire to the Atlantic periphery, providing another mechanism for reaffirming a shared British identity.

The argument that the 1760s were only tangentially part of the traditional narrative of the coming of the American Revolution may seem less convincing when we consider the celebrated colonists—John Adams and John Dickinson, for example—who published impressive statements defending colonial rights against parliamentary oppression. These writers whose works figure centrally in modern collections of revolutionary pamphlets were not heralds of an independent republic. Like the so-called Irish patriots of the late seventeenth and early eighteenth centuries—John Toland, William Molyneux, and Jonathan Swift, to name a few—the colonists who chronicled the American grievances were members of a creole elite, in other words, a group of wealthy, privileged, and well-educated men who felt marginalized within an imperial structure.

What these ambitious Americans wanted was respect, to be accepted by leading British political figures as fully British and not as lesser beings inhabiting the distant marchlands of empire. George Washington sulked when he was not given a proper commission in the British army. John Adams, looking to make a legal career in Massachusetts, complained bitterly about the Hutchinson clan, which he thought received an unfair amount of imperial patronage. Protesting his imagined inferiority in British eyes, Adams announced, "I say we are as handsome as old English folks, and so should be free."[9] James Otis agreed. Benjamin Franklin held on to the hope of acceptance to the very eve of revolution, and it was only when Alexander Wedderburn, the British solicitor-general under Lord North, humiliated Franklin during a public hearing that the American felt the full sting of rejection. Other creole leaders experienced similar resentment at what they perceived as their second-class status within the empire.

The point of these observations is not that men such as Adams and Otis were hypocrites mouthing the language of rights when they really desired office and honor. They wrote nobly about freedom and liberty within the context of what they regarded as a very appealing imperial system. They desired acceptance, not separation. Francis Bernard, royal governor of Massachusetts during the 1760s, understood how easy it would be to accommodate these restive colonials. He advised the Earl of Hillsborough (4 February 1769) that if Parliament created an upper house in each colony—a sort of provincial House of Lords—filled with wealthy Americans appointed by the king, it would "go a great way to remedy the disorders to which the Governments of America are subject to." He predicted, no doubt correctly, that eager Americans would fall all over themselves to have "Baron prefixed to their Name." The beauty of the change would be that the addition of so "many royal honors in the new form of Government, will assist the establishment of it, by engaging men who are ripe for honors to the reconciling the people to the System which introduces them."[10] Nothing came of the plan, since parliamentary leaders did in fact look at the Americans, as well as the Irish and Scots, as inferior subjects of the king.

What once appeared as simply the run-up to the American Revolution, therefore, takes on a very different character when we view the period as a general crisis of empire. Americans wanted more authority; they demanded a meaningful voice in shaping the Atlantic economy. Indeed, if there was a moment when the notion of an integrated history of the Atlantic World has particular salience, it was during the middle decades of the eighteenth century. This was the moment when the British, French, and Spanish discovered that they were not fully in control of all the lands and peoples they claimed to rule. The New World remained uncharted territory for European administrators.[11] Developing commercial opportunities and unprecedented military challenges required constant adjustment and accommodation. Men who claimed to be in charge of imperial affairs desperately sought local knowledge.[12]

The demanding, fluid, and experimental aspect of eighteenth-century imperial expansion is a central theme that a group of historians explore so thoughtfully in this volume: Timothy J. Shannon, Owen Stanwood, Christopher Hodson, James Coltrain, and Patricia Cleary. They bring to a period of imperial crisis a wonderfully nuanced sense of the unprecedented perils and possibilities of European ambitions in the New World. It is a complex story of people of different races and backgrounds struggling to accommodate accelerating change. Ian Saxine, for example, documents in convincing detail how Native Americans living on the Maine frontier were drawn into a vast imperial network of conflicting interests. There is nothing about the work of these scholars of the Atlantic World that looks ahead to the Declaration of Independence or the Constitution. They depict a chronology of mid-eighteenth-century imperial challenges in a context that contemporaries would have understood.

A radical break in the standard revolutionary narrative occurred during 1774. It marked the second stage of a revised account of the political origins of the United States. This crucial year witnessed a rending of time, a dramatic caesura in the flow of events, for although memories of an earlier history shaped the political consciousness of ordinary Americans, the landscape of power underwent a sudden and profound shift. The trigger for massive change was not as the traditional story of the coming of the Revolution would have it: the Boston Tea Party. Many Americans saw the destruction of private property as an extreme form of protest, even an unwarranted provocation, and there was no immediate outpouring of support for the people of Boston who organized the action.

What fundamentally transformed the character of colonial politics was the reaction of Parliament to news of the Tea Party. Lord North and his allies passed a series of harsh retaliatory acts, known in the colonies as the Coercive Acts, which not only closed the port of Boston to all commerce but also authorized an army of occupation to police the port city. This legislation alienated Americans who had not previously voiced much enthusiasm for the Boston rioters. One encounters for the first time in the records of town meetings throughout Massachusetts ordinary farmers wrestling with questions about the limits of political allegiance. For colonists living in distant places such as South Carolina and Virginia, the punishment of Boston seemed totally out of proportion with the seriousness of the crime. After all, an entire city population was being forced to take responsibility for the behavior of a small group.

The Coercive Acts sparked widespread sympathy for the suffering poor and unemployed people of Boston.[13] Extreme retaliation brought forth a massive mobilization the likes of which were unimaginable before 1774; from New Hampshire to Georgia, people began to speak of an "American Cause." Again, we should appreciate that there was nothing unique about the swift development of new political solidarities in the American colonies. The Easter Rising in Dublin in 1916, for example, did not spark a general revolt against Great Britain. But, as in America, the cruel and humiliating suppression of dissent that followed the Rising persuaded Irish people who had been neutral or afraid to participate in armed rebellion.[14] In both cases, a revision of revolutionary time takes the interpretive focus away from the actions and writings of leaders—the Founding Fathers—and restores to the story the people who actually showed up at Bunker Hill and figured out what revolution meant in their lives without having to read learned pamphlets.

The Irish participation in the American Revolution also renders the traditional teleological narrative problematic. During the early 1770s, tens of thousands of Irish migrants flooded into the middle colonies. Most of them were Protestants, driven from their homes in part by British regulations restricting the export of linen, an industry on which the income of many Irish families depended. Even as the First Continental Congress was meeting in Philadelphia in September 1774, boatloads of Irish men and women arrived almost daily in the city. They marched in huge numbers past Carpenters' Hall.

What is significant about this migration is that a very large percentage of the Continental Lines that fought with distinction during the war were Irish. These men had no personal memory of the Stamp Act protests of 1765 or the Boston Massacre of 1770. They were not part of the story we tell ourselves about a decadelong series of grievances that led inevitably to independence.[15] And since so many of the American soldiers during the Revolution had only been small children at the time of the Stamp Act, it is hard to comprehend their commitment to independence outside the context of the British army's occupation of Boston and its use of armed force against ordinary people in the countryside. They certainly did not have personal memories of earlier moments of protest.

We should also recognize that organized resistance to British rule in 1775 did not signal the start of a genuine revolution. That development came later. At first, most Americans hoped that Lord North and his political supporters would come to their senses and find a way to negotiate an acceptable solution to the imperial crisis. Small communities throughout New England, for example, protested their allegiance to George III while struggling for the first time with the possibility of armed resistance against the abuse of power. From this perspective almost all the Americans were loyalists in that they sincerely hoped that the British would back down and restore an imperial system that had brought the colonists prosperity and security. As Thomas Jefferson noted in his rough draft of the Declaration of Independence, British stubbornness had forced the issue by denying them their constitutional rights as British subjects. "We might have been a free & great people together," he argued, "but a communication of grandeur & of freedom it seems is below their dignity. Be it so, since they will have it: the road to glory & happiness is open to us too; we will climb it in a separate state, and acquiesce in the necessity which pronounces our ever-lasting Adieu."[16]

At the start of the war, therefore, the American insurgents clashed over strategies of reconciliation, not over fundamental political ideas. Even colonial leaders who later opposed independence championed at the beginning of resistance standard republican values of virtue and liberty. By 1776, however, a protest against British oppression that had begun as a colonial rebellion became a genuine revolution. The transformation did not involve a shift in fundamental political principles. Ideology did not turn rebellion into revolution. After all, the idea that the people are the only legitimate source of political power had a long history in the colonies.

The new element in the revolutionary equation was experience, quite simply the excitement, the fear, the disappointments, the betrayals, and denunciations associated with living—with just surviving—through a time of violent political change. We direct the analytic focus properly on the actual challenge of waging war that lasted eight years. During this period Americans discovered that it was one thing to discuss rights and equality in the abstract, to read philosophic pamphlets, or to analyze ancient Renaissance texts or seventeenth-century English political tracts, and quite another to experience republicanism in newly formed army units that elected their own officers or on committees of safety and inspection that recruited scores of men who had never before served in significant positions of authority. Gone suddenly were the trappings of monarchical and aristocratic society. There would be no more doffing of the cap to one's betters. Participation in political resistance created new emotional bonds that carried radical possibilities.[17] White American males came to believe in a crude sense of equality. To draw once again on Irish history, a terrible beauty was born.

To be sure, the language of rights inspired American Revolutionaries. The traditional story of revolution correctly chronicles the centrality of ennobling principles of liberty and freedom. But that approach discounts other binding elements, some of which make modern commentators on the Revolution uncomfortable. As Michael Guenther reminds us, complex networks as much as ideas sustained radical change. Moreover, the actual experience of war included not only republican ideas, fear of power and ubiquity of corruption, the importance of virtue and the necessity of constant vigilance, but also a demanding lexicon of largely forgotten, unsettling words such as *fear, vengeance, retaliation, betrayal,* and *violence.* This is the analytic vocabulary of other revolutions from France and Haiti to Russia and China. To erase these experiential concepts from the American Revolution, as so many historians have done, only serves to reinforce problematic notions of our own exceptionalism, as if our revolution somehow turned on an Enlightenment discourse while the other revolutions of the world succumbed to fear and violence. It is this more realistic aspect of revolutionary society as seen from the ground that Donald Johnson reconstructs so persuasively. As he demonstrates, with persuasive archival evidence, securing the revolution was difficult and dangerous. Both essays invite fruitful comparative discussion. After all, the creation of revolutionary networks, suspicion of neighbors, policing a revolutionary agenda, accommodating to the demands of military occupation, and taking property from alleged domestic enemies are commonly thought to be part of the story of other revolutions.[18]

After the victory at Yorktown, Americans entered what is best described as a postrevolutionary period. This terminology deflects attention away from the Constitution of the United States, a document of such significance in the nation's subsequent history that we tend to see the entire decade of the 1780s as a prologue to its drafting and ratification. George Washington, Alexander Hamilton, and James Madison—the dominant characters in a campaign to establish a strong federal government—certainly worried about the danger of political fragmentation. They became so anxious about the threat to the stability of the new republic, in fact, that they greatly exaggerated the danger posed by a small rising led by Daniel Shays. Insistence that Shays and a group of impoverished farmers in central Massachusetts betrayed the goals of the revolution only serves to make the Constitution appear to be the proper and inevitable end of the revolutionary era. Indeed, histories that dwell on the alleged fear of anarchy only reinforce the self-serving and teleological notion that the country had to be saved from the ordinary people who had lost their political way.

Perhaps more than other veterans, Washington sensed that revolutions most often fail after the military battles have ended.[19] In his role as a postrevolutionary leader, he defined the political landscape much as Mahatma Gandhi and Nelson Mandela did in more recent times. Washington warned that faction would erode a sense of common purpose; narrow and self-serving interests at the state level appeared to imperil the union that he had worked so hard to preserve during the war. So passionately did the country's leaders fear a general breakdown of authority that they refused to address pressing issues such as slavery. They knew that an unfree labor system was morally objectionable, but as David Gellman demonstrates so well in his examination of race and freedom in the extended Jay family, it was often easier to avoid confrontation with hard questions than to reform society.

However much we may admire Washington, we do not have to accept his analysis of the postrevolutionary decade. If one concentrates on elite fears of looming anarchy, one discounts the buoyant optimism that characterized the American people as a whole. There is not much evidence that they were paralyzed by anxiety over the country's future. The revolution unleashed an extraordinary burst of energy and optimism. Suddenly, after years of British economic regulation, ordinary Americans devised new schemes to better their lives. Everyone seemed to have a plan, a proposal to build a canal, a chance to make money through land speculation, or a dream of striking it rich through trade with China. They moved west in huge numbers, brutally pushing Native Americans aside, in hope of establishing the independent farms that they had been unable to acquire in colonies such as Virginia and Connecticut. And they had lots of children, a family decision often seen as an index to a positive vision of the future. Washington and his friends may have regarded ambitious speculators and urban projectors as threats to classic republican values, but whatever their apprehensions, in the postrevolutionary United States that kind of thinking did not have deep roots among the people.

A rejection of the standard narrative of revolution—a smooth, almost predestined tale of gifted leaders guiding the people from colonial protest to political stability under the Constitution—brings into focus fresh and challenging interpretive concerns. The payoff seems obvious. First, the run-up to independence becomes a genuinely comparative story within the context of the imperial rivalries that defined the Atlantic World. The competition for military and commercial dominance shaped the lives of ordinary Europeans and African slaves as well as indigenous peoples. Second, an account of the actual experience of living through a revolution restores the ordinary people to a tale previously dominated by a small group of leaders. And third, by rejecting the teleological analysis that depicts the Constitution as an almost providential remedy to the imagined breakdown of governing authority, we appreciate more fully the promise and energy generated within a postrevolutionary society. The new periodization of the revolutionary era developed here is inclusive, dynamic, and open to people who did not pen founding documents or serve as generals or statesmen. As Seth Cotlar reminds us, our interpretation of time will change as the context of our own lives changes. But however we conduct a conversation among ourselves about political origins, we can be assured that we will repeatedly ask, "What time was the American Revolution?"

Notes

1. For a splendid discussion of periodization, see Jacques Le Goff, *Must We Divide History into Periods?* (New York, 2015).

2. See, for example, Bernard Bailyn, *Ideological Origins of the American Revolution* (Cambridge, MA, 1992). On the long interpretive history of the Revolution, see Gwenda Morgan, *The Debate on the American Revolution* (Manchester, 2007).

3. This claim is not meant to deny the extraordinary importance of R. R. Palmer's pioneering work, *The Age of the Democratic Revolution: A Political History of Europe and America, 1760–1800* (Princeton, 2014). Also helpful in inviting a broader comparative perspective are Eliga H. Gould, *Among the Powers of the Earth: The American Revolution and the Making of a New World* (Cambridge, MA, 2014), and *Revolution! The Atlantic World Reborn*, ed. by Thomas Bender, Laurent Dubois, and Richard Rabinowitz (New York, 2011).

4. Two innovative and provocative attempts to redefine revolutionary chronology are Gordon S. Wood, *The Radicalism of the American Revolution* (New York, 1993), and Brendan McConville, *The King's Three Faces: The Rise and Fall of Royal America, 1688–1776* (Chapel Hill, NC, 2007).

5. Thomas Paine, *Rights of Man*, ed. Hypatia B. Bonner (London, 1937), 119. For a different view, see Eric Nelson, *The Royalist Revolution: Monarchy and the American Founding* (Cambridge, MA, 2014).

6. See Paul Langford, *A Polite and Commercial People: England, 1727–1783* (Oxford, 1994); John Brewer and John Styles, *An Ungovernable People: The English and Their Law in the Seventeenth and Eighteenth Centuries* (New Brunswick, NJ, 1980); and R. F. Foster, *Modern Ireland, 1600–1972* (London, 1989).

7. See Edmund S. Morgan and Helen M. Morgan, *The Stamp Act Crisis: Prologue to Revolution* (Chapel Hill, NC, 1995).

8. Linda Colley, *Britons: Forging the Nation, 1707–1837* (New Haven, CT, 2009); and T. H. Breen, "Ideology and Nationalism on the Eve of the American Revolution: Revisions Once More in Need of Revising," *Journal of American History* 84 (1997): 13–39.

9. *Boston Gazette*, 14 October 1765.

10. Colin Nicolson, ed., *Papers of Francis Bernard, Governor of Colonial Massachusetts, 1760–69* (Charlottesville, VA, 2015), 5:187. See John Clive and Bernard Bailyn, "England's Cultural Provinces: Scotland and America," *William and Mary Quarterly*, 3rd ser., vol. 11 (1954), 200–213.

11. Paul W. Mapp, *The Elusive West and the Contest of Empire, 1713–1763* (Chapel Hill, NC, 2013).

12. John H. Elliott, *Empires of the Atlantic World: Britain and Spain in America, 1492–1830* (New Haven, 2007); Anthony Pagden, *Lords of All the Worlds: Ideologies of Empire in Spain, Britain, and France c. 1500–c.1800* (New Haven, CT, 1998); James Pritchard, *In Search of Empire: The French in the Americas, 1670–1730* (Cambridge, 2007); and P. J. Marshall, ed., *Oxford History of the British Empire: The Eighteenth Century* (Oxford, 2001).

13. T. H. Breen, *American Insurgents, American Patriots: The Revolution of the People* (New York, 2011).

14. T. H. Breen, "Reflections on the American and Irish Revolutions," lecture given at the O'Connell House, Dublin (29 August 2011).

15. T. H. Breen, "An Irish Rebellion in America?" *Field Day Review* 2 (2006): 275–85, and Breen, *American Insurgents, American Patriots.* Also see Bernard Bailyn, *Voyagers to the West: A Passage in the Peopling of America on the Eve of Revolution* (New York, 1988).

16. Julian P. Boyd, ed., *Papers of Thomas Jefferson* (Princeton, 1950), 1:427.

17. See Charles Royster, *A Revolutionary People at War: The Continental Army and American Character, 1775–1783* (Chapel Hill, NC, 1996); and John Shy, *A People Numerous and Armed: Reflections on the Military Struggle for American Independence* (Ann Arbor, MI, 1990).

18. Sheila Fitzpatrick, *Everyday Stalinism: Ordinary Life in Extraordinary Times: Soviet Russia in the 1930s* (Oxford, 2000); Timothy Tackett, *The Coming of the Terror in the French Revolution* (Cambridge, MA, 2015); and Wendy Z. Goldman, *Inventing the Enemy: Denunciation and Terror in Stalin's Russia* (Cambridge, 2011).

19. T. H. Breen, *George Washington's Journey: The President Forges a New Nation* (New York, 2016).

Afterword

Joyce E. Chaplin

At the time I first consulted it, on May 3, 2013, Timothy H. Breen's online curriculum vitae included eleven items under the heading of "Books" and sixty-three under "Articles." I felt discouraged—not over the prospect of writing an assessment of Breen's oeuvre but because he has been so shamingly productive. I could reassure myself, slightly, that he has had an almost fifty-year scope for his outpouring. But then there was the astonishing productivity in every register available to a senior scholar, from academic monograph to *TLS* review essay, from major peer-reviewed articles to a commercial textbook in its tenth edition. There is also the fact that, since 2013, Breen's publications have only continued to accumulate. Above all, there is the critical truth that Breen's work has been central and centrally productive to almost every major argument and intellectual turn within the field of early American history from the 1960s to the 2010s (and very likely beyond).

There is little point to surveying the Breen corpus work by work, with a mention of every last item. It is the major intellectual interventions within this scholarly edifice that matter. These are his lasting contributions, the kind that any real scholar wants to make and of a multitude and magnitude that are remarkable for any scholar—indeed, enviable. There is a difference between jealousy and envy. The former sentiment is what you might feel about someone whose gift or accomplishment you wish they did not have because you want it exclusively for yourself and worry that their possession of it somehow dispossesses you; the latter feeling is wanting what the other person has, but not begrudging it to them, because you know they deserve it. According to that distinction, this is a very envious essay but not at all a jealous one.

Particularly enviable is Breen's consistent interrogation of two themes that have been at the heart of the field: authority and liberty, those vexedly connected possibilities for the different peoples in the different early Americas that existed from the late 1500s to the early 1800s. In this, Breen of course is not unique. He follows many scholars who have pointed out the coexistence of American freedom and American slavery, all of them somewhat indebted to G. W. F. Hegel's famous Master-Slave dialectic. But Breen's gift was to make clear that these opposing states were not theoretical categories but lived experiences for actual people, millions of them. And what is especially notable is that Breen was always to be found on the cutting edge of some new way of understanding these two historical realities. He was ever defining and pursuing new ways of seeing how authority was defended (or assaulted) and how liberty expanded or contracted. His multiple publications have, accordingly, occupied both the center of early American history and its innovative peripheries. Again, that's enviable.

Breen's first published work appeared about a half century before the publication of this essay, in 1966, in the journal *Church History*, and although the author was still in graduate school, his article already exhibited the patient and productive exasperation with foolishness that would continue to characterize his work. "The Non-Existent Controversy: Puritan and Anglican Attitudes on Work and Wealth, 1600–1640," addressed the question of whether early modern religions were basically socioeconomic ideologies. Breen was here taking on Max Weber's famous thesis about a putative "Protestant Ethic" of hard work that had somehow laid the ideological foundations for capitalism, though his immediate target was the then canonical figure Christopher Hill. That English historian's recent *Society and Puritanism in Pre-Revolutionary England* (1964) was among a suite of studies that argued for puritanism as the vanguard of modern economic society, as opposed to the traditional and agrarian order upheld by Anglicans. "Nonsense," Breen retorted, supplying ample evidence of complexity of ideas where others insisted on simple ideologies and of similarities between puritan and Church of England responses to the problems of work, idleness, and wealth.[1]

Given that essay's focus on religion in the seventeenth century, it may have seemed surprising that Breen's next publication shot forward in time to consider "John Adams's Fight against Innovation in the New England Constitution: 1776," which appeared in the *New England Quarterly* in 1967. And it may have seemed even more surprising that his subsequent publication, "'The Conflict in the Golden Bough': Frazer's Two Images of Man" (*South Atlantic Quarterly*, also 1967), spun laterally toward social science theory. But by publishing these three articles just as he was completing his dissertation, Breen had quickly staked out the entire habitat that he would continue to inhabit throughout his subsequent career. Already there was the Breen claim to the long chronology of early American history: both the seventeenth and eighteenth centuries, from the founding of colonies to the ending of the first British Empire. There was also the characteristic curiosity about both behavior and ideas and, even more important, how historians could and should consider those two realms of evidence about the past (and about humanity) as interconnected. Obviously there was the persistent reminder that power and powerlessness (religious, economic, political) were constitutive of nearly every kind of historical experience. And there was the prescient knowledge of the disciplines beyond history that might productively inform historians' inquiries about the past, which the article on the anthropologist Sir James George Frazer quite definitely announced.[2]

Breen's commitment to the connected realms of ideas and of actions, both halves of lived experience, was present in his first book, based on his dissertation, *The Character of the Good Ruler: A Study of Puritan Political Ideas in New England, 1630–1730* (1970). It is unrivaled because it is still the closest examination of how New England's Puritans thought about their government and put their thoughts into action. The book is therefore a serious intervention into the historiography on political thought, formal analysis of the theories that lay behind or beyond the institutionalization of power. And yet *The Character of the Good Ruler* would also be essential reading for the authors of the many New England "town studies" that looked at how people behaved (or misbehaved) in the communities of England's northernmost American settler society. The book was rare in being appreciated, therefore, by two emerging groups of scholars: those around Quentin Skinner's Cambridge (England) school of contextualized examination of political thought, and those who were emerging from France and England and would go about their work under the extremely messy name of "social historians."[3]

Breen never relinquished his belief that ideas matter, but most of the works he would go on to publish in the 1970s and early 1980s were important and indeed germinal contributions to what Americanists once called "the new social history." The decades of his contributions to this subfield represented the heyday of social history which, in its American incarnation, focused on recovering the words and deeds of people whose recorded existence had fallen outside the main lines of historical inquiry, which had tended to privilege the lives of those who were powerful and visible, particularly elite men whose actions (political, military, economic, intellectual) had dominated the received narrative about the past. To excavate the lives of others, meaning the vast majority of human beings, required the identification and interrogation of different sources, ones that often noted people more incidentally. The subjects of social history were not authors of major texts, leaders of troops, or heads of state, but instead were writers of diaries, wills, and letters, persons of interest to magistrates and warrant officers, wielders of tools or weapons, and makers of wealth for others, rarely for themselves.

At first, the early Americanists who pursued social history sources and methodologies focused on white settlers, the counterparts of the peasants and proto-proletarians who were at the heart of social history in Europe. That project included the direct tracking of the English lower orders to the American colonies. Those emphases were certainly apparent in Breen's major contributions to the field in the 1970s. Foremost among these were the essay "Moving to the New World: The Character of Early Massachusetts Immigration," coauthored with Stephen Foster (*William and Mary Quarterly*, 1973), and his own "Persistent Localism: English Social Change and the Shaping of New England Institutions" (also for the *William and Mary Quarterly*, 1975, awarded the prize for best article in the journal that year). Breen also broadened his geographic remit by looking south, first in *Shaping Southern Society: The Colonial Experience* (1976), an edition of collected essays by a variety of colleagues and a strategic way for Breen to survey the then current work on the southern colonies as he began to consider moving beyond New England in his own scholarship.[4]

In parallel, and impressively, Breen kept up his analysis of the past as more than a mere record of what had been done—deeds without motives—and thus he made several notable contributions to cultural history, defined in an anthropological sense of culture. This was not yet the kind of cultural history (which would blossom in the 1990s) informed by literary theory and focused on the exegesis of texts and other human artifacts as culturally distinctive objects. Instead, this 1980s iteration of cultural history followed one of the intellectual debts of social history to the social sciences, principally anthropology and sociology, in order to represent past lives wholly, as embedded within and expressive of broader cultural practice and nexuses. That emphasis on society as a totality, as a dynamic context for humanity, was apparent in the essay Breen published with Stephen Foster, "The Puritans' Greatest Achievement: A Study of Social Cohesion in Seventeenth-Century Massachusetts" (*Journal of American History*, 1973), in his own "Transfer of Culture: Chance and Design in Shaping Massachusetts Bay, 1630–1660" (*New England Historical and Genealogical Register*, 1978), and in the shrewdly named "Looking Out for Number One: Conflicting Cultural Values in Early Seventeenth-Century Virginia" (*South Atlantic Quarterly*, 1979).[5]

Without questioning the value of any of these pieces, I nevertheless think that the greatest among his cultural history contributions resulted from Breen's deployment of the symbolic anthropology of Clifford Geertz. That scholar's name may no longer carry the weight it did in the 1970s and 1980s, when Geertz's *Interpretation of Cultures* (1973) was pretty much ubiquitous among academics. Geertz's essay on Balinese cockfighting, in particular, had great resonance among historians, who used its basic insight—that social activities were forms of cultural expression through which people displayed inter-nested motivations and desires and achieved notable gains and losses—to examine a variety of things people did in the past. Breen's own contribution, "Horses and Gentlemen: The Cultural Significance of Gambling among the Gentry of Virginia" (*William and Mary Quarterly*, 1979), is exemplary, perhaps the finest interpretation of early America that was ever done within the terms of symbolic anthropology.[6]

It is worth noting that Breen not only read and used the intellectual strategies of social science but undertook another of its distinctive methods: collaboration. This is still an approach most historians find foreign, even as it is the standard within the social sciences, not to mention the natural sciences. In contrast, most historians continue to follow a humanities model of working solo. But many of Breen's efforts have been collaborative. He worked this way first with Stephen Foster in "Moving to the New World" and in "The Puritans' Greatest Achievement." These essays were, moreover, published in prime locations, the *William and Mary Quarterly* (where "Moving to the New World" won the prize for the best article that year) and the *Journal of American History.* They were neither marginalized nor experimental as coauthored articles, and this is still a counterexample if not rebuke to the individualized efforts that continue to characterize the work of academic historians and constrain the kinds of questions we ask and answer.[7]

Even so, it was apparent that Breen had not relinquished his oldest interests but rather was augmenting them with contributions to the newest trends in the field. Two of his essays, "Who Governs: The Town Franchise in Seventeenth-Century Massachusetts" (*William and Mary Quarterly*, 1970) and "English Origins and New World Development: The Case of the Covenanted Militia in Seventeenth-Century Massachusetts" (*Past and Present,* 1972), developed themes on government and political ideology he had first laid out in *The Character of the Good Ruler.* But in good social history fashion, Breen had expanded his analysis of colonial political culture to include the men who might never hold high political office but whose status as householders nonetheless qualified them to vote or serve in militias, activities that set them apart from women, children, the poor, Indians, servants, and slaves. In this way (and for the moment distinctively) Breen blended old and new ways of considering authority to include the men of middling rank who were politicized entities though not actual rulers, sharp recognition of how power and lack of power operated on a daily basis. Yet another contribution to the *William and Mary Quarterly*, "George Donne's 'Virginia Reviewed': A 1638 Plan to Reform Colonial Society" (1973), was a piece in the "Notes and Documents" section of the journal, and it presented scholars with a transcription of Donne's proposal, which displayed Breen's status as a supreme "archive rat." The archive in this case was the British Library, where Donne's work had languished for over three centuries after having been presented to Charles I.[8]

It was at this point that Breen's three established strengths as a historian— as a scholar of power relations, as a social historian, and as an archival adept—converged to produce his work on race and slavery in early Virginia. His article on "A Changing Labor Force and Race Relations in Virginia, 1660– 1710" (*Journal of Social History*, 1973) was an initial salvo, a significant (and for the time unusual) move beyond the new social history's focus on the ordinary white settlers who, however subordinate within the contemporary social hierarchy and therefore less visible in the historical record, were nonetheless either free or only temporarily in servitude. Slavery was different—and understanding that difference is crucial to our understanding of how power and liberty acquired the fatefully racist American configurations they did. Indeed, Breen's essay was one of several works that followed the earliest efforts to trace the emergence of racial slavery in what would become the United States. A longer collaborative work, the book that Breen wrote with Stephen Innes, *"Myne Owne Ground": Race and Freedom on Virginia's Eastern Shore* (1980), explored not only the deepening entrenchment of chattel slavery in the first southern colony but also the paradoxical status of blacks who were free as well as landholders within a slave society. Breen offered another look at the uneven and uneasy correlation between race and status in an essay he wrote with Stephen Innes, "Seventeenth-Century Virginia's Forgotten Yeomen: The Free Blacks" (*Virginia Cavalcade*, 1981), which placed the new insights of social history and of the histories of racism and slavery admirably into a publication for general readers. In another register, Breen presented, along with two younger scholars (James Lewis and Keith Schlesinger), another notable archival find into the "Notes and Documents" section of the *William and Mary Quarterly*. This contribution was "Motive for Murder: A Servant's Life in Virginia, 1678" (1983), a chilling documentary insight into the miserable colonial life conditions that could drive an indentured servant to murder.[9]

By this stage of his career, between fifteen and twenty years after his first publication, Breen began to add several synthetic works to his portfolio. He gathered his most forceful essays into a collection, *Puritans and Adventurers: Change and Persistence in Early America* (1980), and tried his hand at writing a textbook. The latter was done with several coauthors, including his Northwestern University colleague George Fredrickson, but also R. Hal Williams and Robert Divine, to produce *America Past and Present.* First published in 1984, the text has, with a changing set of authors—yet always including Breen—been in print continuously and is now in its tenth edition, longevity here being significant evidence that the authors of the first edition had absolutely known what they were doing.[10]

After Breen had explored many of the reigning topics within social history, he turned next to one that represented a new focus for his work: agriculture. Although the parallel fields of historical geography and environmental history were at the time and in other ways reviving agricultural history (which until then had begun to seem like a dull and dusty subject), many historians of the colonies and the United States had yet to follow the lead of European social historians to consider seriously the agricultural foundations of early modern society, which would have included the societies of the neo-Europes in the Americas. Breen moved first to lay out a rationale for doing agricultural history, "Back to Sweat and Toil: Suggestions for the Study of Agricultural Work in Early America" (*Pennsylvania History,* 1982), but he quickly amalgamated that assertion about the centrality of rural production to colonial life with a reminder of the ethnographic significance of whatever people might have been doing every day as a constituent element of their overall culture, whether out in the fields or elsewhere. "The Culture of Agriculture: The Symbolic World of the Tidewater Planter, 1760–1790," published in an edited volume of essays on early American history, made this argument in miniature, followed by an extended treatment in Breen's *Tobacco Culture: The Mentality of the Great Tidewater Planters on the Eve of Revolution* (1985), winner of the Theodore Saloutos Prize for outstanding book on agricultural history. These quite Geertzian analyses were followed by another essay for general readers, "'Making a Crop': Tobacco and the Tidewater Planters on the Eve of Revolution" (*Virginia Cavalcade,* 1986), which disseminated news about the significance of premodern rural economies to an audience beyond academia.[11]

The agricultural turn was at the time quite apparent in several subfields within American history, and here Breen confronted anew questions about capitalism he had first considered in his very first essay on the Weber thesis. Some scholars were looking at rural production as a way to track the arrival and spread of an early capitalist economy into the American hinterland. Others argued that colonial agriculture was not quite capitalist, but neither was it a mere subsistence strategy, although the large monocultural plantations that produced tobacco, rice, and sugar were obvious exceptions. For farming in the north, as well as on smaller farms in the tobacco colonies, a mix of market orientation and household production seemed to be common, as the environmental historian William Cronon and the colonial historian Richard L. Bushman argued elsewhere. Breen took this view even as his focus on tobacco planters stressed, necessarily, their manifest dedication to commercial profits. Southern and Caribbean plantations lay, after all, at the far end of the early modern spectrum running between subsistence and commerce. (And if the author may be allowed a personal interpolation, it was precisely Professor Breen's work on the culture of agriculture that lured her into early American history, and then to graduate school, and thus to other analyses of the human place within the natural world.)[12]

What next? Already Breen's contributions to academic historiography had been considerable and done in several registers, pursuing long established themes relating to political power, on the one hand, and making newer inquiries into the experiences of people long absent from the dominant narrative of history, on the other, and altogether parsing each level of colonial society, from the privileged to the enslaved. Breen did take time, going into the 1990s, to consolidate several of his important statements about the colonial past. Foremost among these was a synthetic essay, "Creative Adaptations: Peoples and Cultures in Early America," that he produced for a volume edited by Jack P. Greene and J. R. Pole, *Colonial British America: Essays in the New History of the Early Modern Era* (1984). He also made a pair of forays into the history of Native Americans, in collaboration with the D'Arcy McNickle Center for the History of the American Indian at the Newberry Library in Chicago. And Breen made his first contribution to discussions of early America in the major media, in a review essay on two recent works analyzing the Seven Years' War (by Fred Anderson and E. Wayne Carp) called "Founding Sons," published in the *New York Review of Books* in December 1985, which inaugurated a career as a book reviewer for popular media on two sides of the Atlantic.[13]

Breen's next major historiographic move came one year after he published that initial popular review, when he commenced a significant engagement with material culture and the history of consumer economics. Addressing questions about economic development that had also informed his studies of agricultural economies, Breen used the consumer culture of the colonies to deliver a firm verdict not only that colonists had been enmeshed in early capitalist and manufacturing economies but also that their consumption of British manufactures was part of a complex cultural affiliation with the imperial nation across the sea. "An Empire of Goods: The Anglicization of Colonial America" (*Journal of British Studies*, 1986) introduced early Americanists to these claims, and the closely associated "'Baubles of Britain': The Consumer Culture of Eighteenth-Century America and the Coming Revolution" (*Past and Present*, 1988), invited scholars of the early modern period more generally to consider that argument. This was an important move, as the journal in question was still the clearinghouse for all scholars who focused on historical eras before industrialization. Two other important interventions into the politics of consumer culture followed. Breen published "Narrative of Commercial Life: Consumption, Ideology, and Community on the Eve of the American Revolution" in the *William and Mary Quarterly* of 1993, plus "The Meaning of Things: Consumption and Ideology in the Eighteenth-Century," in an important collection, *Consumption, Culture, and Society* (1993), edited by John Brewer and Roy Porter. The first of these essays has remained particularly influential; it won the prize for best essay in the *William and Mary Quarterly* for 1993, then the Douglas Adair Prize (1994) for the outstanding essay to appear in the journal over the previous five years, and was subsequently republished in two scholarly collections.[14]

Breen's work on consumerism gained its widest impact with his monograph *Marketplace of Revolution: How Consumer Politics Shaped American Independence* (2004). Although the question of economic motives for revolutionary politics had been an important one for early American history at least since the publication of Charles Beard's *Economic Interpretation of the Constitution of the United States* (1913), the "Beard Thesis" that propertied Americans had instantiated their economic interests within the founding documents of the republic has been divisive and disputed. Breen's intervention was much more subtle: free colonists' desire to resemble their British counterparts materially, through the consumption of certain manufactured goods (and in their willingness to acquire debt in order to do the consuming), was prime evidence of their voluntaristic affiliation with Britain, yet also the source of their anger at being taxed for their patriotic consumerism. That Breen thus established himself as the leading scholar on consumption before 1776 was apparent in his contribution to a forum on consumerism in the fall 2006 issue of the *Journal of American History*, under the title "Will American Consumers Buy a Second American Revolution?" As topics in economic history and the history of capitalism now return to the historiographic center, Breen's analysis of consumerism and his argument for its implied voluntaristic power (for members of some social classes) seem prescient and worthy of fresh debate.[15]

These major interventions, on a topic of renewed historical interest, would have been enough for any major scholar to call it a day. And yet Timothy Breen found within him at least one more historical argument, this one about the nature of the political ideas that had driven at least some colonists into a revolt against Great Britain. Here Breen assessed several generations' worth of scholarship on that question, with greatest attention to the oldest focus on specific traditions of rights and to the newest definition of revolutionary ideology as a modern nexus of meaning that supplied motives for revolt. The former school had emphasized either the traditional rights of Englishmen (sometimes represented as extending back to the Magna Carta or else to an unwritten "Ancient Constitution") or else John Locke's modern formulation of rights, as possessed by rational men who shared an identity as political actors. The latter position had been most memorably staked out by Bernard Bailyn in his *Ideological Origins of the American Revolution* (1967), in an analysis that utilized, most prominently, the pamphlet literature in which proponents of a break with Great Britain argued their case. Bailyn maintained that their ideology had emphasized an English Whig or republican fear, if not panic, about political corruption, especially the kind of political rot that had undermined Rome's ancient republic, replacing it with the corrupt imperial ambitions that ominously resembled those of eighteenth-century Britain's leaders. That focus on republican ideology was present as well in J. G. A. Pocock's equally influential book, *The Machiavellian Moment: Florentine Political Thought and the Atlantic Republican Tradition* (1975).[16]

At least partly because his very earliest work had been engaged with political ideas, Breen was well equipped to judge the character and flow of the many counterclaims about the American Revolution's ideological underpinnings. He cited his long-standing expertise in an essay, "Ideology and Experience in Eighteenth-Century American Political Culture and the Concept of the 'Good Ruler,'" within a collection that compared German and American constitutional thought and in which Breen pushed his knowledge of political thought from the seventeenth century and into the revolutionary era. For the most part, he concluded that rights, and Lockean rights in particular, had been unjustly dismissed, as he would argue in two more essays for edited collections, as well as in his article for the *New England Quarterly*, "Subjecthood and Citizenship: The Context of James Otis's Radical Critique of John Locke" (1998). Finally Breen placed the case for Lockean rights at the center of his 2001 Harmsworth Inaugural Lecture at Oxford University, *The Lockean Mo-*

ment: The Language of Rights on the Eve of the American Revolution, which, under that manifestly counter-Pocockean title, was published in 2001.[17]

His insistence on the relevance of modern definitions of rights (overlooked in the rush to investigate multiple variations of republicanism) was not Breen's only salvo, however. Perhaps even more innovatively, he introduced the element of nationalism, specifically a transition from British nationalism to something that could credibly be described as a proto-American sense of community and identity. To make these points, Breen drew upon his graduate mentor's work. In 1957 Edmund S. Morgan had written a review essay for the *William and Mary Quarterly,* "The American Revolution: Revisions in Need of Revising," which assessed the literature about imperialism and national identity that had characterized British history at the time. Breen pointed out that early Americanists would do well to take on board updated assessments of nationalism, including British nationalism. He put himself in dialogue with many such works, including Benedict Anderson's *Imagined Communities: Reflections on the Origin and Spread of Nationalism* (1983) and Linda Colley's *Britons: Forging the Nation, 1707–1737* (1992). Of several relevant publications, Breen's still magisterial essay "Ideology and Nationalism on the Eve of the American Revolution: Revisions *Once More* in Need of Revising" (*Journal of American History,* 1997) was his most robust assessment of the problem of American nationalism (and of imperial or post-imperial nationalisms more generally) in the age of Atlantic revolutions.[18]

In a closely related series of publications, Breen examined the motives not just for a political break with Great Britain but as a commitment to fight for that separation. He embraced the term that the British ministry might have preferred for the American rebels, "insurgents," and, returning to his earlier focus on political mobilization in colonial militias, examined how and why individual men decided to take up arms and fight for national independence. In essence, this topic represented what was perhaps the most important way in which Americans who were only barely endowed with political authority displayed and protected their liberty. They were subjects who resisted their objectification. Breen's essays on this problem included several written for edited volumes, "Revolutionary Mobilization: New Perspectives" (2006), "Where Have All the People Gone? Reflections on Popular Mobilization on the Eve of American Independence" (2010), and "Samuel Thompson's War: The Career of an American Insurgent" (2010), as well as a book-length investigation, *American Insurgents, American Patriots: The Revolution of the People* (2010).[19]

The focus on military engagement was bold in two ways. First, it reminded early Americanists that war (and not just in the case of the American Revolution) was a crucial element of early modern history, and especially the history of empires, which were won in battle more often than by other means and only the victors could afford to pretend otherwise. Second, the focus on war reminded contemporary Americans, precisely at a moment of highly contested U.S. military effort abroad, that war was still a considerable political action and therefore a historical activity that should always be critically examined. Power and liberty still matter after all.

In the meantime, Breen kept up a stream of synthetic assessments of the field and of contributions for audiences beyond the academy. These included his review essays on "The Miracle of Print: Shaping Popular Religion in Seventeenth-Century New England" (*Reviews in American History,* 1991), and (with Timothy Hall) "Structuring Provincial Imagination: The Rhetoric and Experience of Social Change in Eighteenth-Century New England" (*American Historical Review,* 1998). His wide-ranging popular essays included some considered thoughts on George Washington and John Winthrop: "At Mount Vernon, Reflections on an Elusive Man" (*New York Times Magazine,* 1993), and "The Puritan's Puritan" (*New York Times Book Review,* 1997). Never keen to avoid controversy, Breen opened the second of those reviews with the admonishing words: "As Congress hacks away at the Federal endowments for the arts and humanities, we should greet the release of a major early American text with enthusiasm." Breen also produced a sprawling two-volume reader, *Power of Words: Documents of American History* (1995), along with a focused synthesis, *American Colonies in an Atlantic World: A Story of Creative Interaction* (2003), coauthored with Timothy Hall.[20]

The oeuvre of T. H. Breen is impossible to summarize, and yet it forms an enviable summit. It could be said that Breen's interests always swing toward examinations of power; certainly, his investigations of politics, slavery, economic life, and military service are in various ways analyses of early modern authority. It could equally be said that he is fascinated by liberty, leading to his contributions to the study of free blacks, the pleasures of consumption, and the prospects of political independence. His perspective has been invigorating within the field because he not only has pursued these themes but has come at them from multiple directions. Breen has always been the kind of scholar who identifies some new document, method, or critical mode of analysis. He has in essence, and over his entire career, made an argument for the historiographic inescapability of power and liberty. Each of the studies that did this are admirable for their scholarly rigor, their inventiveness, and their engagement with other scholars and other scholarship.

Of course, this is an ex post facto summary. Did Breen always plan to make these contributions, in this order, according to this pattern? Obviously not. That would have been a dumb way to go about it, dully returning to the same topic in the exact same way, time after time. It is Breen's ongoing assessment of potential new methods—from other fields of history, from other disciplines—and his modification of these methodologies to early American history that show *his* creative adaptation to shifts within the academy. He provides a good and formidable model because the result has been this enviable stream of publications. Even if they had nothing else in common, they had this above all: excellence.

Notes

1. Christopher Hill, *Society and Puritanism in Pre-Revolutionary England* (London, 1964); T. H. Breen, "The Non-Existent Controversy: Puritan and Anglican Attitudes on Work and Wealth, 1600–1640," *Church History* 35 (1966): 273–87.

2. T. H. Breen, "John Adams's Fight against Innovation in the New England Constitution: 1776," *New England Quarterly* 40 (1967): 501–20; Breen, "'The Conflict in the Golden Bough': Frazer's Two Images of Man," *South Atlantic Quarterly* 56 (1967): 174–94.

3. T. H. Breen, *The Character of the Good Ruler: A Study of Puritan Political Ideas in New England, 1630–1730* (New Haven, CT, 1970). Quentin Skinner's very influential "Meaning and Understanding in the History of Ideas" had appeared one year earlier in *History and Theory* 8 (1969): 3–53. On social history, see Paul Cartledge, "What Is Social History Now?" in *What Is History Now?* ed. David Cannadine (New York, 2002).

4. T. H. Breen and Stephen Foster, "Moving to the New World: The Character of Early Massachusetts Immigration," *William and Mary Quarterly,* 3rd ser., 30 (1973): 189–222; Breen, "Persistent Localism: English Social Change and the Shaping of New England Institutions," *William and Mary Quarterly,* 3rd ser., 32 (1975): 3–28; Breen, ed., *Shaping Southern Society: The Colonial Experience* (Oxford, 1976).

5. T. H. Breen and Stephen Foster, "The Puritans' Greatest Achievement: A Study of Social Cohesion in Seventeenth-Century Massachusetts," *Journal of American History* 60 (1973): 5–22; Breen, "Transfer of Culture: Chance and Design in Shaping Massachusetts Bay, 1630–1660," *New England Historical and Genealogical Register* 132 (1978): 3–17; Breen, "Looking Out for Number One: Conflicting Cultural Values in Early Seventeenth-Century Virginia," *South Atlantic Quarterly* 38 (1979): 341–60.

6. Clifford Geertz, "Deep Play: Notes on the Balinese Cockfight," in *The Interpretation of Cultures* (New York, 1973); T. H. Breen, "Horses and Gentlemen: The Cultural Significance of Gambling among the Gentry of Virginia," *William and Mary Quarterly,* 3rd ser., 34 (1979): 239–57.

7. T. H. Breen and Stephen Foster, "Moving to the New World: The Character of Early Massachusetts Immigration," *William and Mary Quarterly,* 3rd ser., 30 (1973): 189–222;

T. H. Breen and Stephen Foster, "The Puritans' Greatest Achievement: A Study of Social Cohesion in Seventeenth-Century Massachusetts," 5–22.

8. T. H. Breen, "Who Governs: The Town Franchise in Seventeenth-Century Massachusetts," *William and Mary Quarterly*, 3rd ser., 27 (1970): 460–74; Breen, "English Origins and New World Development: The Case of the Covenanted Militia in Seventeenth-Century Massachusetts," *Past and Present* 57, no. 1 (1972): 74–96; Breen, "George Donne's 'Virginia Reviewed': A 1638 Plan to Reform Colonial Society," *William and Mary Quarterly*, 3rd ser., 30 (1973): 449–66.

9. T. H. Breen, "A Changing Labor Force and Race Relations in Virginia, 1660–1710," *Journal of Social History* 7 (1973): 3–25; Breen and Stephen Innes, *"Myne Owne Ground": Race and Freedom on Virginia's Eastern Shore* (Oxford, 1980); Breen and Innes, "Seventeenth-Century Virginia's Forgotten Yeomen: The Free Blacks," *Virginia Cavalcade* 32 (1981): 5–12; Breen, James Lewis, and Keith Schlesinger, "Motive for Murder: A Servant's Life in Virginia, 1678," *William and Mary Quarterly*, 3rd ser., 40 (1983): 106–20.

10. T. H. Breen, *Puritans and Adventurers: Change and Persistence in Early America* (New York, 1980); Robert A. Divine, T. H. Breen, George M. Fredrickson, and R. Hal Williams, *America Past and Present* (Glenview, IL, 1984). Breen would produce a later textbook with H. W. Brands et al., *American Stories: A History of the United States* (New York, 2009), now in its third edition.

11. T. H. Breen "Back to Sweat and Toil: Suggestions for the Study of Agricultural Work in Early America," *Pennsylvania History* 49 (1982): 241–58; Breen, "The Culture of Agriculture: The Symbolic World of the Tidewater Planter, 1760–1790," in *Saints and Revolutionaries: Essays in Early American History*, ed. Thad Tate, David D. Hall, and John Murrin (New York, 1984), 247–84; Breen, *Tobacco Culture: The Mentality of the Great Tidewater Planters on the Eve of Revolution* (Princeton, 1985); "'Making a Crop': Tobacco and the Tidewater Planters on the Eve of Revolution," *Virginia Cavalcade* 36 (1986): 52–65.

12. See William Cronon, *Changes in the Land: Indians, Colonists, and the Ecology of New England* (New York, 1983); Richard Lyman Bushman, "Markets and Composite Farms in Early America," *William and Mary Quarterly*, 3d ser., 55 (1998): 351–74.

13. T. H. Breen, "Creative Adaptations: Peoples and Cultures in Early America," in *Colonial British America: Essays in the New History of the Early Modern Era*, ed. Jack P. Green and J. R. Pole (Baltimore, 1984), 195–232; Breen, "Searching for the Mainstream: The State of Native American Studies in the Colonial Period," in *Occasional Papers in Curriculum Series, D'Arcy McNickle Center for the History of the American Indian* (Chicago, 1985), 1–15; Breen, "Varieties of Clear Thinking. A Critique of Positivism in Native American Studies," in *Towards a Quantitative Approach to American Indian History: Papers and Commentaries from a Research Conference Held at the Newberry Library*, ed. Fred Hoxie, Occasional Papers Series (Chicago, 1987), sec.1; Breen, "Founding Sons," *New York Review of Books* (December 5, 1985). See also Breen, *Imagining the Past: East Hampton Histories* (Boston, 1989).

14. T. H. Breen, "An Empire of Goods: The Anglicization of Colonial America," *Journal of British Studies* (1986): 467–99; Breen, "'Baubles of Britain': The Consumer Culture of Eighteenth-Century America and the Coming Revolution," *Past and Present*, no. 119 (1988): 73–104; Breen, "The Meaning of 'Likeness': Portrait Painting in an Eighteenth-Century Consumer Society," *Word and Image* 6 (1990): 325–50; Breen, "Narrative of Commercial

Life: Consumption, Ideology, and Community on the Eve of the American Revolution," *William and Mary Quarterly*, 3rd ser., 50 (1993): 471–501 (reprinted in two collections); Breen, "The Meaning of Things: Consumption and Ideology in the Eighteenth Century," in *Consumption, Culture, and Society*, ed. John Brewer and Roy Porter (New York, 1993); Breen, "Meanings in the Marketplace: A Political Interpretation of Late Eighteenth-Century Commerce," in *Oceanic Trade, Colonial Wares, and Industrial Development, 1600–1800: Eleventh International Economic History Congress*, ed. Maxine Berg (London, 1994); Breen, "Trade and Community: East Hampton's Curious Commercial Origins," in Tom Twomey, ed., *Awakening the Past: The East Hampton 350th Anniversary Lecture Series* (New York, 1999), 268–83.

15. See Charles Beard, *An Economic Interpretation of the Constitution of the United States* (New York, 1913); plus Richard Hofstadter's thoughtful if somewhat dismissive, "Beard and the Constitution: The History of an Idea," *American Quarterly* 2 (1950): 195–213, whose title prematurely suggested the demise of Beard's idea. T. H. Breen, *Marketplace of Revolution: How Consumer Politics Shaped American Independence* (New York, 2004); Breen, "Will American Consumers Buy a Second American Revolution?" *Journal of American History* 93 (2006): 404–8.

16. Bernard Bailyn, *The Ideological Origins of the American Revolution* (Cambridge, MA, 1967); J. G. A. Pocock, *The Machiavellian Moment: Florentine Political Thought and the Atlantic Republican Tradition* (Princeton, 1975).

17. T. H. Breen, "Ideology and Experience in Eighteenth-Century American Political Culture and the Concept of the 'Good Ruler,'" in *German and American Constitutional Thought: Contexts, Interaction, and Historical Realities*, ed. Hermann Wellenreuther (New York, 1990); Breen, "Retrieving Common Sense: Rights, Liberties, and the Religious Public Sphere in Late Eighteenth-Century America," in *To Secure the Blessings of Liberty: Rights in American History*, ed. Josephine F. Pacheco (Fairfax, VA, 1993); Breen, "Subjecthood and Citizenship: The Context of James Otis's Radical Critique of John Locke," *New England Quarterly* 71 (1998): 378–403; Breen, *The Lockean Moment: The Language of Rights on the Eve of the American Revolution*, Harmsworth Inaugural Lecture, Oxford University, May 15, 2001 (Oxford, 2001); Breen, "'An Appeal to Heaven': Rights Talk on the Eve of the American Revolution," in *The Future of Liberal Democracy: Thomas Jefferson and the Contemporary World*, ed. Robert Fatton Jr. and R. K. Ramazani (New York, 2004). See also Daniel T. Rodgers, "Republicanism: The Career of a Concept," *Journal of American History* 79 (1992): 11–38.

18. Edmund S. Morgan, "The American Revolution: Revisions in Need of Revising," *William and Mary Quarterly* 14 (1957): 3–15; Benedict Anderson, *Imagined Communities: Reflections on the Origin and Spread of Nationalism* (London, 1983); Linda Colley, *Britons: Forging the Nation, 1707–1737* (New Haven, CT, 1992); T. H. Breen, "Ideology and Nationalism on the Eve of the American Revolution: Revisions *Once More* in Need of Revising," *Journal of American History* 84 (1997): 13–39; Breen, "Interpreting New World Nationalism," in *Nationalism in the New World*, ed. Don Doyle and Marco Pamplona (Athens, GA, 2006), 41–60.

19. T. H. Breen, "Revolutionary Mobilization: New Perspectives," in *Atlantic Understandings: Essays on European and American History in Honor of Hermann Wellenreuther*, ed. Claudia Schnurmann and Hartmut Lehmann (Hamburg, 2006), 231–44; T. H. Breen,

American Insurgents, American Patriots; Breen, "Where Have All the People Gone? Reflections on Popular Mobilization on the Eve of American Independence," in *Wars in the Age of Revolution, 1775–1815,* ed. Roger Chickering and Stig Foerster (New York, 2010); Breen, "Samuel Thompson's War: The Career of an American Insurgent," in *Revolutionary Founders: Rebels, Radicals, and Reformers in the Making of the Nation,* ed. Alfred Young, Gary B. Nash, and Ray Raphael (New York, 2011).

20. Review essays: T. H. Breen, "The Miracle of Print: Shaping Popular Religion in Seventeenth-Century New England," *Reviews in American History* 19 (1991): 166–70; Breen and Timothy Hall, "Structuring Provincial Imagination: The Rhetoric and Experience of Social Change in Eighteenth-Century New England," *American Historical Review* 103 (1998): 1411–39. Popular essays: Breen, "At Mount Vernon, Reflections on an Elusive Man," *New York Times Magazine,* pt. 2, May 16, 1993, 26–27, 40–42; Breen, "The Puritan's Puritan," *New York Times Book Review,* 24 August 1997, endnote; Breen, "The Tea Party," *Times Literary Supplement* (April 2011); Breen, "Paul Revere's Ride," *Times Literary Supplement* (July 2011). Textbooks and readers: Breen, ed., *Power of Words: Documents of American History,* 2 vols. (New York, 1995); Breen and Timothy Hall, *American Colonies in an Atlantic World: A Story of Creative Interaction* (New York, 2003). See also "Making History: The Force of Public Opinion and the Last Years of Slavery in Revolutionary Massachusetts," in *Through a Glass Darkly: Reflections on Personal Identity in Early America,* ed. Ronald Hoffman, Mechal Sobel, and Fredrika J. Teute (Chapel Hill, NC, 1997).

Contributors

T. H. Breen, author of several volumes on colonial and revolutionary American history, is the William Smith Mason Professor of American History Emeritus at Northwestern University and the James Marsh Professor-at-Large at the University of Vermont. He is also currently the Kluge Professor of American Law and Governance at the Library of Congress.

Joyce E. Chaplin is the James Duncan Phillips Professor of Early American History at Harvard University. Her most recent book is entitled *Round about the Earth: Circumnavigation from Magellan to Orbit* (2012).

Patricia Cleary, Professor of U.S. History at California State University, Long Beach, is the author of *The World, the Flesh, and the Devil: A History of Colonial St. Louis* (2011) and *Elizabeth Murray: A Woman's Pursuit of Independence in Eighteenth-Century America* (2000).

James Coltrain is an Assistant Professor of History and a Faculty Fellow in the Center for Digital Research in the Humanities at the University of Nebraska.

Seth Cotlar is a Professor of History at Willamette University in Salem, Oregon. His first book, *Tom Paine's America: The Rise and Fall of Transatlantic Radicalism in the Early Republic* (2011), was awarded the James Broussard Best First Book Prize by the Society for Historians of the Early American Republic. This essay is drawn from his current book project entitled "When the Olden Days Were New: The Cultural History of Nostalgia in Modernizing America, 1776–1860."

David N. Gellman is Andrew Wallace Crandall Professor of History and Chair of the Department of History at DePauw University.

PATRICK GRIFFIN is the Madden-Hennebry Professor of History at the University of Notre Dame. He is the author of a number of books, the most recent of which is *The Townsend Moment: The Making of Empire and Revolution in the Eighteenth Century* (2017).

MICHAEL GUENTHER is an Assistant Professor of History at Grinnell College, where he teaches courses on environmental history, the history of science and technology, and the Atlantic world. His current book project focuses on the political impact of eighteenth-century science and its connection to the age of revolution.

CHRISTOPHER HODSON is Associate Professor in the Department of History at Brigham Young University. He is the author of *The Acadian Diaspora: An Eighteenth-Century History* (2012) and is currently completing a book on the French Atlantic world from the medieval period through the early nineteenth century.

DONALD F. JOHNSON is an Assistant Professor of History at North Dakota State University. His research focuses on popular politics of revolutionary movements, the interplay between war and society during the formative years of the republic, and history and memory in early America.

IAN SAXINE is a Visiting Assistant Professor of History at St. Mary's College of Maryland. His research focuses on the intersection of race, class, and property in the early modern Atlantic World. He won the Walter Muir Whitehill Prize in Early American History for "The Performance of Peace: Indians, Speculators, and the Politics of Property on the Maine Frontier, 1735–1737." Saxine is the author of the forthcoming *Properties of Empire: Indians, Colonists, and Land Speculators on the Maine Frontier.*

TIMOTHY J. SHANNON is a Professor of History at Gettysburg College. His books include *Indians and Colonists at the Crossroads of Empire: The Albany Congress of 1754* (2000) and *Iroquois Diplomacy on the Early American Frontier* (2008). His current project is a biography of Peter Williamson.

OWEN STANWOOD is Associate Professor of History at Boston College. He is the author of *The Empire Reformed: English America in the Age of the Glorious Revolution* (2011) and is working on a history of the Huguenot diaspora in the early modern world.

Index

Early American Histories